CREATED BY SPIKE CHUNSOFT
MANGA BY KUROKI Q

GOODBYE DESPAIR

TRANSLATION BY JACKIE MCCLURE

LETTERING AND TOUCHUP BY JOHN CLARK

EDITED BY CARL GUSTAV HORN

SPECIAL THANKS TO RACHEL FUJII, MIMI SAITO,
AND ARIANNE ADVINCULA AT SPIKE CHUNSOFT

DR2: **2**

CONTENTS

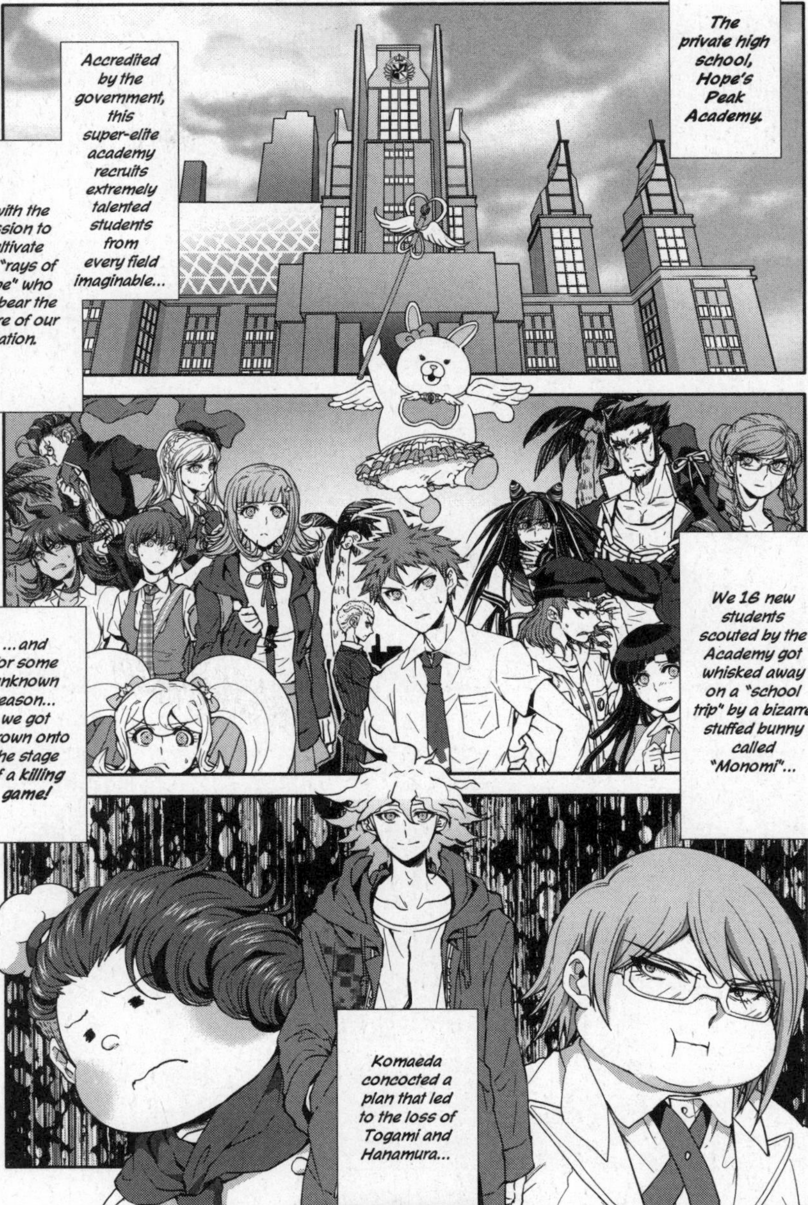
The private high school, Hope's Peak Academy.
Accredited by the government, this super-elite academy recruits extremely talented students from every field imaginable...
...with the mission to cultivate the "rays of hope" who will bear the future of our nation.
We 16 new students scouted by the Academy got whisked away on a "school trip" by a bizarre stuffed bunny called "Monomi"...
...and for some unknown reason... we got thrown onto the stage of a killing game!
Komaeda concocted a plan that led to the loss of Togami and Hanamura...

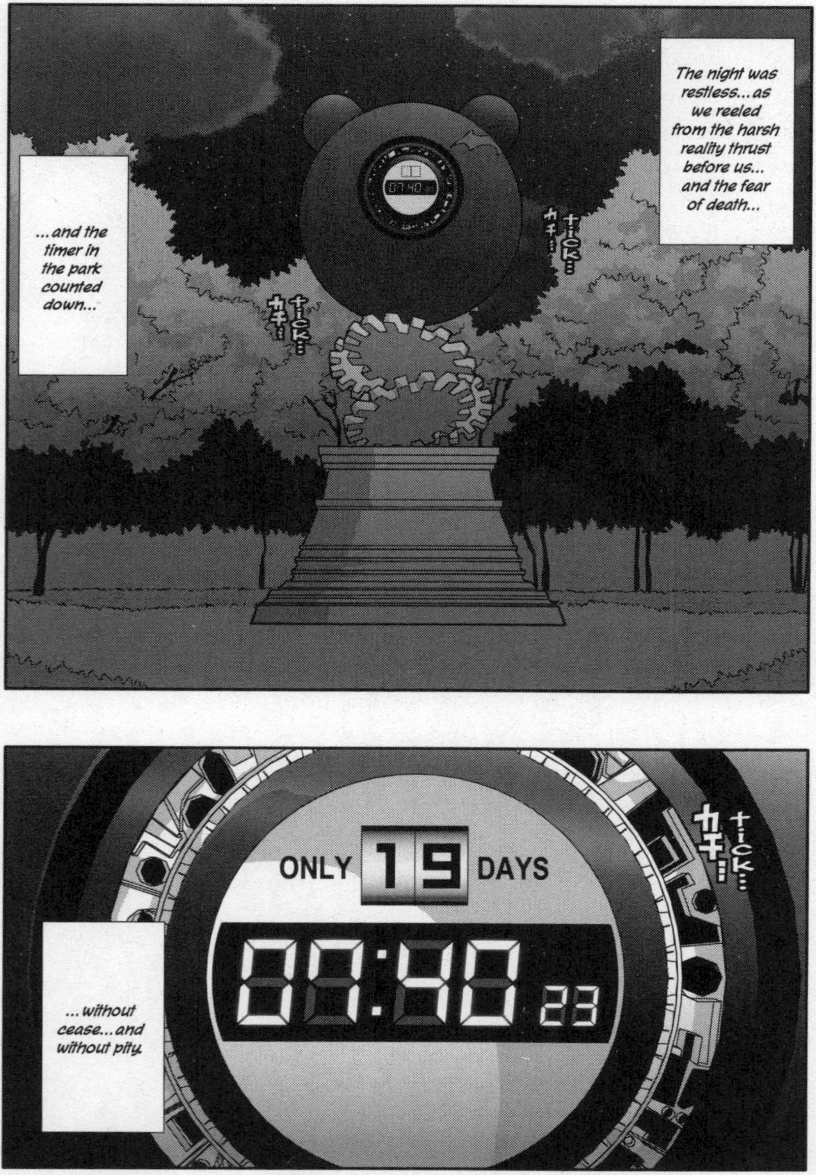
The night was restless...as we reeled from the harsh reality thrust before us... and the fear of death...
カチ... tick...
...and the timer in the park counted down...
カチ... tick...
カチ... tick...
ONLY 19 DAYS
07:40 23
...without cease...and without pity.

CHAPTER 7: THE DAY AFTER THE TRIAL

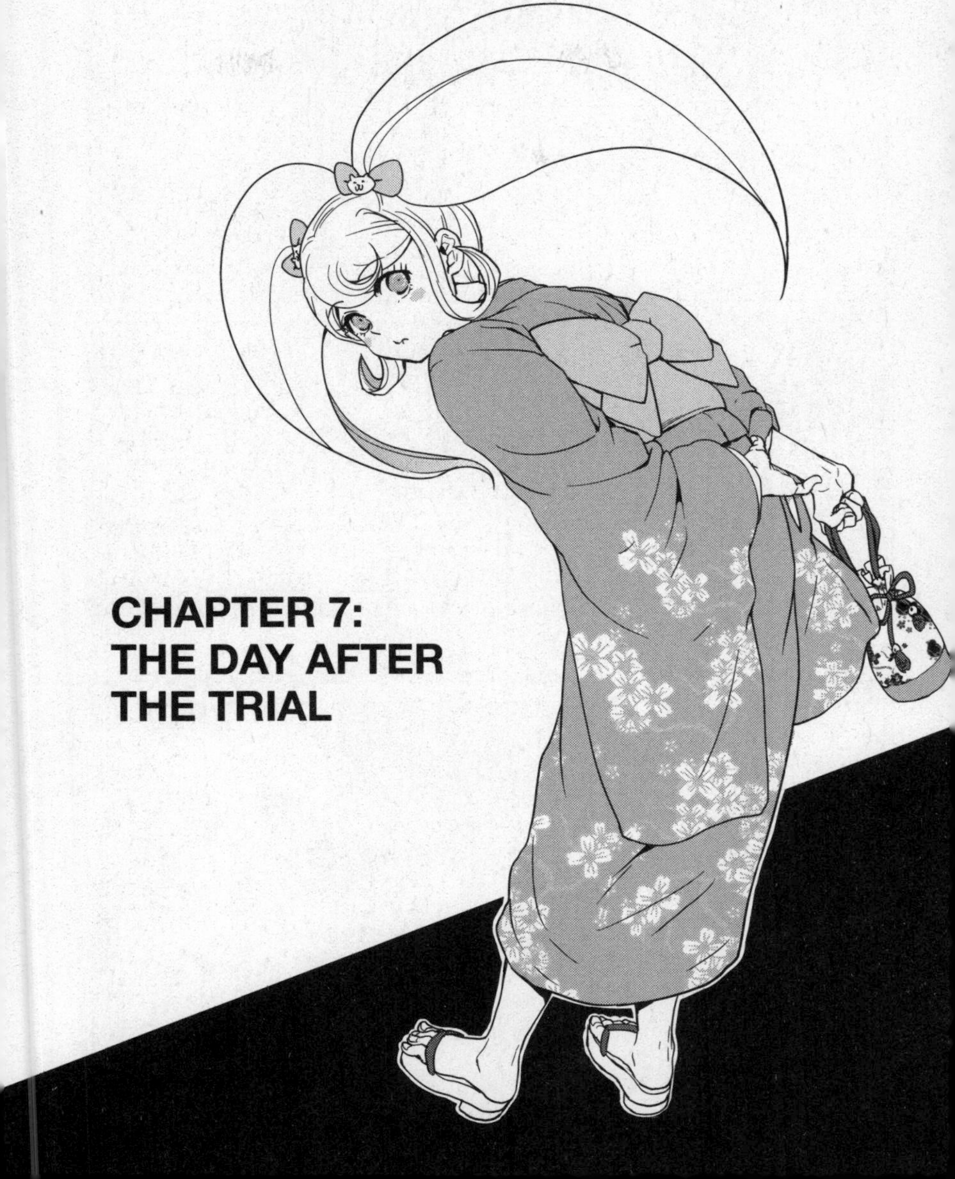

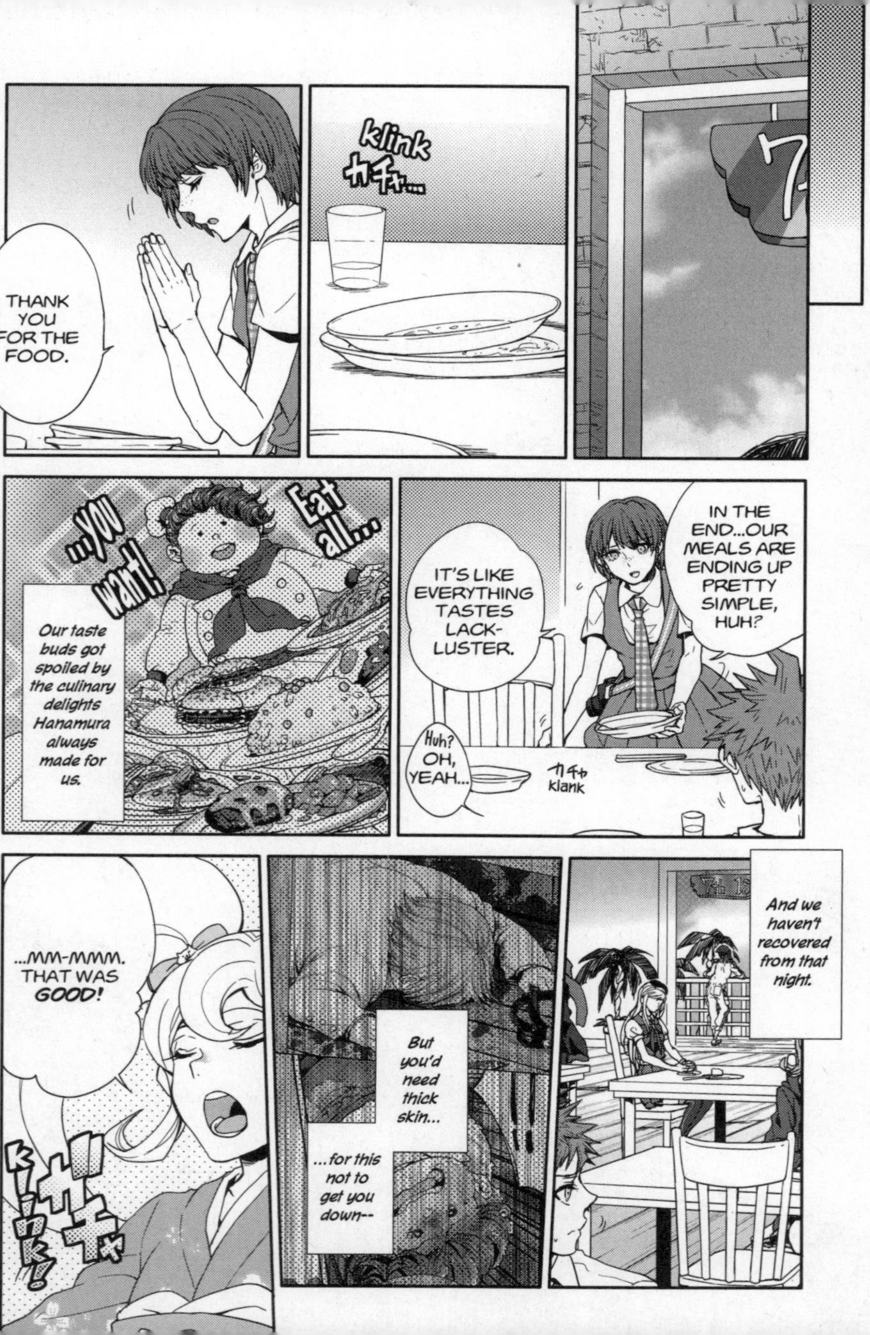

klink
カチャ...
THANK YOU FOR THE FOOD.
IN THE END...OUR MEALS ARE ENDING UP PRETTY SIMPLE, HUH?
IT'S LIKE EVERYTHING TASTES LACK-LUSTER.
カチャ
klank
Huh? OH, YEAH...
Eat all...
...you want!
Our taste buds got spoiled by the culinary delights Hanamura always made for us.
And we haven't recovered from that night.
But you'd need thick skin...
...for this not to get you down--
...MM-MMM. THAT WAS GOOD!
K-link!
カチャ

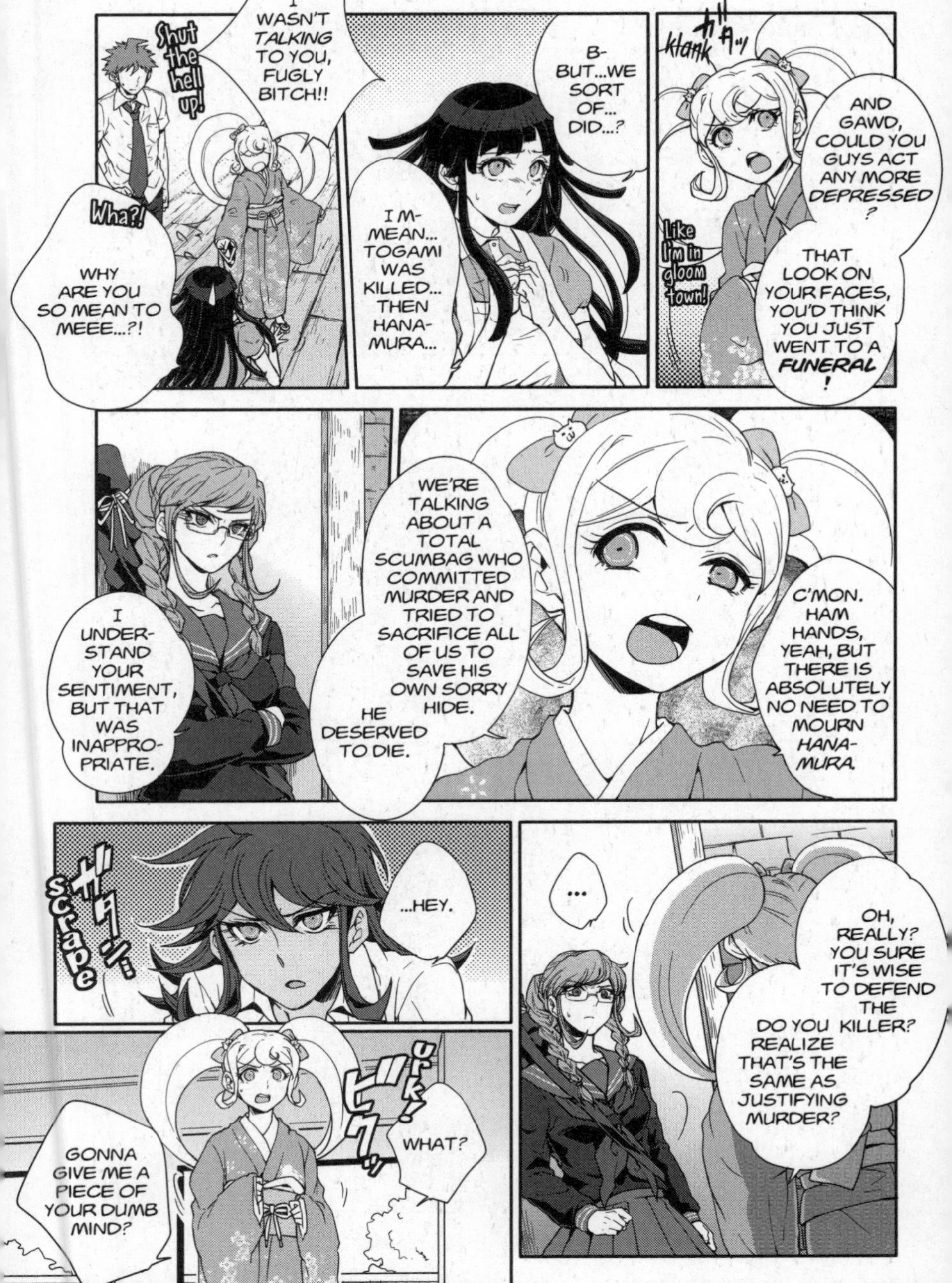
klank
AND GAWD, COULD YOU GUYS ACT ANY MORE DEPRESSED?
THAT LOOK ON YOUR FACES, YOU'D THINK YOU JUST WENT TO A FUNERAL!
Like I'm in gloom town!
B- BUT...WE SORT OF... DID...?
I M- MEAN... TOGAMI WAS KILLED... THEN HANA- MURA...
I WASN'T TALKING TO YOU, FUGLY BITCH!!
Shut the hell up!
Wha?!
WHY ARE YOU SO MEAN TO MEEE...?!
C'MON. HAM HANDS, YEAH, BUT THERE IS ABSOLUTELY NO NEED TO MOURN HANA- MURA.
WE'RE TALKING ABOUT A TOTAL SCUMBAG WHO COMMITTED MURDER AND TRIED TO SACRIFICE ALL OF US TO SAVE HIS OWN SORRY HIDE.
HE DESERVED TO DIE.
I UNDER- STAND YOUR SENTIMENT, BUT THAT WAS INAPPRO- PRIATE.
...
OH, REALLY? YOU SURE IT'S WISE TO DEFEND THE KILLER?
DO YOU REALIZE THAT'S THE SAME AS JUSTIFYING MURDER?
scrape
...HEY.
urk!
WHAT?
GONNA GIVE ME A PIECE OF YOUR DUMB MIND?

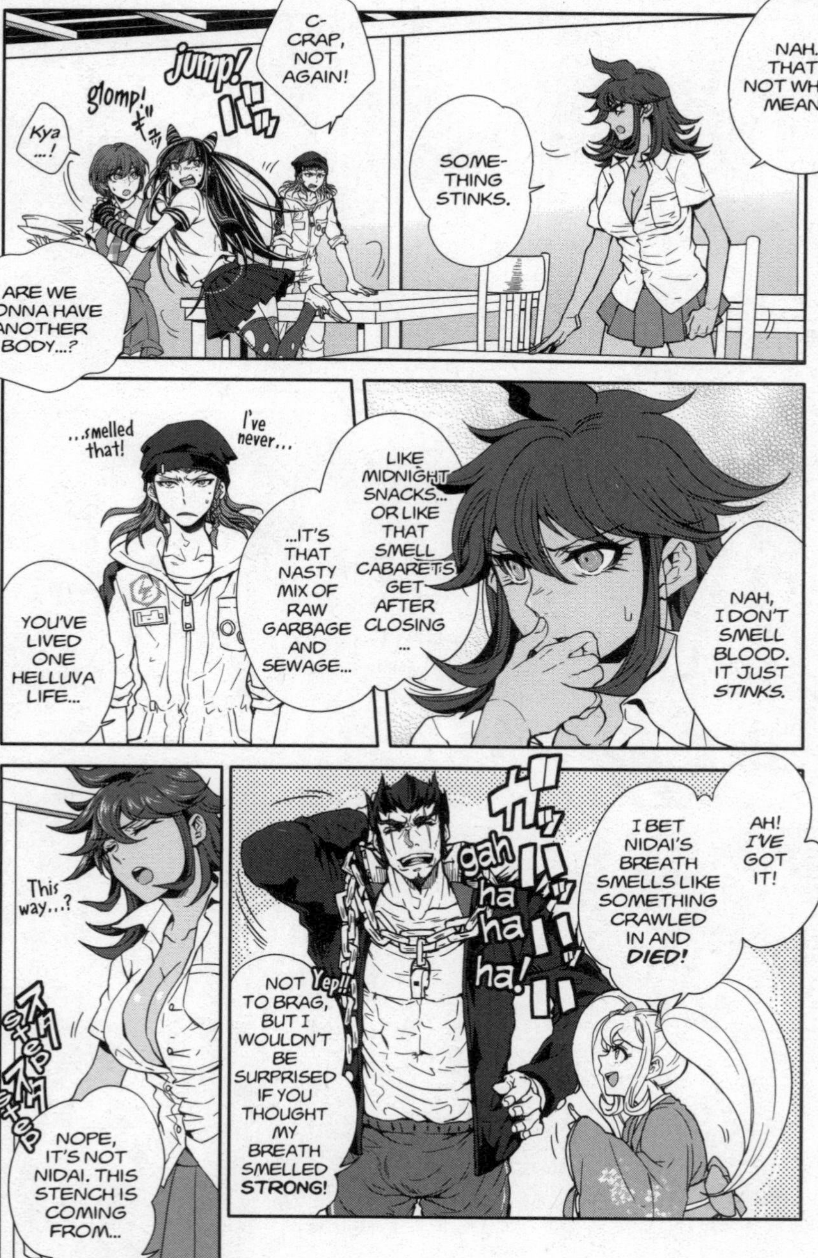
NAH... THAT'S NOT WHAT I MEANT.
SOME-THING STINKS.
C-CRAP, NOT AGAIN!
jump!
glomp!
Kya...!
ARE WE GONNA HAVE ANOTHER BODY...?
NAH, I DON'T SMELL BLOOD. IT JUST *STINKS.*
...IT'S THAT NASTY MIX OF RAW GARBAGE AND SEWAGE...
LIKE MIDNIGHT SNACKS... OR LIKE THAT SMELL CABARETS GET AFTER CLOSING...
I've never...
...smelled that!
YOU'VE LIVED ONE HELLUVA LIFE...
AH! *I'VE* GOT IT!
I BET NIDAI'S BREATH SMELLS LIKE SOMETHING CRAWLED IN AND **DIED!**
gah ha ha ha!
Yep!!
NOT TO BRAG, BUT I WOULDN'T BE SURPRISED IF YOU THOUGHT MY BREATH SMELLED **STRONG!**
This way...?
step step
NOPE, IT'S NOT NIDAI. THIS STENCH IS COMING FROM...

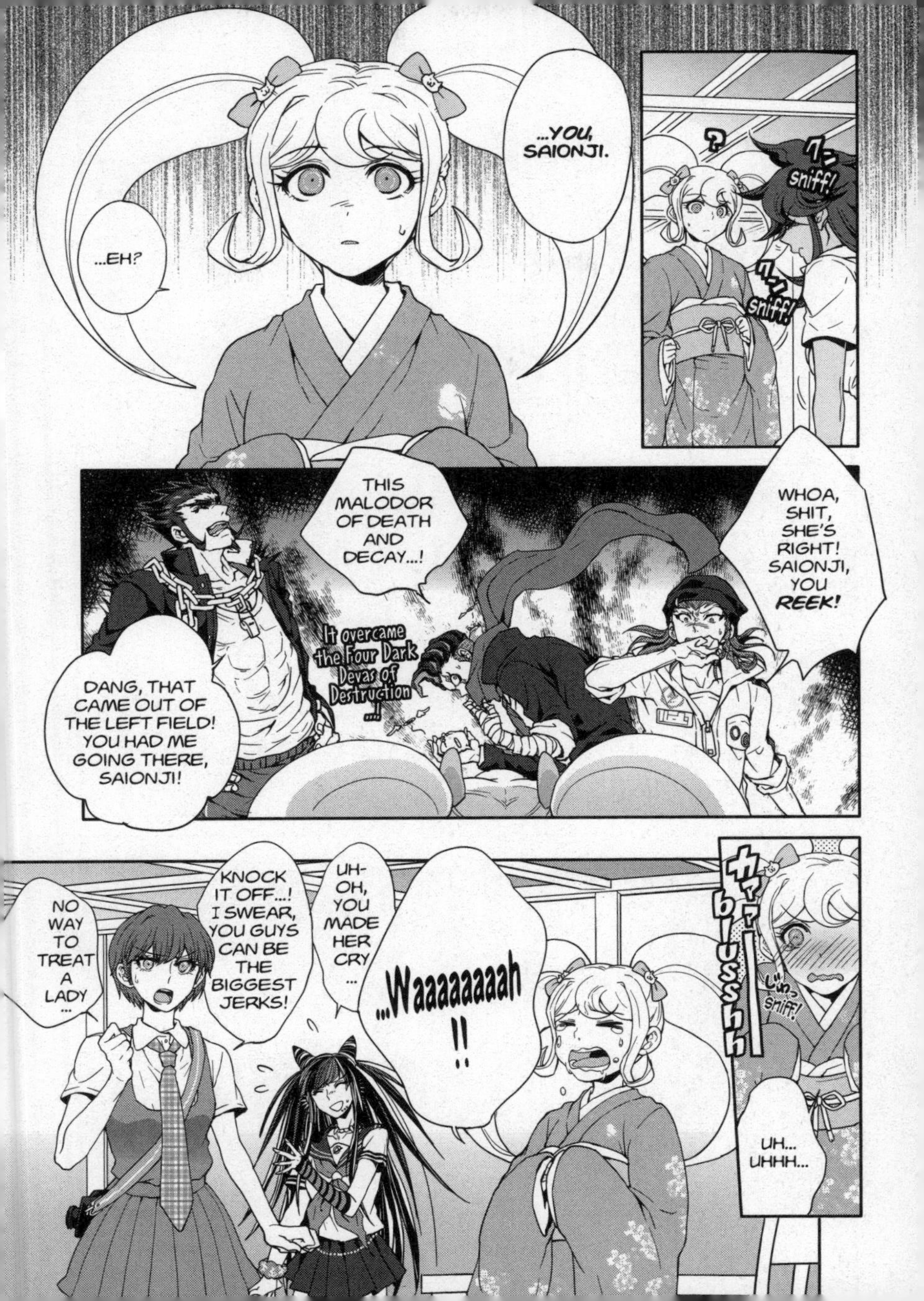
?
クン sniff!
クン sniff!
...YOU, SAIONJI.
...EH?
WHOA, SHIT, SHE'S RIGHT! SAIONJI, YOU REEK!
THIS MALODOR OF DEATH AND DECAY...!
It overcame the Four Dark Devas of Destruction...!
DANG, THAT CAME OUT OF THE LEFT FIELD! YOU HAD ME GOING THERE, SAIONJI!
カァァ b-lusshh
sniff!
UH... UHHH...
...Waaaaaaaah!!
UH-OH, YOU MADE HER CRY...
KNOCK IT OFF...! I SWEAR, YOU GUYS CAN BE THE BIGGEST JERKS!
NO WAY TO TREAT A LADY...

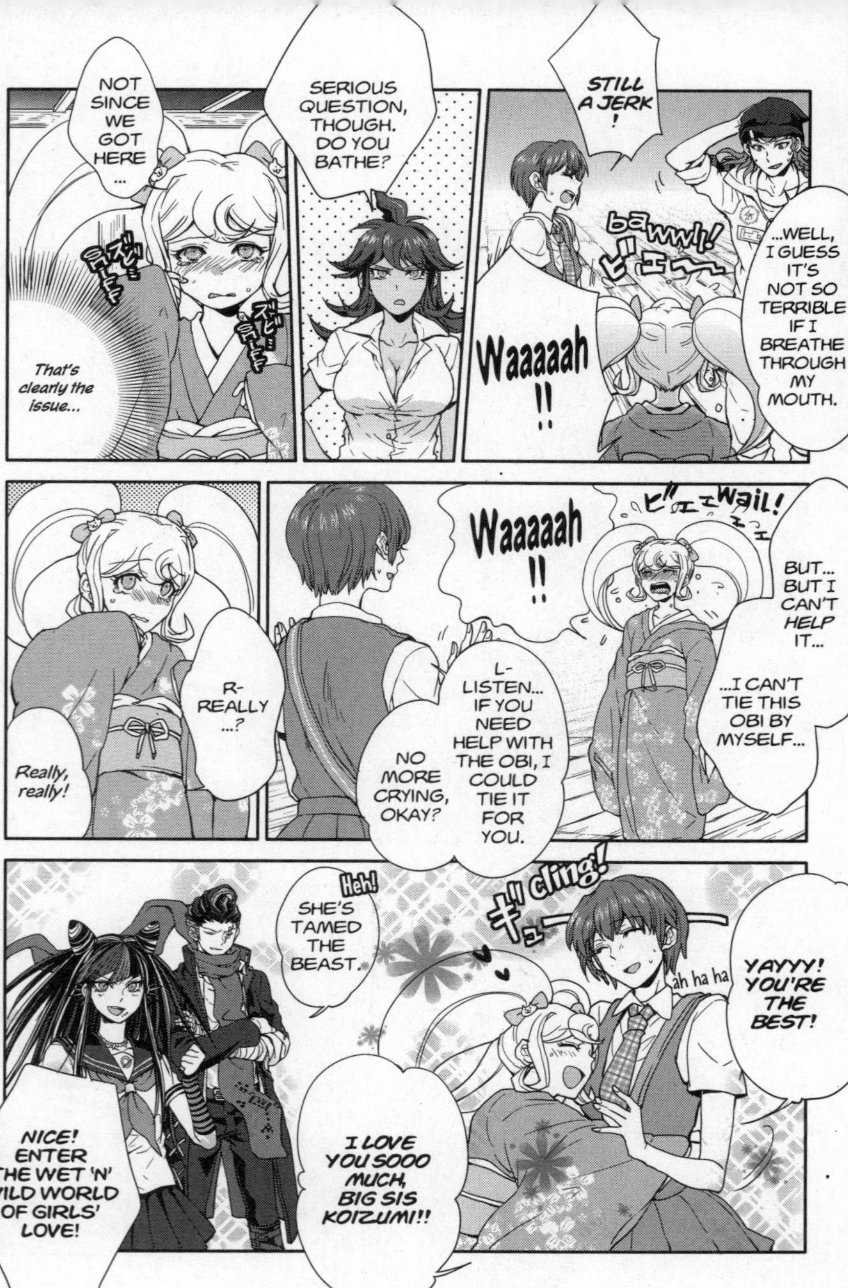
STILL A JERK!
...WELL, I GUESS IT'S NOT SO TERRIBLE IF I BREATHE THROUGH MY MOUTH.
bawwl!
Waaaaah!!
SERIOUS QUESTION, THOUGH. DO YOU BATHE?
NOT SINCE WE GOT HERE...
sniff
sniff
That's clearly the issue...
Waaaaah!!
wail!
BUT... BUT I CAN'T HELP IT...
...I CAN'T TIE THIS OBI BY MYSELF...
L-LISTEN... IF YOU NEED HELP WITH THE OBI, I COULD TIE IT FOR YOU.
NO MORE CRYING, OKAY?
R-REALLY...?
Really, really!
cling!
YAYYY! YOU'RE THE BEST!
ah ha ha
Heh!
SHE'S TAMED THE BEAST.
I LOVE YOU SOOO MUCH, BIG SIS KOIZUMI!!
NICE! ENTER THE WET 'N' WILD WORLD OF GIRLS' LOVE!

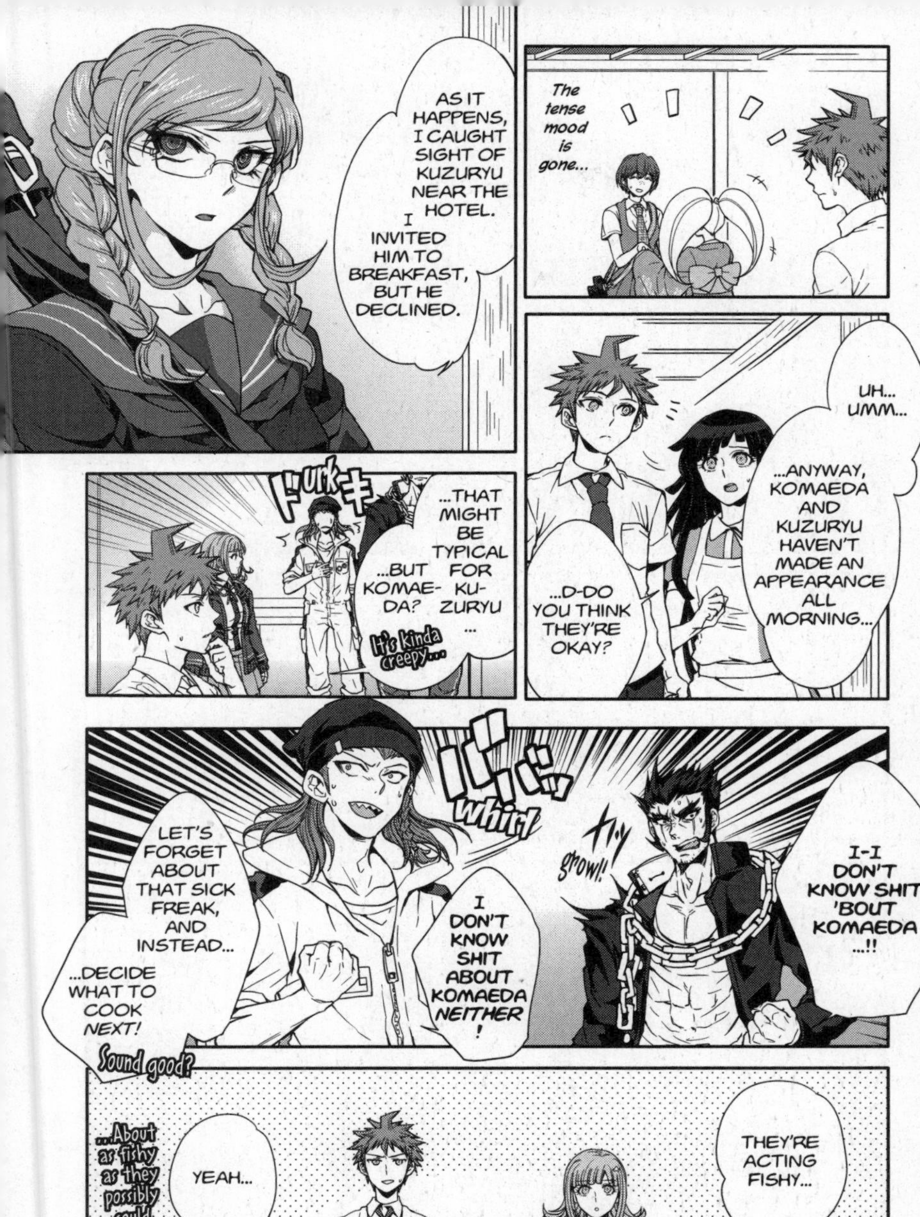

The tense mood is gone...
UH... UMM...
...ANYWAY, KOMAEDA AND KUZURYU HAVEN'T MADE AN APPEARANCE ALL MORNING...
...D-DO YOU THINK THEY'RE OKAY?
AS IT HAPPENS, I CAUGHT SIGHT OF KUZURYU NEAR THE HOTEL.
I INVITED HIM TO BREAKFAST, BUT HE DECLINED.
urk
...THAT MIGHT BE TYPICAL FOR KUZURYU...
...BUT KOMAEDA?
It's kinda creepy...
whirl
growl!
I-I DON'T KNOW SHIT 'BOUT KOMAEDA...!!
I DON'T KNOW SHIT ABOUT KOMAEDA NEITHER!
LET'S FORGET ABOUT THAT SICK FREAK, AND INSTEAD...
...DECIDE WHAT TO COOK NEXT!
Sound good?
THEY'RE ACTING FISHY...
YEAH...
...About as fishy as they possibly could.

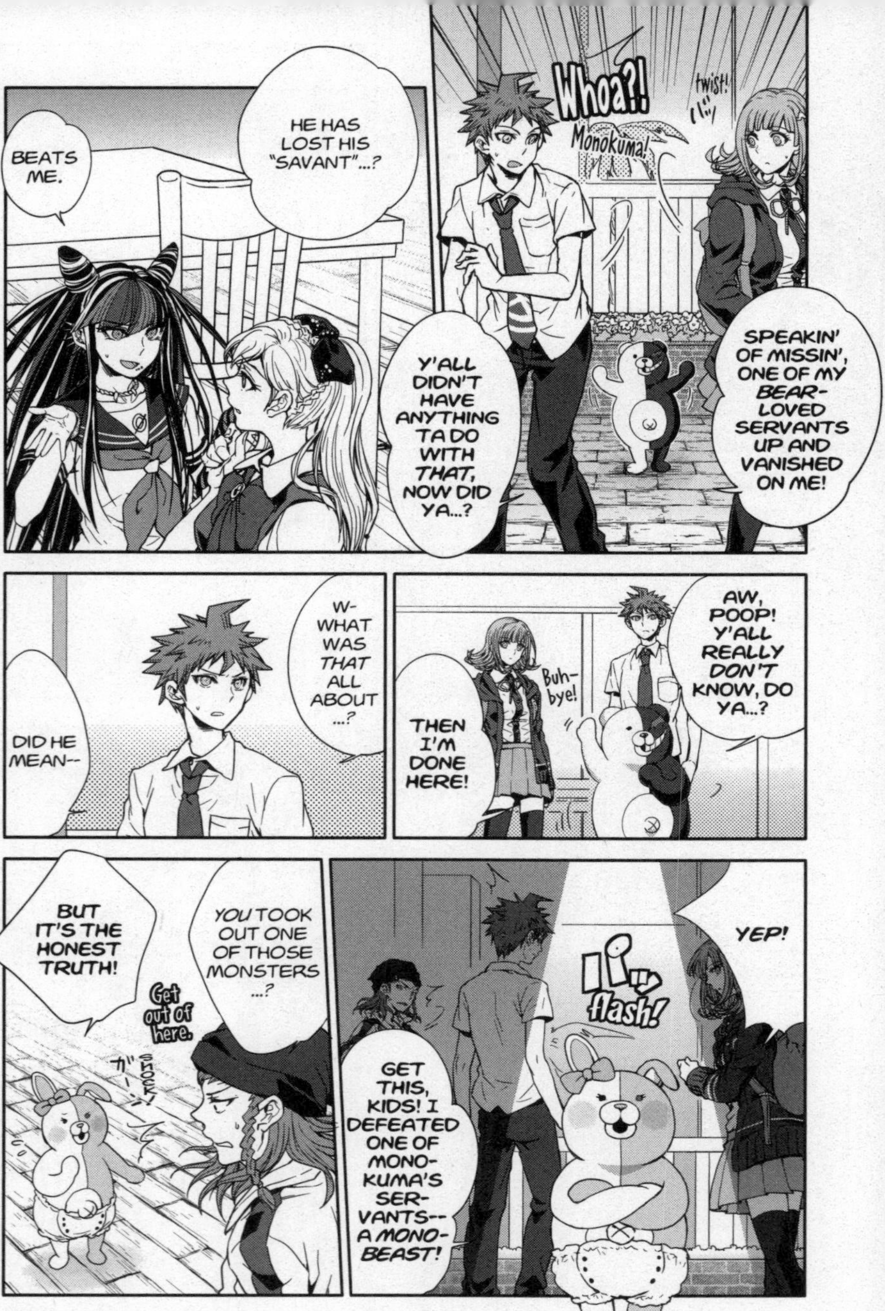
twist!
Whoa?!
Monokuma!
SPEAKIN' OF MISSIN', ONE OF MY *BEAR*-LOVED SERVANTS UP AND VANISHED ON ME!
Y'ALL DIDN'T HAVE ANYTHING TA DO WITH *THAT*, NOW DID YA...?
HE HAS LOST HIS "SAVANT"...?
BEATS ME.
AW, POOP! Y'ALL REALLY DON'T KNOW, DO YA...?
Buh-bye!
THEN I'M DONE HERE!
W-WHAT WAS *THAT* ALL ABOUT ...?
DID HE MEAN--
YEP!
flash!
GET THIS, KIDS! I DEFEATED ONE OF MONO-KUMA'S SER-VANTS-- A *MONO-BEAST*!
YOU TOOK OUT ONE OF THOSE MONSTERS ...?
BUT IT'S THE HONEST TRUTH!
Get out of here.
SHOCK!

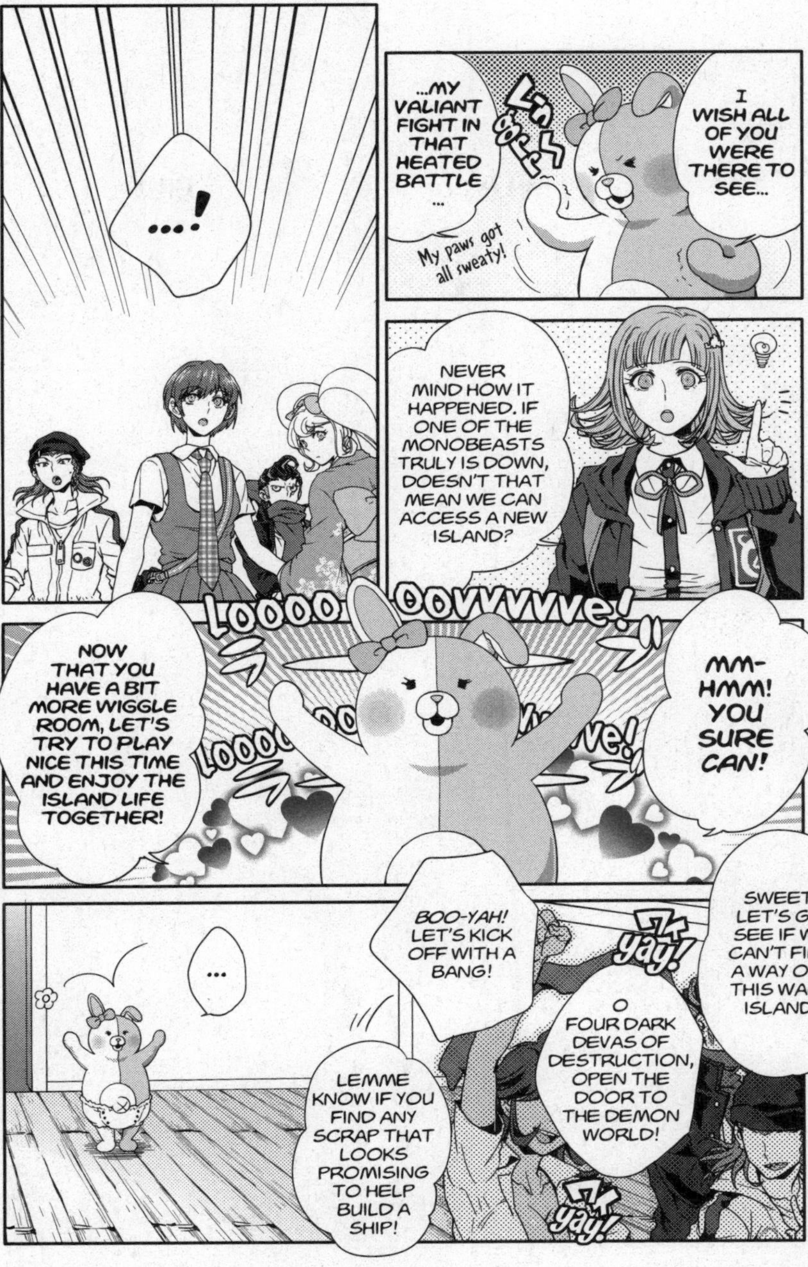
I WISH ALL OF YOU WERE THERE TO SEE...
...MY VALIANT FIGHT IN THAT HEATED BATTLE ...
My paws got all sweaty!
NEVER MIND HOW IT HAPPENED. IF ONE OF THE MONOBEASTS TRULY IS DOWN, DOESN'T THAT MEAN WE CAN ACCESS A NEW ISLAND?
...!
LOOOOOOOVVVVVVE!
MM-HMM! YOU SURE CAN!
NOW THAT YOU HAVE A BIT MORE WIGGLE ROOM, LET'S TRY TO PLAY NICE THIS TIME AND ENJOY THE ISLAND LIFE TOGETHER!
SWEET! LET'S GO SEE IF WE CAN'T FIND A WAY OFF THIS WACK ISLAND!
yay!
BOO-YAH! LET'S KICK OFF WITH A BANG!
O FOUR DARK DEVAS OF DESTRUCTION, OPEN THE DOOR TO THE DEMON WORLD!
LEMME KNOW IF YOU FIND ANY SCRAP THAT LOOKS PROMISING TO HELP BUILD A SHIP!
yay!
...

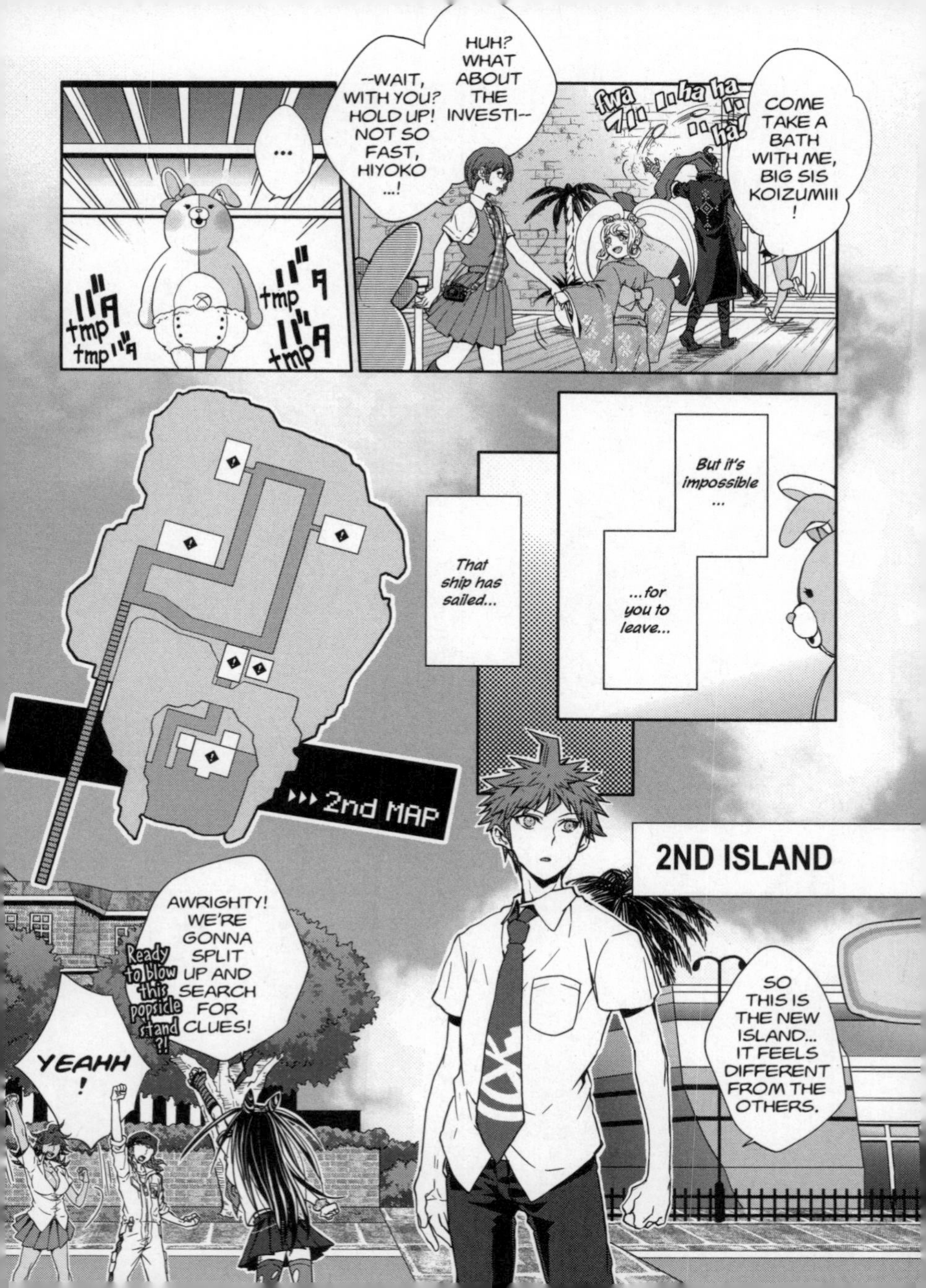

fwa ..ha ha .. ..ha!
COME TAKE A BATH WITH ME, BIG SIS KOIZUMIII!
HUH? WHAT ABOUT THE INVESTI--
--WAIT, WITH YOU? HOLD UP! NOT SO FAST, HIYOKO...!
...
バタ tmp バタ tmp
バタ tmp バタ tmp
But it's impossible...
...for you to leave...
That ship has sailed...
▸▸▸ 2nd MAP
2ND ISLAND
SO THIS IS THE NEW ISLAND... IT FEELS DIFFERENT FROM THE OTHERS.
AWRIGHTY! WE'RE GONNA SPLIT UP AND SEARCH FOR CLUES!
Ready to blow this popsicle stand?!
YEAHH!

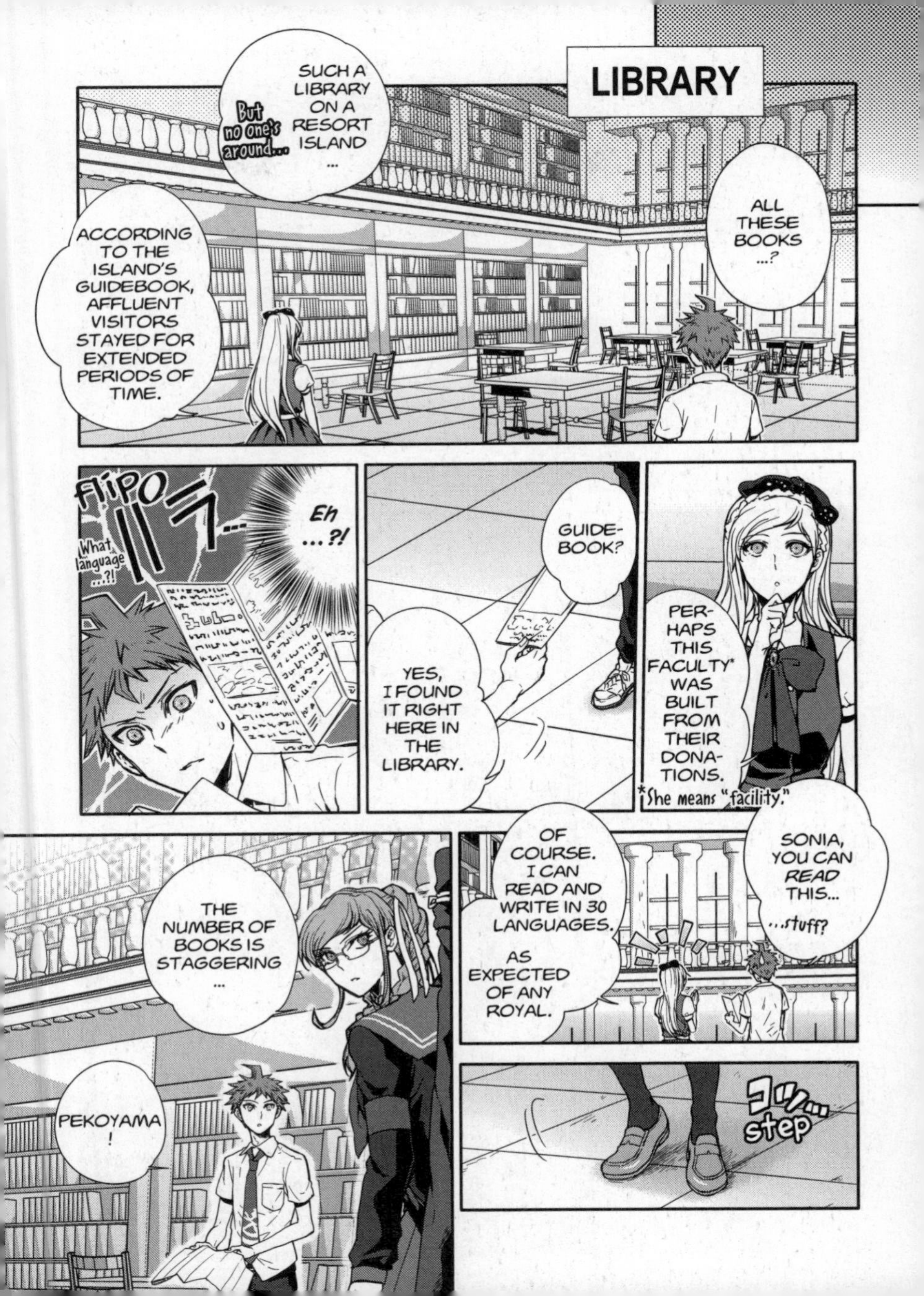
LIBRARY
ALL THESE BOOKS ...?
SUCH A LIBRARY ON A RESORT ISLAND ...
But no one's around...
ACCORDING TO THE ISLAND'S GUIDEBOOK, AFFLUENT VISITORS STAYED FOR EXTENDED PERIODS OF TIME.
PER-HAPS THIS FACULTY* WAS BUILT FROM THEIR DONA-TIONS.
*She means "facility."
GUIDE-BOOK?
YES, I FOUND IT RIGHT HERE IN THE LIBRARY.
Eh ...?!
Flipo
What language ...?!
SONIA, YOU CAN READ THIS...
...stuff?
OF COURSE. I CAN READ AND WRITE IN 30 LANGUAGES.
AS EXPECTED OF ANY ROYAL.
step
THE NUMBER OF BOOKS IS STAGGERING ...
PEKOYAMA !

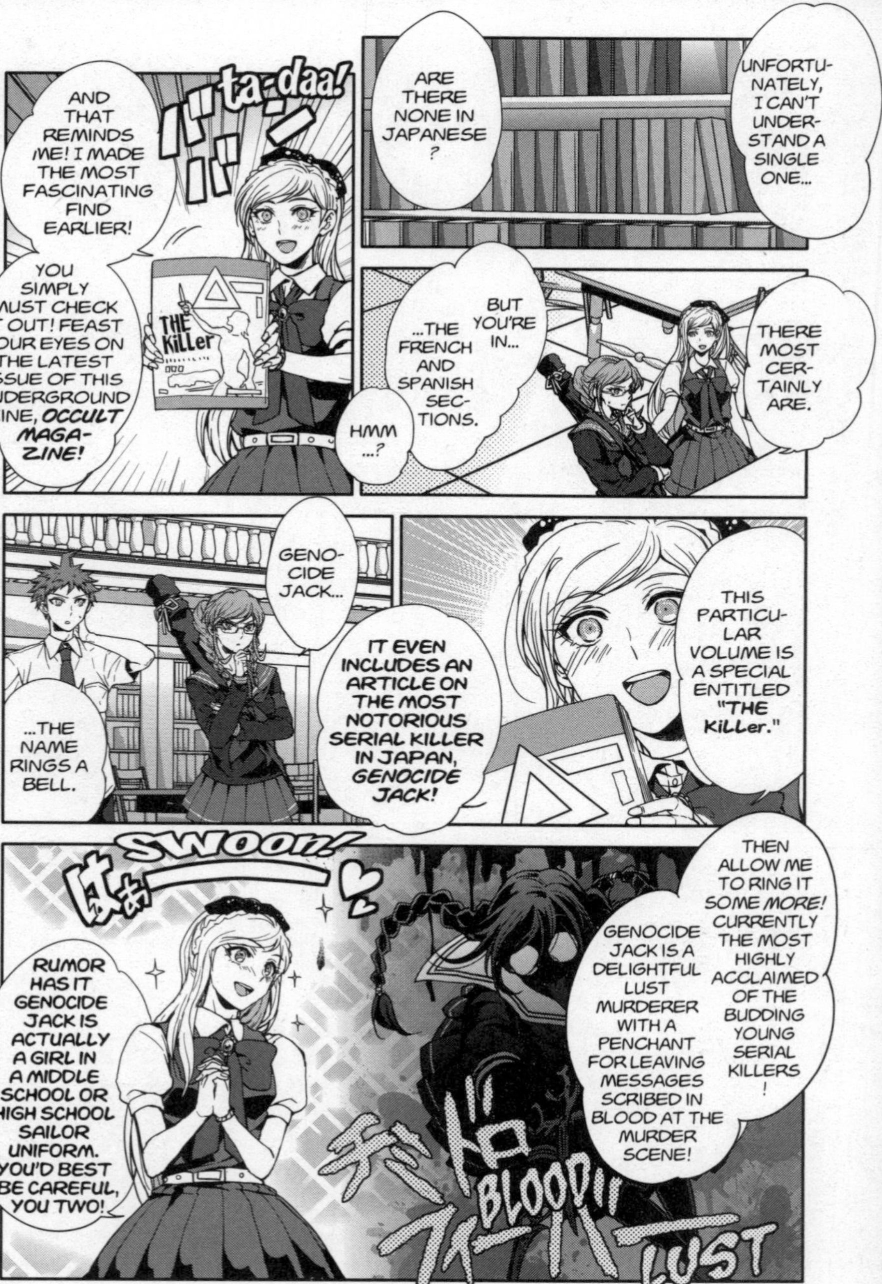

UNFORTUNATELY, I CAN'T UNDERSTAND A SINGLE ONE...
ARE THERE NONE IN JAPANESE?
THERE MOST CERTAINLY ARE.
BUT YOU'RE IN...
...THE FRENCH AND SPANISH SECTIONS.
HMM...?
ta-daa!
AND THAT REMINDS ME! I MADE THE MOST FASCINATING FIND EARLIER!
YOU SIMPLY MUST CHECK IT OUT! FEAST YOUR EYES ON THE LATEST ISSUE OF THIS UNDERGROUND ZINE, *OCCULT MAGAZINE!*
THE KiLLer
THIS PARTICULAR VOLUME IS A SPECIAL ENTITLED "THE KiLLer."
GENOCIDE JACK...
IT EVEN INCLUDES AN ARTICLE ON THE MOST NOTORIOUS SERIAL KILLER IN JAPAN, *GENOCIDE JACK!*
...THE NAME RINGS A BELL.
THEN ALLOW ME TO RING IT SOME *MORE!* CURRENTLY THE MOST HIGHLY ACCLAIMED OF THE BUDDING YOUNG SERIAL KILLERS!
GENOCIDE JACK IS A DELIGHTFUL LUST MURDERER WITH A PENCHANT FOR LEAVING MESSAGES SCRIBED IN BLOOD AT THE MURDER SCENE!
SWOON!
RUMOR HAS IT GENOCIDE JACK IS ACTUALLY A GIRL IN A MIDDLE SCHOOL OR HIGH SCHOOL SAILOR UNIFORM. YOU'D BEST BE CAREFUL, YOU TWO!
BLOOD LUST

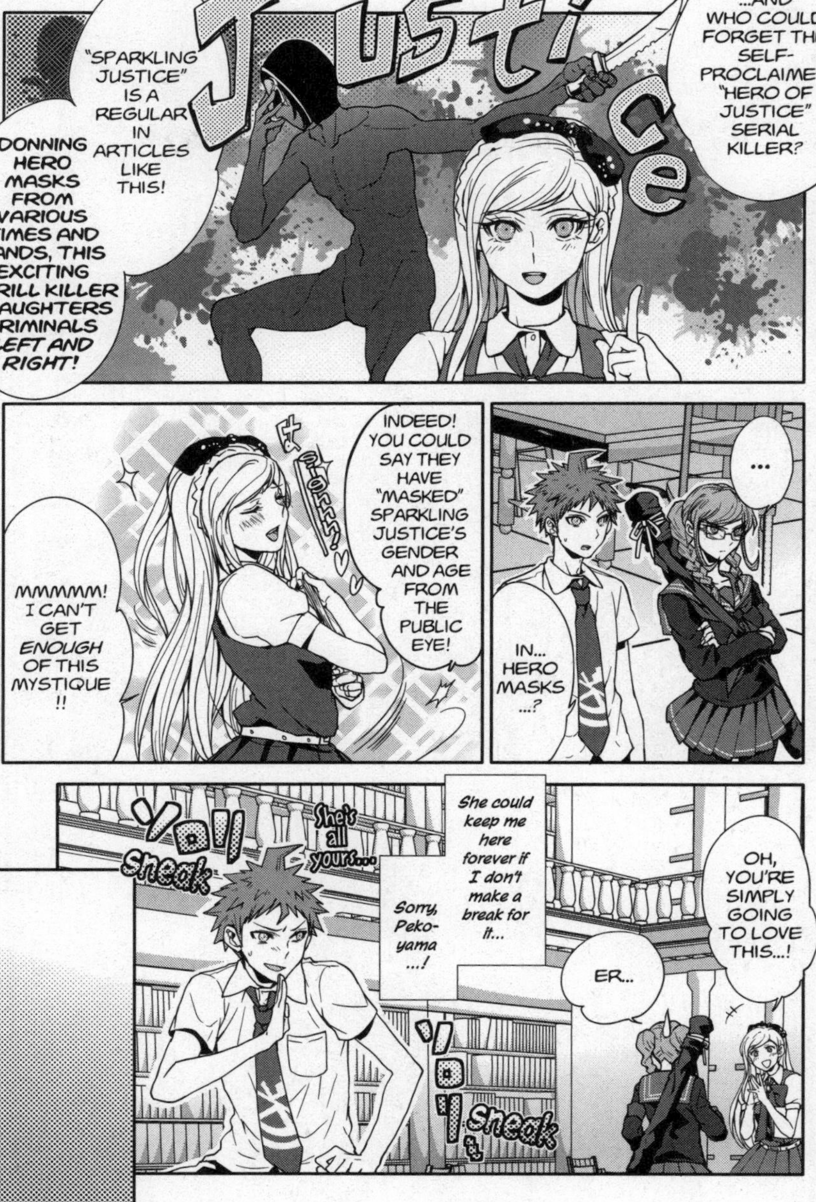
...AND WHO COULD FORGET THE SELF-PROCLAIMED "HERO OF JUSTICE" SERIAL KILLER?
Justice
"SPARKLING JUSTICE" IS A REGULAR IN ARTICLES LIKE THIS!
DONNING HERO MASKS FROM VARIOUS TIMES AND LANDS, THIS EXCITING THRILL KILLER SLAUGHTERS CRIMINALS *LEFT AND RIGHT!*
...
IN... HERO MASKS ...?
INDEED! YOU COULD SAY THEY HAVE "MASKED" SPARKLING JUSTICE'S GENDER AND AGE FROM THE PUBLIC EYE!
MMMMM! I CAN'T GET *ENOUGH* OF THIS MYSTIQUE !!
OH, YOU'RE SIMPLY GOING TO LOVE THIS...!
ER...
sneak
She could keep me here forever if I don't make a break for it...
Sorry, Peko-yama ...!
She's all yours...
sneak

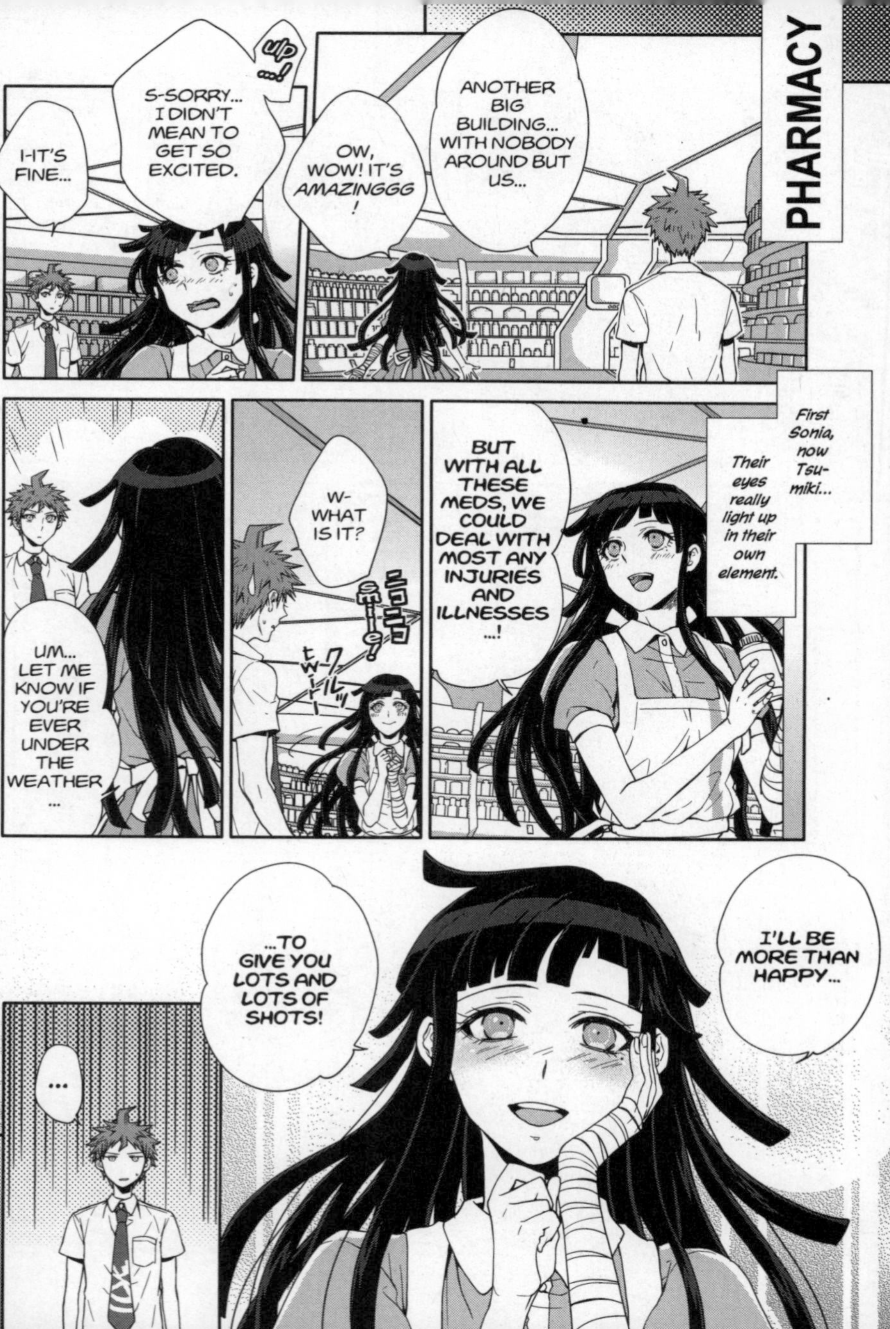
PHARMACY
ANOTHER BIG BUILDING... WITH NOBODY AROUND BUT US...
OW, WOW! IT'S AMAZINGGG!
up...!
S-SORRY... I DIDN'T MEAN TO GET SO EXCITED.
I-IT'S FINE...
First Sonia, now Tsumiki...
Their eyes really light up in their own element.
BUT WITH ALL THESE MEDS, WE COULD DEAL WITH MOST ANY INJURIES AND ILLNESSES ...!
W-WHAT IS IT?
smile
twirl
UM... LET ME KNOW IF YOU'RE EVER UNDER THE WEATHER ...
I'LL BE MORE THAN HAPPY...
...TO GIVE YOU LOTS AND LOTS OF SHOTS!
...

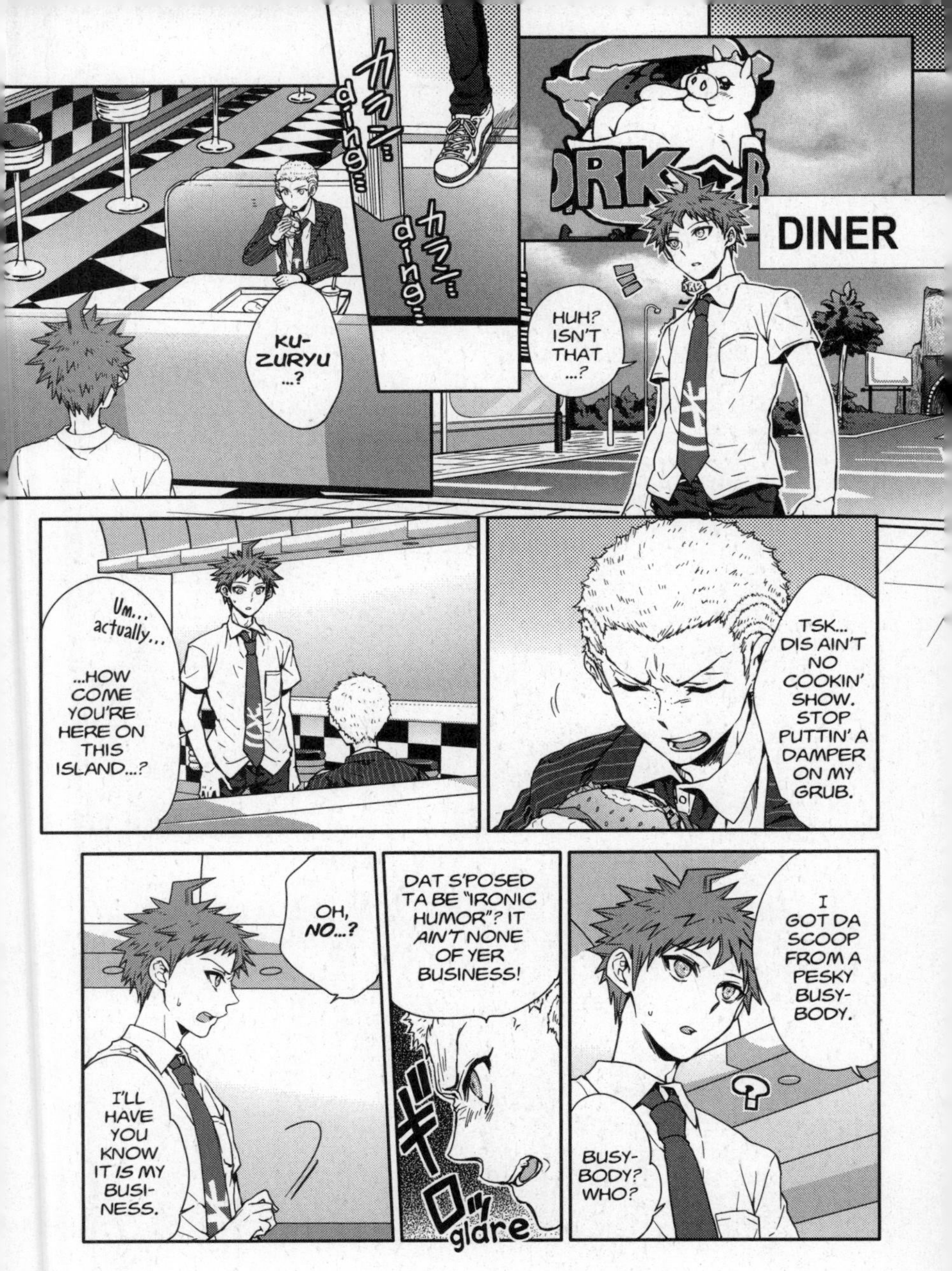
DINER
HUH? ISN'T THAT ...?
カラン… ding…
カラン… ding…
KU-ZURYU ...?
TSK... DIS AIN'T NO COOKIN' SHOW. STOP PUTTIN' A DAMPER ON MY GRUB.
Um... actually...
...HOW COME YOU'RE HERE ON THIS ISLAND...?
I GOT DA SCOOP FROM A PESKY BUSY-BODY.
BUSY-BODY? WHO?
DAT S'POSED TA BE "IRONIC HUMOR"? IT AIN'T NONE OF YER BUSINESS!
ギロッ glare
OH, NO...?
I'LL HAVE YOU KNOW IT IS MY BUSI-NESS.

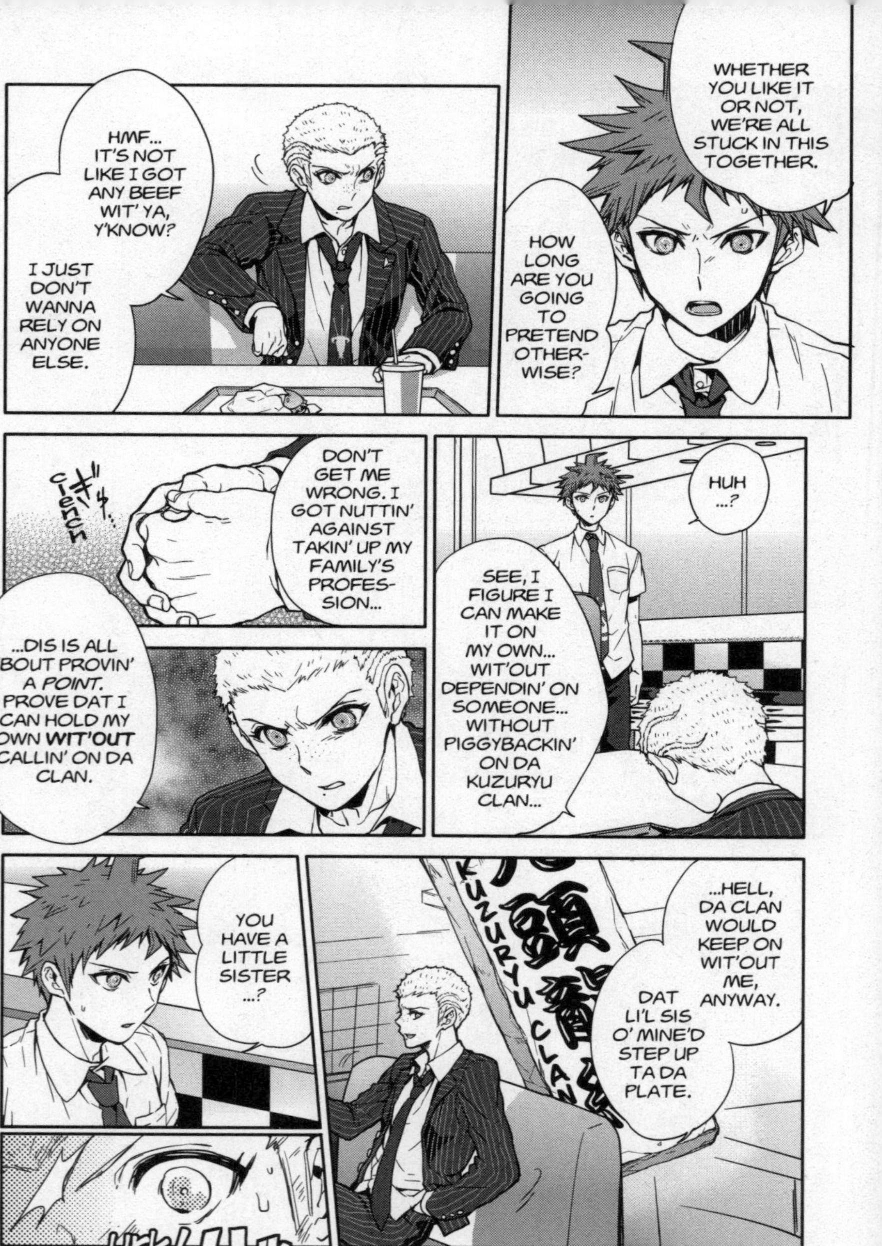
WHETHER YOU LIKE IT OR NOT, WE'RE ALL STUCK IN THIS TOGETHER.
HOW LONG ARE YOU GOING TO PRETEND OTHER-WISE?
HMF... IT'S NOT LIKE I GOT ANY BEEF WIT' YA, Y'KNOW?
I JUST DON'T WANNA RELY ON ANYONE ELSE.
HUH ...?
SEE, I FIGURE I CAN MAKE IT ON MY OWN... WIT'OUT DEPENDIN' ON SOMEONE... WITHOUT PIGGYBACKIN' ON DA KUZURYU CLAN...
DON'T GET ME WRONG. I GOT NUTTIN' AGAINST TAKIN' UP MY FAMILY'S PROFES-SION...
clench
...DIS IS ALL 'BOUT PROVIN' A *POINT*. PROVE DAT I CAN HOLD MY OWN **WIT'OUT** CALLIN' ON DA CLAN.
...HELL, DA CLAN WOULD KEEP ON WIT'OUT ME, ANYWAY.
DAT LI'L SIS O' MINE'D STEP UP TA DA PLATE.
KUZURYU CLAN
YOU HAVE A LITTLE SISTER ...?
urk!

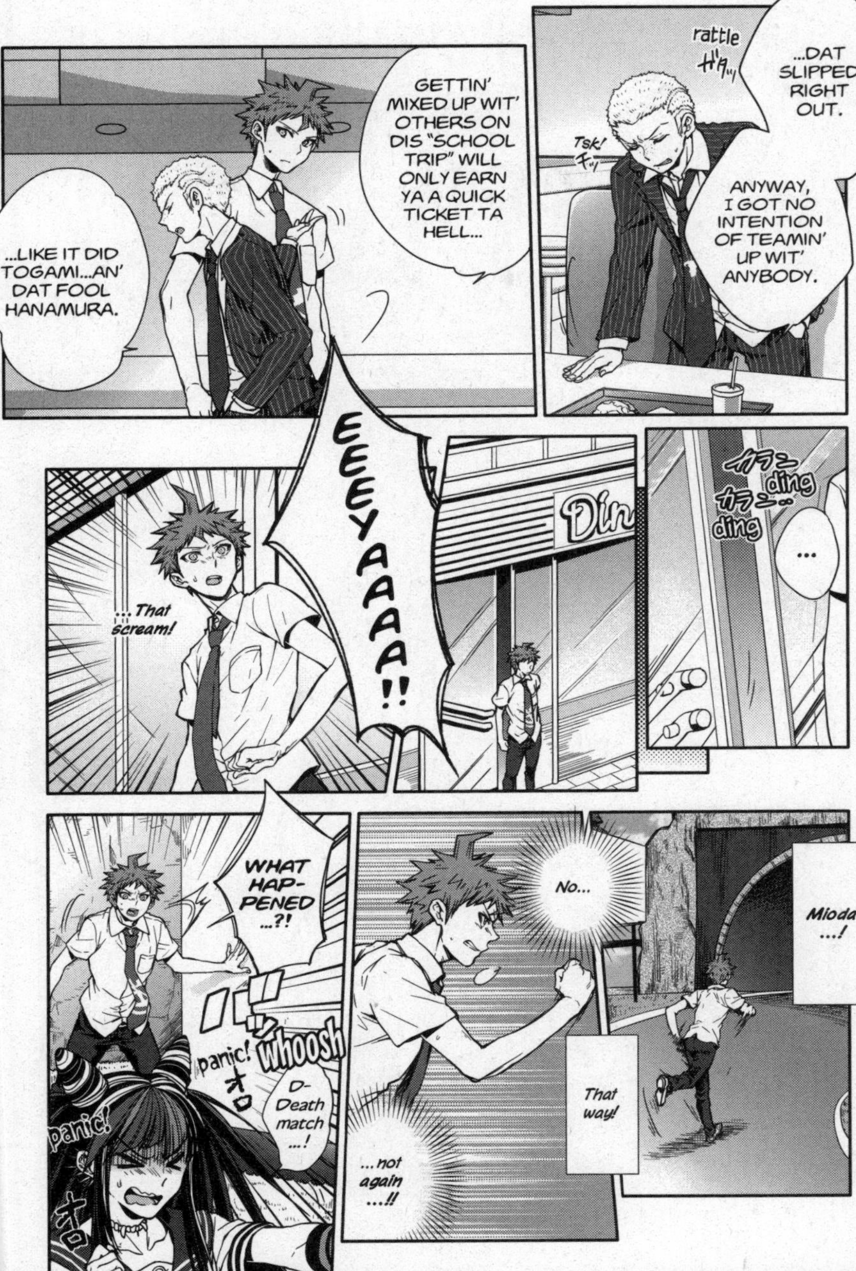
...DAT SLIPPED RIGHT OUT.
rattle
ガタッ
Tsk!
チッ
ANYWAY, I GOT NO INTENTION OF TEAMIN' UP WIT' ANYBODY.
GETTIN' MIXED UP WIT' OTHERS ON DIS "SCHOOL TRIP" WILL ONLY EARN YA A QUICK TICKET TA HELL...
...LIKE IT DID TOGAMI...AN' DAT FOOL HANAMURA.
カラン
ding
カラン
ding
...
Din
EEEEYAAAAA!!
...That scream!
Mioda ...!
That way!
No...
...not again ...!!
WHAT HAP-PENED ...?!
whoosh
panic!
オロ
D-Death match ...!
panic!
オロ

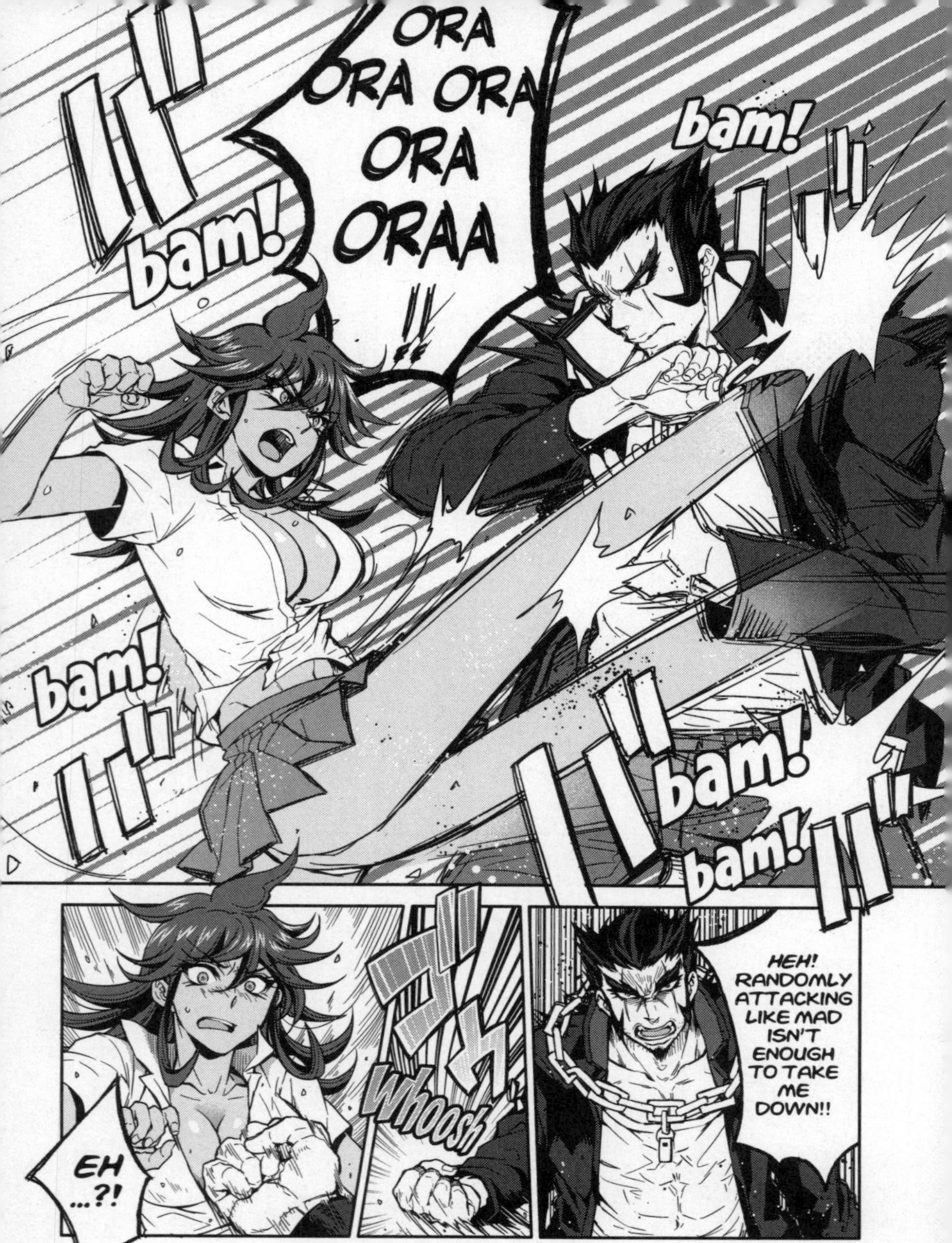
bam!
ORA ORA ORA ORA ORA ORAA !!
bam!
bam!
bam!
bam!
HEH! RANDOMLY ATTACKING LIKE MAD ISN'T ENOUGH TO TAKE ME DOWN!!
whoosh
EH ...?!

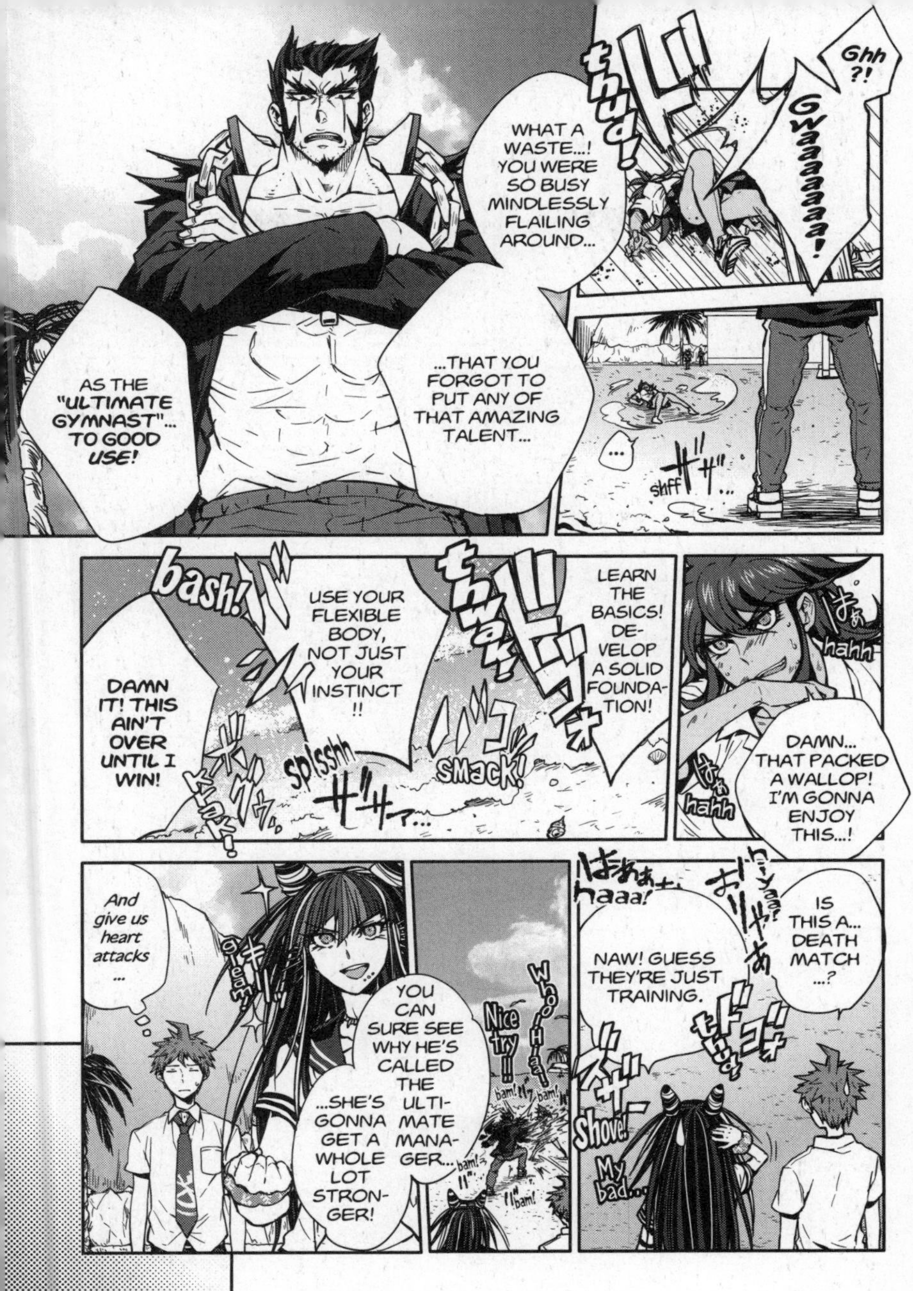

thud!
Ghh?!
Gwaaaaaaaa!
...
shff...
WHAT A WASTE...! YOU WERE SO BUSY MINDLESSLY FLAILING AROUND...
...THAT YOU FORGOT TO PUT ANY OF THAT AMAZING TALENT...
AS THE "ULTIMATE GYMNAST"... TO GOOD USE!
hahh
hahh
DAMN... THAT PACKED A WALLOP! I'M GONNA ENJOY THIS...!
thwak!
LEARN THE BASICS! DE-VELOP A SOLID FOUNDA-TION!
USE YOUR FLEXIBLE BODY, NOT JUST YOUR INSTINCT!!
bash!
DAMN IT! THIS AIN'T OVER UNTIL I WIN!
SMACK!
splsshh
haaa!
IS THIS A... DEATH MATCH...?
NAW! GUESS THEY'RE JUST TRAINING.
Shove!
My bad...
Whooo-Hah!
Nice try!!
bam!
bam!
bam!
bam!
YOU CAN SURE SEE WHY HE'S CALLED THE ULTI-MATE MANA-GER...
...SHE'S GONNA GET A WHOLE LOT STRON-GER!
gleam
And give us heart attacks...

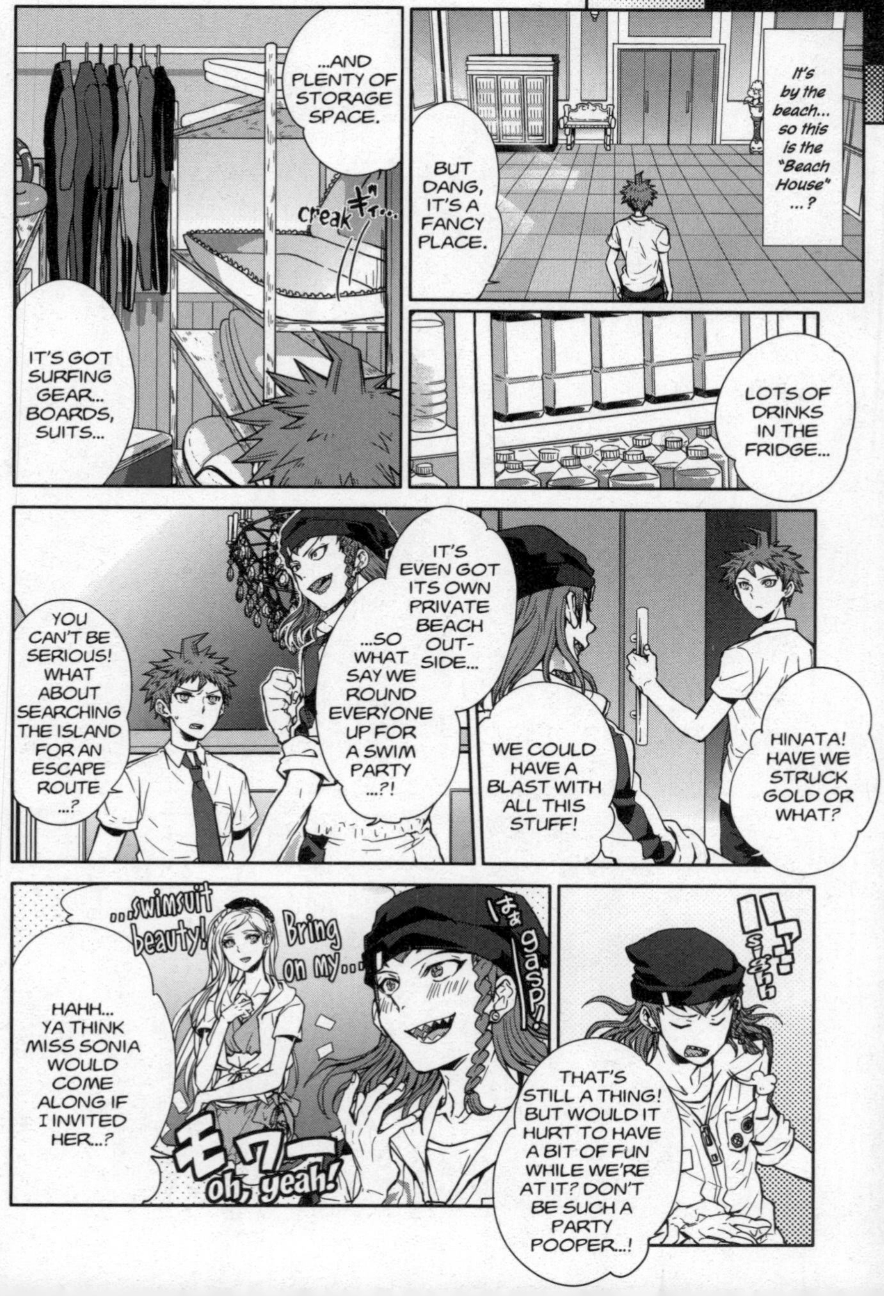
It's by the beach... so this is the "Beach House" ...?
BUT DANG, IT'S A FANCY PLACE.
LOTS OF DRINKS IN THE FRIDGE...
...AND PLENTY OF STORAGE SPACE.
creak
IT'S GOT SURFING GEAR... BOARDS, SUITS...
HINATA! HAVE WE STRUCK GOLD OR WHAT?
WE COULD HAVE A BLAST WITH ALL THIS STUFF!
IT'S EVEN GOT ITS OWN PRIVATE BEACH OUT-SIDE...
...SO WHAT SAY WE ROUND EVERYONE UP FOR A SWIM PARTY ...?!
YOU CAN'T BE SERIOUS! WHAT ABOUT SEARCHING THE ISLAND FOR AN ESCAPE ROUTE ...?
sigh
THAT'S STILL A THING! BUT WOULD IT HURT TO HAVE A BIT OF FUN WHILE WE'RE AT IT? DON'T BE SUCH A PARTY POOPER...!
gasp!
Bring on my... ...swimsuit beauty!
HAHH... YA THINK MISS SONIA WOULD COME ALONG IF I INVITED HER...?
oh, yeah!

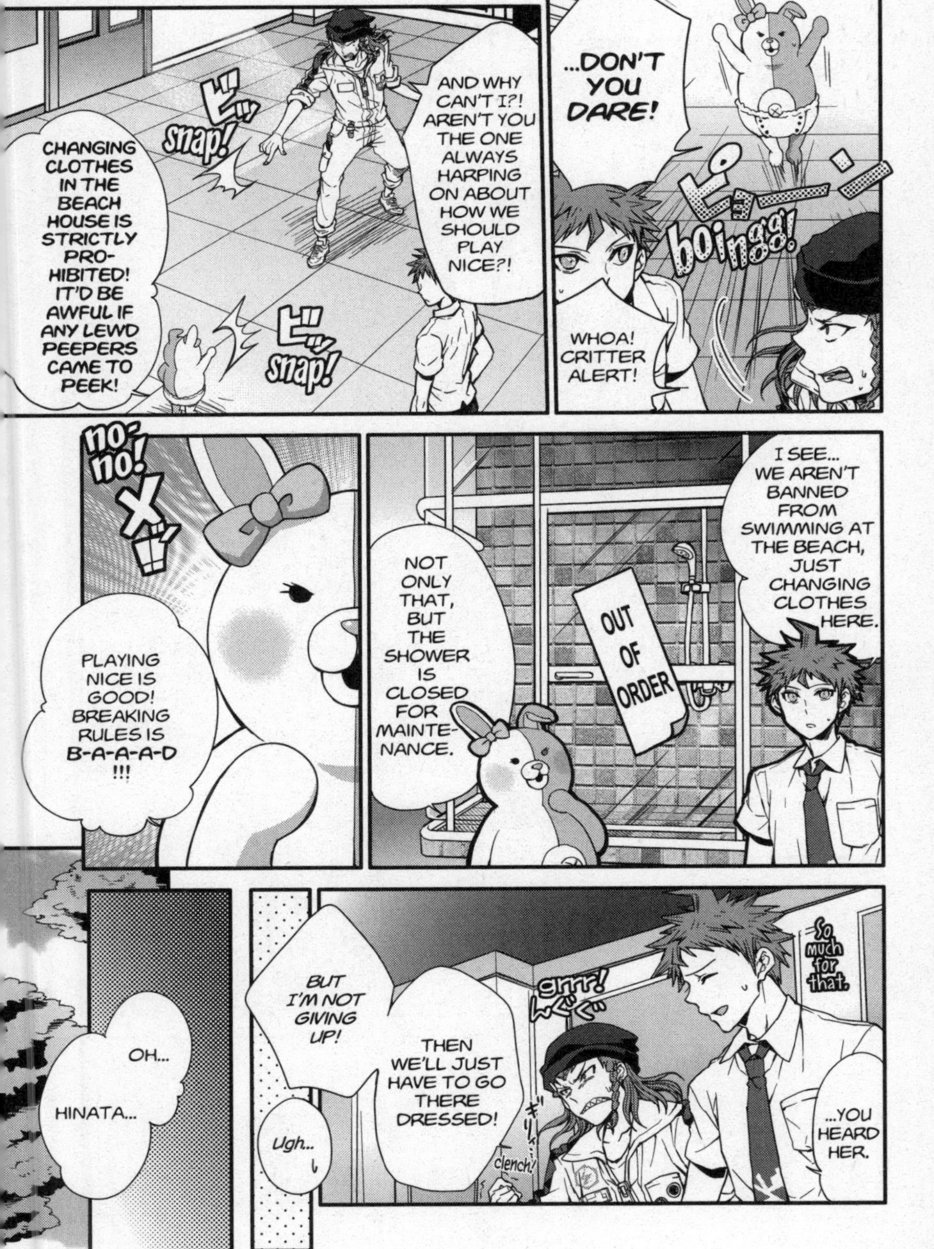
...DON'T YOU DARE!
boingg!
WHOA! CRITTER ALERT!
AND WHY CAN'T I?! AREN'T YOU THE ONE ALWAYS HARPING ON ABOUT HOW WE SHOULD PLAY NICE?!
snap!
CHANGING CLOTHES IN THE BEACH HOUSE IS STRICTLY PRO-HIBITED! IT'D BE AWFUL IF ANY LEWD PEEPERS CAME TO PEEK!
snap!
I SEE... WE AREN'T BANNED FROM SWIMMING AT THE BEACH, JUST CHANGING CLOTHES HERE.
NOT ONLY THAT, BUT THE SHOWER IS CLOSED FOR MAINTE-NANCE.
OUT OF ORDER
no-no!
PLAYING NICE IS GOOD! BREAKING RULES IS B-A-A-A-D !!!
So much for that.
grrr!
BUT I'M NOT GIVING UP!
...YOU HEARD HER.
THEN WE'LL JUST HAVE TO GO THERE DRESSED!
clench!
Ugh...
OH...
HINATA...

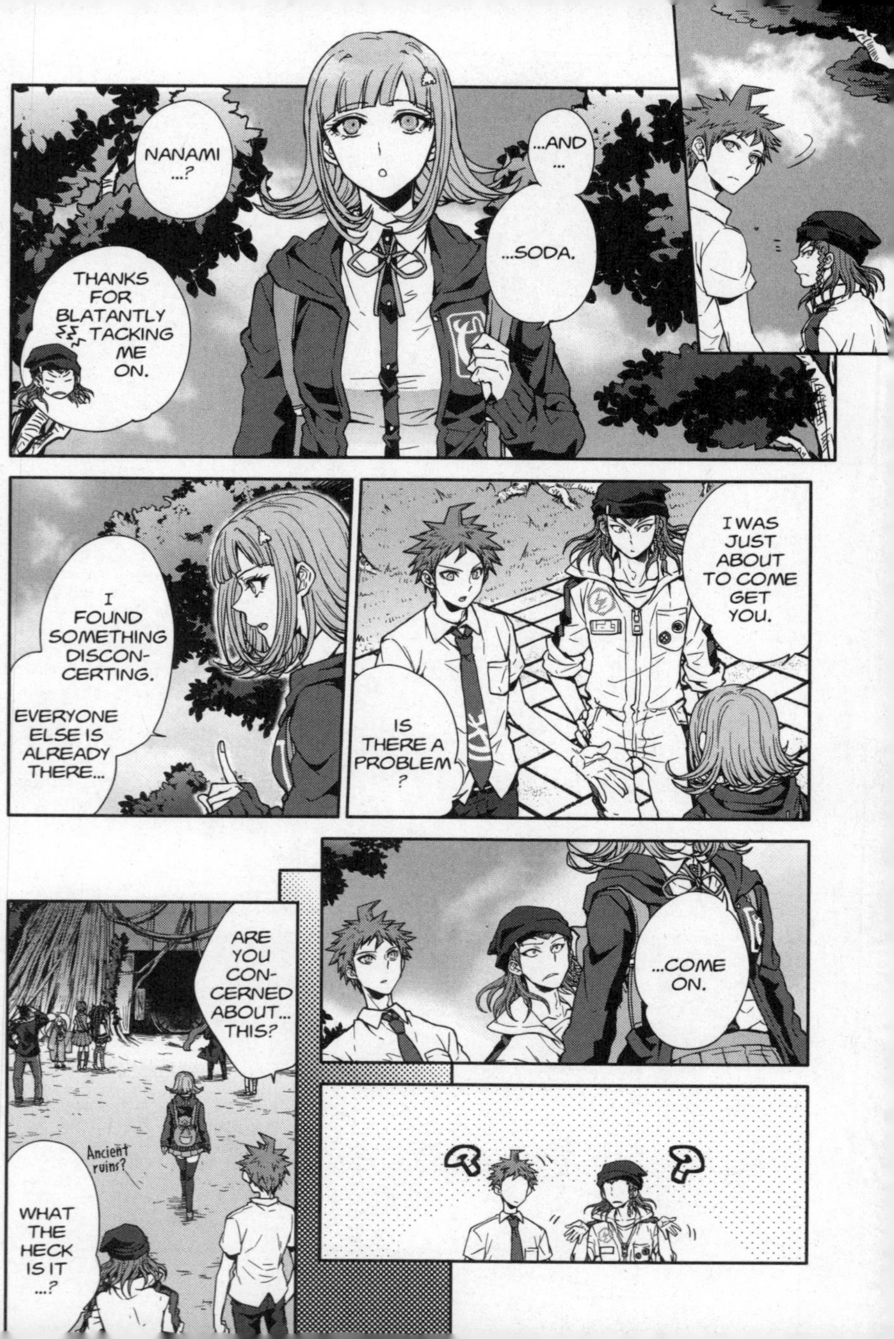
...AND ...
...SODA.
NANAMI ...?
THANKS FOR BLATANTLY TACKING ME ON.
I WAS JUST ABOUT TO COME GET YOU.
IS THERE A PROBLEM ?
I FOUND SOMETHING DISCONCERTING.
EVERYONE ELSE IS ALREADY THERE...
...COME ON.
?
?
ARE YOU CONCERNED ABOUT... THIS?
Ancient ruins?
WHAT THE HECK IS IT ...?

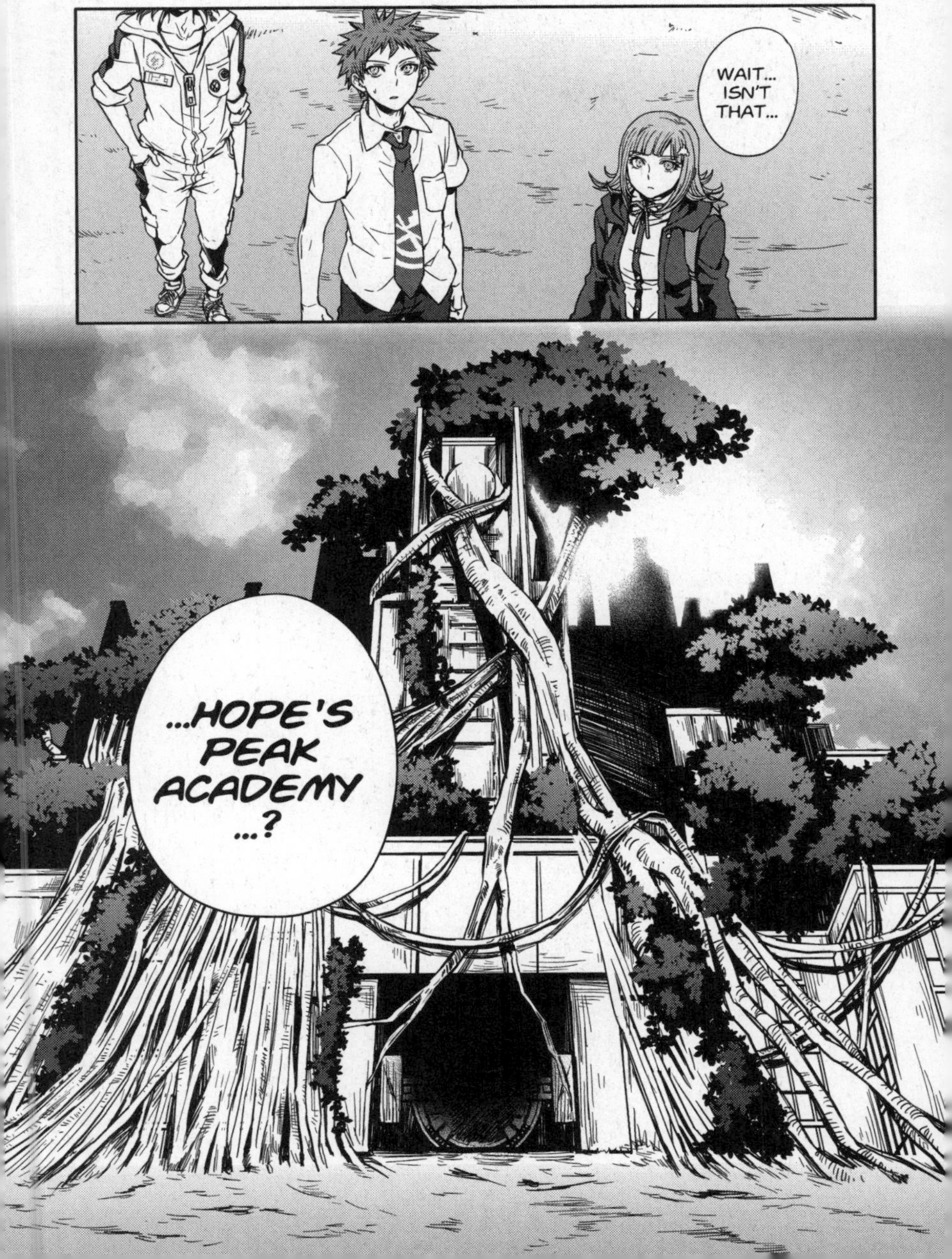
WAIT... ISN'T THAT...
...HOPE'S PEAK ACADEMY ...?

DANGAN RONPA 2

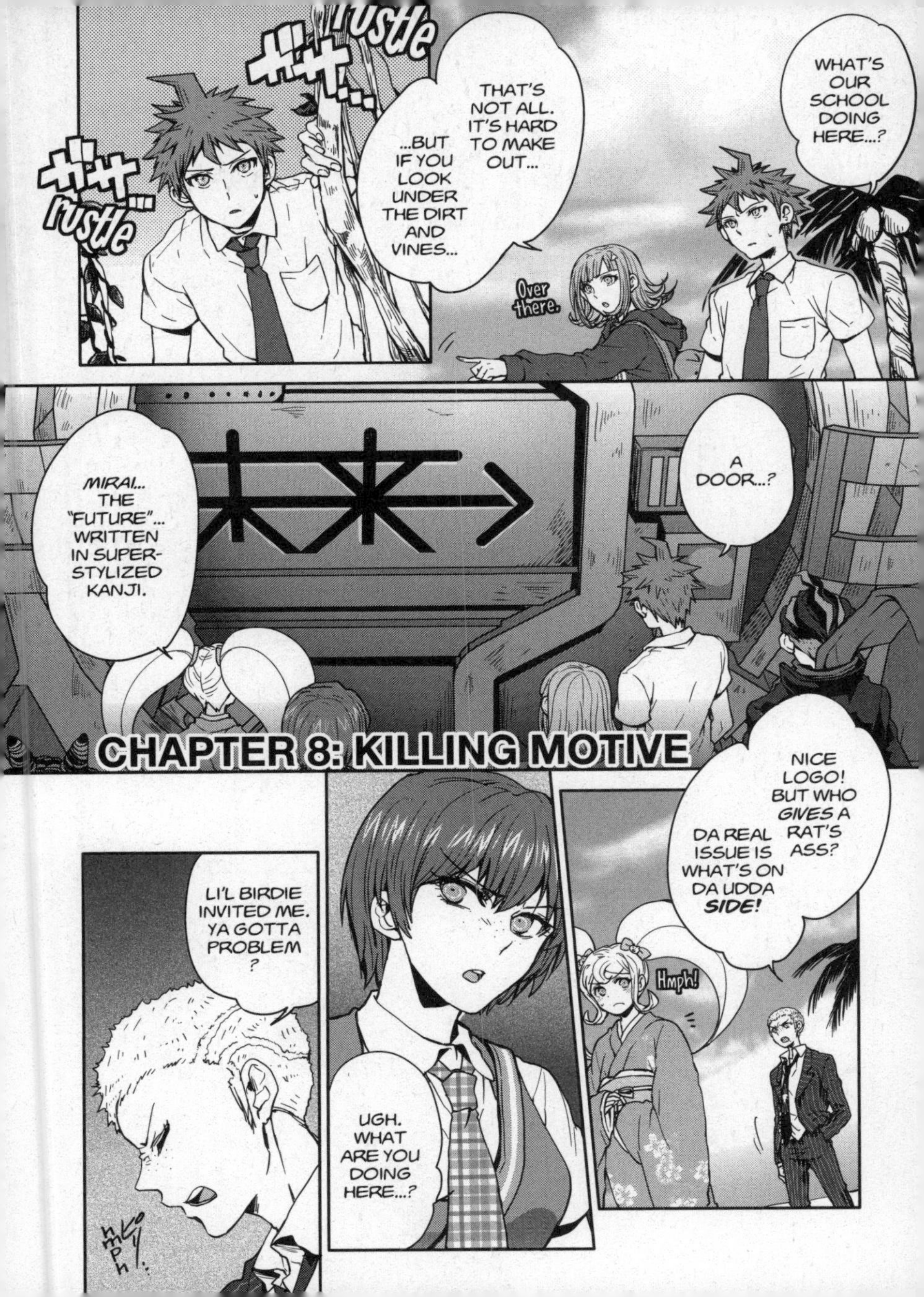
WHAT'S OUR SCHOOL DOING HERE...?
Over there.
rustle
THAT'S NOT ALL. IT'S HARD TO MAKE OUT...
...BUT IF YOU LOOK UNDER THE DIRT AND VINES...
rustle
A DOOR...?
MIRAI... THE "FUTURE"... WRITTEN IN SUPER-STYLIZED KANJI.
CHAPTER 8: KILLING MOTIVE
NICE LOGO! BUT WHO GIVES A RAT'S ASS?
DA REAL ISSUE IS WHAT'S ON DA UDDA SIDE!
Hmph!
UGH. WHAT ARE YOU DOING HERE...?
LI'L BIRDIE INVITED ME. YA GOTTA PROBLEM?
hmph

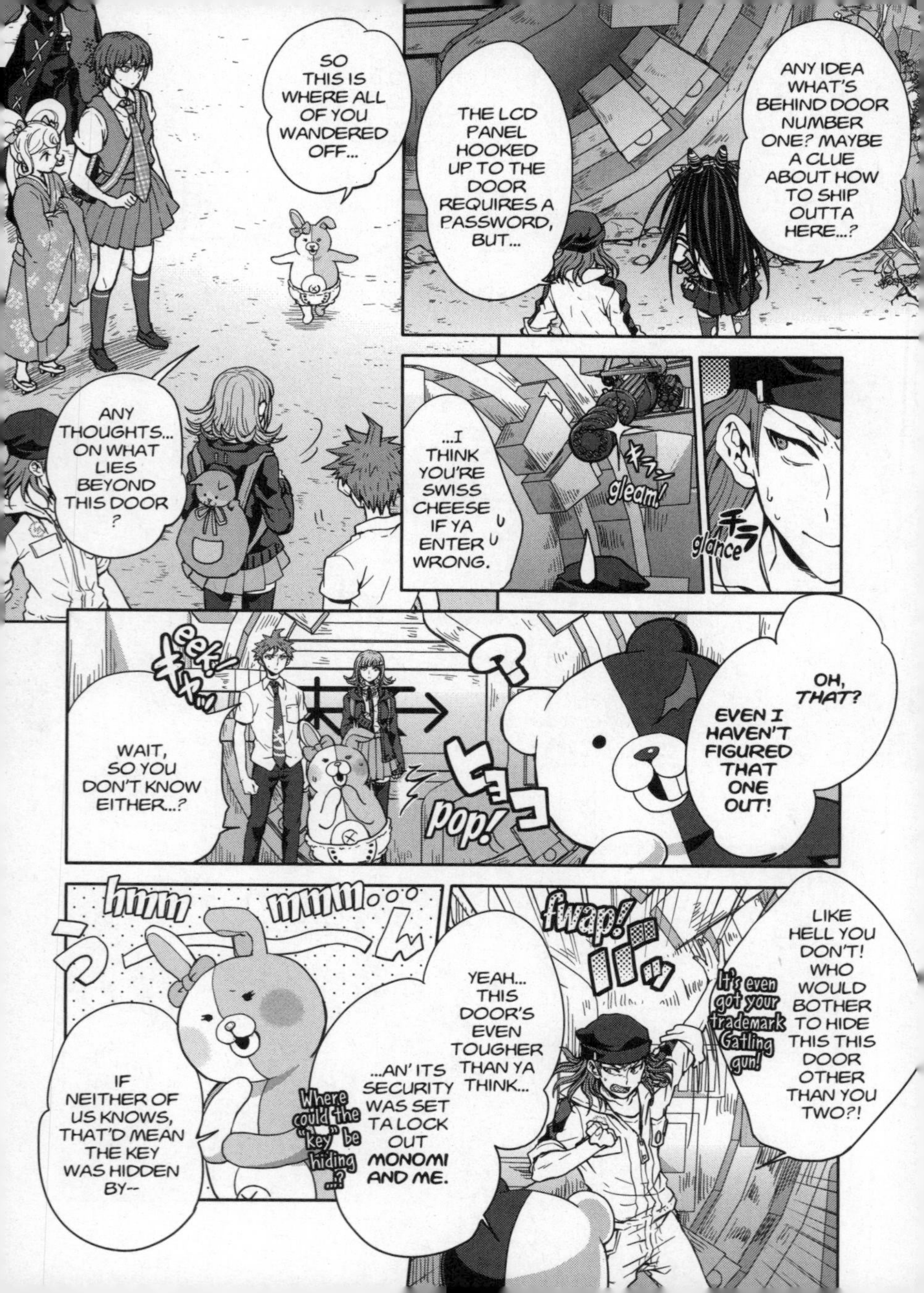

ANY IDEA WHAT'S BEHIND DOOR NUMBER ONE? MAYBE A CLUE ABOUT HOW TO SHIP OUTTA HERE...?
THE LCD PANEL HOOKED UP TO THE DOOR REQUIRES A PASSWORD, BUT...
チラ
glance
gleam!
...I THINK YOU'RE SWISS CHEESE IF YA ENTER WRONG.
SO THIS IS WHERE ALL OF YOU WANDERED OFF...
ANY THOUGHTS... ON WHAT LIES BEYOND THIS DOOR?
OH, THAT? EVEN I HAVEN'T FIGURED THAT ONE OUT!
ヒョコ
pop!
eek! キャッ
WAIT, SO YOU DON'T KNOW EITHER...?
LIKE HELL YOU DON'T! WHO WOULD BOTHER TO HIDE THIS THIS DOOR OTHER THAN YOU TWO?!
It's even got your trademark Gatling gun!
fwap! バッ
YEAH... THIS DOOR'S EVEN TOUGHER THAN YA THINK...
...AN' ITS SECURITY WAS SET TA LOCK OUT MONOMI AND ME.
Where could the "key" be hiding...?
hmm
mmmooo
IF NEITHER OF US KNOWS, THAT'D MEAN THE KEY WAS HIDDEN BY--

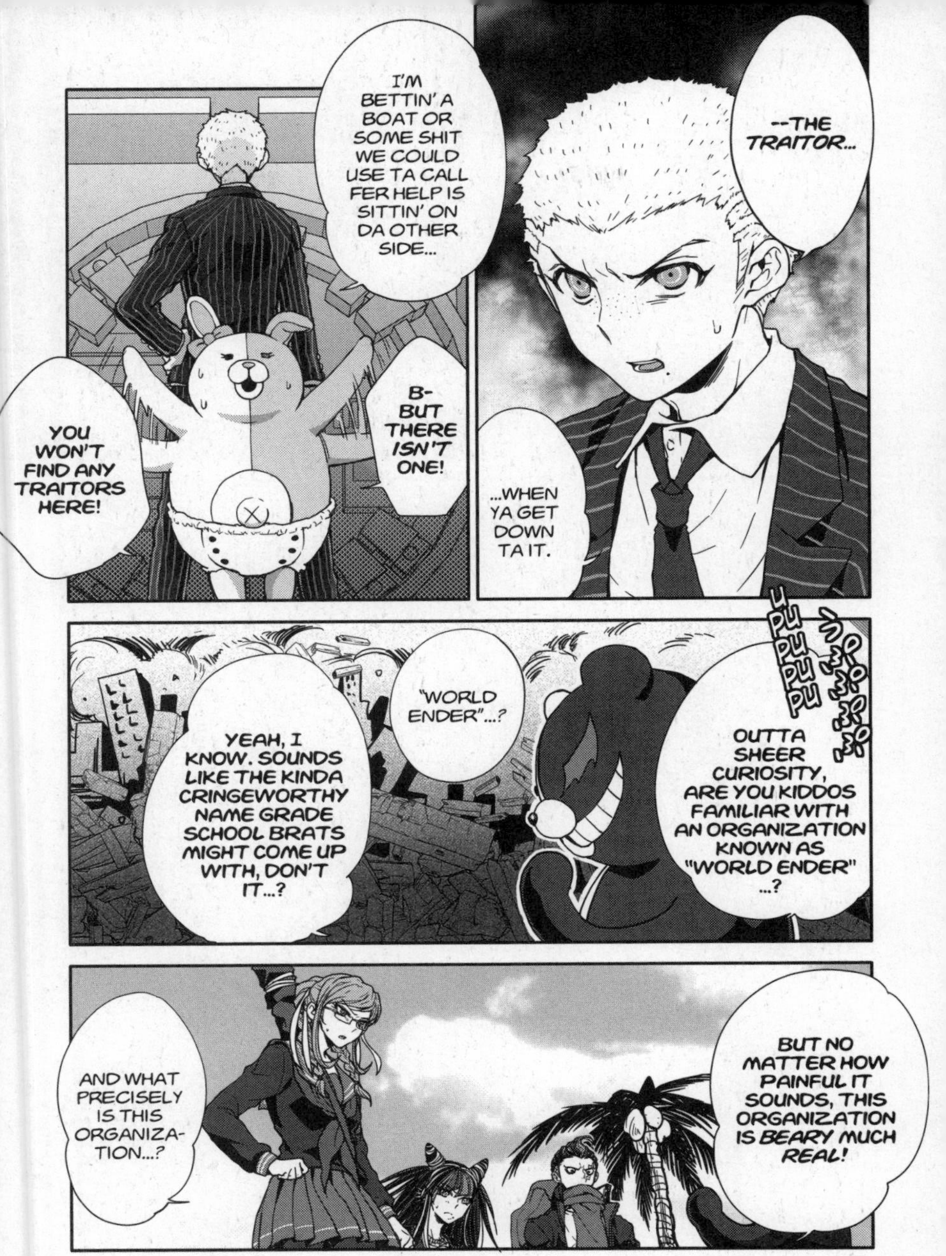
--THE TRAITOR...
...WHEN YA GET DOWN TA IT.
I'M BETTIN' A BOAT OR SOME SHIT WE COULD USE TA CALL FER HELP IS SITTIN' ON DA OTHER SIDE...
B-BUT THERE ISN'T ONE!
YOU WON'T FIND ANY TRAITORS HERE!
UPUPUPUPU
OUTTA SHEER CURIOSITY, ARE YOU KIDDOS FAMILIAR WITH AN ORGANIZATION KNOWN AS "WORLD ENDER" ...?
"WORLD ENDER"...?
YEAH, I KNOW. SOUNDS LIKE THE KINDA CRINGEWORTHY NAME GRADE SCHOOL BRATS MIGHT COME UP WITH, DON'T IT...?
BUT NO MATTER HOW PAINFUL IT SOUNDS, THIS ORGANIZATION IS BEARY MUCH REAL!
AND WHAT PRECISELY IS THIS ORGANIZA-TION...?

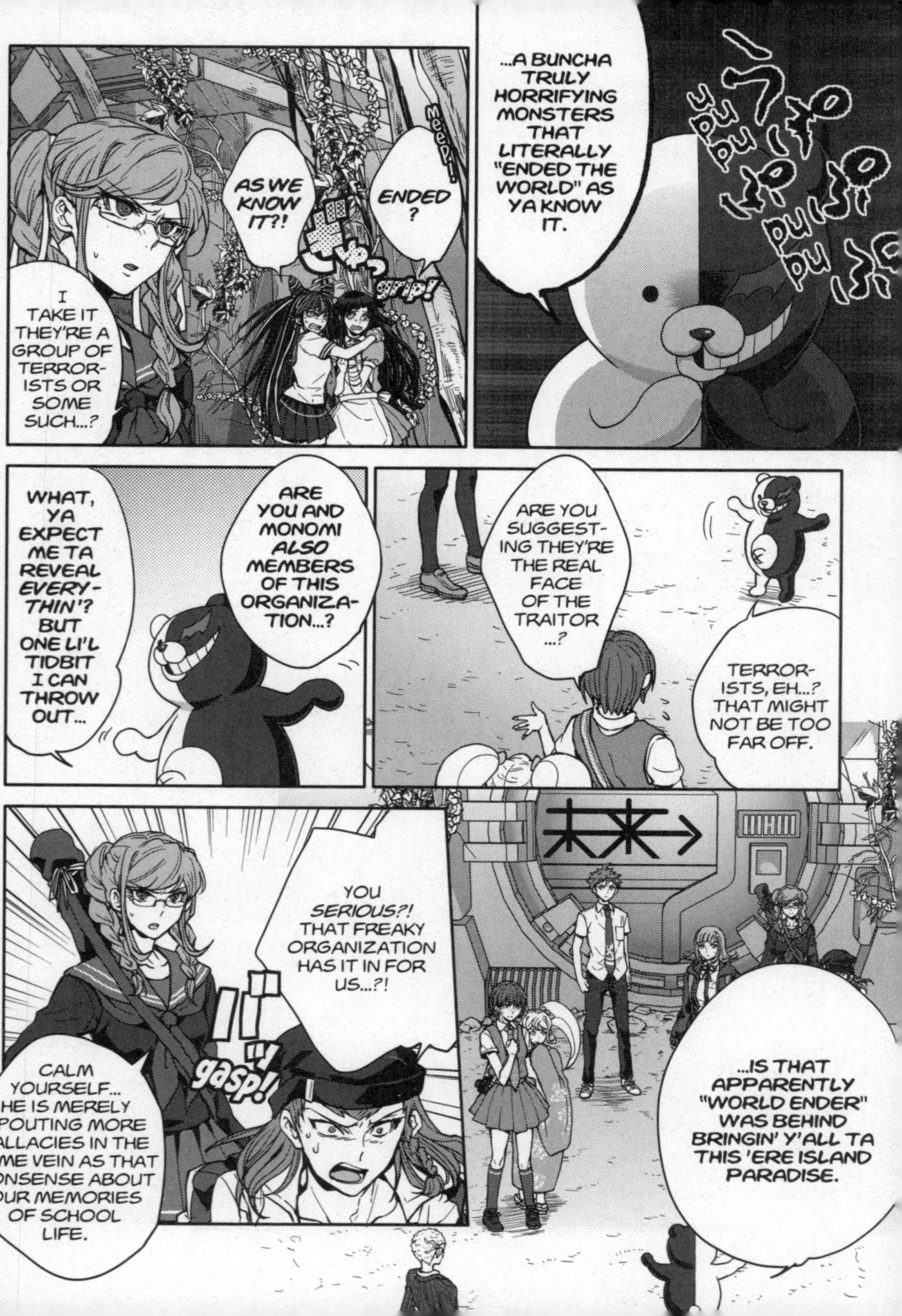
...A BUNCHA TRULY HORRIFYING MONSTERS THAT LITERALLY "ENDED THE WORLD" AS YA KNOW IT.
ENDED?
Meep!!
AS WE KNOW IT?!
grip!
I TAKE IT THEY'RE A GROUP OF TERROR-ISTS OR SOME SUCH...?
ARE YOU SUGGEST-ING THEY'RE THE REAL FACE OF THE TRAITOR ...?
TERROR-ISTS, EH...? THAT MIGHT NOT BE TOO FAR OFF.
ARE YOU AND MONOMI ALSO MEMBERS OF THIS ORGANIZA-TION...?
WHAT, YA EXPECT ME TA REVEAL EVERY-THIN'? BUT ONE LI'L TIDBIT I CAN THROW OUT...
未来
...IS THAT APPARENTLY "WORLD ENDER" WAS BEHIND BRINGIN' Y'ALL TA THIS 'ERE ISLAND PARADISE.
YOU SERIOUS?! THAT FREAKY ORGANIZATION HAS IT IN FOR US...?!
gasp!
CALM YOURSELF... HE IS MERELY SPOUTING MORE FALLACIES IN THE SAME VEIN AS THAT NONSENSE ABOUT OUR MEMORIES OF SCHOOL LIFE.

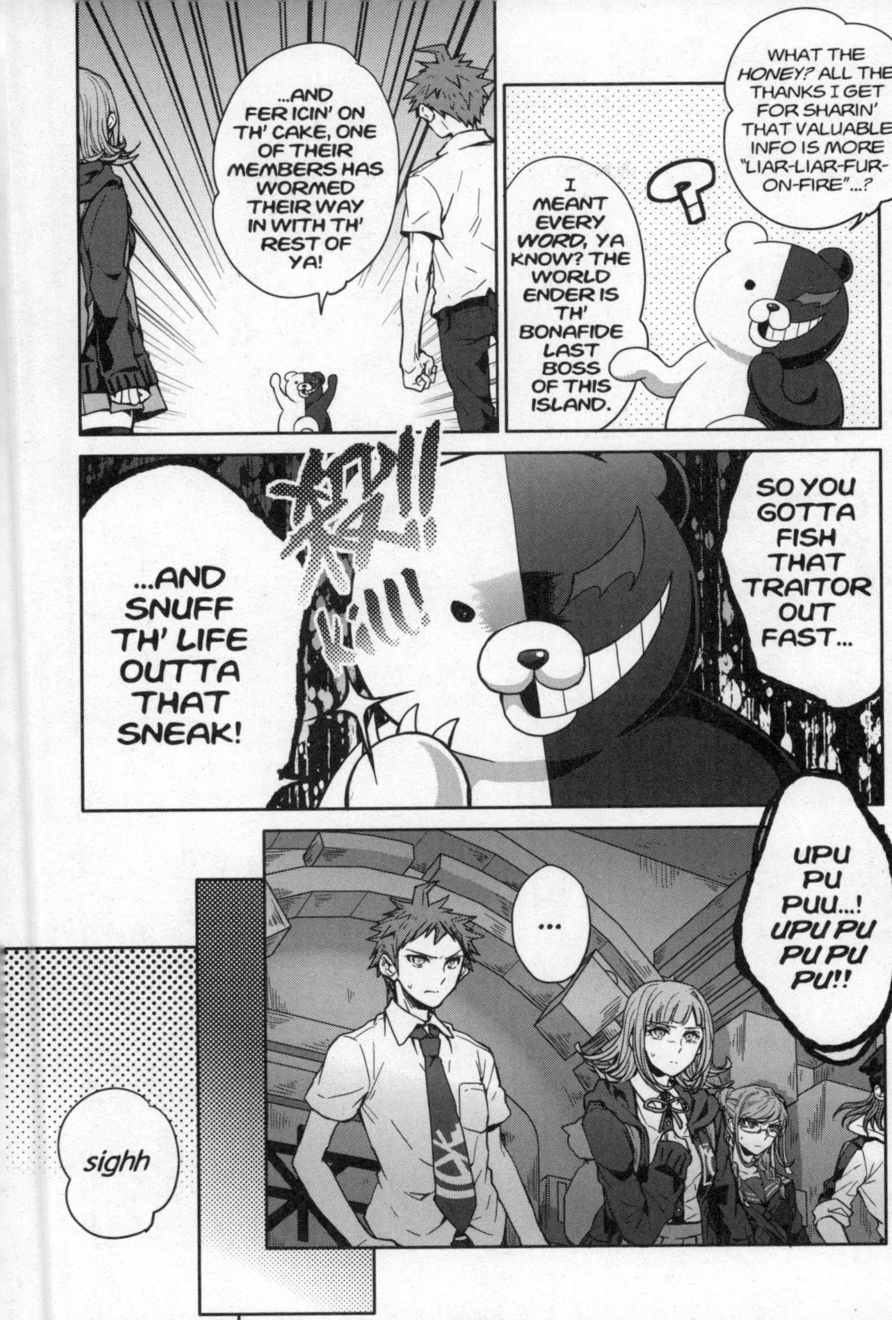
WHAT THE HONEY? ALL THE THANKS I GET FOR SHARIN' THAT VALUABLE INFO IS MORE "LIAR-LIAR-FUR-ON-FIRE"...?
I MEANT EVERY WORD, YA KNOW? THE WORLD ENDER IS TH' BONAFIDE LAST BOSS OF THIS ISLAND.
...AND FER ICIN' ON TH' CAKE, ONE OF THEIR MEMBERS HAS WORMED THEIR WAY IN WITH TH' REST OF YA!
SO YOU GOTTA FISH THAT TRAITOR OUT FAST...
...AND SNUFF TH' LIFE OUTTA THAT SNEAK!
UPU PU PUU...! UPU PU PU PU PU!!
...
sighh

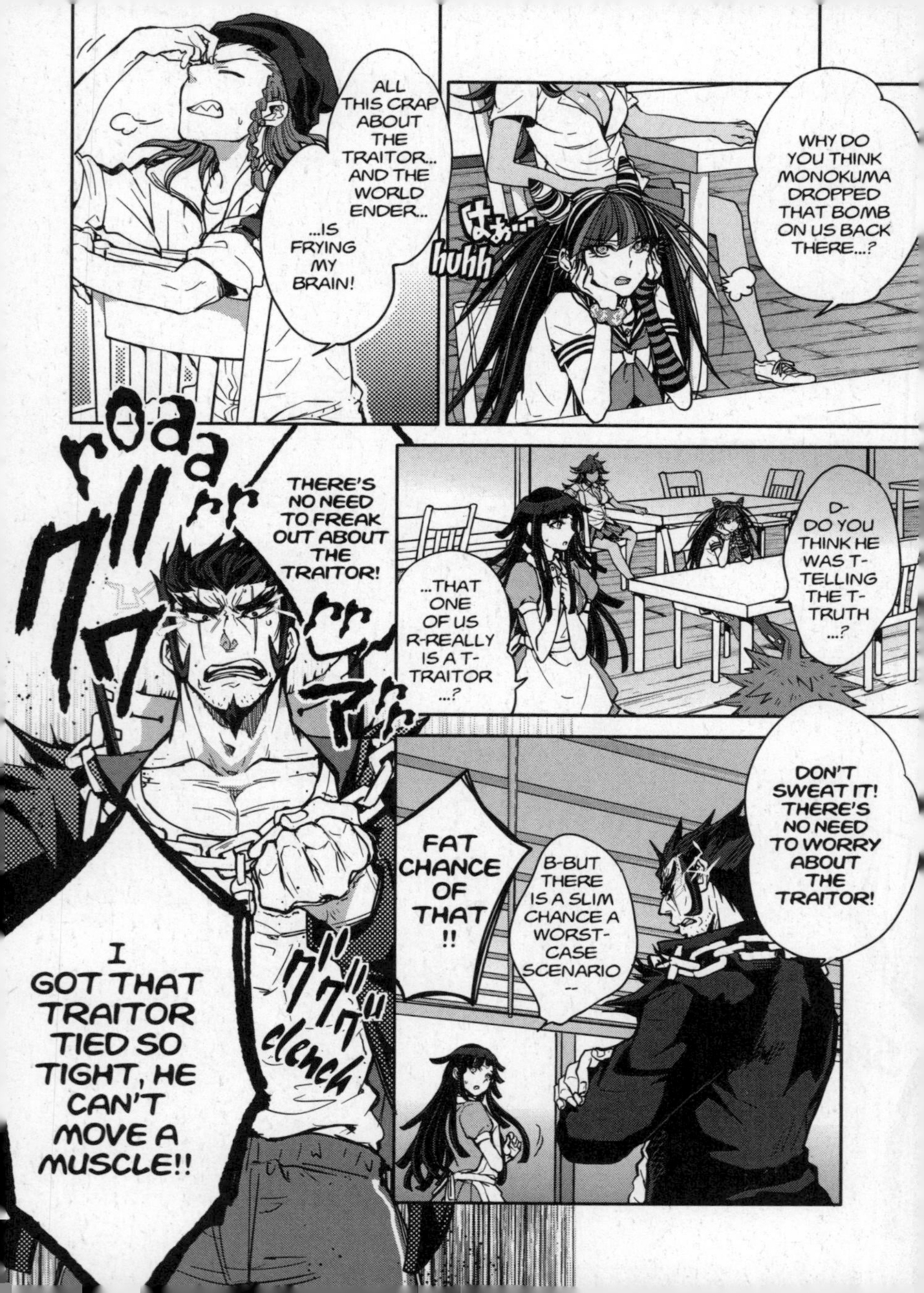
WHY DO YOU THINK MONOKUMA DROPPED THAT BOMB ON US BACK THERE...?
huhh
ALL THIS CRAP ABOUT THE TRAITOR... AND THE WORLD ENDER...
...IS FRYING MY BRAIN!
D-DO YOU THINK HE WAS T-TELLING THE T-TRUTH ...?
...THAT ONE OF US R-REALLY IS A T-TRAITOR ...?
DON'T SWEAT IT! THERE'S NO NEED TO WORRY ABOUT THE TRAITOR!
B-BUT THERE IS A SLIM CHANCE A WORST-CASE SCENARIO --
FAT CHANCE OF THAT !!
roaarr
THERE'S NO NEED TO FREAK OUT ABOUT THE TRAITOR!
crr
clench
I GOT THAT TRAITOR TIED SO TIGHT, HE CAN'T MOVE A MUSCLE!!

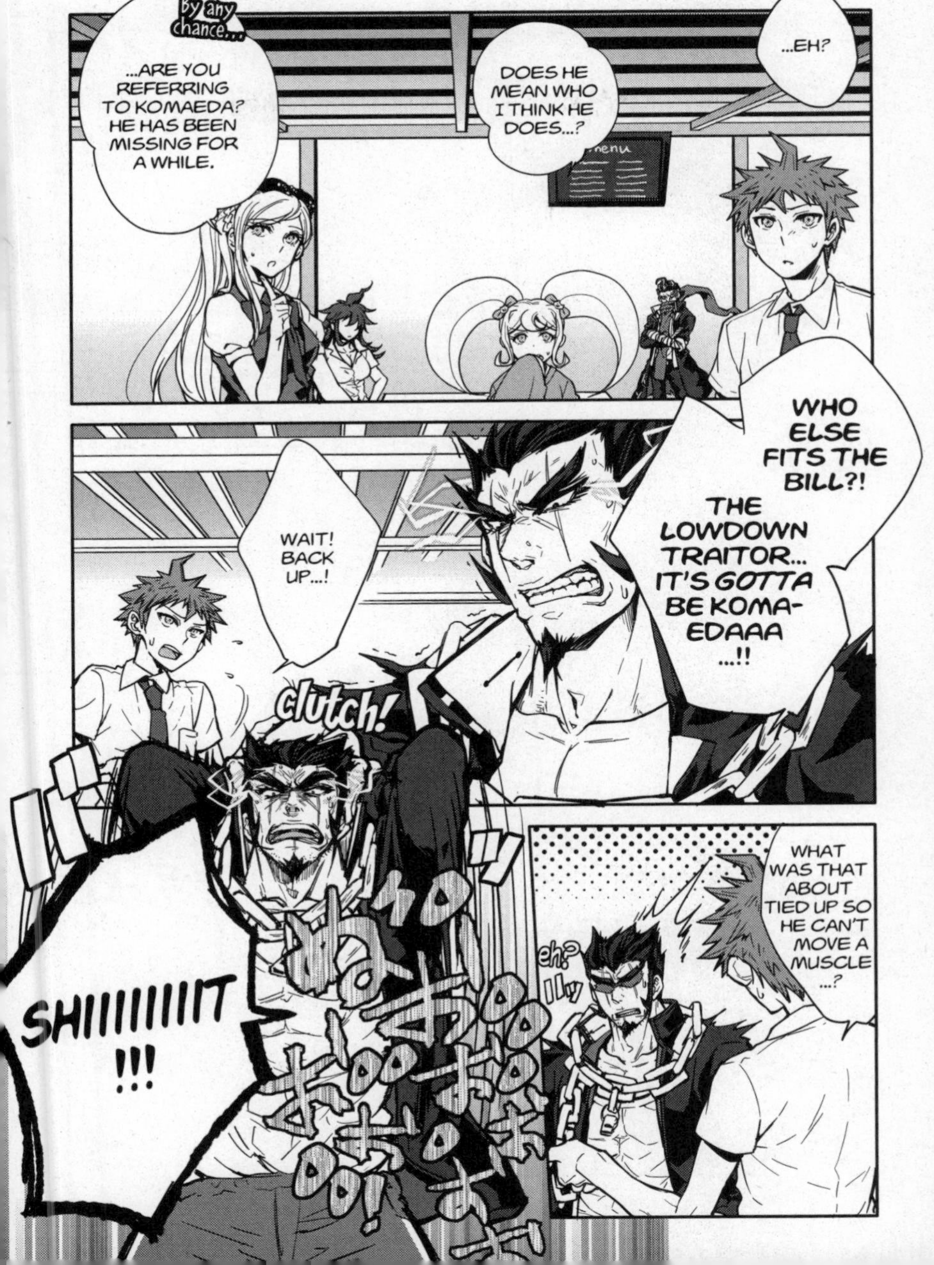
...EH?
DOES HE MEAN WHO I THINK HE DOES...?
By any chance...
...ARE YOU REFERRING TO KOMAEDA? HE HAS BEEN MISSING FOR A WHILE.
WHO ELSE FITS THE BILL?!
THE LOWDOWN TRAITOR... IT'S GOTTA BE KOMA-EDAAA ...!!
WAIT! BACK UP...!
clutch!
WHAT WAS THAT ABOUT TIED UP SO HE CAN'T MOVE A MUSCLE ...?
eh?
ハッ
SHIIIIIIIIT !!!

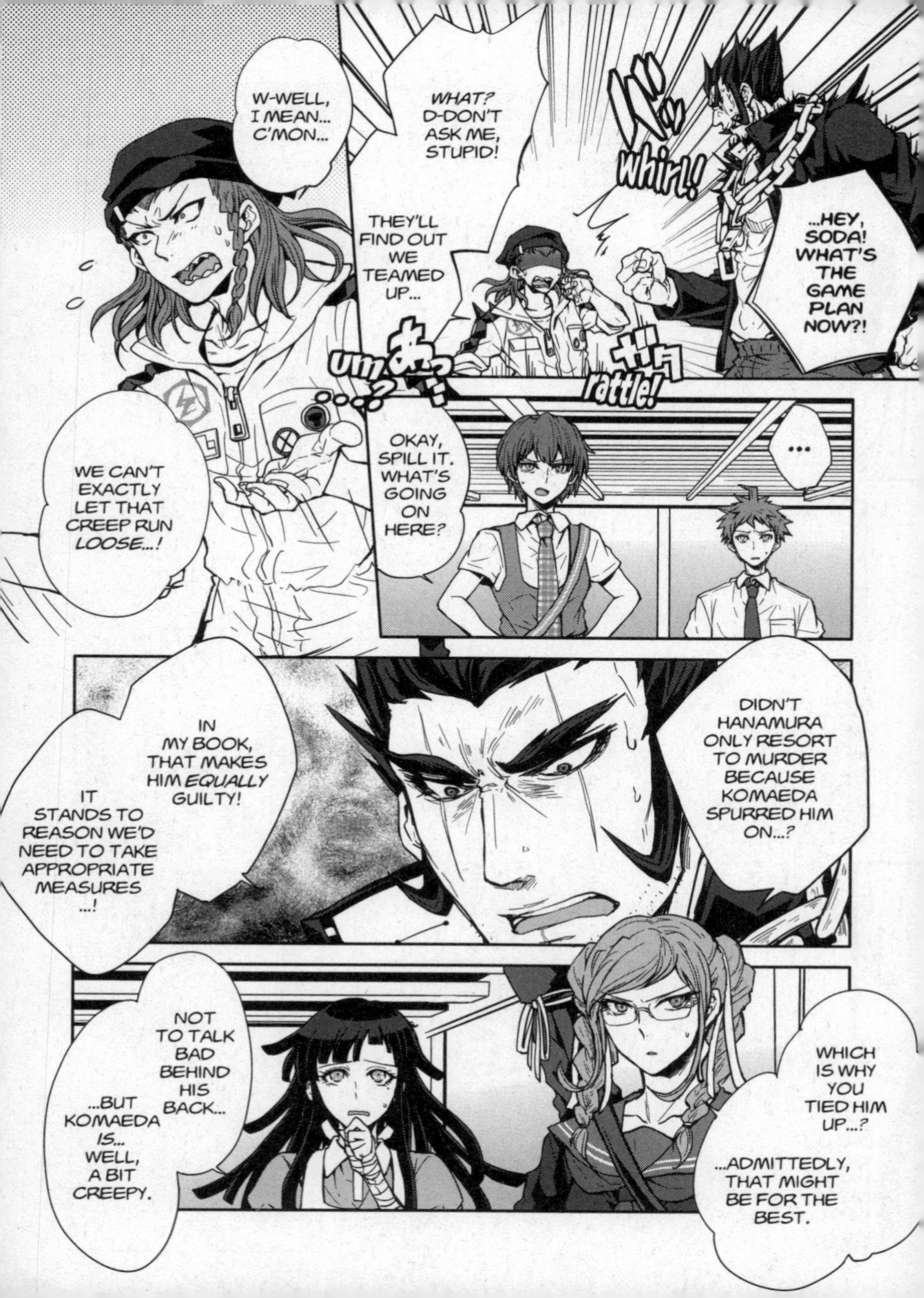
バッ
whirl!
...HEY, SODA! WHAT'S THE GAME PLAN NOW?!
WHAT? D-DON'T ASK ME, STUPID!
THEY'LL FIND OUT WE TEAMED UP...
rattle!
あっ
um...?
OKAY, SPILL IT. WHAT'S GOING ON HERE?
...
W-WELL, I MEAN... C'MON...
WE CAN'T EXACTLY LET THAT CREEP RUN LOOSE...!
DIDN'T HANAMURA ONLY RESORT TO MURDER BECAUSE KOMAEDA SPURRED HIM ON...?
IN MY BOOK, THAT MAKES HIM EQUALLY GUILTY!
IT STANDS TO REASON WE'D NEED TO TAKE APPROPRIATE MEASURES ...!
WHICH IS WHY YOU TIED HIM UP...?
...ADMITTEDLY, THAT MIGHT BE FOR THE BEST.
NOT TO TALK BAD BEHIND HIS BACK...
...BUT KOMAEDA IS... WELL, A BIT CREEPY.

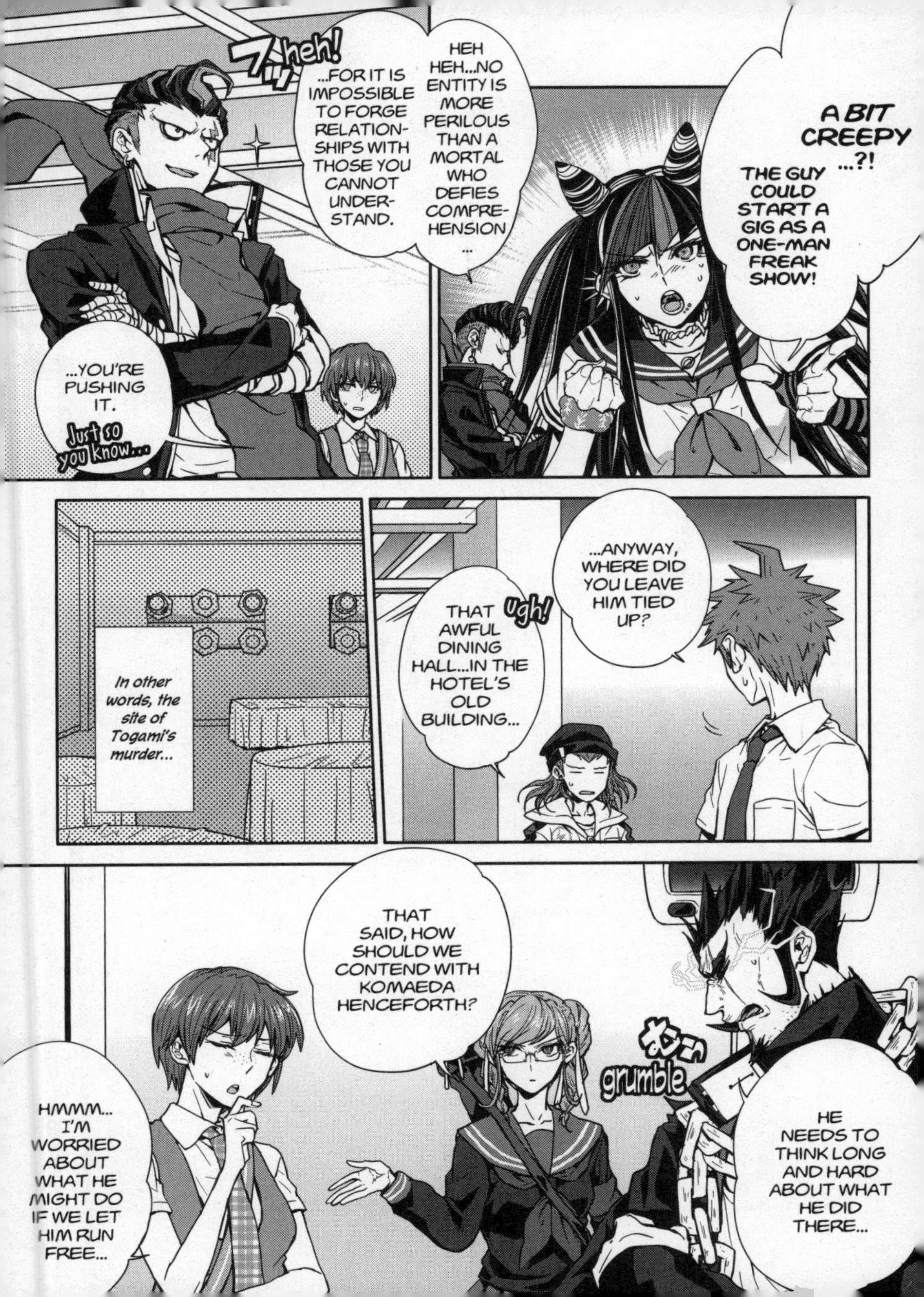
A BIT CREEPY ...?!
THE GUY COULD START A GIG AS A ONE-MAN FREAK SHOW!
HEH HEH...NO ENTITY IS MORE PERILOUS THAN A MORTAL WHO DEFIES COMPREHENSION ...
...FOR IT IS IMPOSSIBLE TO FORGE RELATIONSHIPS WITH THOSE YOU CANNOT UNDERSTAND.
heh!
...YOU'RE PUSHING IT.
Just so you know...
...ANYWAY, WHERE DID YOU LEAVE HIM TIED UP?
ugh!
THAT AWFUL DINING HALL...IN THE HOTEL'S OLD BUILDING...
In other words, the site of Togami's murder...
HE NEEDS TO THINK LONG AND HARD ABOUT WHAT HE DID THERE...
grumble
THAT SAID, HOW SHOULD WE CONTEND WITH KOMAEDA HENCEFORTH?
HMMM... I'M WORRIED ABOUT WHAT HE MIGHT DO IF WE LET HIM RUN FREE...

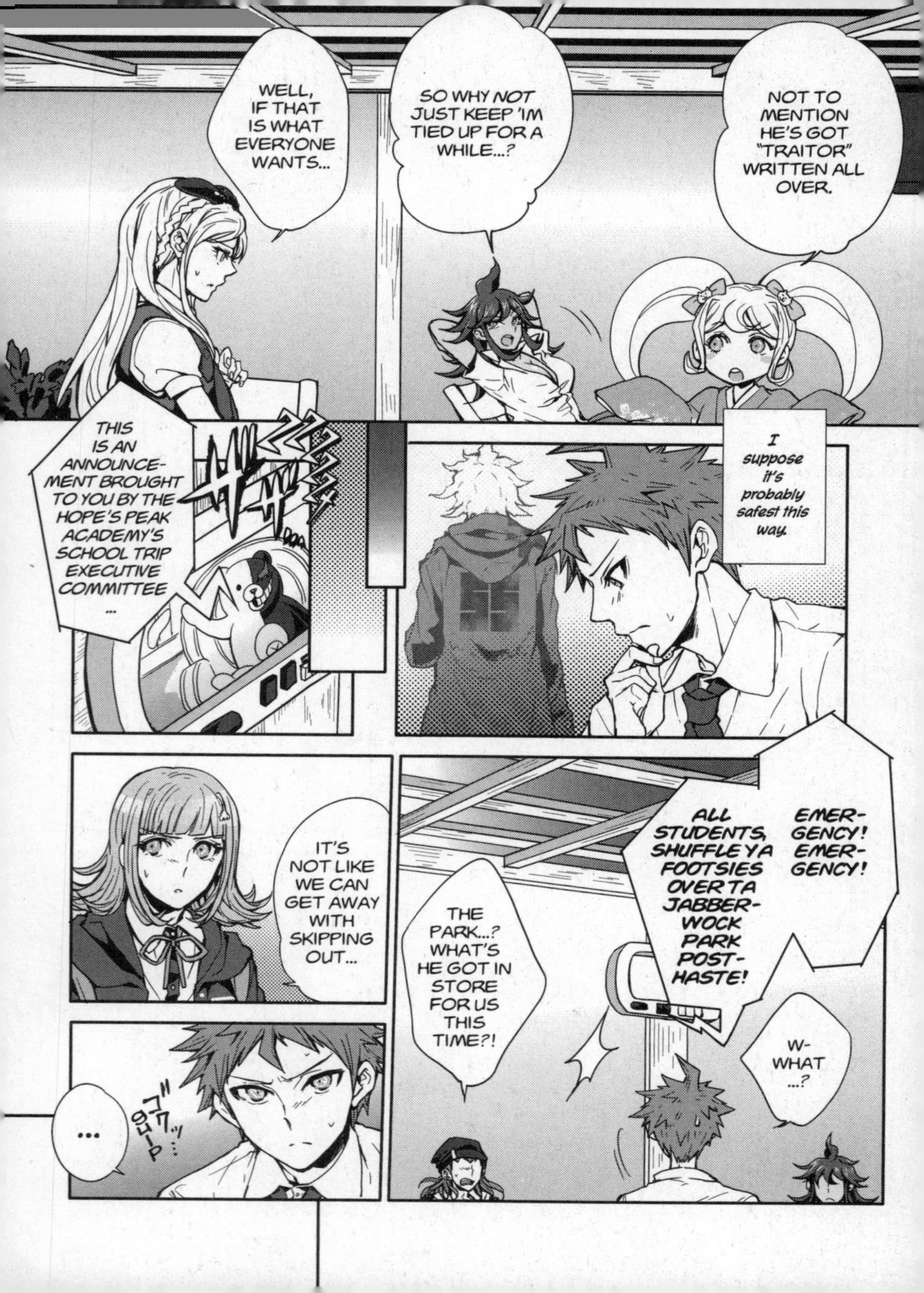
NOT TO MENTION HE'S GOT "TRAITOR" WRITTEN ALL OVER.
SO WHY *NOT* JUST KEEP 'IM TIED UP FOR A WHILE...?
WELL, IF THAT IS WHAT EVERYONE WANTS...
I suppose it's probably safest this way.
THIS IS AN ANNOUNCEMENT BROUGHT TO YOU BY THE HOPE'S PEAK ACADEMY'S SCHOOL TRIP EXECUTIVE COMMITTEE...
EMERGENCY! EMERGENCY!
ALL STUDENTS, SHUFFLE YA FOOTSIES OVER TA JABBERWOCK PARK POST-HASTE!
W-WHAT...?
THE PARK...? WHAT'S HE GOT IN STORE FOR US THIS TIME?!
IT'S NOT LIKE WE CAN GET AWAY WITH SKIPPING OUT...
GULP
...

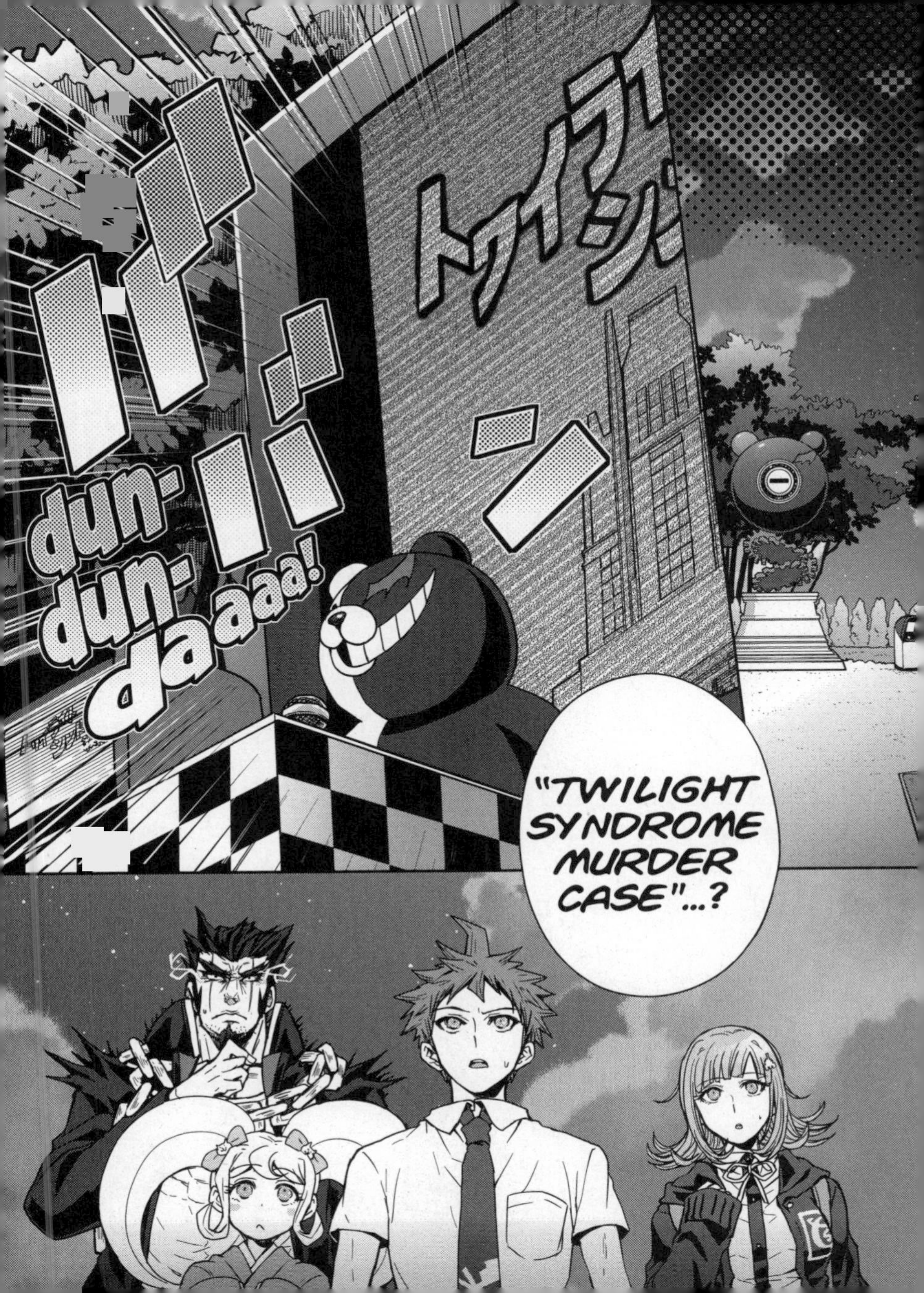
dun-
dun-
daaaaa!
トワイライトシンドローム
"TWILIGHT SYNDROME MURDER CASE"...?

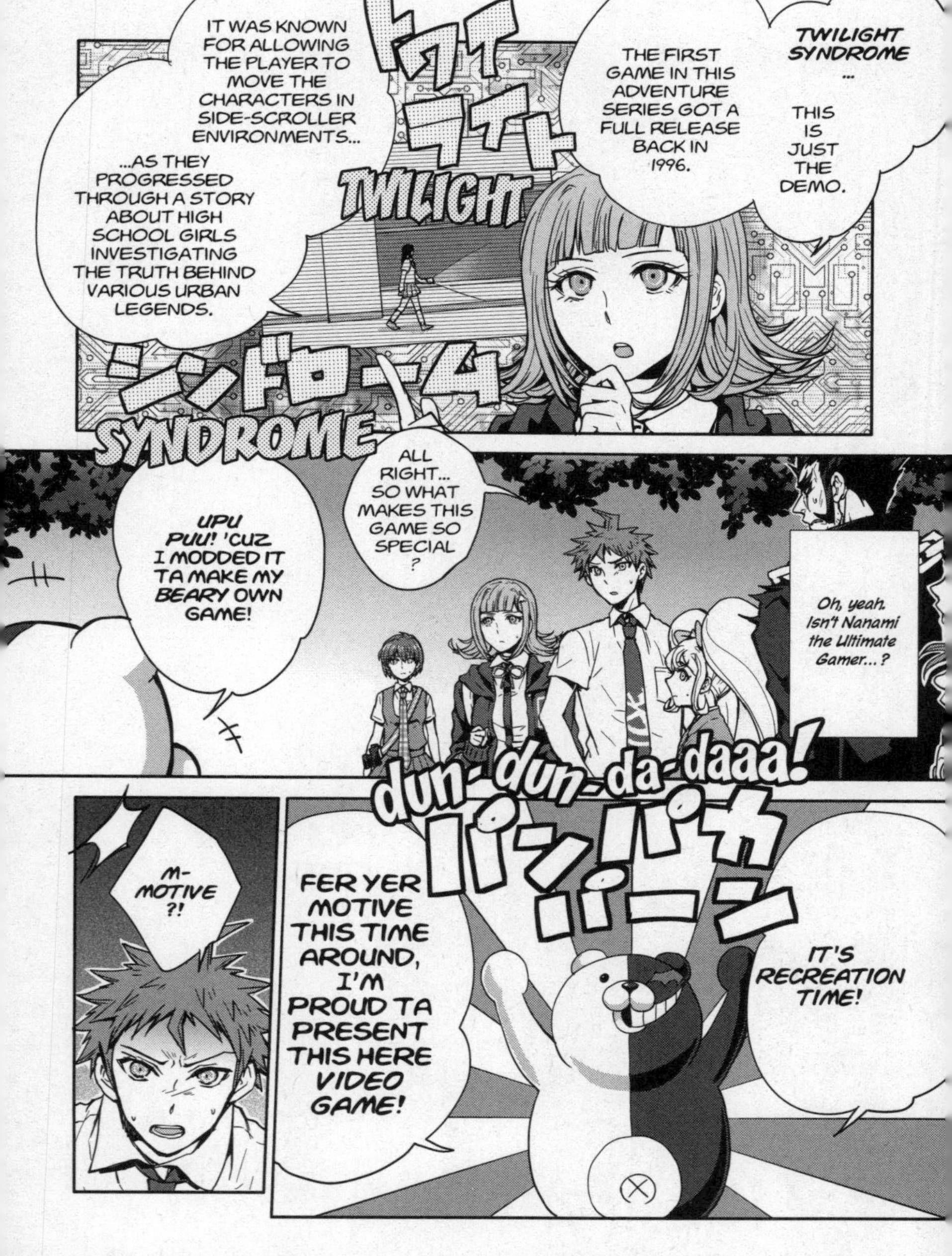
TWILIGHT SYNDROME ... THIS IS JUST THE DEMO.
THE FIRST GAME IN THIS ADVENTURE SERIES GOT A FULL RELEASE BACK IN 1996.
トワイライト
TWILIGHT
IT WAS KNOWN FOR ALLOWING THE PLAYER TO MOVE THE CHARACTERS IN SIDE-SCROLLER ENVIRONMENTS...
...AS THEY PROGRESSED THROUGH A STORY ABOUT HIGH SCHOOL GIRLS INVESTIGATING THE TRUTH BEHIND VARIOUS URBAN LEGENDS.
シンドローム
SYNDROME
Oh, yeah. Isn't Nanami the Ultimate Gamer...?
ALL RIGHT... SO WHAT MAKES THIS GAME SO SPECIAL?
UPU PUU! 'CUZ I MODDED IT TA MAKE MY BEARY OWN GAME!
IT'S RECREATION TIME!
dun-dun-da-daaa!
パンパカパーン
FER YER MOTIVE THIS TIME AROUND, I'M PROUD TA PRESENT THIS HERE VIDEO GAME!
M-MOTIVE?!

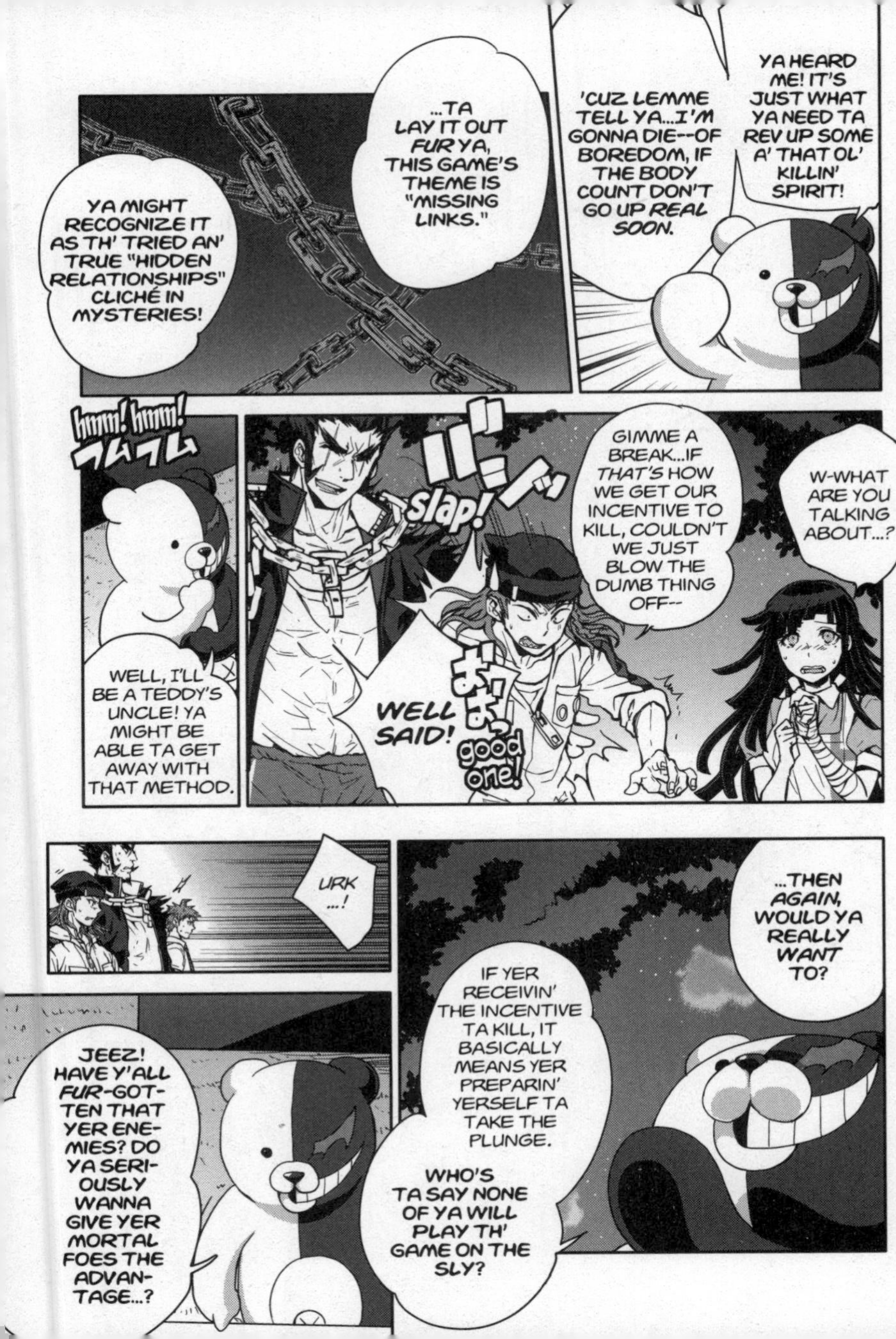

YA HEARD ME! IT'S JUST WHAT YA NEED TA REV UP SOME A' THAT OL' KILLIN' SPIRIT!
'CUZ LEMME TELL YA...I'M GONNA DIE--OF BOREDOM, IF THE BODY COUNT DON'T GO UP *REAL* SOON.
...TA LAY IT OUT *FUR* YA, THIS GAME'S THEME IS "MISSING LINKS."
YA MIGHT RECOGNIZE IT AS TH' TRIED AN' TRUE "HIDDEN RELATIONSHIPS" CLICHÉ IN MYSTERIES!
W-WHAT ARE YOU TALKING ABOUT...?
GIMME A BREAK...IF *THAT'S* HOW WE GET OUR INCENTIVE TO KILL, COULDN'T WE JUST BLOW THE DUMB THING OFF--
Slap!
WELL SAID!
おおっ
good one!
hmm! hmm!
フムフム
WELL, I'LL BE A TEDDY'S UNCLE! YA MIGHT BE ABLE TA GET AWAY WITH THAT METHOD.
...THEN *AGAIN,* WOULD YA REALLY *WANT* TO?
IF YER RECEIVIN' THE INCENTIVE TA KILL, IT BASICALLY MEANS YER PREPARIN' YERSELF TA TAKE THE PLUNGE.
WHO'S TA SAY NONE OF YA WILL PLAY TH' GAME ON THE SLY?
URK ...!
JEEZ! HAVE Y'ALL *FUR*-GOTTEN THAT YER ENEMIES? DO YA SERIOUSLY WANNA GIVE YER MORTAL FOES THE ADVANTAGE...?

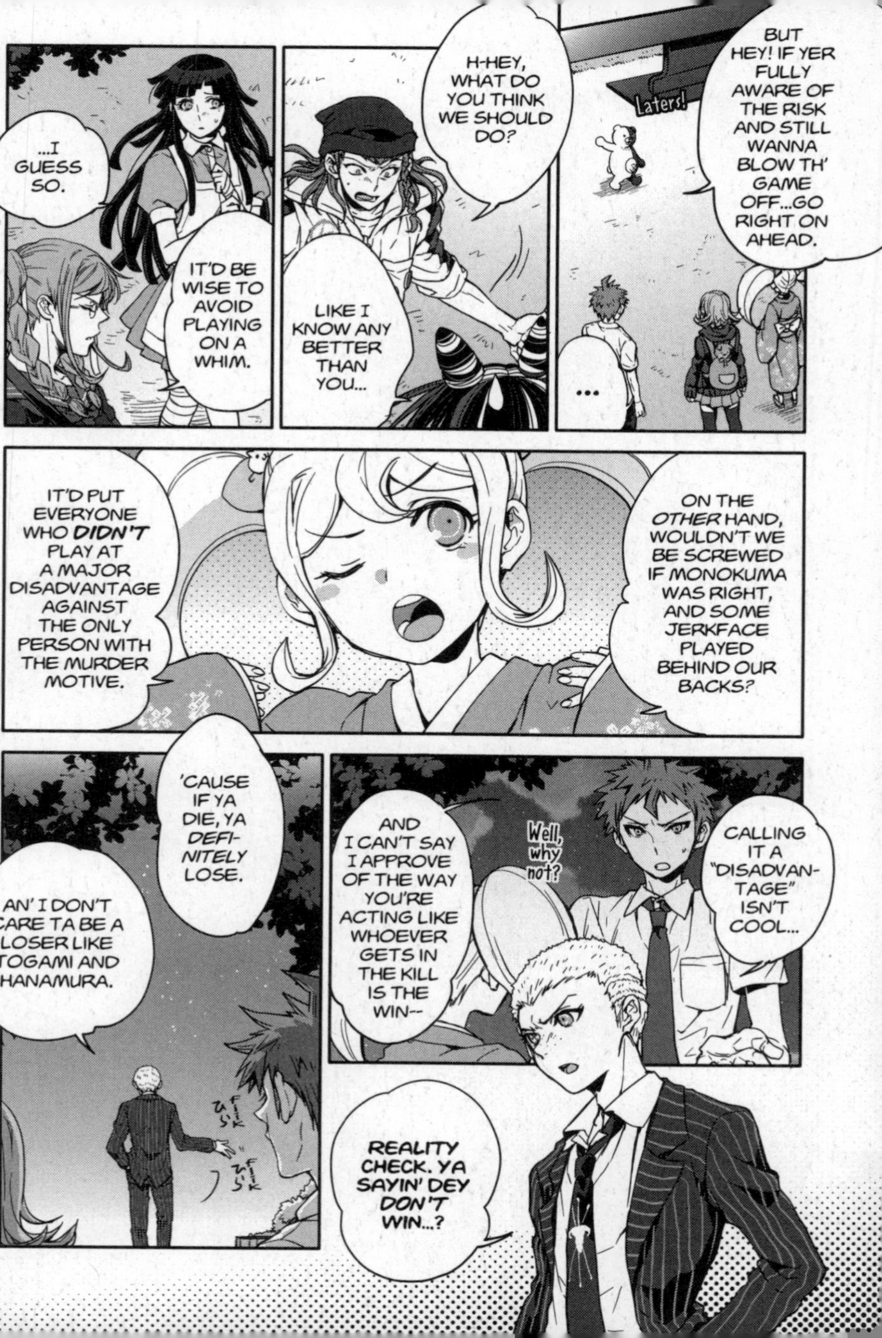
BUT HEY! IF YER FULLY AWARE OF THE RISK AND STILL WANNA BLOW TH' GAME OFF...GO RIGHT ON AHEAD.
Laters!
...
H-HEY, WHAT DO YOU THINK WE SHOULD DO?
LIKE I KNOW ANY BETTER THAN YOU...
...I GUESS SO.
IT'D BE WISE TO AVOID PLAYING ON A WHIM.
ON THE OTHER HAND, WOULDN'T WE BE SCREWED IF MONOKUMA WAS RIGHT, AND SOME JERKFACE PLAYED BEHIND OUR BACKS?
IT'D PUT EVERYONE WHO DIDN'T PLAY AT A MAJOR DISADVANTAGE AGAINST THE ONLY PERSON WITH THE MURDER MOTIVE.
CALLING IT A "DISADVANTAGE" ISN'T COOL...
Well, why not?
AND I CAN'T SAY I APPROVE OF THE WAY YOU'RE ACTING LIKE WHOEVER GETS IN THE KILL IS THE WIN--
REALITY CHECK. YA SAYIN' DEY DON'T WIN...?
'CAUSE IF YA DIE, YA DEFINITELY LOSE.
AN' I DON'T CARE TA BE A LOSER LIKE TOGAMI AND HANAMURA.
FLIK
FLIK

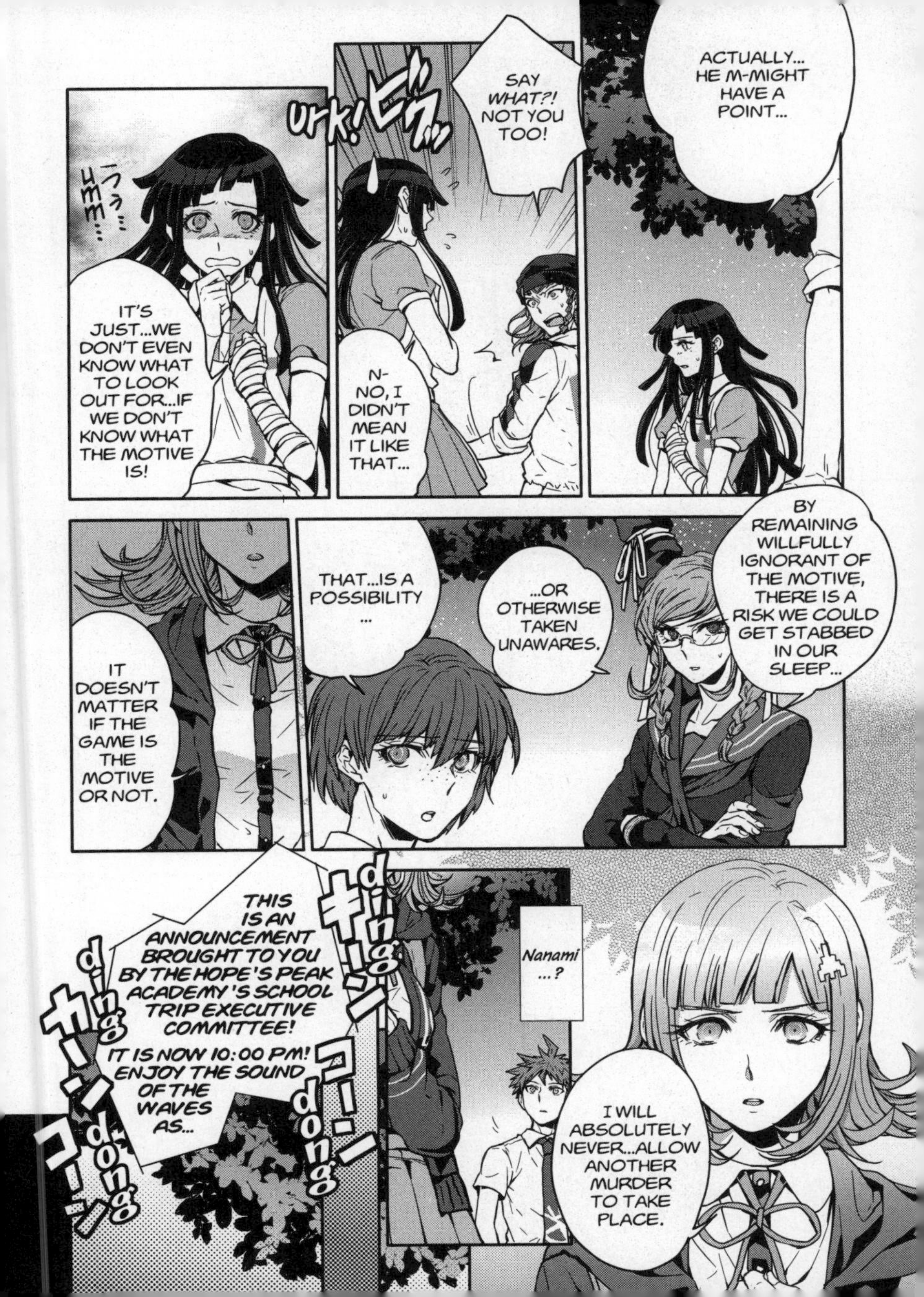
ACTUALLY... HE M-MIGHT HAVE A POINT...
SAY WHAT?! NOT YOU TOO!
URK! ビクッ
N-NO, I DIDN'T MEAN IT LIKE THAT...
うぅ… UMMM...
IT'S JUST...WE DON'T EVEN KNOW WHAT TO LOOK OUT FOR...IF WE DON'T KNOW WHAT THE MOTIVE IS!
BY REMAINING WILLFULLY IGNORANT OF THE MOTIVE, THERE IS A RISK WE COULD GET STABBED IN OUR SLEEP...
...OR OTHERWISE TAKEN UNAWARES.
THAT...IS A POSSIBILITY ...
IT DOESN'T MATTER IF THE GAME IS THE MOTIVE OR NOT.
I WILL ABSOLUTELY NEVER...ALLOW ANOTHER MURDER TO TAKE PLACE.
Nanami ...?
キーン ding
コーン dong
THIS IS AN ANNOUNCEMENT BROUGHT TO YOU BY THE HOPE'S PEAK ACADEMY'S SCHOOL TRIP EXECUTIVE COMMITTEE! IT IS NOW 10:00 PM! ENJOY THE SOUND OF THE WAVES AS...
カーン ding
コーン dong

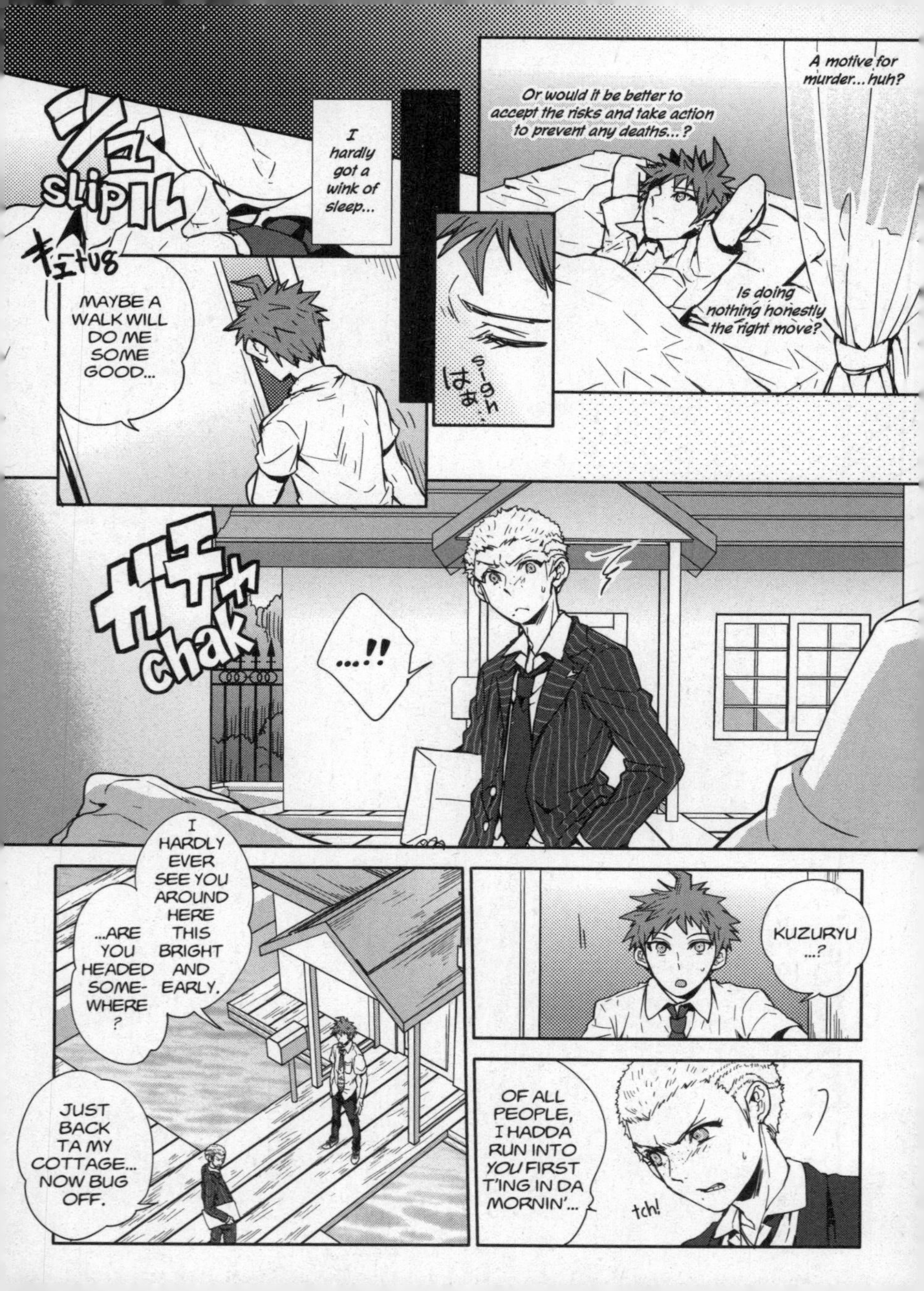
A motive for murder... huh?
Or would it be better to accept the risks and take action to prevent any deaths...?
Is doing nothing honestly the right move?
I hardly got a wink of sleep...
シュ slip ル
キュ tug
はぁ sigh
MAYBE A WALK WILL DO ME SOME GOOD...
ガチャ chak
...!!
KUZURYU ...?
OF ALL PEOPLE, I HADDA RUN INTO *YOU* FIRST T'ING IN DA MORNIN'...
tch!
I HARDLY EVER SEE YOU AROUND HERE THIS BRIGHT AND EARLY.
...ARE YOU HEADED SOME-WHERE?
JUST BACK TA MY COTTAGE... NOW BUG OFF.

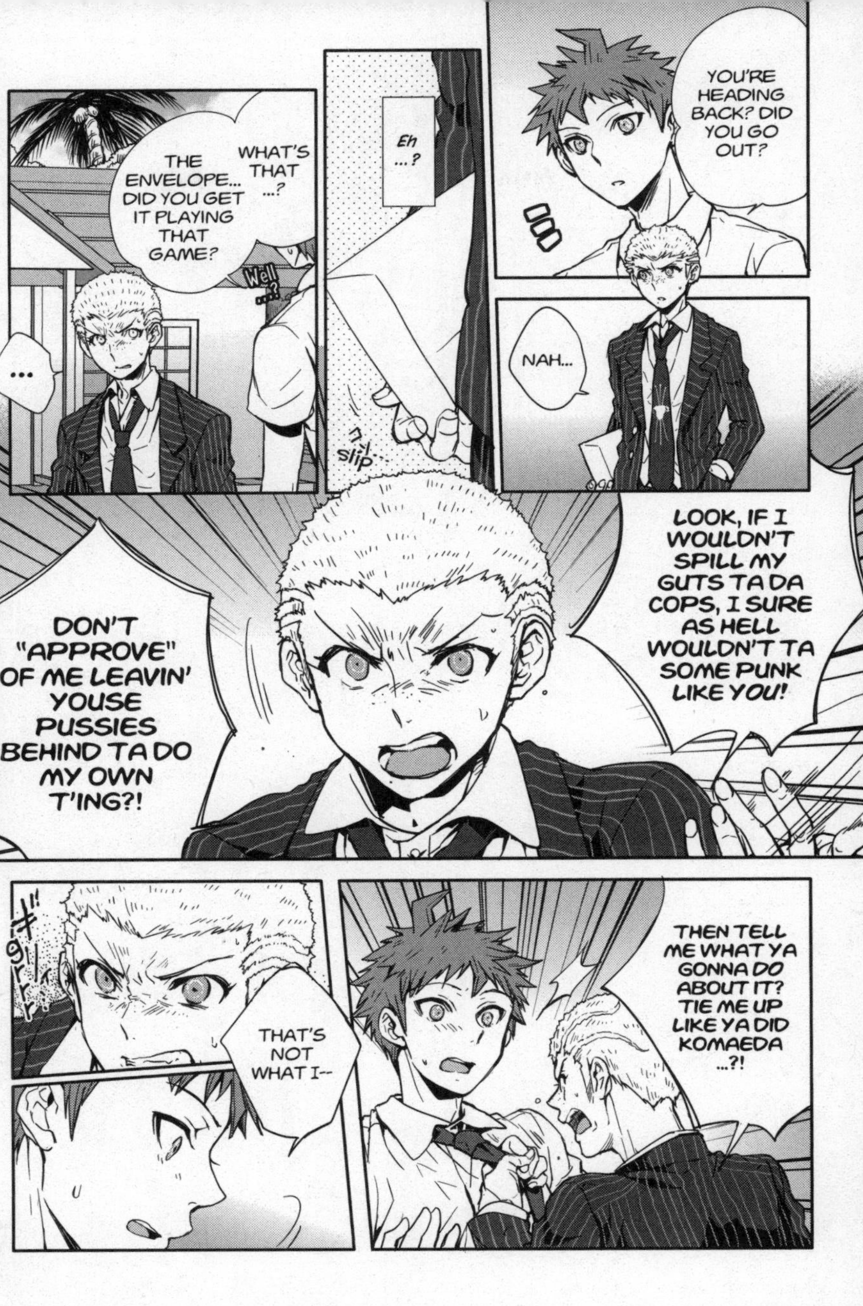
YOU'RE HEADING BACK? DID YOU GO OUT?
NAH...
Eh ...?
slip
WHAT'S THAT ...?
THE ENVELOPE... DID YOU GET IT PLAYING THAT GAME?
Well
...
LOOK, IF I WOULDN'T SPILL MY GUTS TA DA COPS, I SURE AS HELL WOULDN'T TA SOME PUNK LIKE YOU!
DON'T "APPROVE" OF ME LEAVIN' YOUSE PUSSIES BEHIND TA DO MY OWN T'ING?!
THEN TELL ME WHAT YA GONNA DO ABOUT IT? TIE ME UP LIKE YA DID KOMAEDA ...?!
grrr
THAT'S NOT WHAT I--

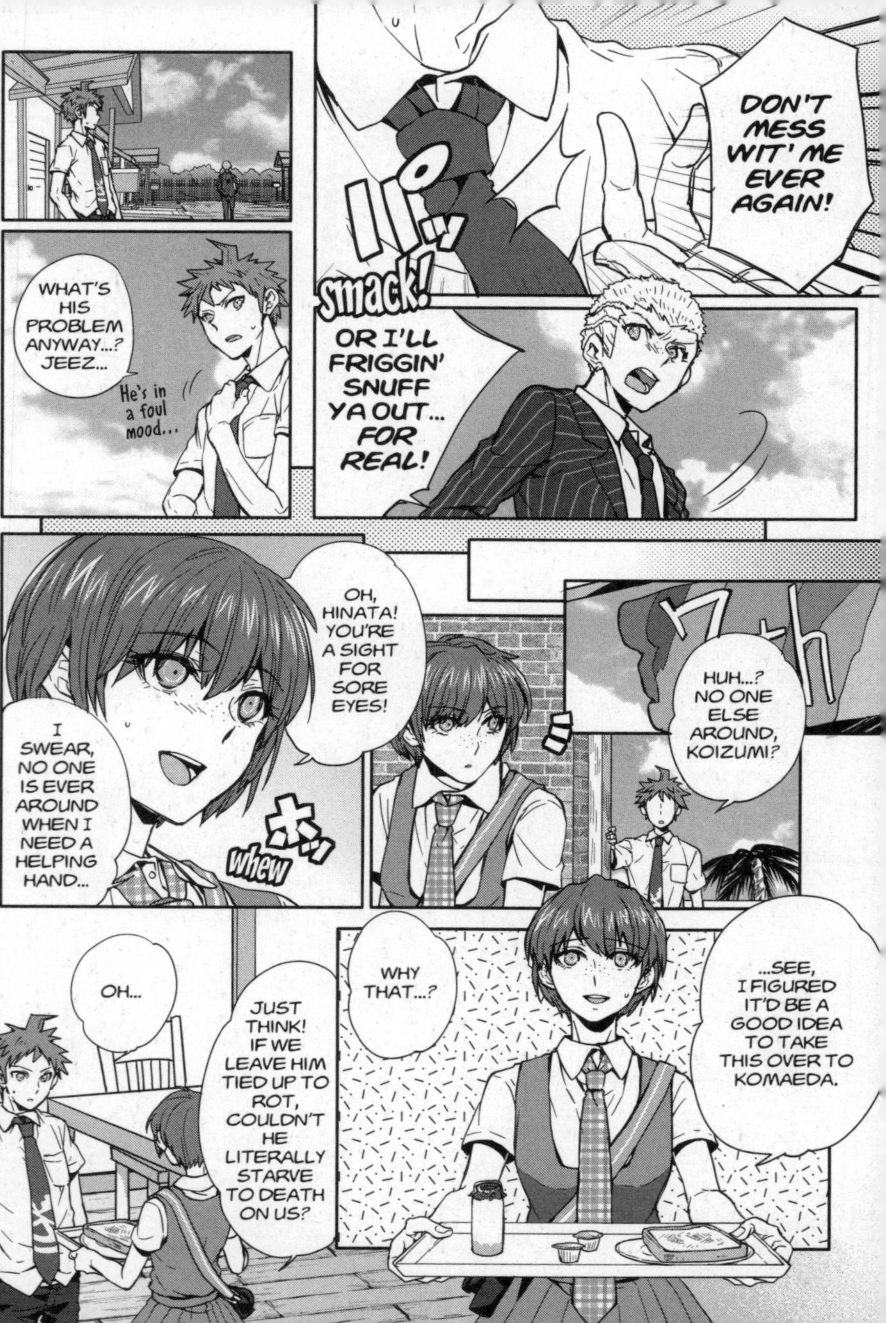
DON'T MESS WIT' ME EVER AGAIN!
smack!
OR I'LL FRIGGIN' SNUFF YA OUT... FOR REAL!
WHAT'S HIS PROBLEM ANYWAY...? JEEZ...
He's in a foul mood...
HUH...? NO ONE ELSE AROUND, KOIZUMI?
OH, HINATA! YOU'RE A SIGHT FOR SORE EYES!
I SWEAR, NO ONE IS EVER AROUND WHEN I NEED A HELPING HAND...
whew
...SEE, I FIGURED IT'D BE A GOOD IDEA TO TAKE THIS OVER TO KOMAEDA.
WHY THAT...?
OH...
JUST THINK! IF WE LEAVE HIM TIED UP TO ROT, COULDN'T HE LITERALLY STARVE TO DEATH ON US?

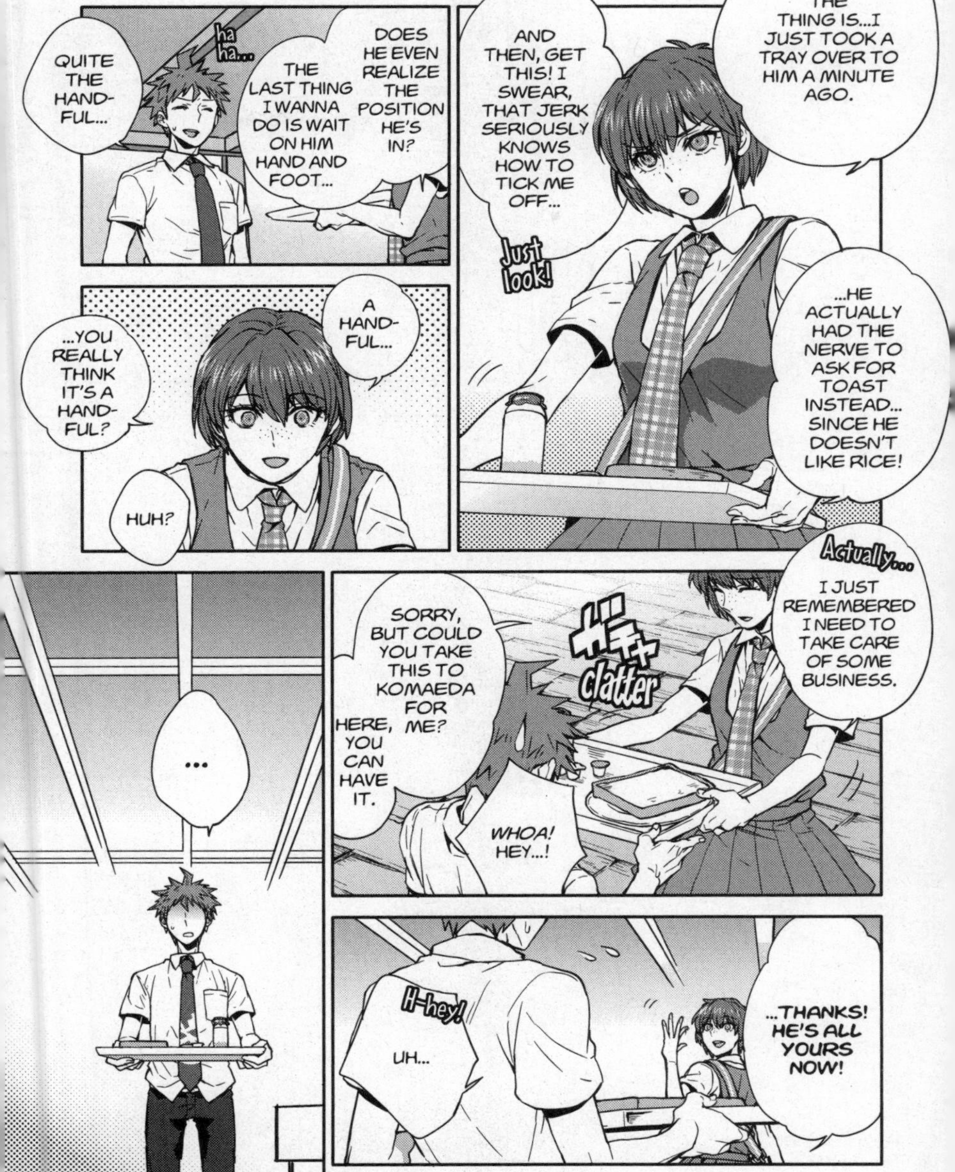
THE THING IS...I JUST TOOK A TRAY OVER TO HIM A MINUTE AGO.
AND THEN, GET THIS! I SWEAR, THAT JERK SERIOUSLY KNOWS HOW TO TICK ME OFF...
Just look!
...HE ACTUALLY HAD THE NERVE TO ASK FOR TOAST INSTEAD... SINCE HE DOESN'T LIKE RICE!
DOES HE EVEN REALIZE THE POSITION HE'S IN?
THE LAST THING I WANNA DO IS WAIT ON HIM HAND AND FOOT...
ha ha...
QUITE THE HANDFUL...
A HANDFUL...
...YOU REALLY THINK IT'S A HANDFUL?
HUH?
Actually...
I JUST REMEMBERED I NEED TO TAKE CARE OF SOME BUSINESS.
clatter
SORRY, BUT COULD YOU TAKE THIS TO KOMAEDA FOR ME?
HERE, YOU CAN HAVE IT.
WHOA! HEY...!
...THANKS! HE'S ALL YOURS NOW!
H-hey!
UH...
...

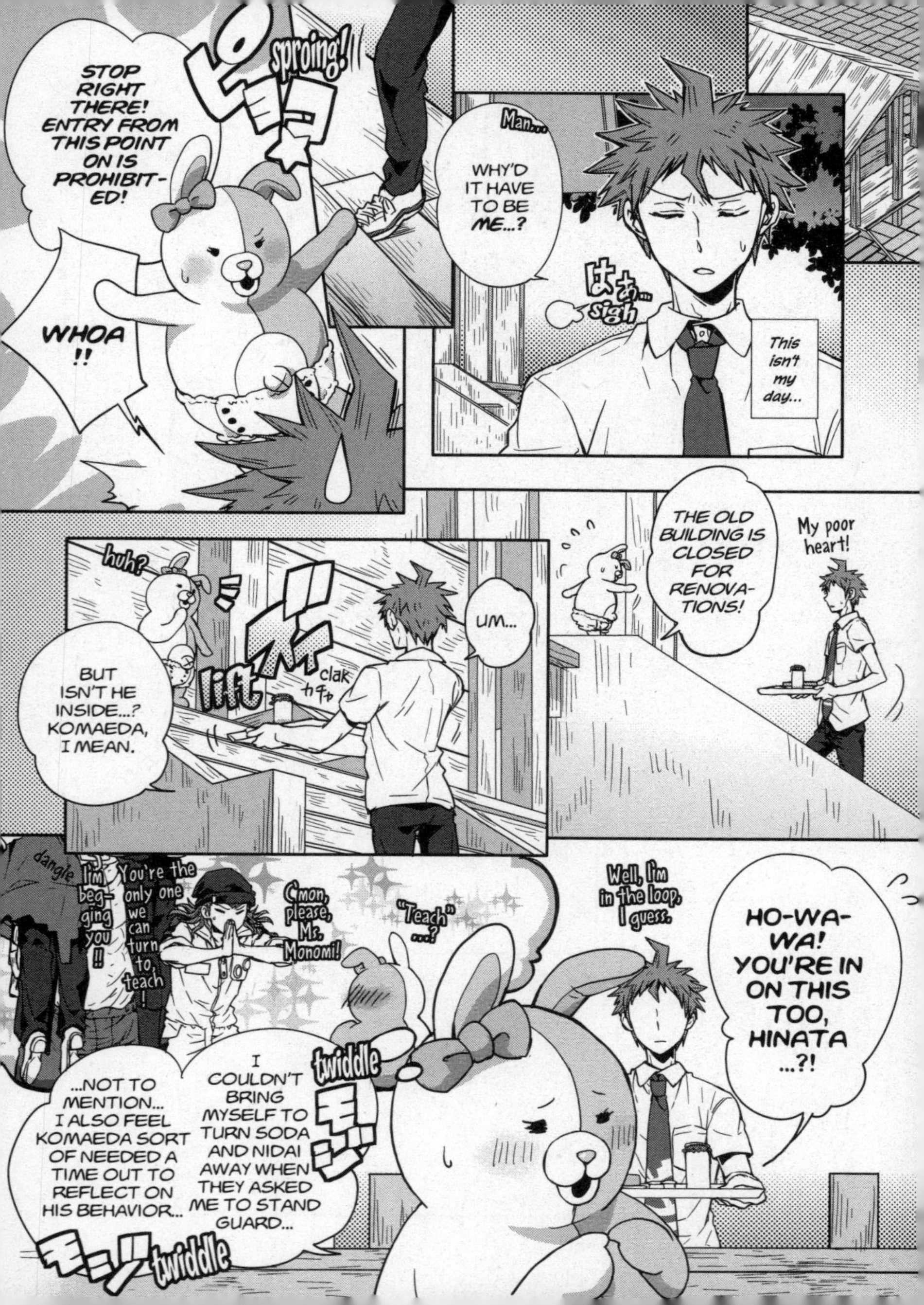
Man...
WHY'D IT HAVE TO BE ME...?
はぁ… sigh
This isn't my day...
sproing!
STOP RIGHT THERE! ENTRY FROM THIS POINT ON IS PROHIBITED!
WHOA !!
My poor heart!
THE OLD BUILDING IS CLOSED FOR RENOVATIONS!
huh?
UM...
lift
clak カチャ
BUT ISN'T HE INSIDE...? KOMAEDA, I MEAN.
HO-WA-WA! YOU'RE IN ON THIS TOO, HINATA...?!
Well, I'm in the loop, I guess.
"Teach"...?
C'mon, please, Ms. Monomi!
You're the only one we can turn to, teach!
I'm begging you !!
dangle
twiddle
I COULDN'T BRING MYSELF TO TURN SODA AND NIDAI AWAY WHEN THEY ASKED ME TO STAND GUARD...
...NOT TO MENTION... I ALSO FEEL KOMAEDA SORT OF NEEDED A TIME OUT TO REFLECT ON HIS BEHAVIOR...
twiddle

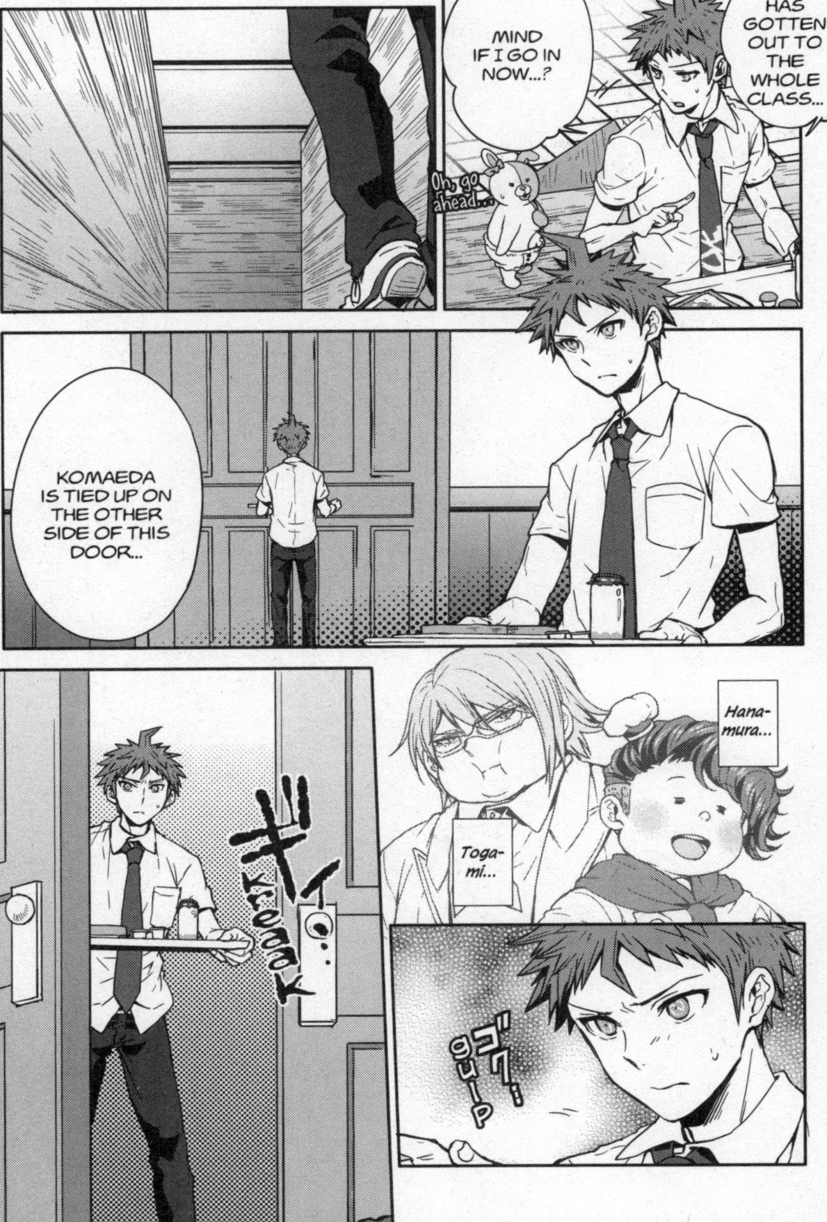
WORD HAS GOTTEN OUT TO THE WHOLE CLASS...
MIND IF I GO IN NOW...?
Oh, go ahead...
KOMAEDA IS TIED UP ON THE OTHER SIDE OF THIS DOOR...
Hana-mura...
Toga-mi...
ゴク
gulp
ギイ
kreaak

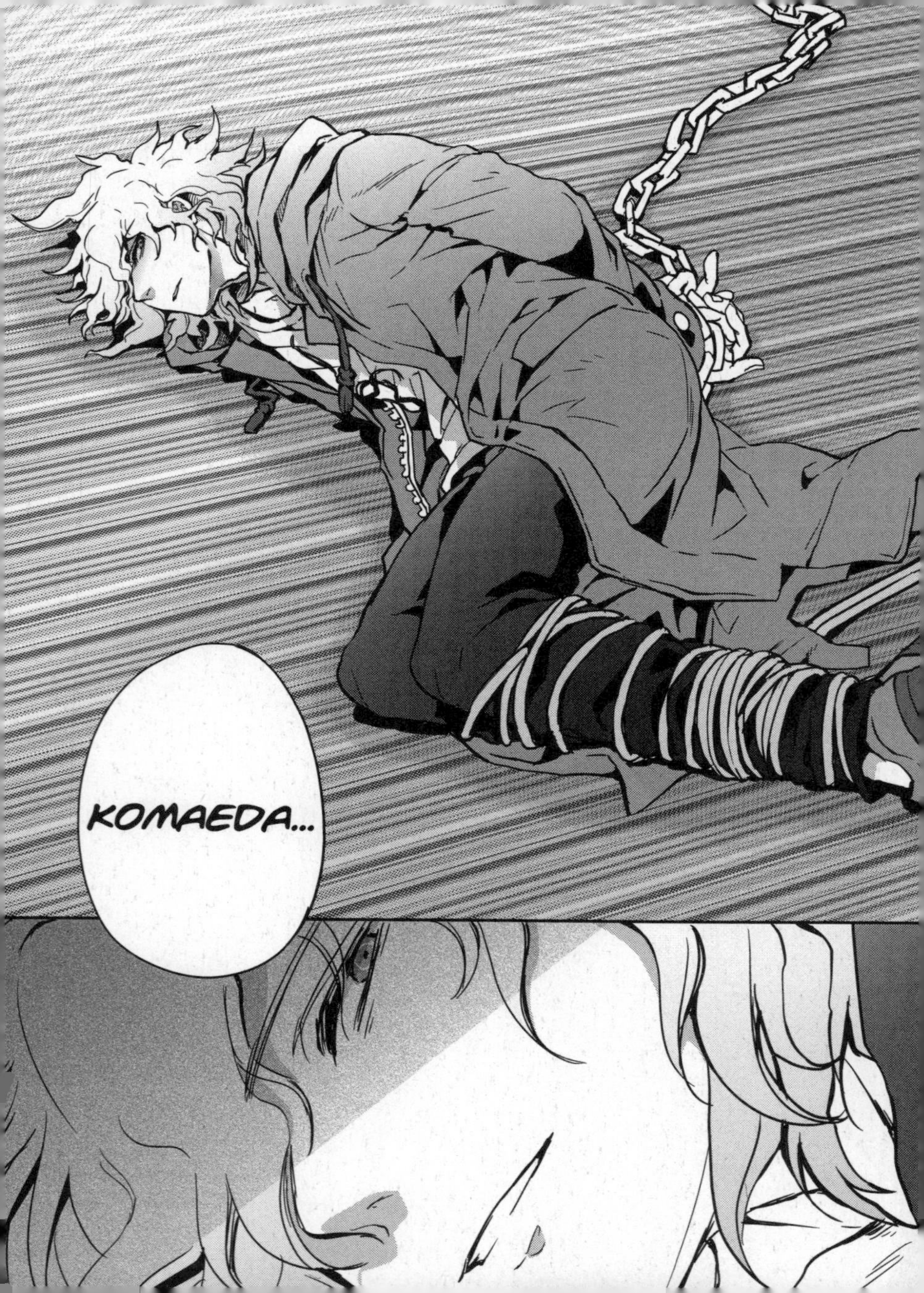
KOMAEDA...

CHAPTER 9: TWILIGHT SYNDROME MURDER CASE

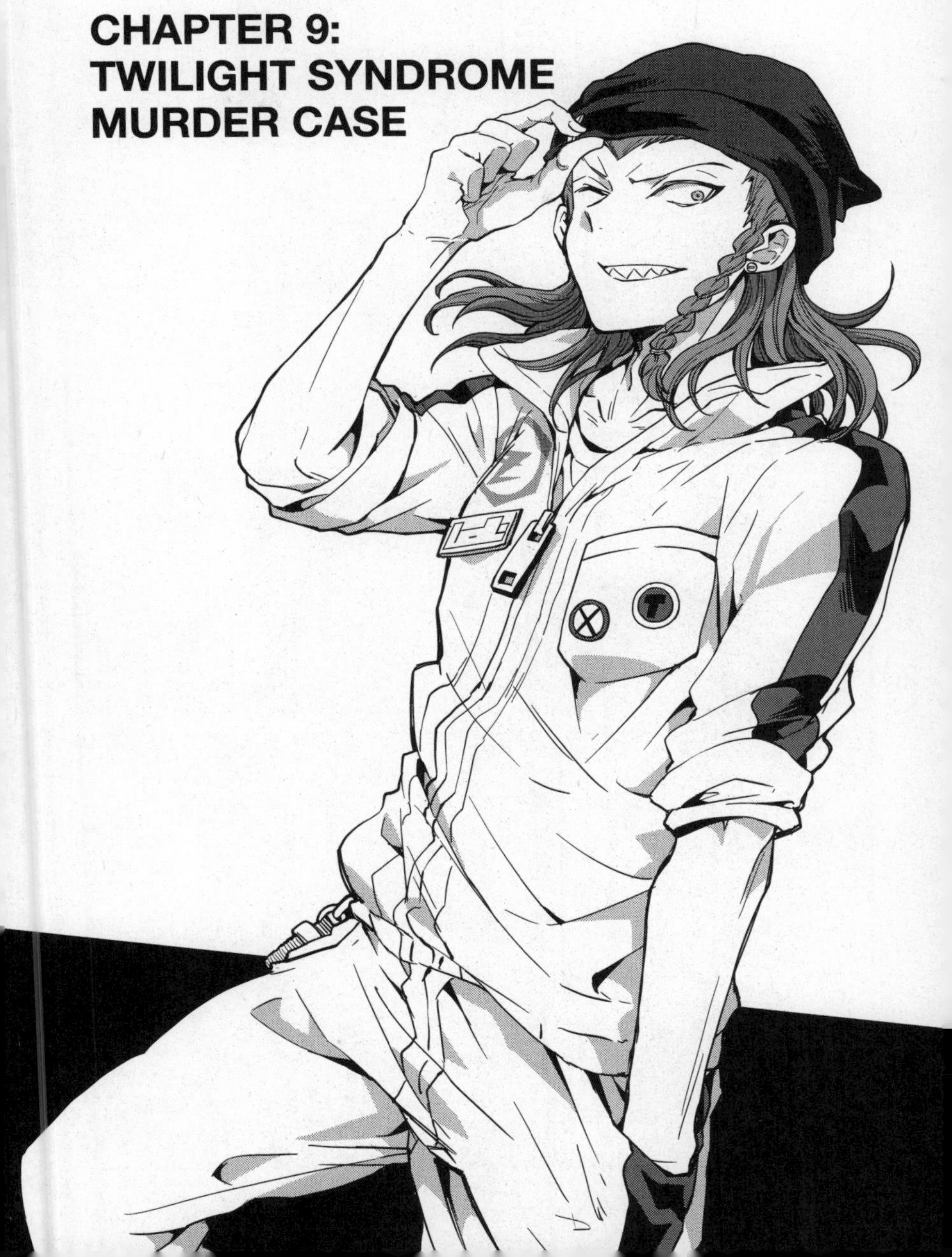

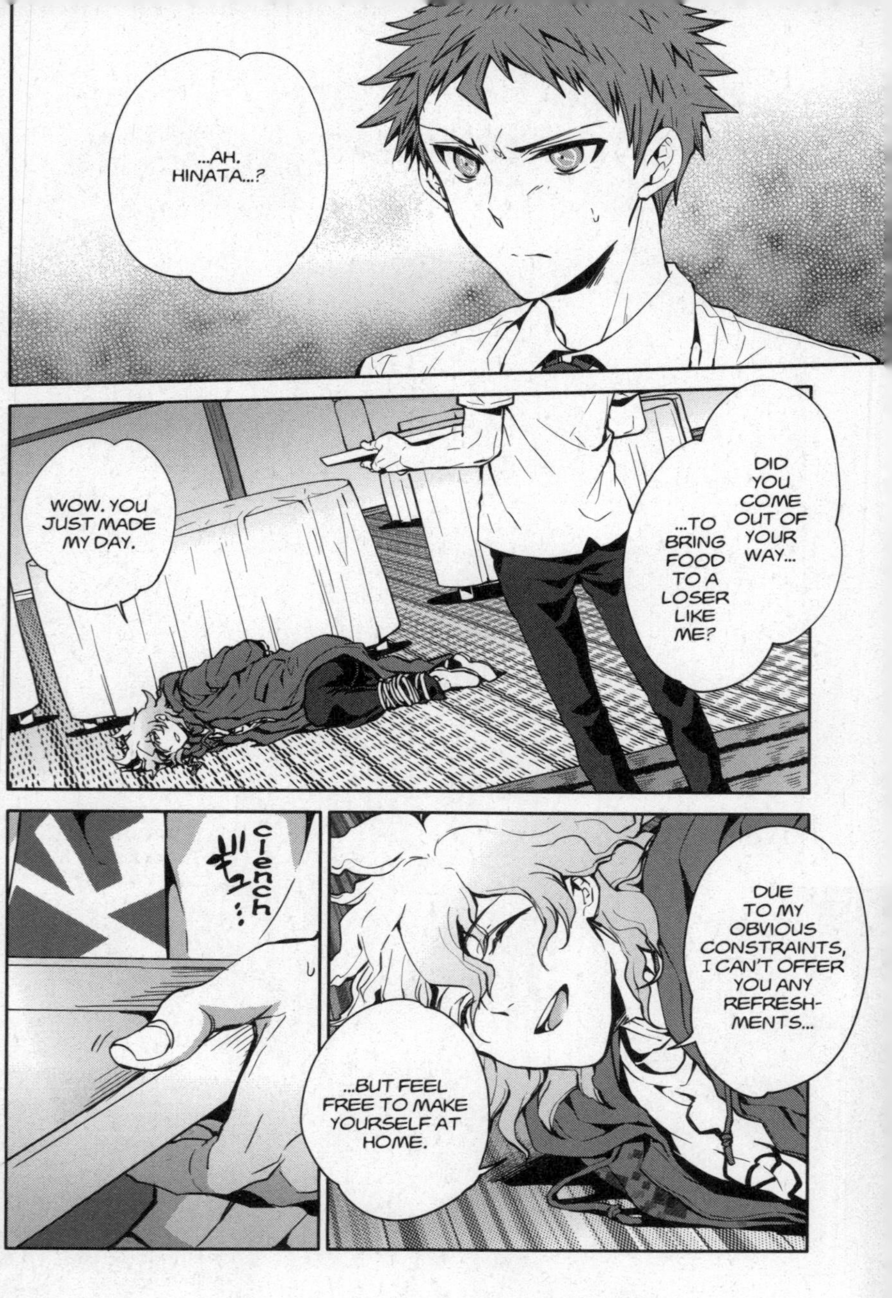
...AH. HINATA...?
DID YOU COME OUT OF YOUR WAY...
...TO BRING FOOD TO A LOSER LIKE ME?
WOW. YOU JUST MADE MY DAY.
DUE TO MY OBVIOUS CONSTRAINTS, I CAN'T OFFER YOU ANY REFRESH- MENTS...
...BUT FEEL FREE TO MAKE YOURSELF AT HOME.
clench

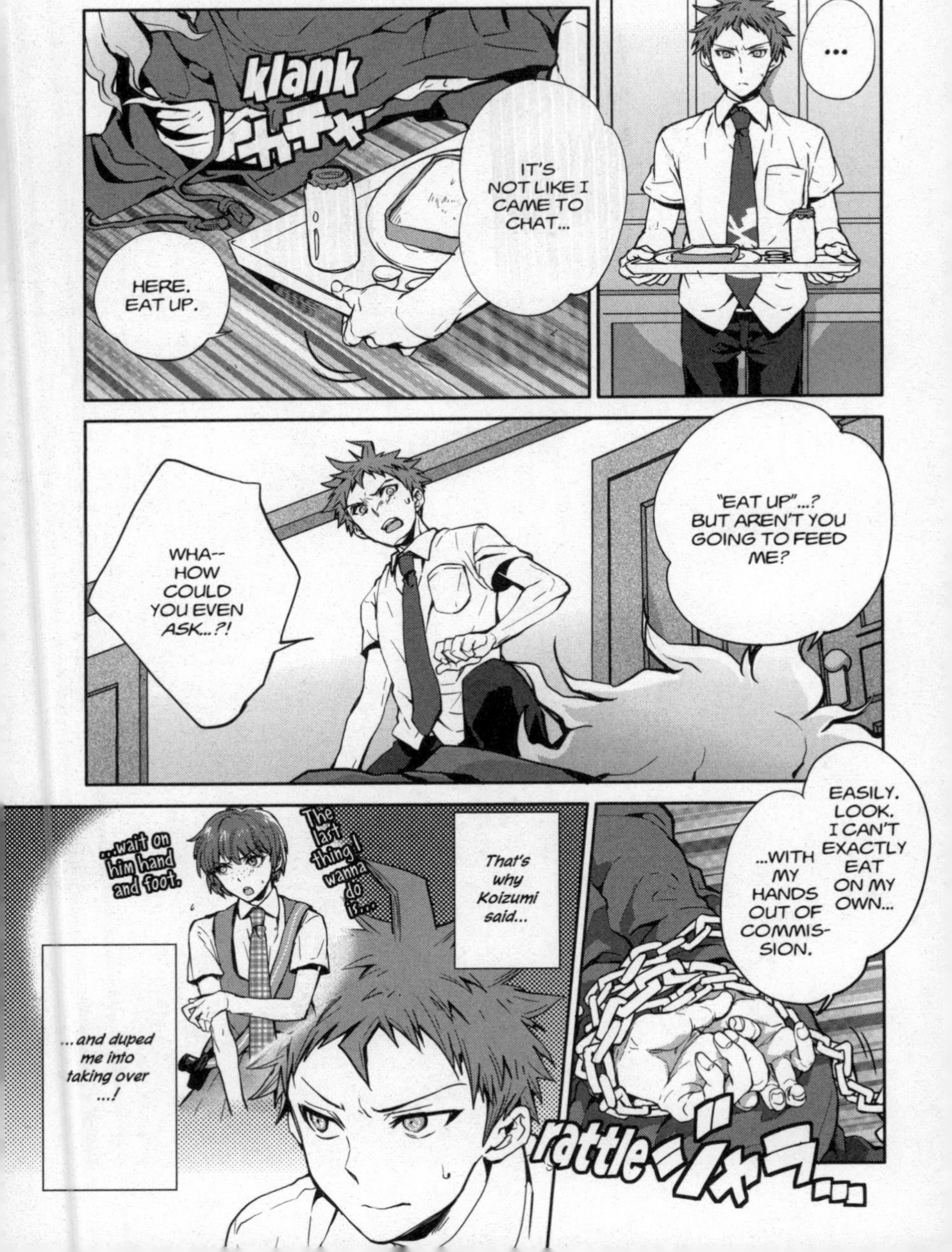
...
IT'S NOT LIKE I CAME TO CHAT...
klank
カチャ
HERE. EAT UP.
"EAT UP"...? BUT AREN'T YOU GOING TO FEED ME?
WHA-- HOW COULD YOU EVEN ASK...?!
EASILY. LOOK. I CAN'T EXACTLY EAT ON MY OWN...
...WITH MY HANDS OUT OF COMMISSION.
rattle
ジャラ...
That's why Koizumi said...
The last thing I wanna do is...
...wait on him hand and foot.
...and duped me into taking over...!

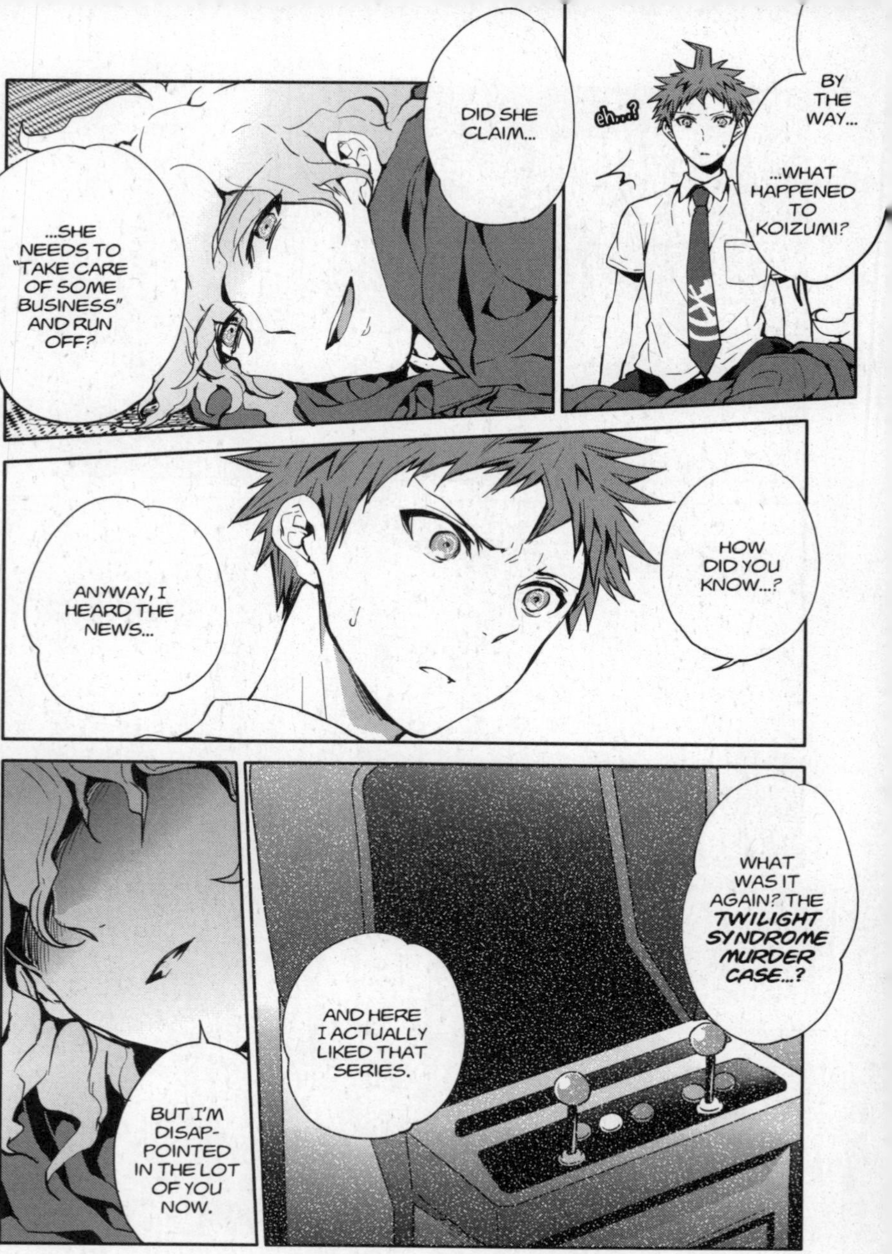
BY THE WAY...
...WHAT HAPPENED TO KOIZUMI?
eh...?
DID SHE CLAIM...
...SHE NEEDS TO "TAKE CARE OF SOME BUSINESS" AND RUN OFF?
HOW DID YOU KNOW...?
ANYWAY, I HEARD THE NEWS...
WHAT WAS IT AGAIN? THE *TWILIGHT SYNDROME MURDER CASE*...?
AND HERE I ACTUALLY LIKED THAT SERIES.
BUT I'M DISAP-POINTED IN THE LOT OF YOU NOW.

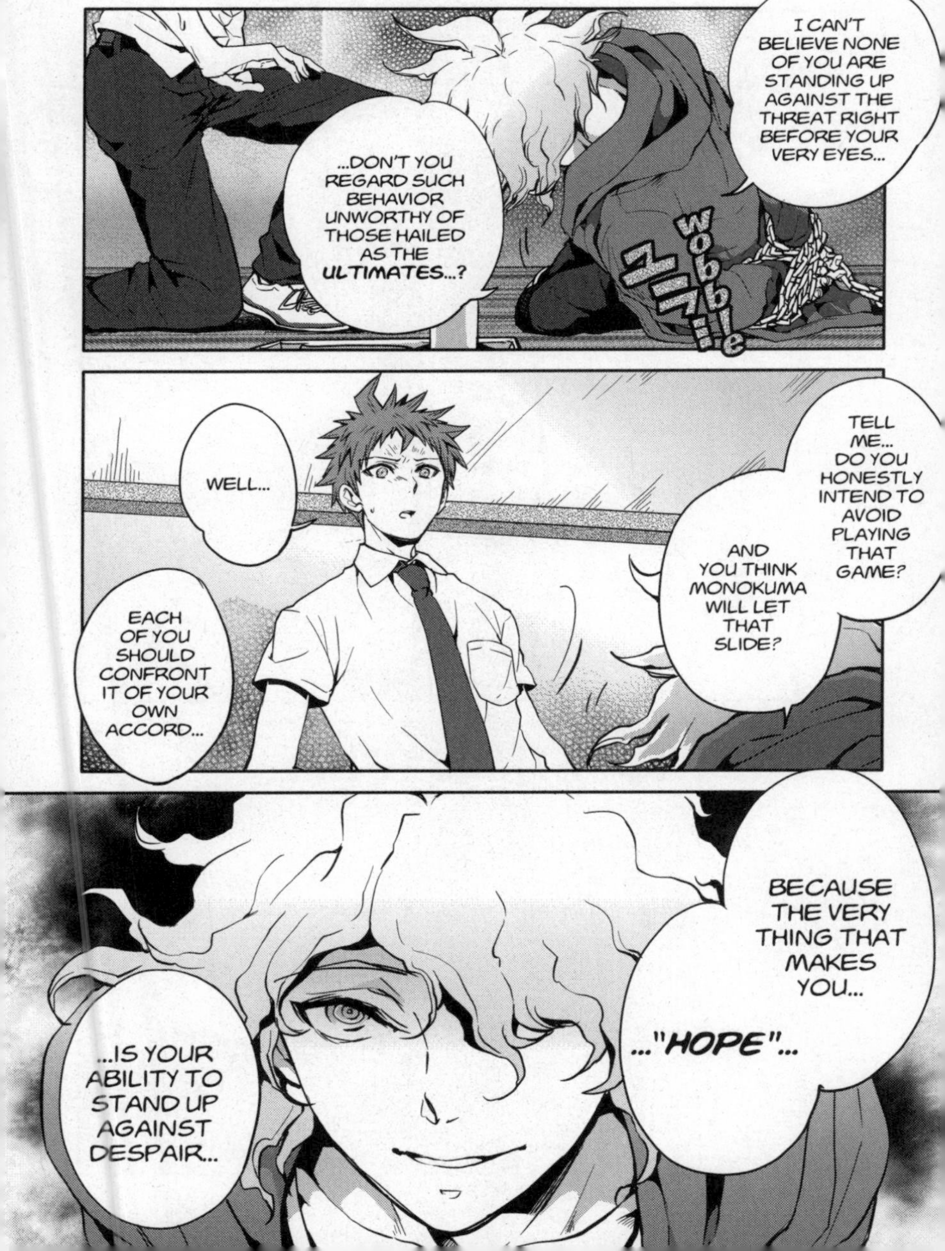
I CAN'T BELIEVE NONE OF YOU ARE STANDING UP AGAINST THE THREAT RIGHT BEFORE YOUR VERY EYES...
...DON'T YOU REGARD SUCH BEHAVIOR UNWORTHY OF THOSE HAILED AS THE **ULTIMATES**...?
wobble
TELL ME... DO YOU HONESTLY INTEND TO AVOID PLAYING THAT GAME?
AND YOU THINK MONOKUMA WILL LET THAT SLIDE?
WELL...
EACH OF YOU SHOULD CONFRONT IT OF YOUR OWN ACCORD...
BECAUSE THE VERY THING THAT MAKES YOU...
..."*HOPE*"...
...IS YOUR ABILITY TO STAND UP AGAINST DESPAIR...

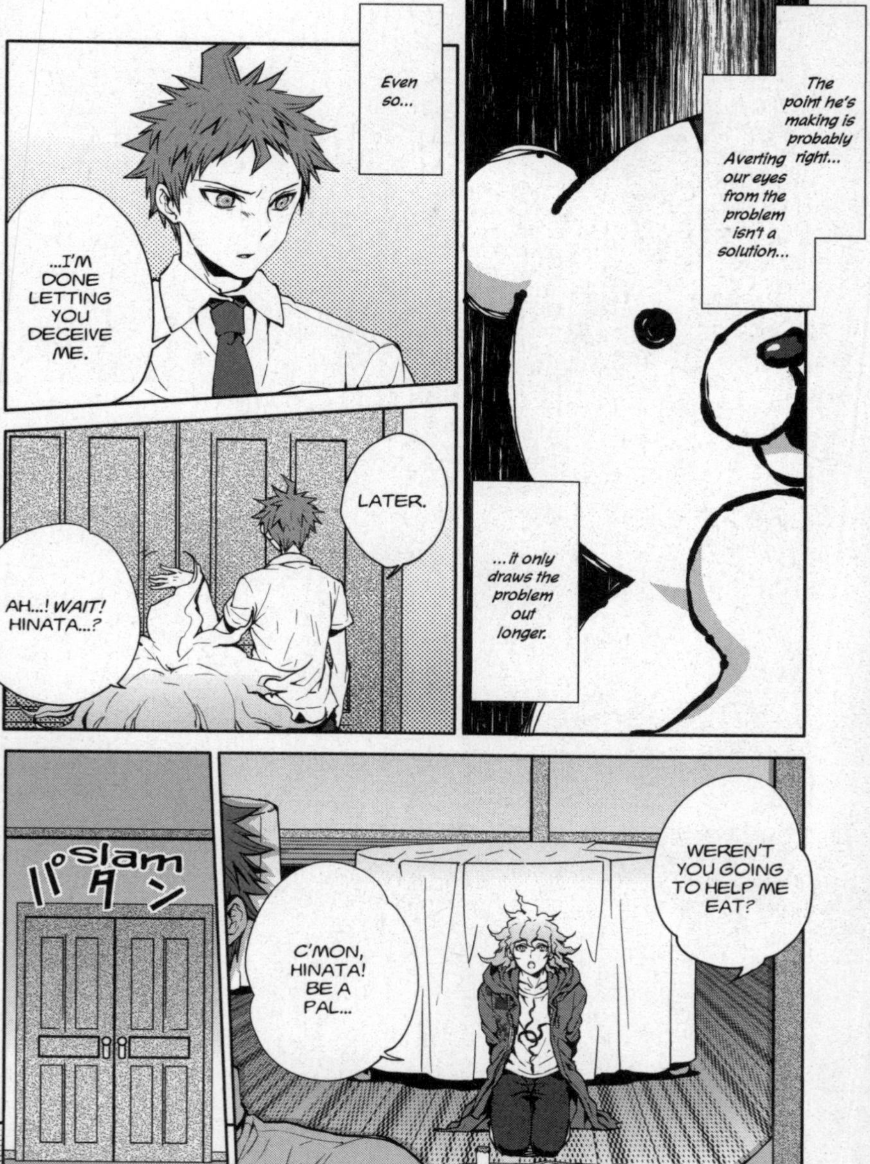
The point he's making is probably right...
Averting our eyes from the problem isn't a solution...
...it only draws the problem out longer.
Even so...
...I'M DONE LETTING YOU DECEIVE ME.
LATER.
AH...! WAIT! HINATA...?
WEREN'T YOU GOING TO HELP ME EAT?
C'MON, HINATA! BE A PAL...
パタン
slam

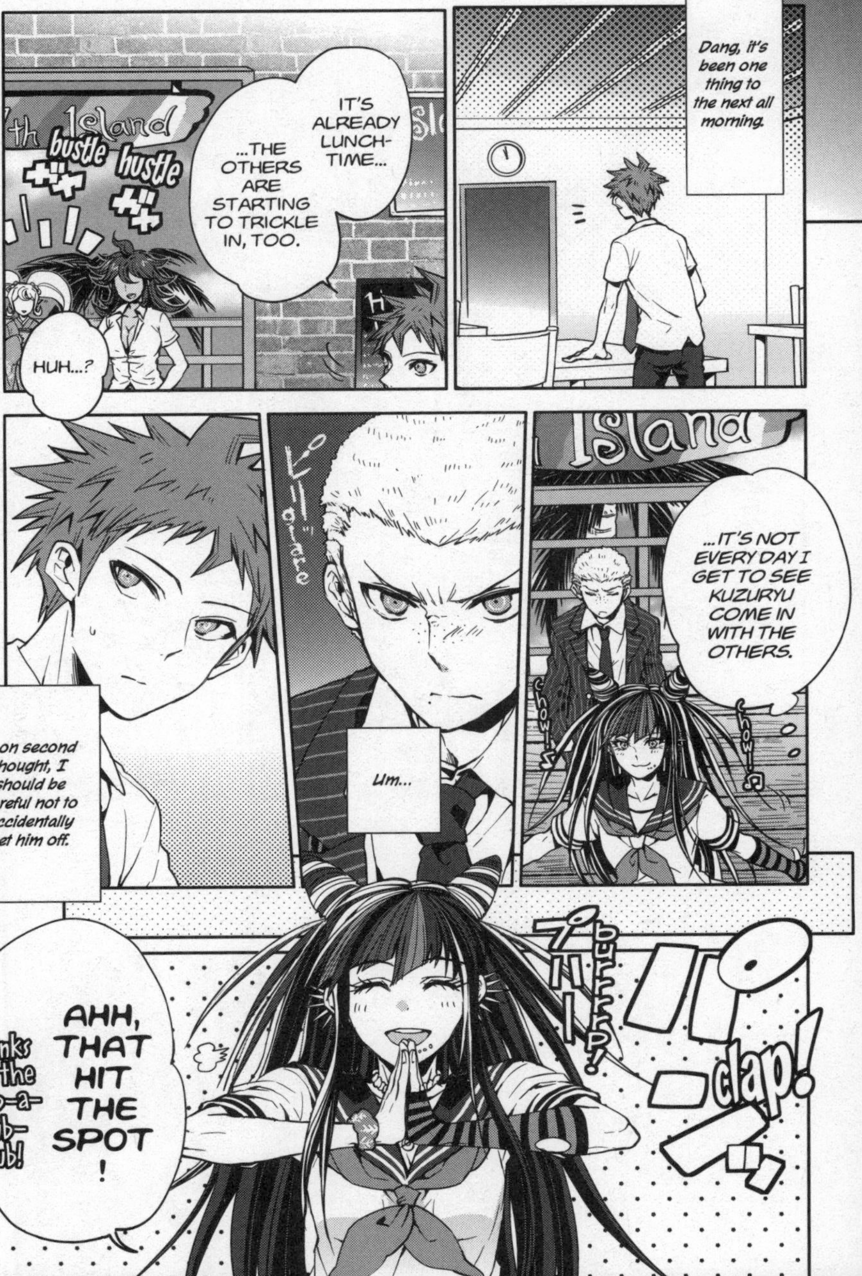
Dang, it's been one thing to the next all morning.
IT'S ALREADY LUNCH-TIME...
...THE OTHERS ARE STARTING TO TRICKLE IN, TOO.
bustle hustle
HUH...?
...IT'S NOT EVERY DAY I GET TO SEE KUZURYU COME IN WITH THE OTHERS.
Um...
...on second thought, I should be careful not to accidentally set him off.
clap!
burrrp!
AHH, THAT HIT THE SPOT!
Thanks for the grub-a-dub-dub!

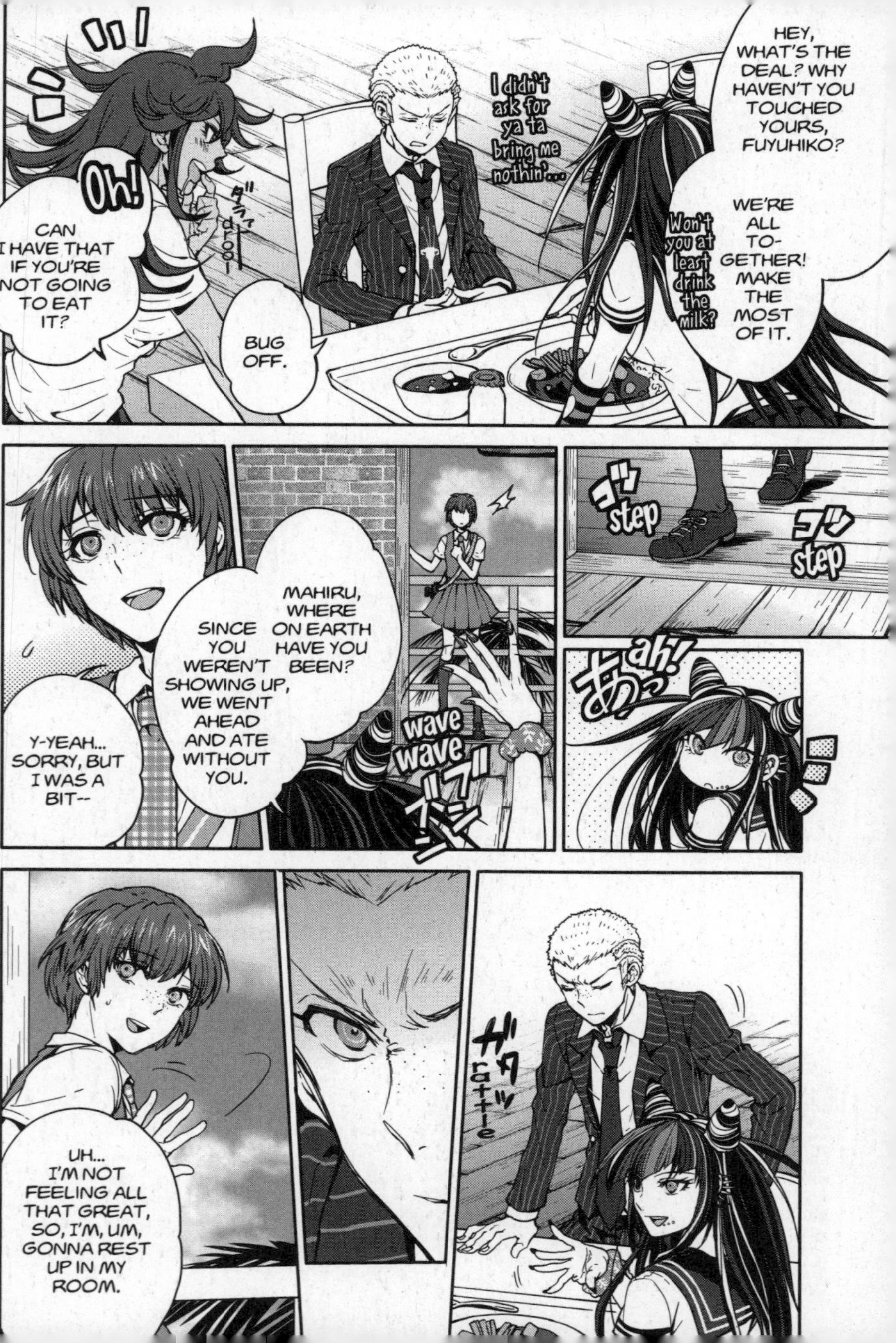
HEY, WHAT'S THE DEAL? WHY HAVEN'T YOU TOUCHED YOURS, FUYUHIKO?
WE'RE ALL TO-GETHER! MAKE THE MOST OF IT.
Won't you at least drink the milk?
I didn't ask for ya ta bring me nothin'...
BUG OFF.
Oh!
CAN I HAVE THAT IF YOU'RE NOT GOING TO EAT IT?
drool
step
step
ah!
wave wave
MAHIRU, WHERE ON EARTH HAVE YOU BEEN?
SINCE YOU WEREN'T SHOWING UP, WE WENT AHEAD AND ATE WITHOUT YOU.
Y-YEAH... SORRY, BUT I WAS A BIT--
rattle
UH... I'M NOT FEELING ALL THAT GREAT, SO, I'M, UM, GONNA REST UP IN MY ROOM.

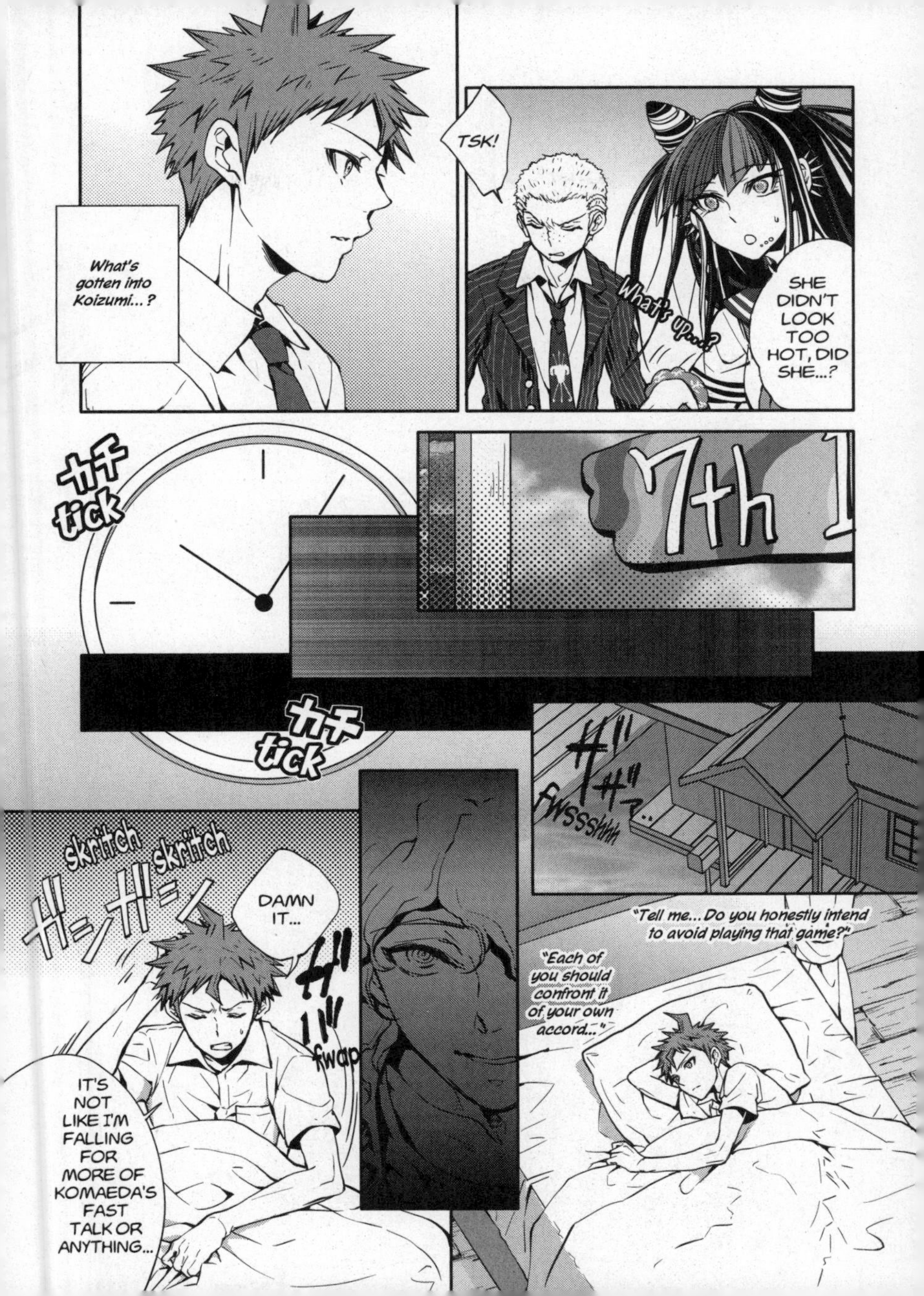

SHE DIDN'T LOOK TOO HOT, DID SHE...?
What's up...?
TSK!
What's gotten into Koizumi...?
7th 1
カチ
tick
カチ
tick
fwssshhh
"Tell me... Do you honestly intend to avoid playing that game?"
"Each of you should confront it of your own accord..."
fwap
skritch skritch
DAMN IT...
IT'S NOT LIKE I'M FALLING FOR MORE OF KOMAEDA'S FAST TALK OR ANYTHING...

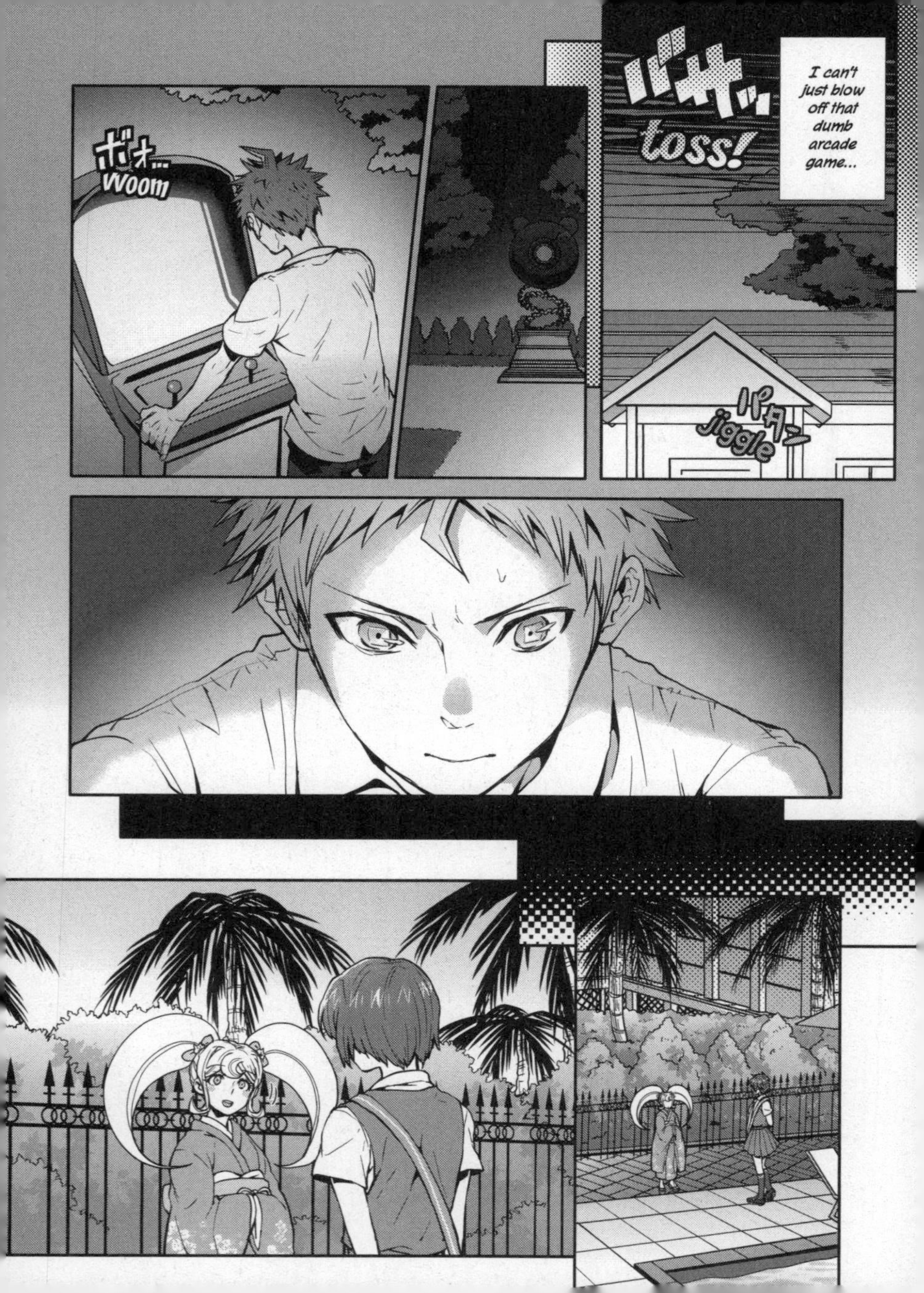
I can't just blow off that dumb arcade game...
バサッ
toss!
パタン
jiggle
ボォ…
vwoom

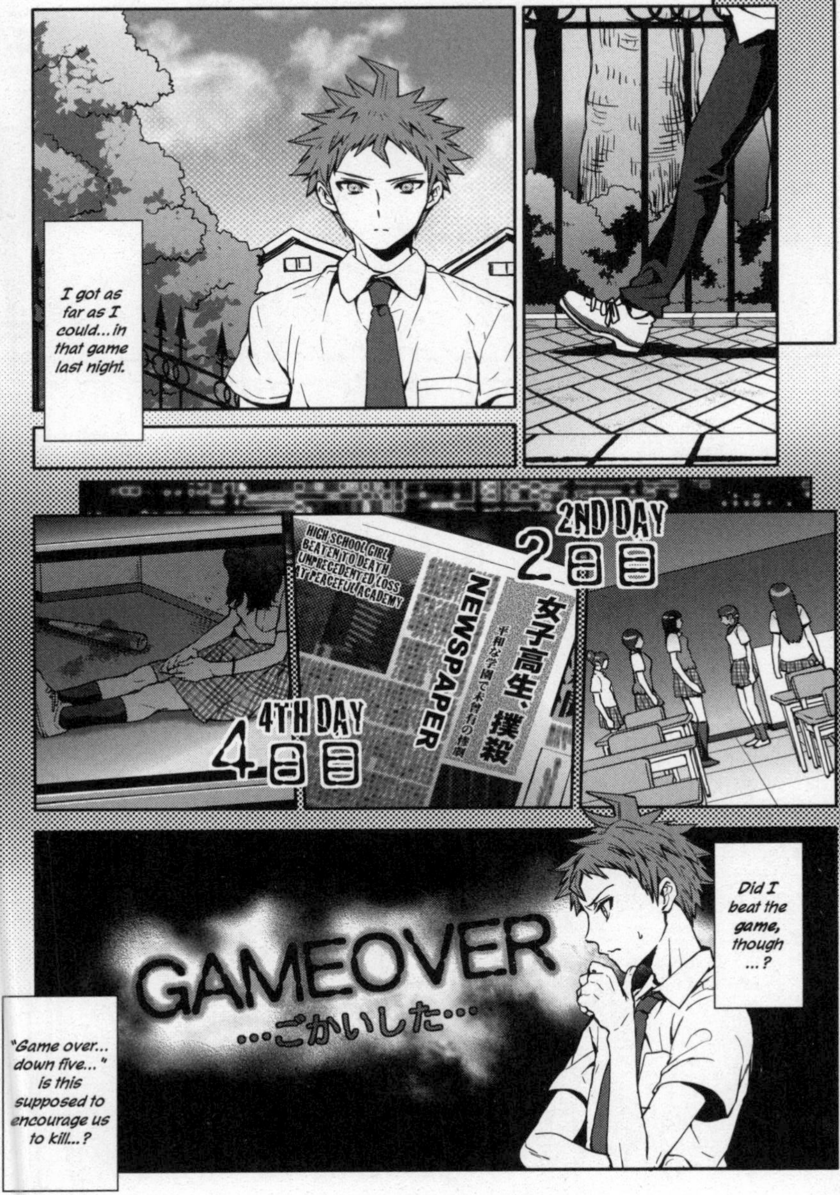
I got as far as I could... in that game last night.
2ND DAY
2日目
女子高生、撲殺
NEWSPAPER
HIGH SCHOOL GIRL BEATEN TO DEATH UNPRECEDENTED LOSS AT PEACEFUL ACADEMY
4TH DAY
4日目
Did I beat the game, though ...?
GAMEOVER
…ごかいした…
"Game over... down five..." is this supposed to encourage us to kill...?

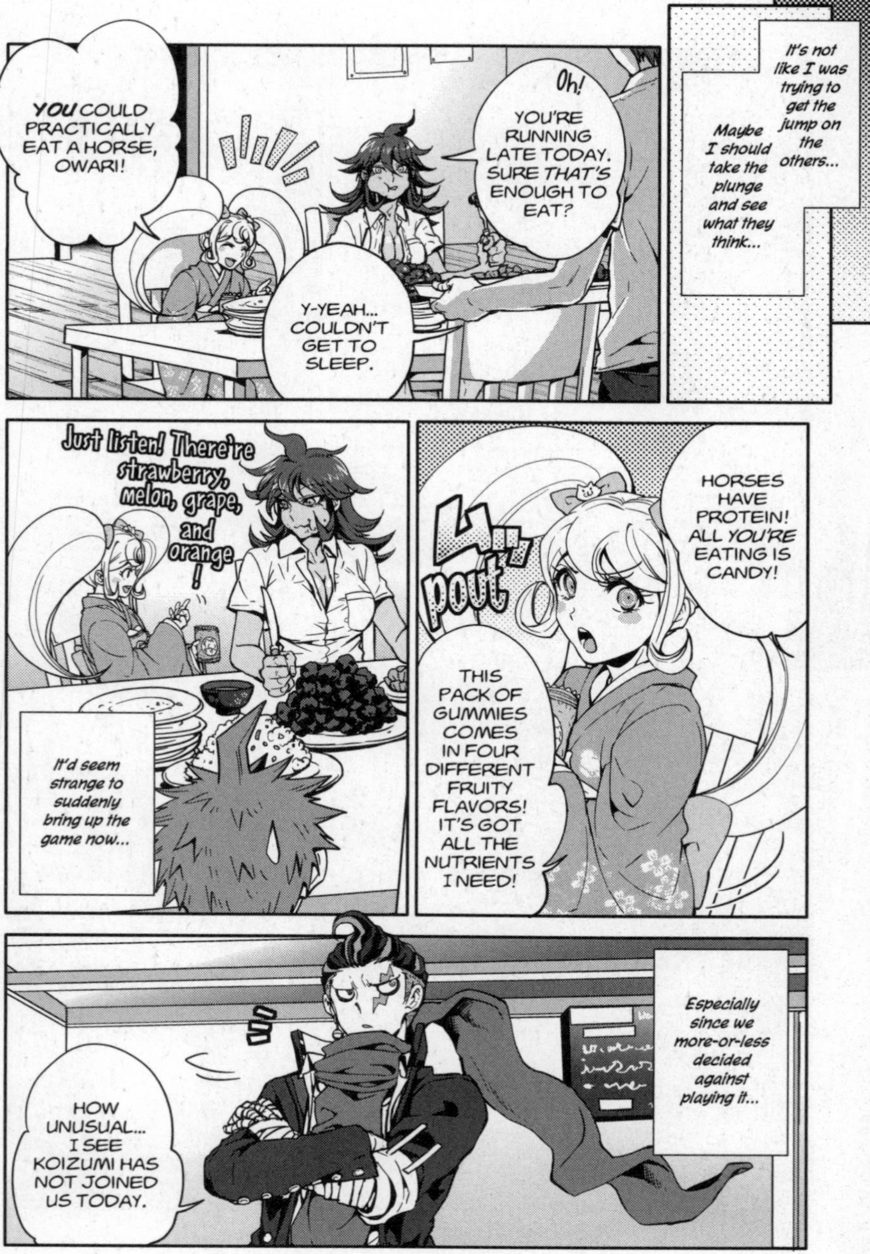
It's not like I was trying to get the jump on the others...
Maybe I should take the plunge and see what they think...
Oh!
YOU'RE RUNNING LATE TODAY. SURE THAT'S ENOUGH TO EAT?
YOU COULD PRACTICALLY EAT A HORSE, OWARI!
Y-YEAH... COULDN'T GET TO SLEEP.
HORSES HAVE PROTEIN! ALL YOU'RE EATING IS CANDY!
pout
THIS PACK OF GUMMIES COMES IN FOUR DIFFERENT FRUITY FLAVORS! IT'S GOT ALL THE NUTRIENTS I NEED!
Just listen! There're strawberry, melon, grape, and orange!
It'd seem strange to suddenly bring up the game now...
Especially since we more-or-less decided against playing it...
HOW UNUSUAL... I SEE KOIZUMI HAS NOT JOINED US TODAY.

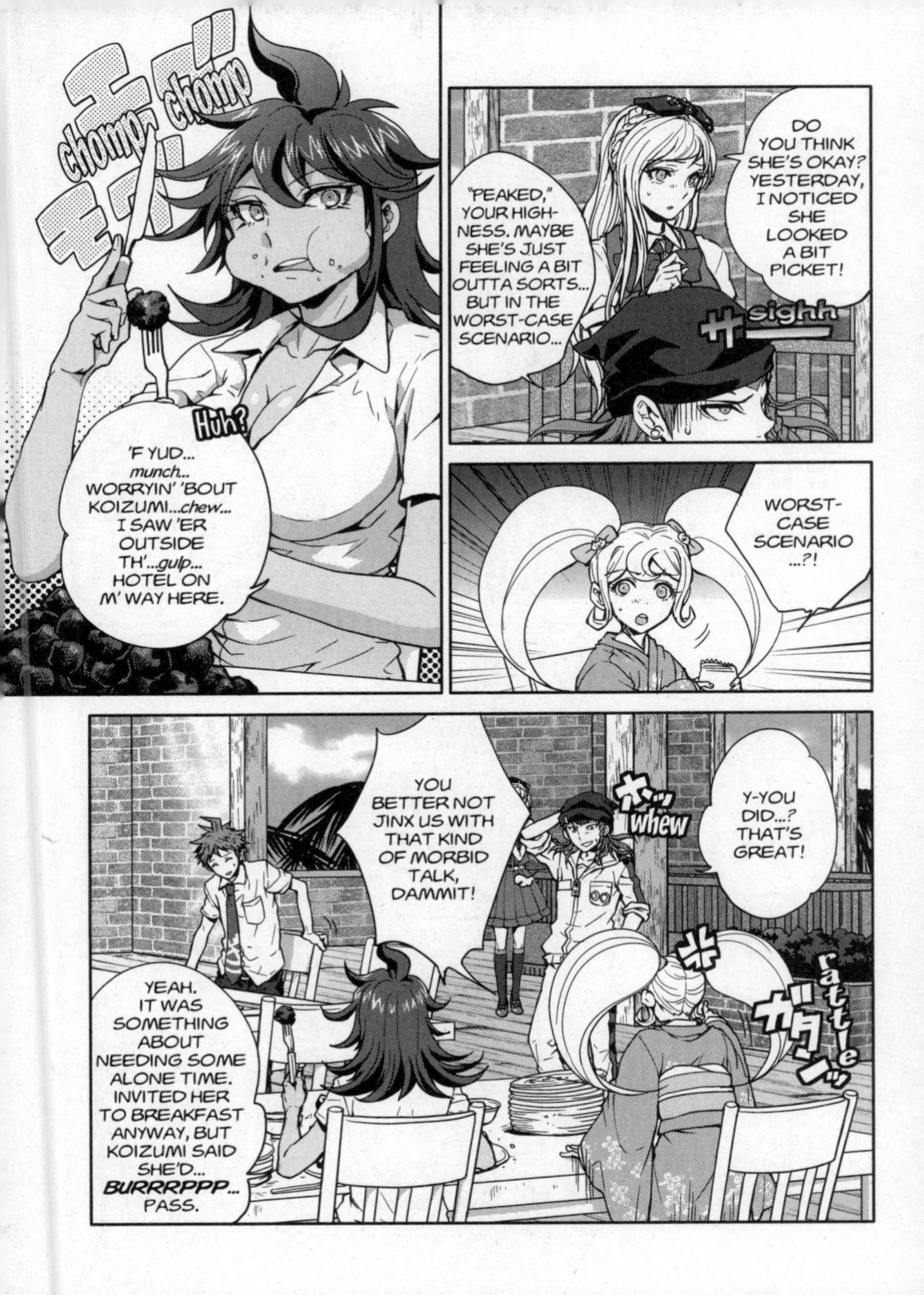
DO YOU THINK SHE'S OKAY? YESTERDAY, I NOTICED SHE LOOKED A BIT PICKET!
sighh
"PEAKED," YOUR HIGHNESS. MAYBE SHE'S JUST FEELING A BIT OUTTA SORTS... BUT IN THE WORST-CASE SCENARIO...
WORST-CASE SCENARIO ...?!
chomp chomp
Huh?
'F YUD... *munch*... WORRYIN' 'BOUT KOIZUMI...*chew*... I SAW 'ER OUTSIDE TH'...*gulp*... HOTEL ON M' WAY HERE.
Y-YOU DID...? THAT'S GREAT!
whew
YOU BETTER NOT JINX US WITH THAT KIND OF MORBID TALK, DAMMIT!
rattle
YEAH. IT WAS SOMETHING ABOUT NEEDING SOME ALONE TIME. INVITED HER TO BREAKFAST ANYWAY, BUT KOIZUMI SAID SHE'D... ***BURRRPPP***... PASS.

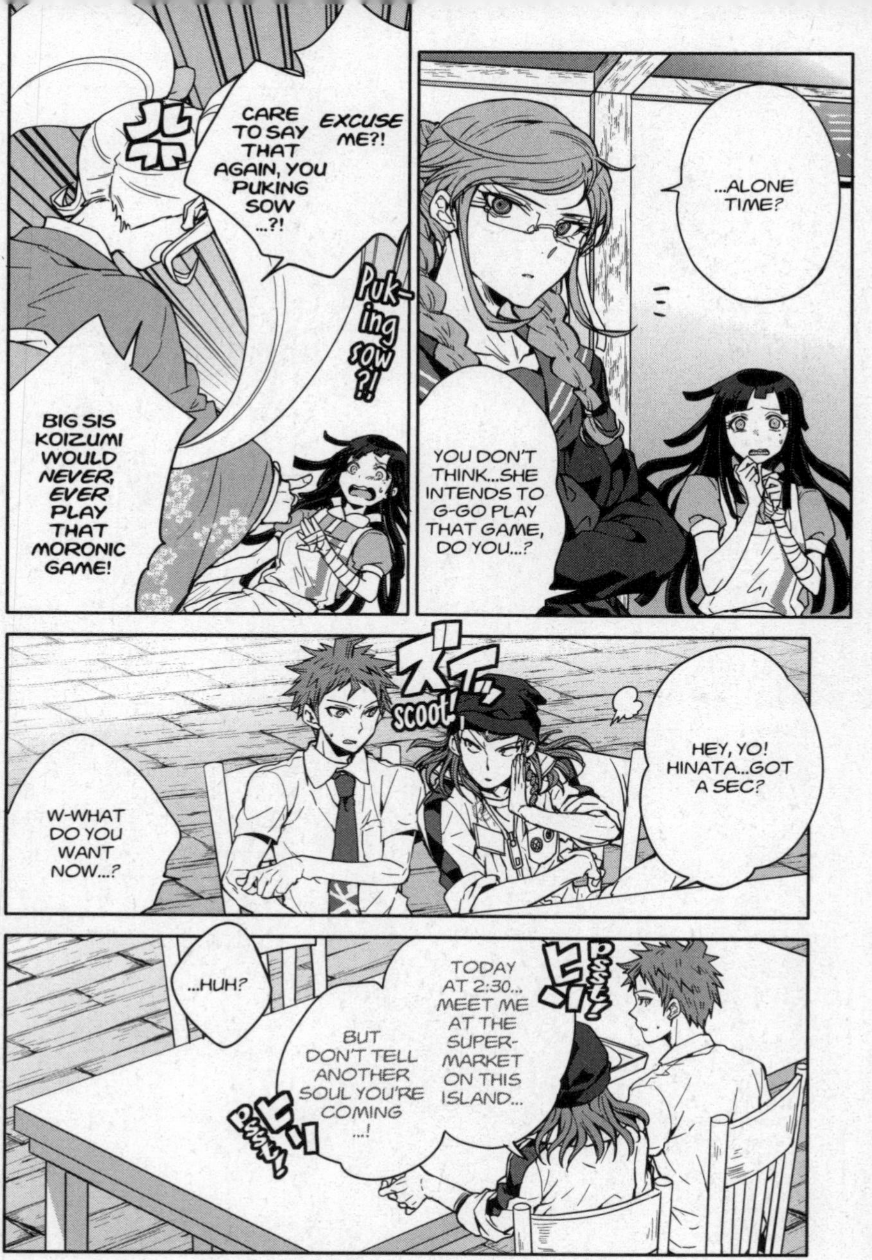
...ALONE TIME?
YOU DON'T THINK...SHE INTENDS TO G-GO PLAY THAT GAME, DO YOU...?
EXCUSE ME?!
CARE TO SAY THAT AGAIN, YOU PUKING SOW ...?!
Puking sow?!
BIG SIS KOIZUMI WOULD NEVER, EVER PLAY THAT MORONIC GAME!
HEY, YO! HINATA...GOT A SEC?
scoot!
W-WHAT DO YOU WANT NOW...?
pssst!
TODAY AT 2:30... MEET ME AT THE SUPER-MARKET ON THIS ISLAND...
BUT DON'T TELL ANOTHER SOUL YOU'RE COMING ...!
pssst!
...HUH?

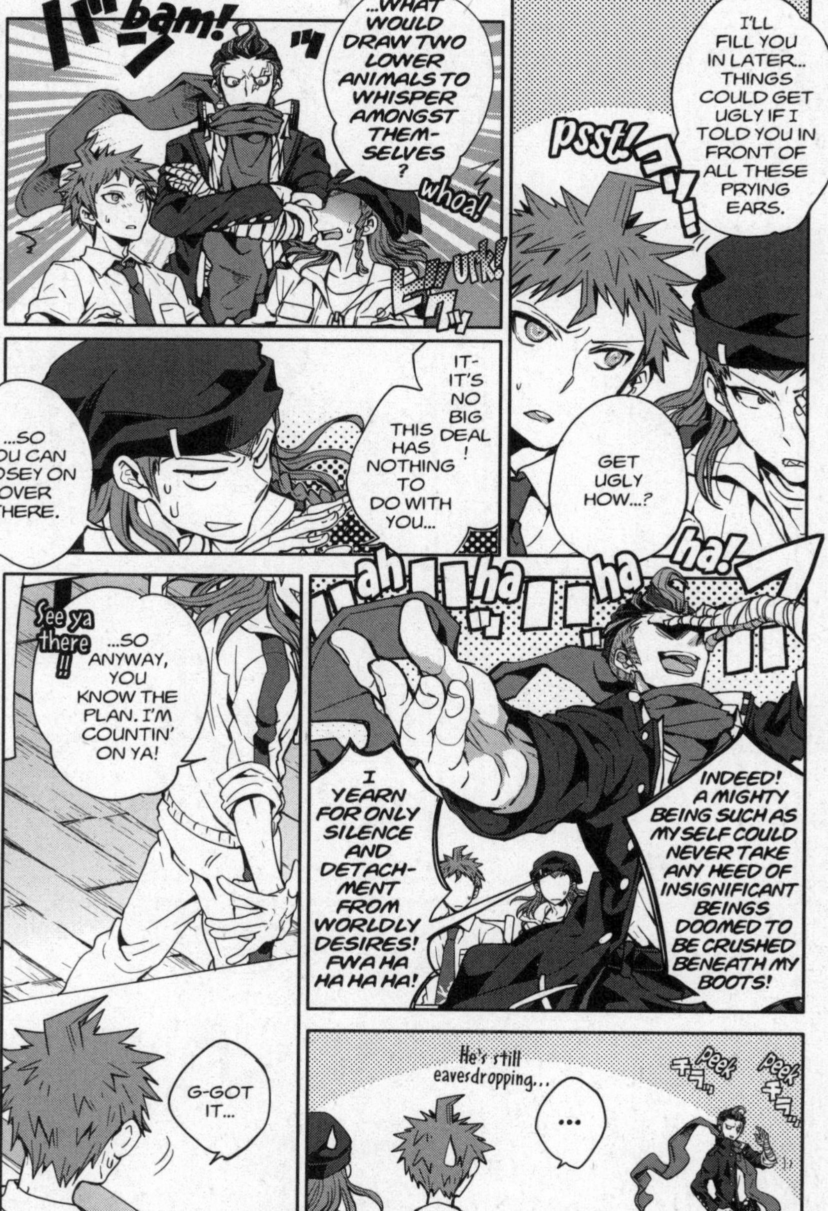
psst!
I'LL FILL YOU IN LATER... THINGS COULD GET UGLY IF I TOLD YOU IN FRONT OF ALL THESE PRYING EARS.
GET UGLY HOW...?
bam!
...WHAT WOULD DRAW TWO LOWER ANIMALS TO WHISPER AMONGST THEM-SELVES?
whoa!
urk!
IT- IT'S NO BIG DEAL! THIS HAS NOTHING TO DO WITH YOU...
...SO YOU CAN MOSEY ON OVER THERE.
ah ha ha ha!
INDEED! A MIGHTY BEING SUCH AS MYSELF COULD NEVER TAKE ANY HEED OF INSIGNIFICANT BEINGS DOOMED TO BE CRUSHED BENEATH MY BOOTS!
I YEARN FOR ONLY SILENCE AND DETACH-MENT FROM WORLDLY DESIRES! FWA HA HA HA HA!
See ya there!!
...SO ANYWAY, YOU KNOW THE PLAN. I'M COUNTIN' ON YA!
peek
peek
He's still eavesdropping...
...
G-GOT IT...

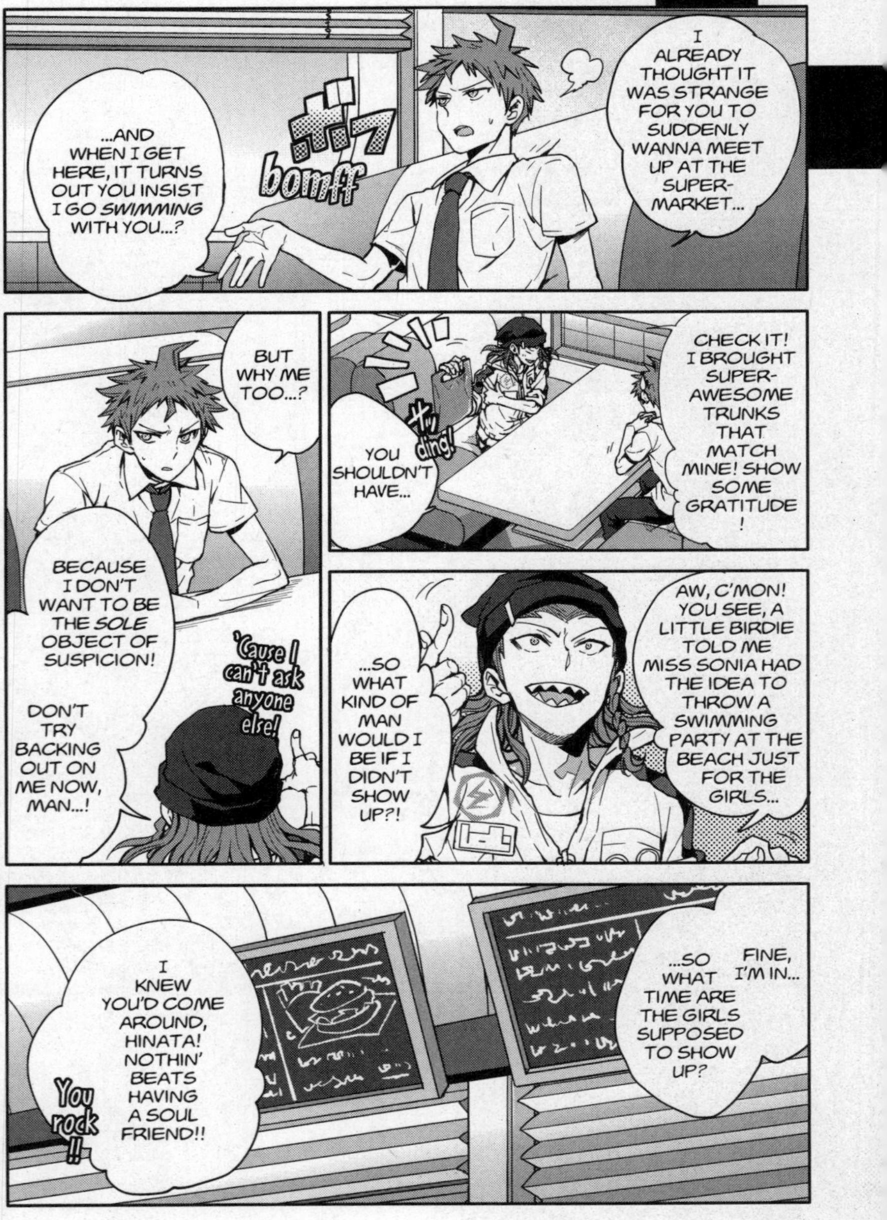
I ALREADY THOUGHT IT WAS STRANGE FOR YOU TO SUDDENLY WANNA MEET UP AT THE SUPER-MARKET...
bomff
...AND WHEN I GET HERE, IT TURNS OUT YOU INSIST I GO *SWIMMING* WITH YOU...?
CHECK IT! I BROUGHT SUPER-AWESOME TRUNKS THAT MATCH MINE! SHOW SOME GRATITUDE!
ding!
YOU SHOULDN'T HAVE...
AW, C'MON! YOU SEE, A LITTLE BIRDIE TOLD ME MISS SONIA HAD THE IDEA TO THROW A SWIMMING PARTY AT THE BEACH JUST FOR THE GIRLS...
...SO WHAT KIND OF MAN WOULD I BE IF I DIDN'T SHOW UP?!
BUT WHY ME TOO...?
BECAUSE I DON'T WANT TO BE THE *SOLE* OBJECT OF SUSPICION!
'Cause I can't ask anyone else!
DON'T TRY BACKING OUT ON ME NOW, MAN...!
FINE, I'M IN...
...SO WHAT TIME ARE THE GIRLS SUPPOSED TO SHOW UP?
I KNEW YOU'D COME AROUND, HINATA! NOTHIN' BEATS HAVING A SOUL FRIEND!!
You rock!!

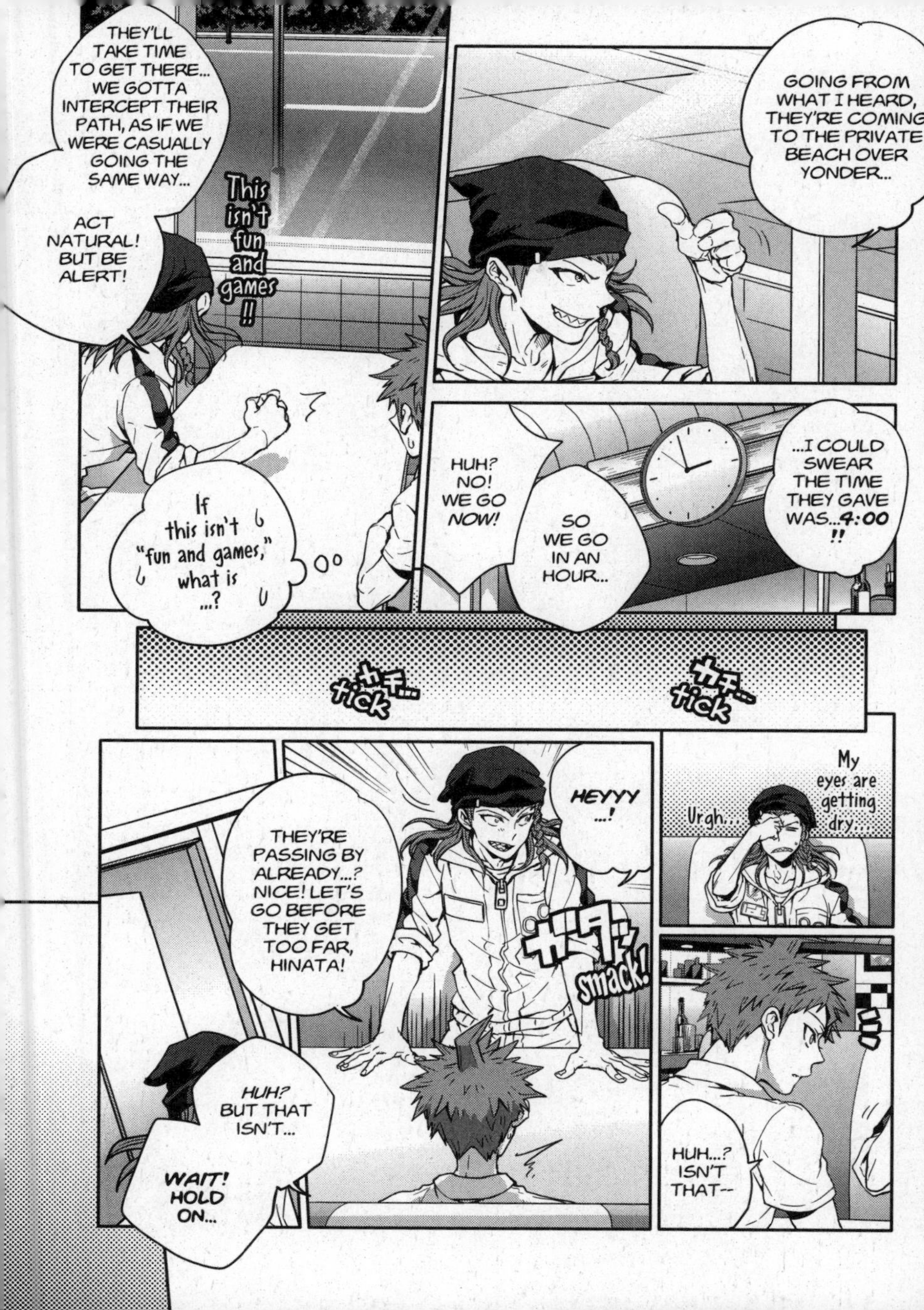
GOING FROM WHAT I HEARD, THEY'RE COMING TO THE PRIVATE BEACH OVER YONDER...
...I COULD SWEAR THE TIME THEY GAVE WAS...4:00!!
SO WE GO IN AN HOUR...
HUH? NO! WE GO NOW!
THEY'LL TAKE TIME TO GET THERE... WE GOTTA INTERCEPT THEIR PATH, AS IF WE WERE CASUALLY GOING THE SAME WAY...
ACT NATURAL! BUT BE ALERT!
This isn't fun and games!!
If this isn't "fun and games," what is ...?
カチ... tick
カチ... tick
My eyes are getting dry...
Urgh...
HUH...? ISN'T THAT--
HEYYY...!
ガタッ smack!
THEY'RE PASSING BY ALREADY...? NICE! LET'S GO BEFORE THEY GET TOO FAR, HINATA!
HUH? BUT THAT ISN'T...
WAIT! HOLD ON...

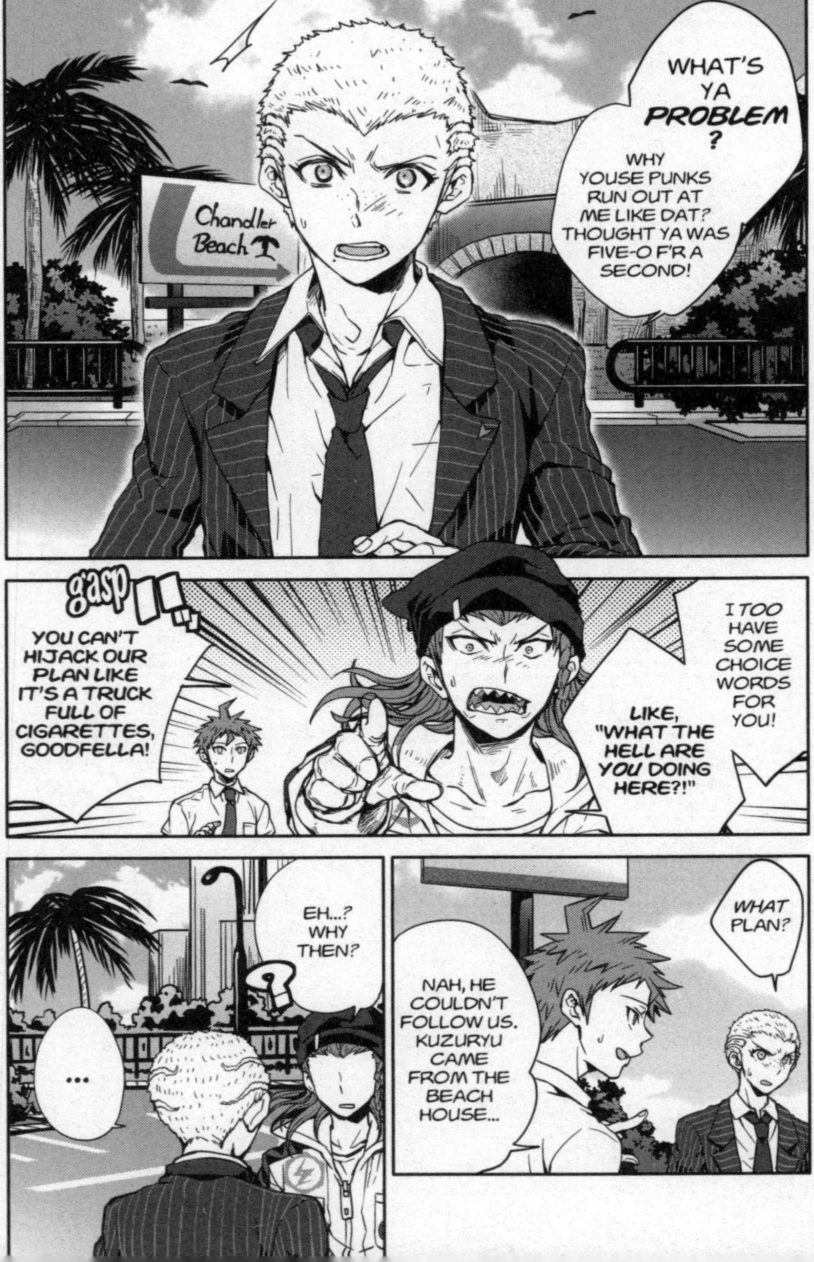
Chandler Beach
WHAT'S YA PROBLEM?
WHY YOUSE PUNKS RUN OUT AT ME LIKE DAT? THOUGHT YA WAS FIVE-O F'R A SECOND!
I TOO HAVE SOME CHOICE WORDS FOR YOU!
LIKE, "WHAT THE HELL ARE YOU DOING HERE?!"
gasp
YOU CAN'T HIJACK OUR PLAN LIKE IT'S A TRUCK FULL OF CIGARETTES, GOODFELLA!
WHAT PLAN?
NAH, HE COULDN'T FOLLOW US. KUZURYU CAME FROM THE BEACH HOUSE...
EH...? WHY THEN?
...

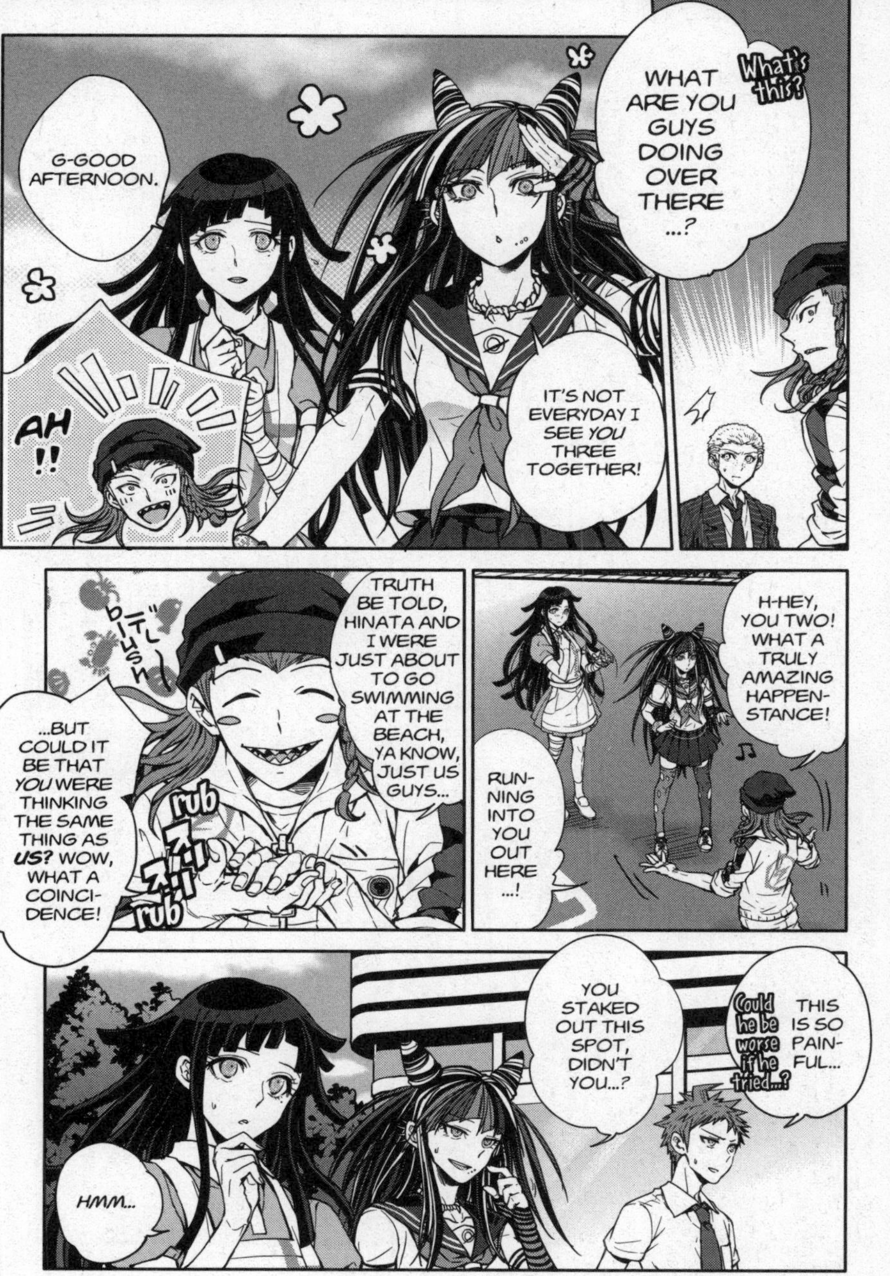
WHAT ARE YOU GUYS DOING OVER THERE ...?
What's this?
G-GOOD AFTERNOON.
IT'S NOT EVERYDAY I SEE *YOU* THREE TOGETHER!
AH !!
H-HEY, YOU TWO! WHAT A TRULY AMAZING HAPPEN-STANCE!
RUN-NING INTO YOU OUT HERE ...!
TRUTH BE TOLD, HINATA AND I WERE JUST ABOUT TO GO SWIMMING AT THE BEACH, YA KNOW, JUST US GUYS...
brush
rub
rub
...BUT COULD IT BE THAT *YOU* WERE THINKING THE SAME THING AS ***US?*** WOW, WHAT A COINCI-DENCE!
THIS IS SO PAIN-FUL...
Could he be worse if he tried...?
YOU STAKED OUT THIS SPOT, DIDN'T YOU...?
HMM...

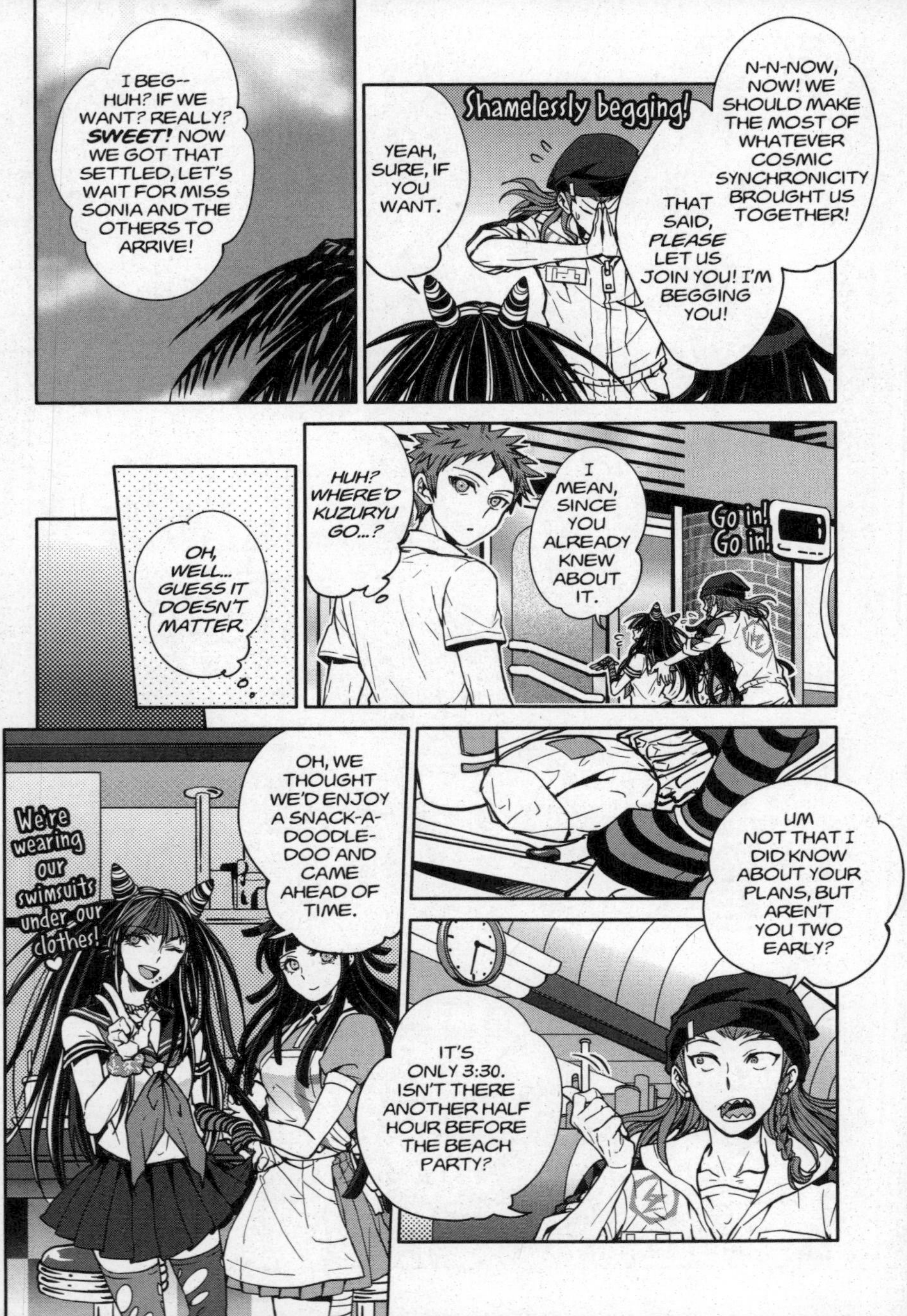
N-N-NOW, NOW! WE SHOULD MAKE THE MOST OF WHATEVER COSMIC SYNCHRONICITY BROUGHT US TOGETHER!
Shamelessly begging!
THAT SAID, *PLEASE* LET US JOIN YOU! I'M BEGGING YOU!
YEAH, SURE, IF YOU WANT.
I BEG-- HUH? IF WE WANT? REALLY? ***SWEET!*** NOW WE GOT THAT SETTLED, LET'S WAIT FOR MISS SONIA AND THE OTHERS TO ARRIVE!
Go in! Go in!
I MEAN, SINCE YOU ALREADY KNEW ABOUT IT.
HUH? WHERE'D KUZURYU GO...?
OH, WELL... GUESS IT DOESN'T MATTER.
UM NOT THAT I DID KNOW ABOUT YOUR PLANS, BUT AREN'T YOU TWO EARLY?
IT'S ONLY 3:30. ISN'T THERE ANOTHER HALF HOUR BEFORE THE BEACH PARTY?
OH, WE THOUGHT WE'D ENJOY A SNACK-A-DOODLE-DOO AND CAME AHEAD OF TIME.
We're wearing our swimsuits under our clothes! ♥

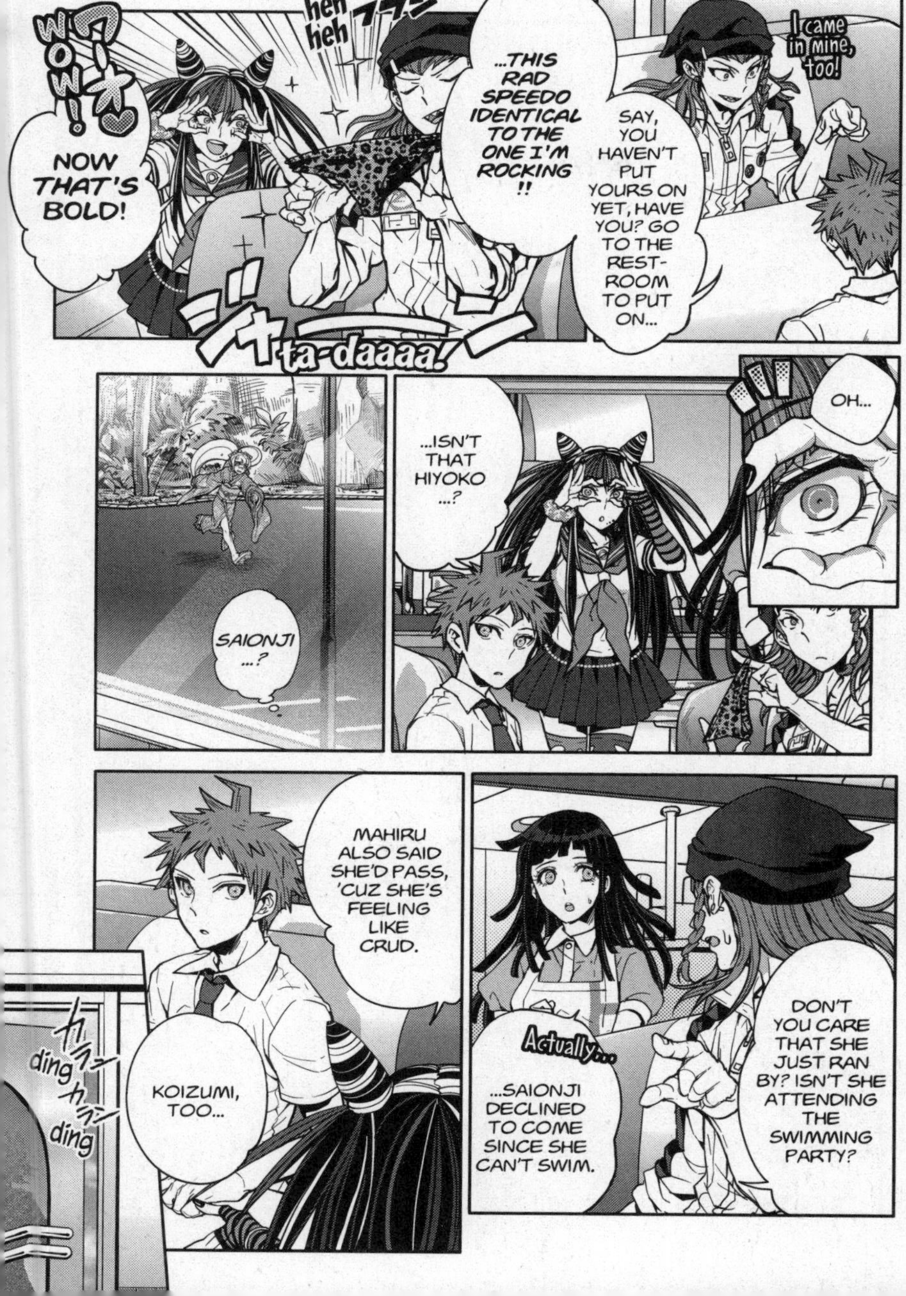

I came in mine, too!
heh heh
...THIS RAD SPEEDO IDENTICAL TO THE ONE I'M ROCKING!!
SAY, YOU HAVEN'T PUT YOURS ON YET, HAVE YOU? GO TO THE REST-ROOM TO PUT ON...
WOW!
NOW THAT'S BOLD!
ta-daaaa!
OH...
...ISN'T THAT HIYOKO...?
SAIONJI...?
DON'T YOU CARE THAT SHE JUST RAN BY? ISN'T SHE ATTENDING THE SWIMMING PARTY?
Actually...
...SAIONJI DECLINED TO COME SINCE SHE CAN'T SWIM.
MAHIRU ALSO SAID SHE'D PASS, 'CUZ SHE'S FEELING LIKE CRUD.
KOIZUMI, TOO...
ding ding

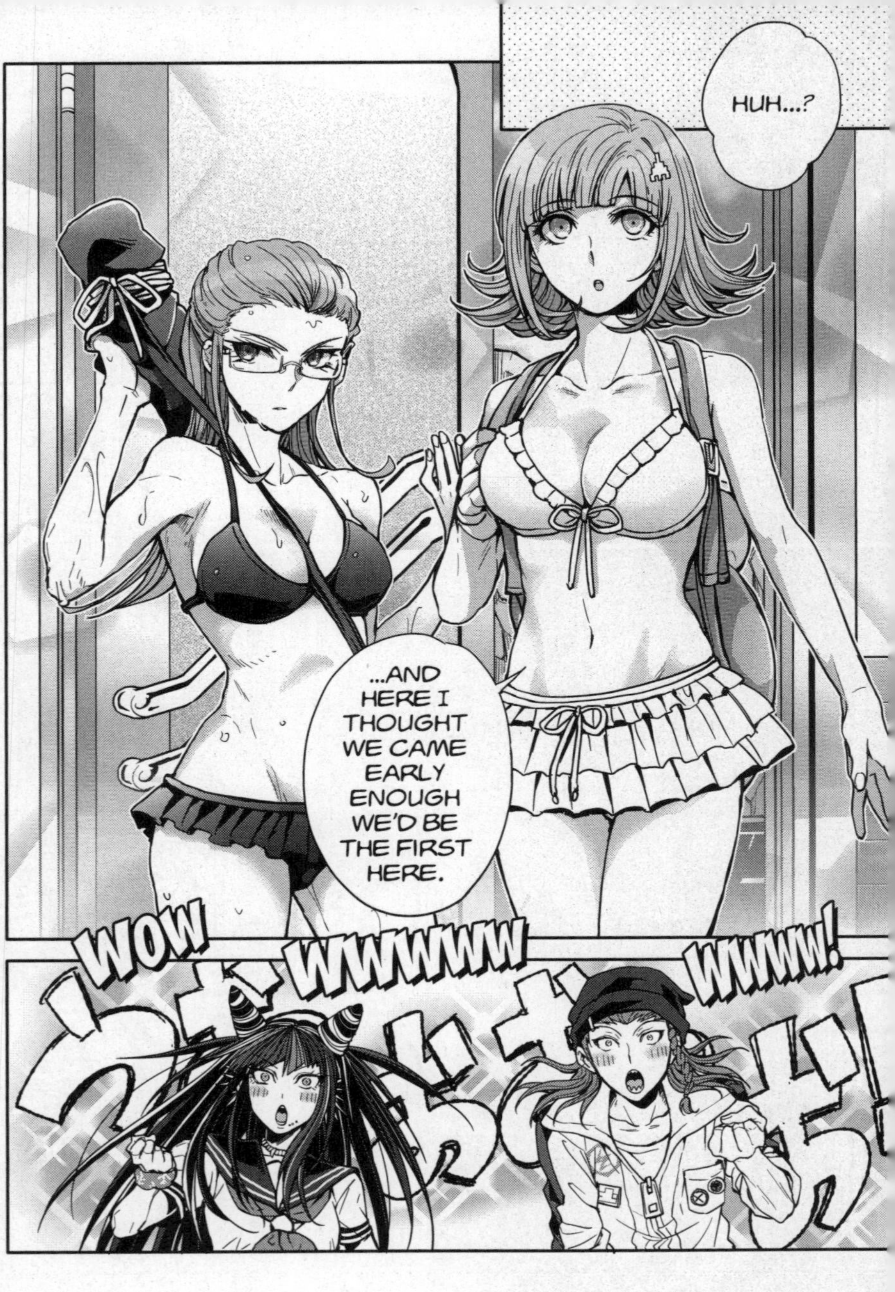
HUH...?
...AND HERE I THOUGHT WE CAME EARLY ENOUGH WE'D BE THE FIRST HERE.
WOW WWWWWW WWWW!

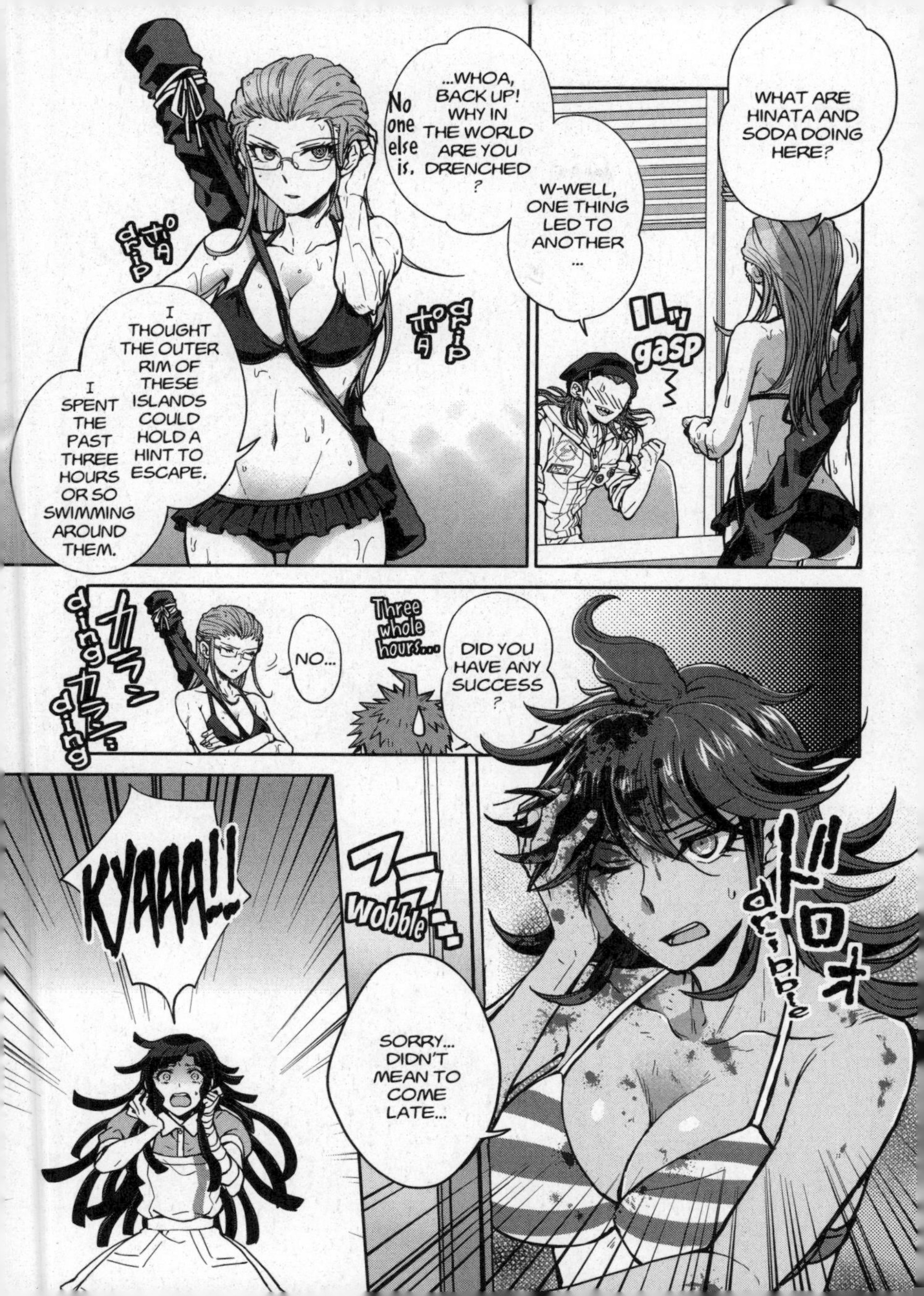
WHAT ARE HINATA AND SODA DOING HERE?
W-WELL, ONE THING LED TO ANOTHER ...
gasp
...WHOA, BACK UP! WHY IN THE WORLD ARE YOU DRENCHED?
No one else is.
drip
drip
I THOUGHT THE OUTER RIM OF THESE ISLANDS COULD HOLD A HINT TO ESCAPE.
I SPENT THE PAST THREE HOURS OR SO SWIMMING AROUND THEM.
DID YOU HAVE ANY SUCCESS?
Three whole hours...
NO...
ding ding
dribble
wobble
SORRY... DIDN'T MEAN TO COME LATE...
KYAAA!!

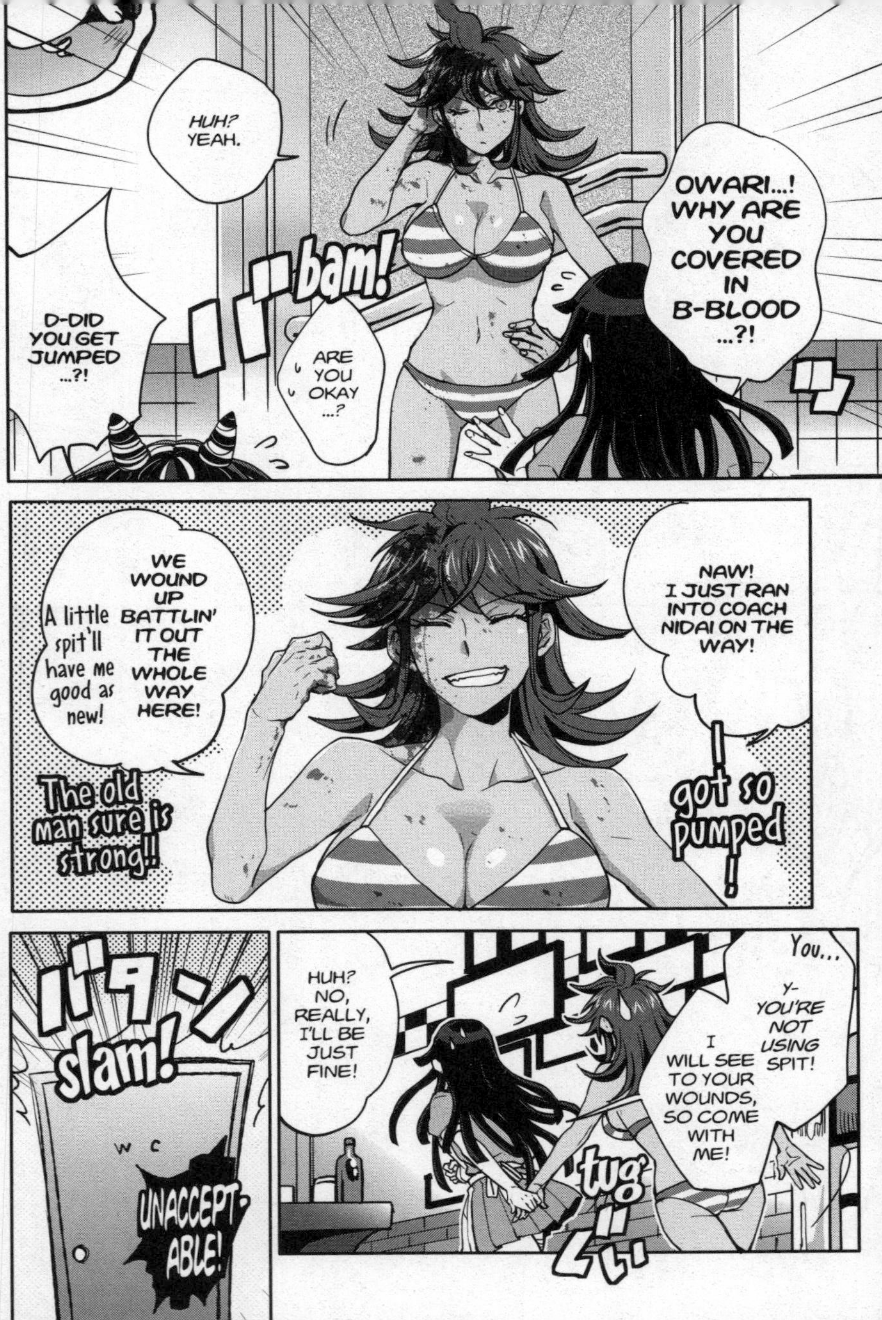
OWARI...! WHY ARE YOU COVERED IN B-BLOOD ...?!
HUH? YEAH.
bam!
ARE YOU OKAY ...?
D-DID YOU GET JUMPED ...?!
NAW! I JUST RAN INTO COACH NIDAI ON THE WAY!
I got so pumped!
WE WOUND UP BATTLIN' IT OUT THE WHOLE WAY HERE!
A little spit'll have me good as new!
The old man sure is strong!!
You...
Y-YOU'RE NOT USING SPIT!
I WILL SEE TO YOUR WOUNDS, SO COME WITH ME!
HUH? NO, REALLY, I'LL BE JUST FINE!
ぐい
tug
バターン
slam!
W C
UNACCEPTABLE!

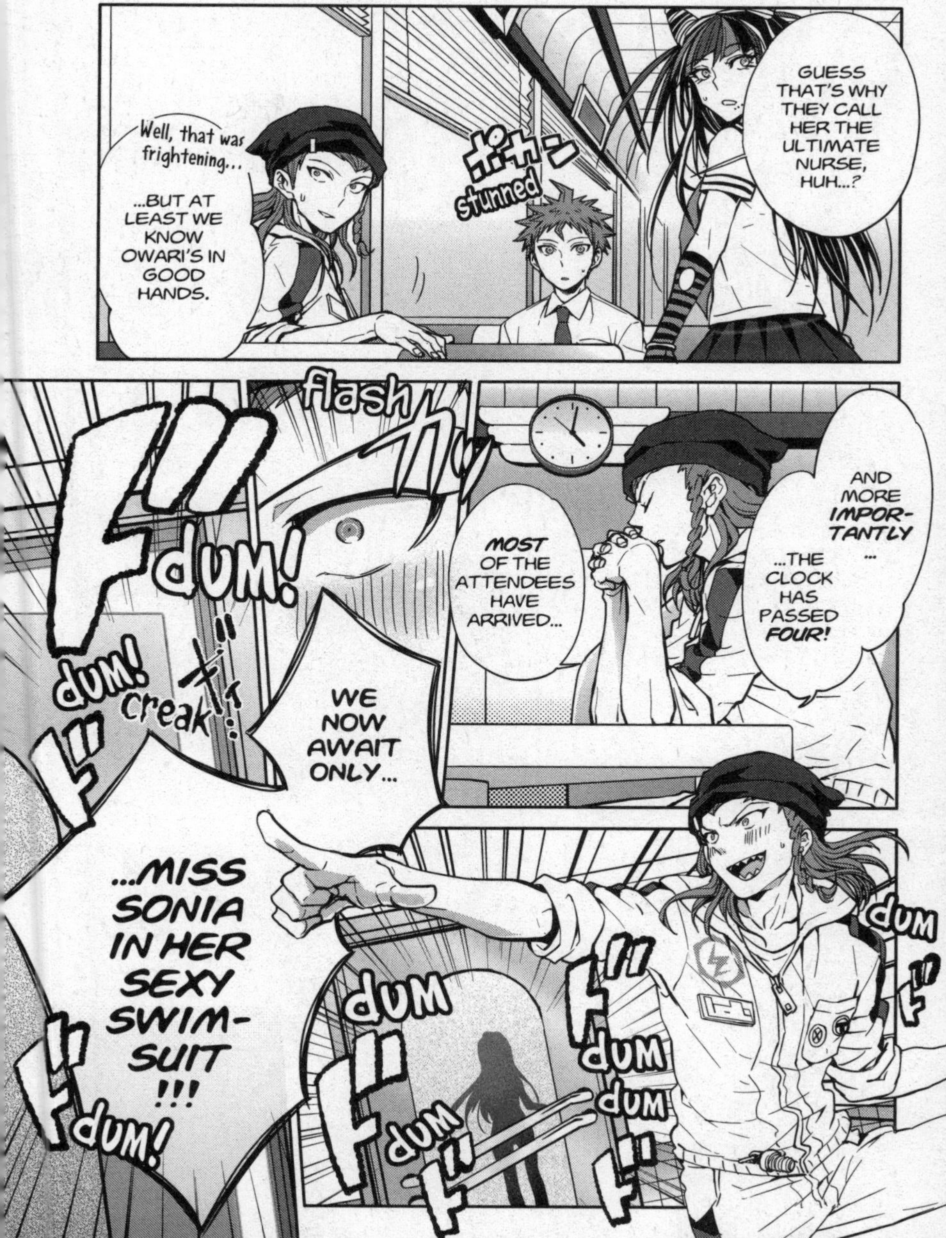
GUESS THAT'S WHY THEY CALL HER THE ULTIMATE NURSE, HUH...?
ポカン
stunned
Well, that was frightening...
...BUT AT LEAST WE KNOW OWARI'S IN GOOD HANDS.
AND MORE IMPORTANTLY ...
...THE CLOCK HAS PASSED FOUR!
MOST OF THE ATTENDEES HAVE ARRIVED...
flash
カッ
ド
dum!
dum!
creak
WE NOW AWAIT ONLY...
...MISS SONIA IN HER SEXY SWIM-SUIT !!!
dum
dum
dum
dum
dum
dum!

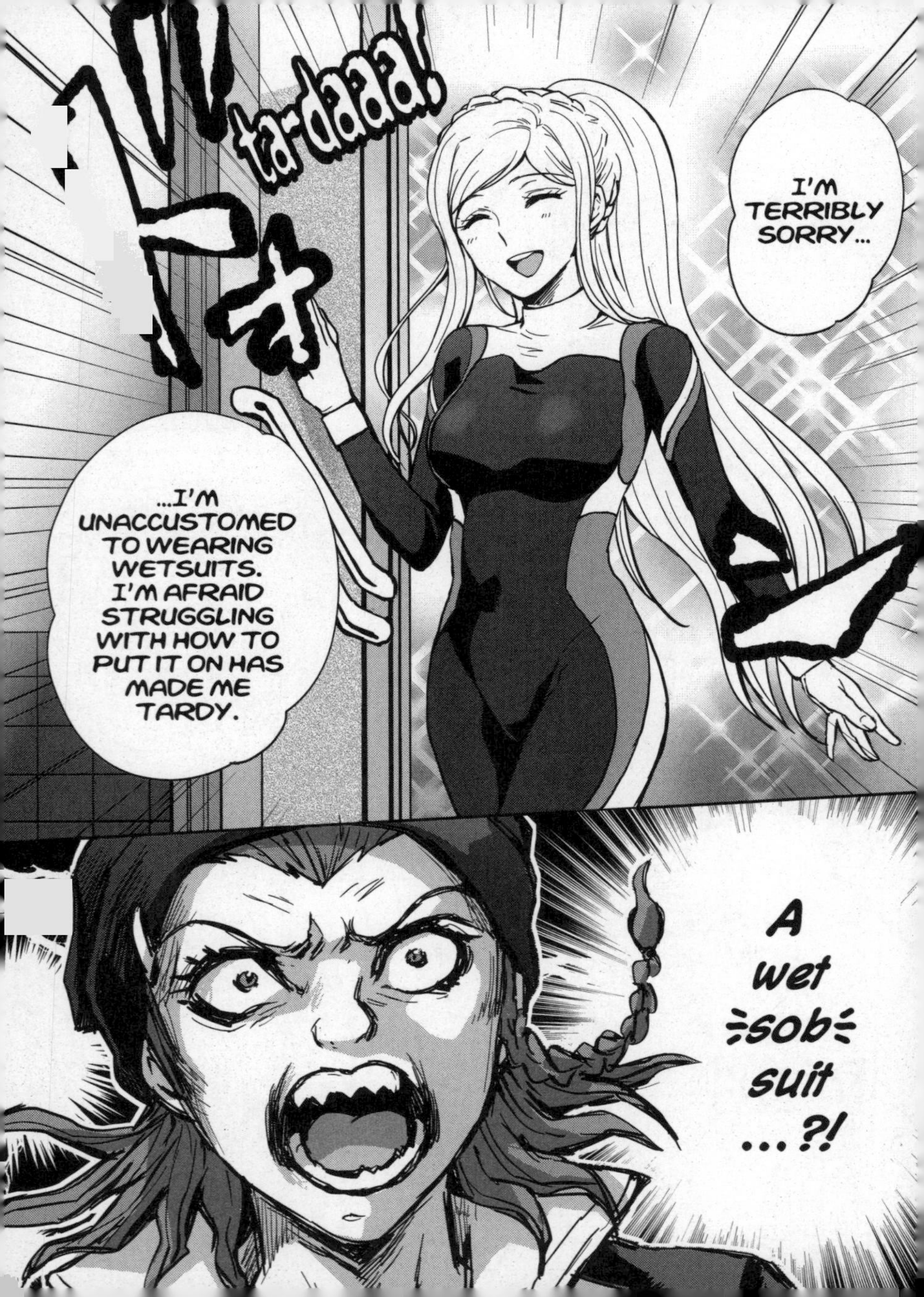
ta-daaa!
I'M TERRIBLY SORRY...
...I'M UNACCUSTOMED TO WEARING WETSUITS. I'M AFRAID STRUGGLING WITH HOW TO PUT IT ON HAS MADE ME TARDY.
A wet sob suit ...?!

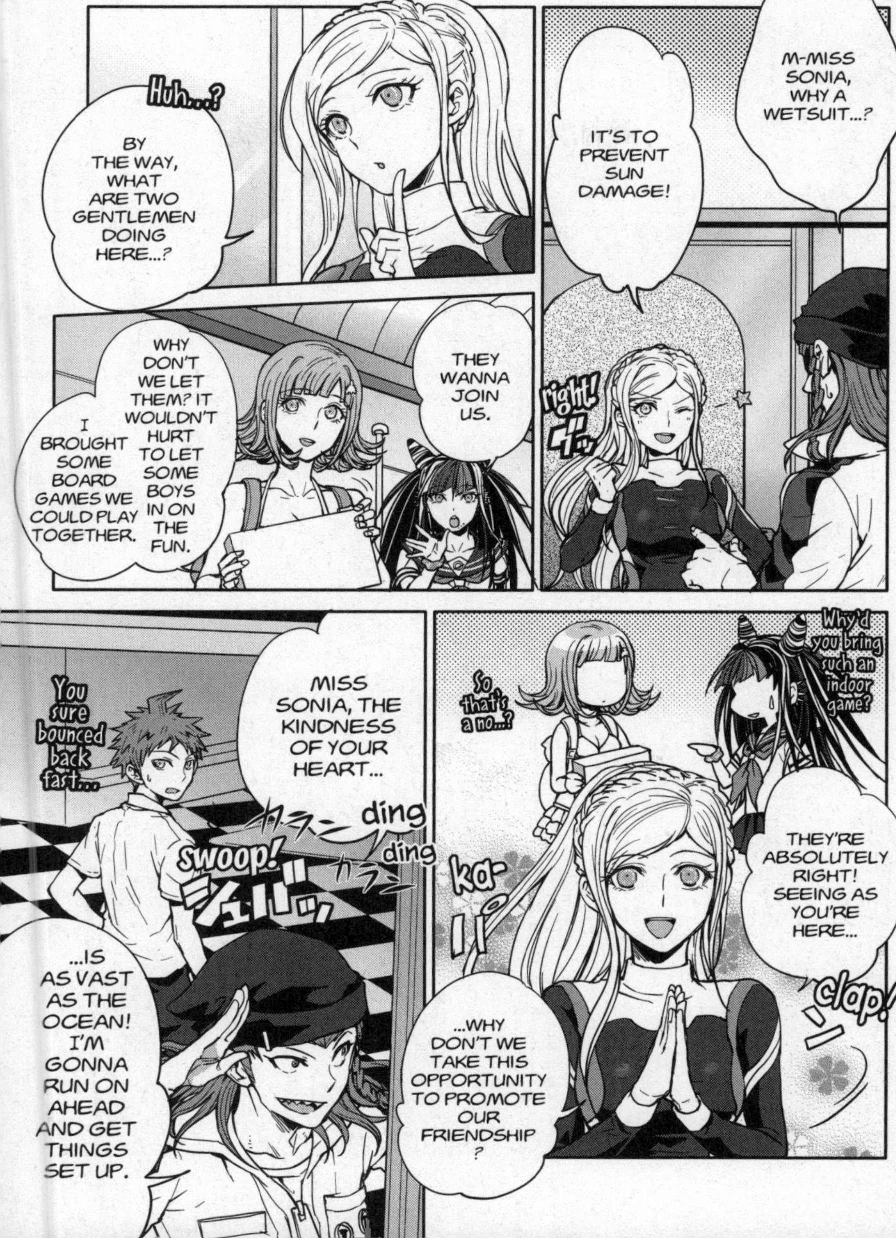
M-MISS SONIA, WHY A WETSUIT...?
IT'S TO PREVENT SUN DAMAGE!
right!
Huh...?
BY THE WAY, WHAT ARE TWO GENTLEMEN DOING HERE...?
THEY WANNA JOIN US.
WHY DON'T WE LET THEM? IT WOULDN'T HURT TO LET SOME BOYS IN ON THE FUN.
I BROUGHT SOME BOARD GAMES WE COULD PLAY TOGETHER.
Why'd you bring such an indoor game?
So that's a no...?
THEY'RE ABSOLUTELY RIGHT! SEEING AS YOU'RE HERE...
ka-
clap!
...WHY DON'T WE TAKE THIS OPPORTUNITY TO PROMOTE OUR FRIENDSHIP?
MISS SONIA, THE KINDNESS OF YOUR HEART...
You sure bounced back fast...
ding
ding
swoop!
...IS AS VAST AS THE OCEAN! I'M GONNA RUN ON AHEAD AND GET THINGS SET UP.

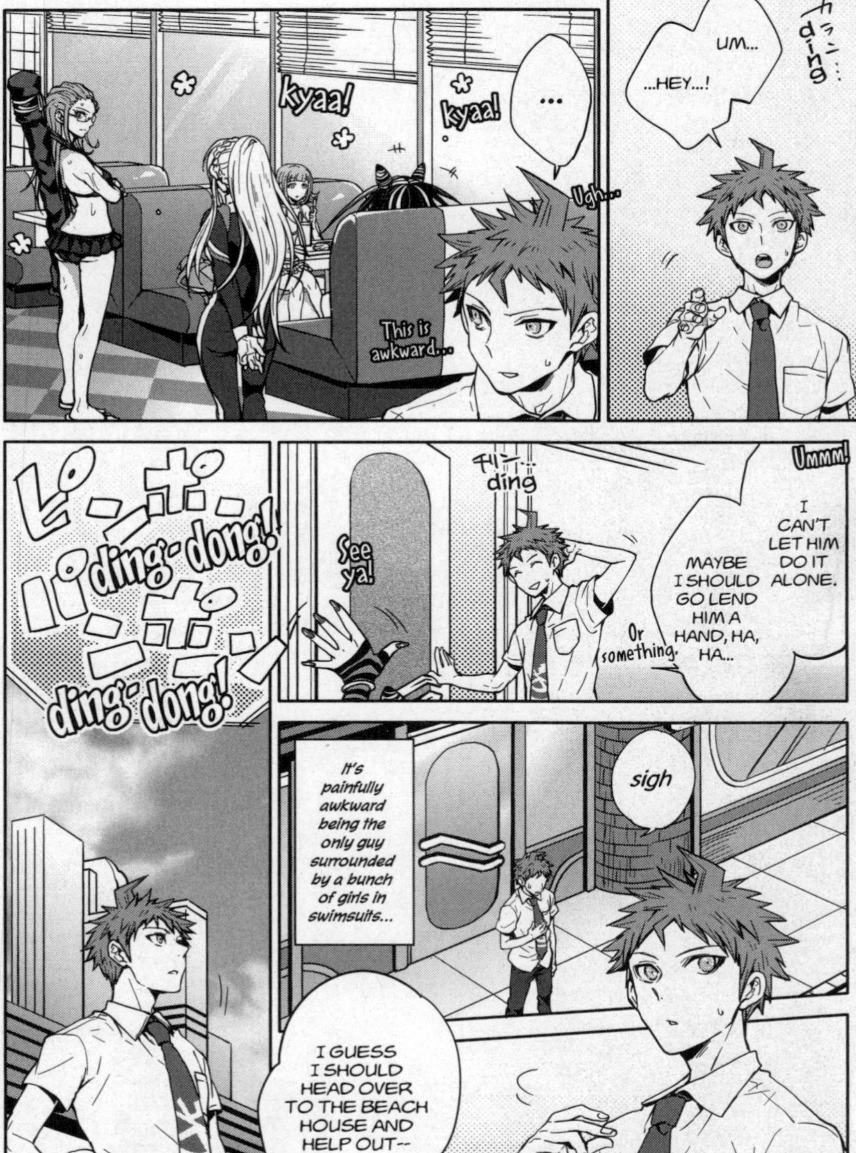

UM...
...HEY...!
ding
...
Ugh...
kyaa!
kyaa!
This is awkward...
Ummm!
I CAN'T LET HIM DO IT ALONE.
MAYBE I SHOULD GO LEND HIM A HAND, HA, HA...
Or something.
ding
See ya!
sigh
It's painfully awkward being the only guy surrounded by a bunch of girls in swimsuits...
I GUESS I SHOULD HEAD OVER TO THE BEACH HOUSE AND HELP OUT--
ding-dong!
ding-dong!

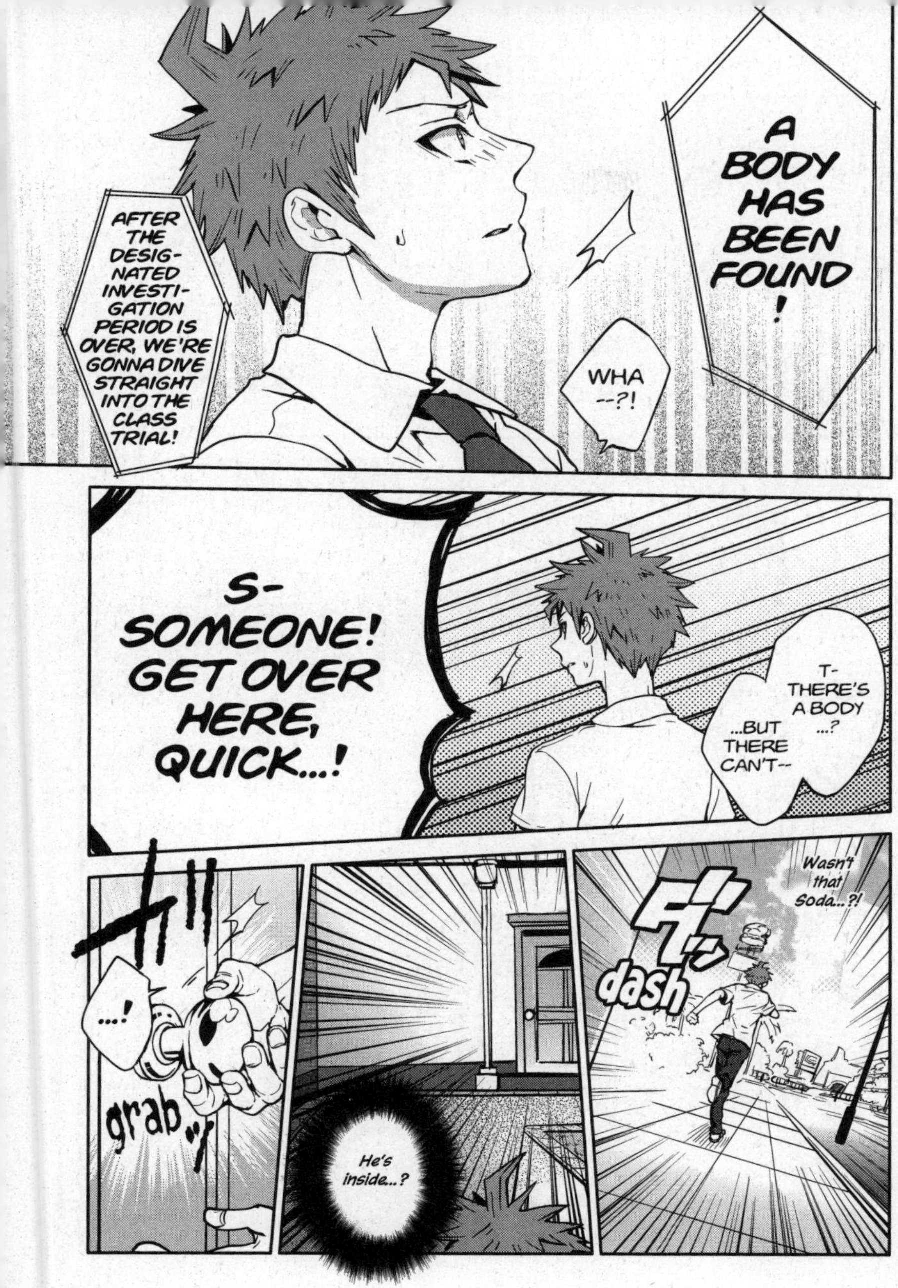
A BODY HAS BEEN FOUND!
WHA--?!
AFTER THE DESIGNATED INVESTIGATION PERIOD IS OVER, WE'RE GONNA DIVE STRAIGHT INTO THE CLASS TRIAL!
T-THERE'S A BODY...?
...BUT THERE CAN'T--
S-SOMEONE! GET OVER HERE, QUICK...!
Wasn't that Soda...?!
dash
He's inside...?
...!
grab

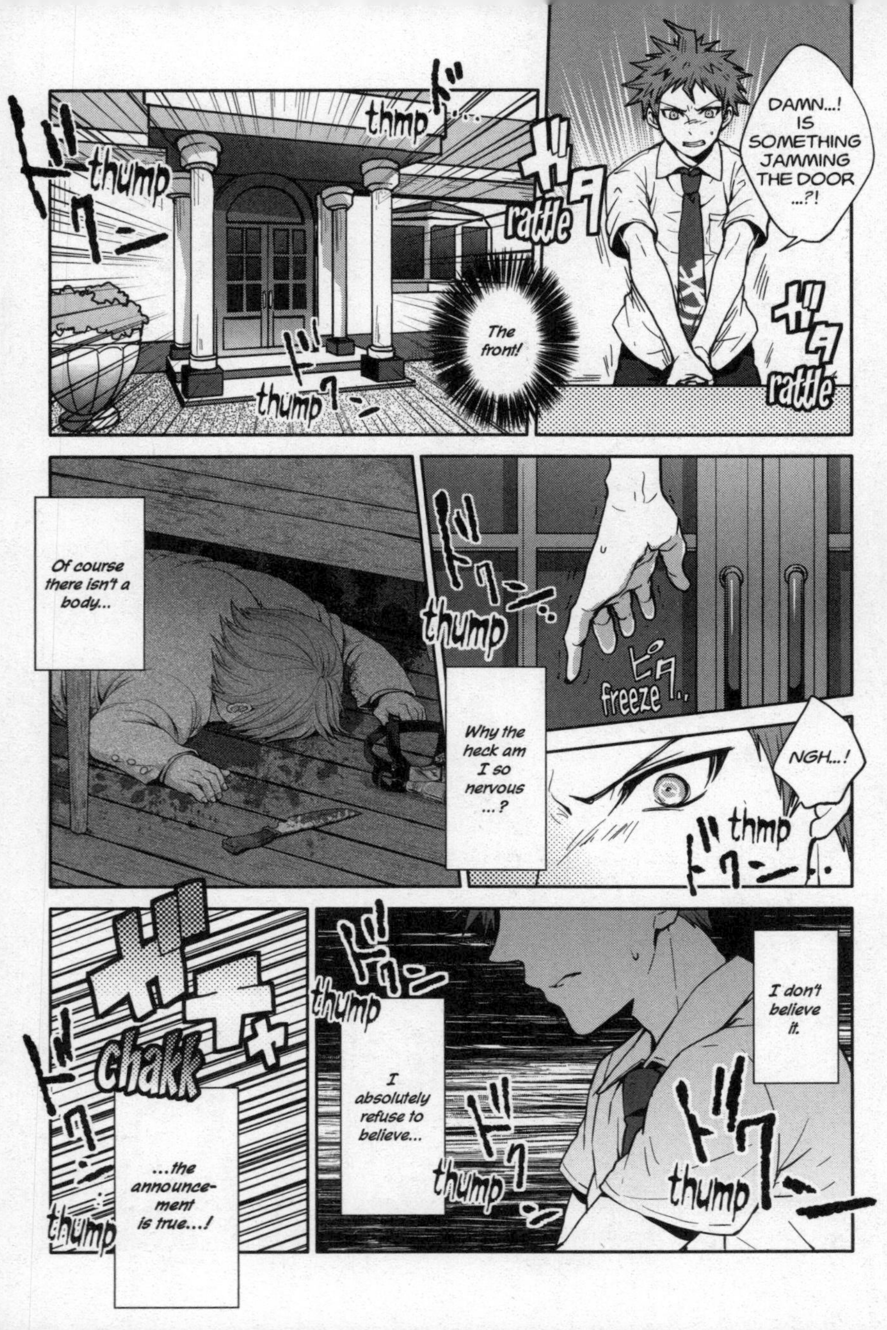
rattle
DAMN...! IS SOMETHING JAMMING THE DOOR ...?!
rattle
thmp
thump
The front!
thump
thump
freeze
Why the heck am I so nervous ...?
NGH...!
thmp
Of course there isn't a body...
I don't believe it.
thump
I absolutely refuse to believe...
thump
thump
chakk
...the announcement is true...!
thump

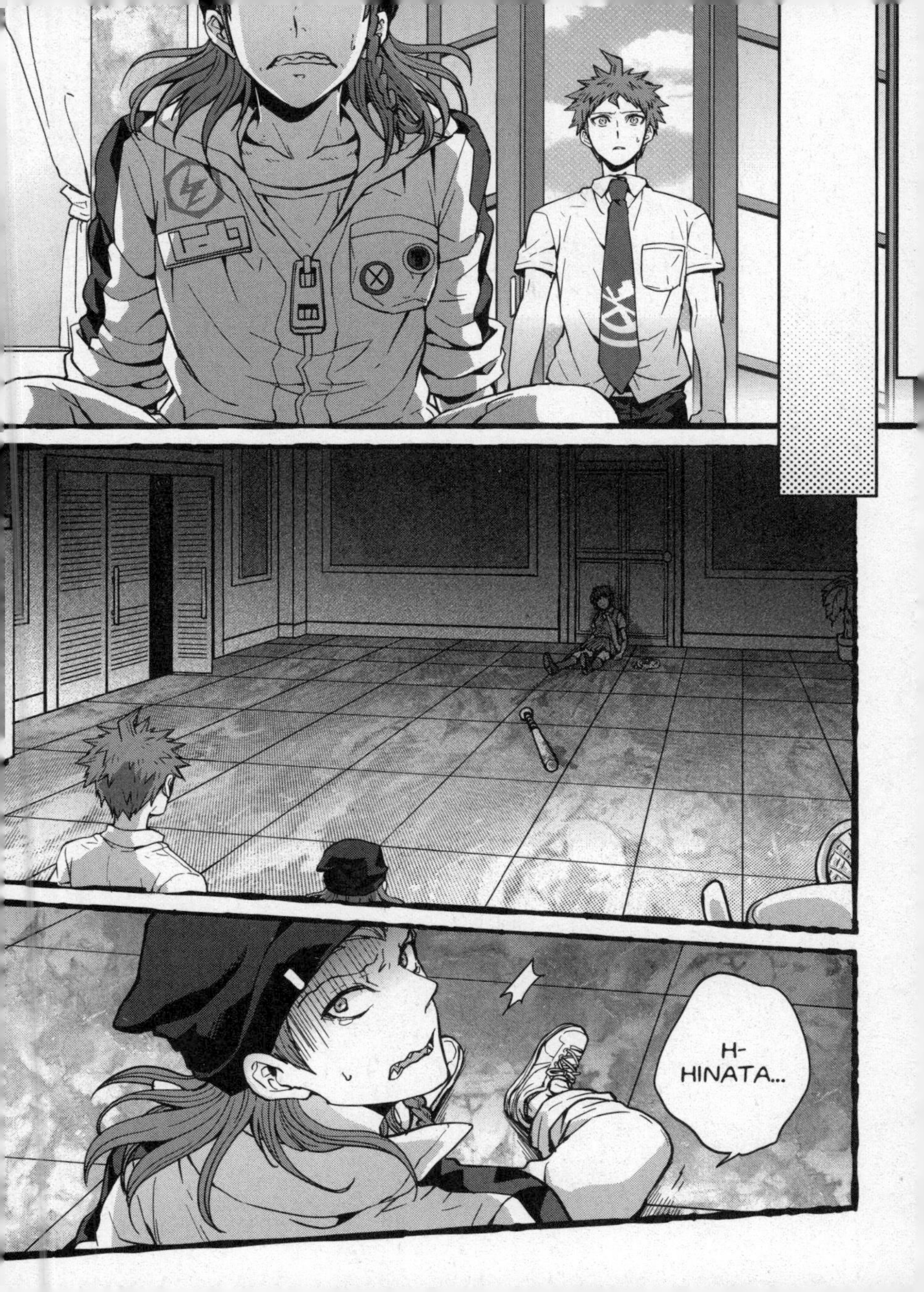
H-
HINATA...

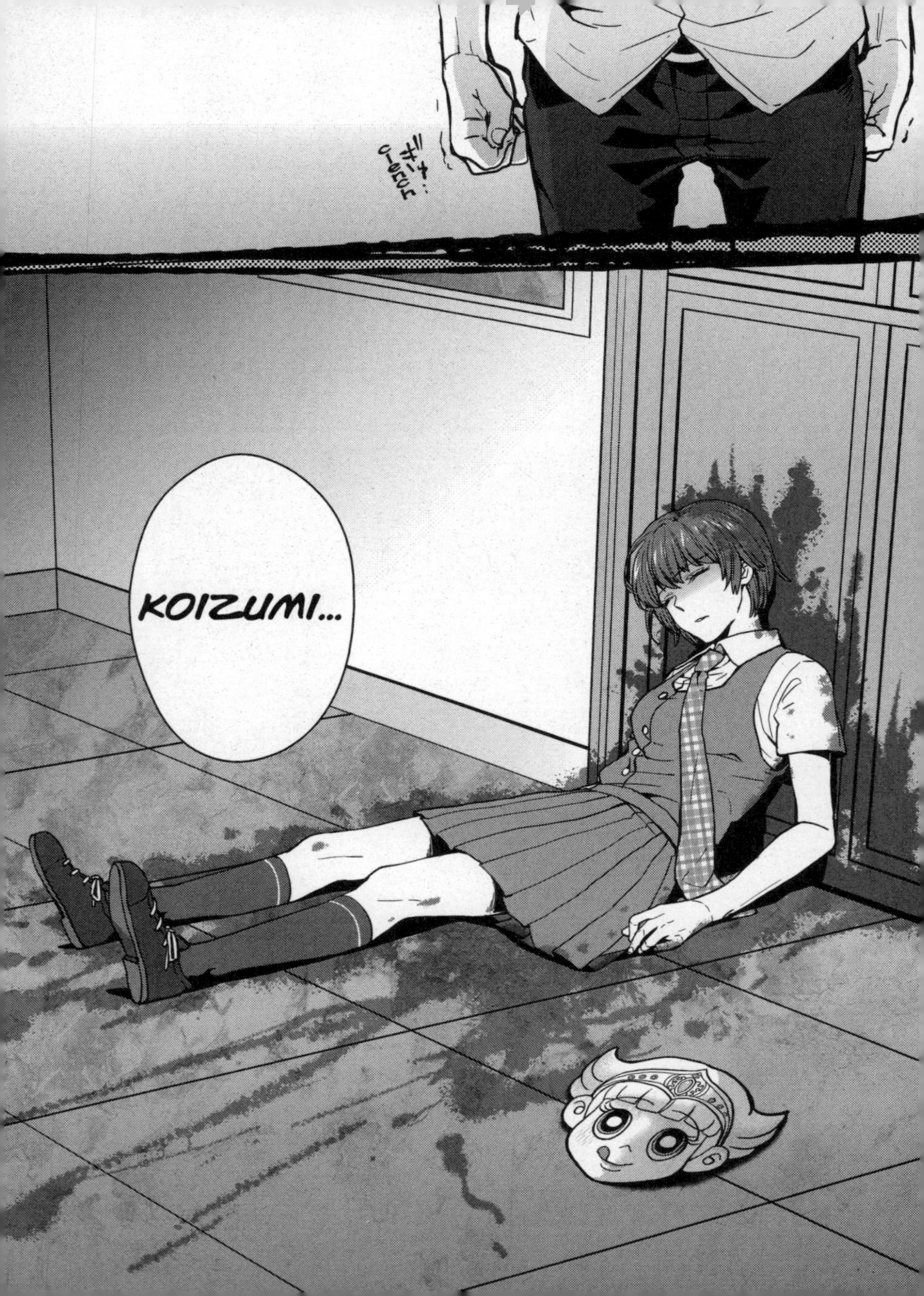
clench
KOIZUMI...

DANGAN
RONPA 2
GOODBYE
DESPAIR

DR2

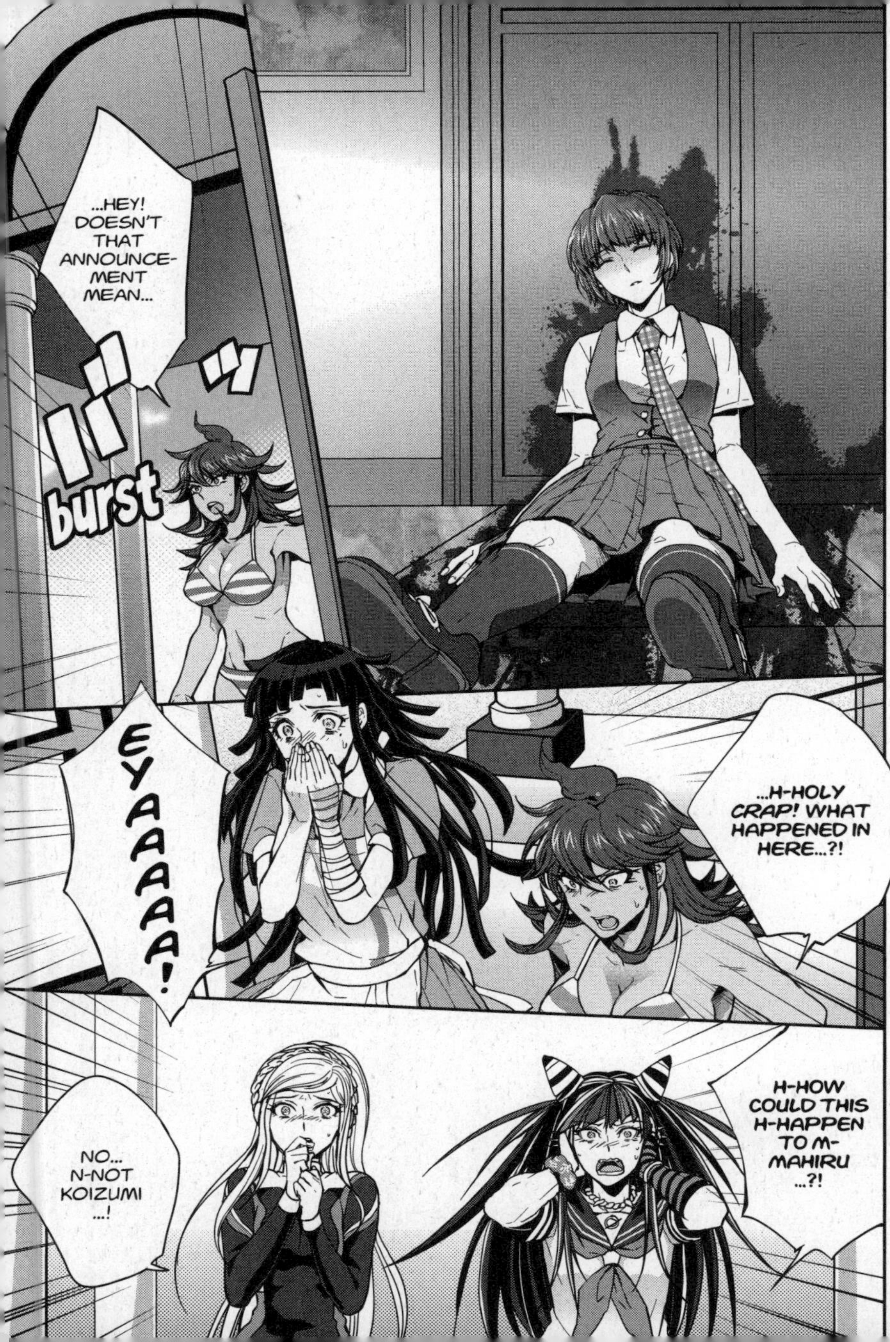
...HEY! DOESN'T THAT ANNOUNCEMENT MEAN...
burst
...H-HOLY CRAP! WHAT HAPPENED IN HERE...?!
EYAAAAAA!
H-HOW COULD THIS H-HAPPEN TO M-MAHIRU ...?!
NO... N-NOT KOIZUMI ...!

CHAPTER 10: THE SECOND MURDER

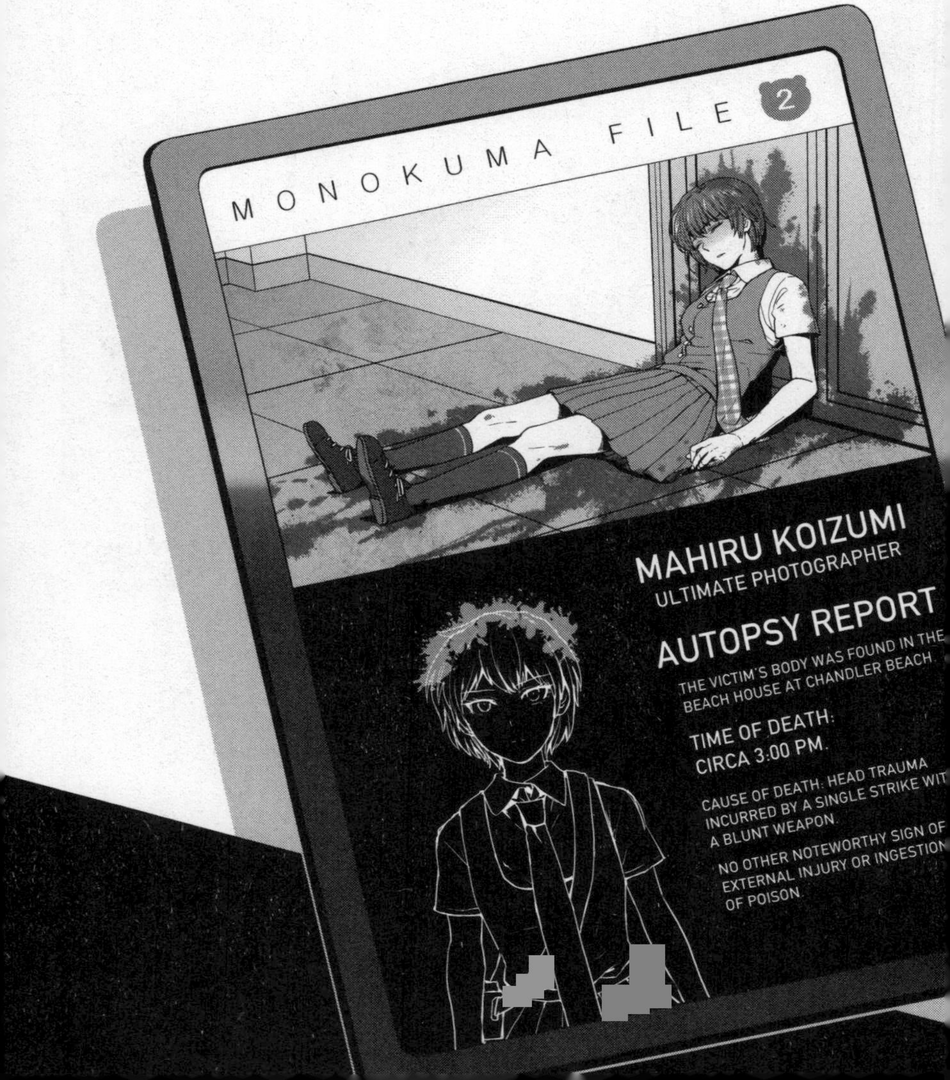
MONOKUMA FILE 2
MAHIRU KOIZUMI
ULTIMATE PHOTOGRAPHER
AUTOPSY REPORT
THE VICTIM'S BODY WAS FOUND IN THE BEACH HOUSE AT CHANDLER BEACH
TIME OF DEATH: CIRCA 3:00 PM.
CAUSE OF DEATH: HEAD TRAUMA INCURRED BY A SINGLE STRIKE WIT[H] A BLUNT WEAPON.
NO OTHER NOTEWORTHY SIGN OF EXTERNAL INJURY OR INGESTION OF POISON.

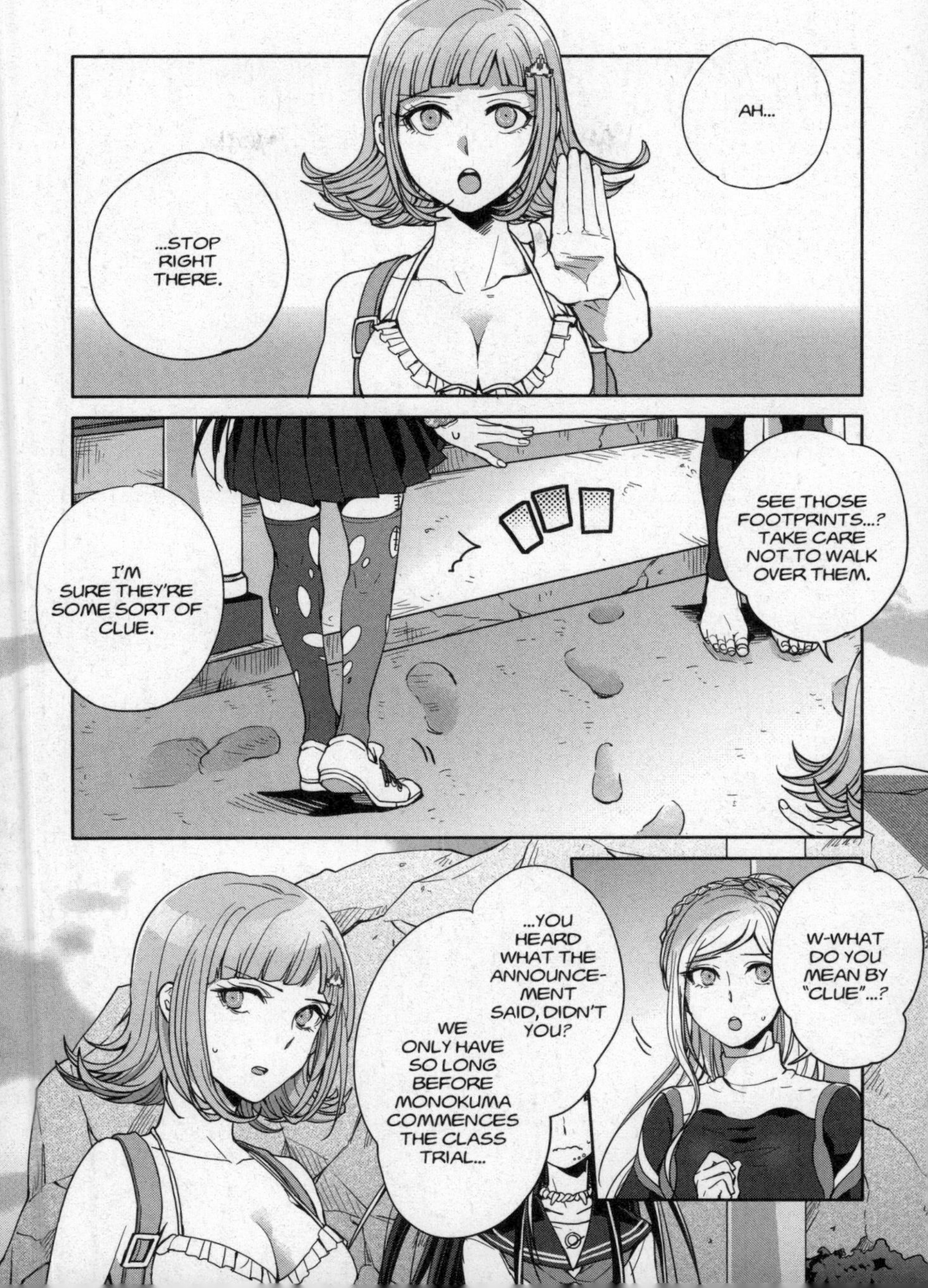
AH...
...STOP RIGHT THERE.
SEE THOSE FOOTPRINTS...? TAKE CARE NOT TO WALK OVER THEM.
I'M SURE THEY'RE SOME SORT OF CLUE.
W-WHAT DO YOU MEAN BY "CLUE"...?
...YOU HEARD WHAT THE ANNOUNCEMENT SAID, DIDN'T YOU?
WE ONLY HAVE SO LONG BEFORE MONOKUMA COMMENCES THE CLASS TRIAL...

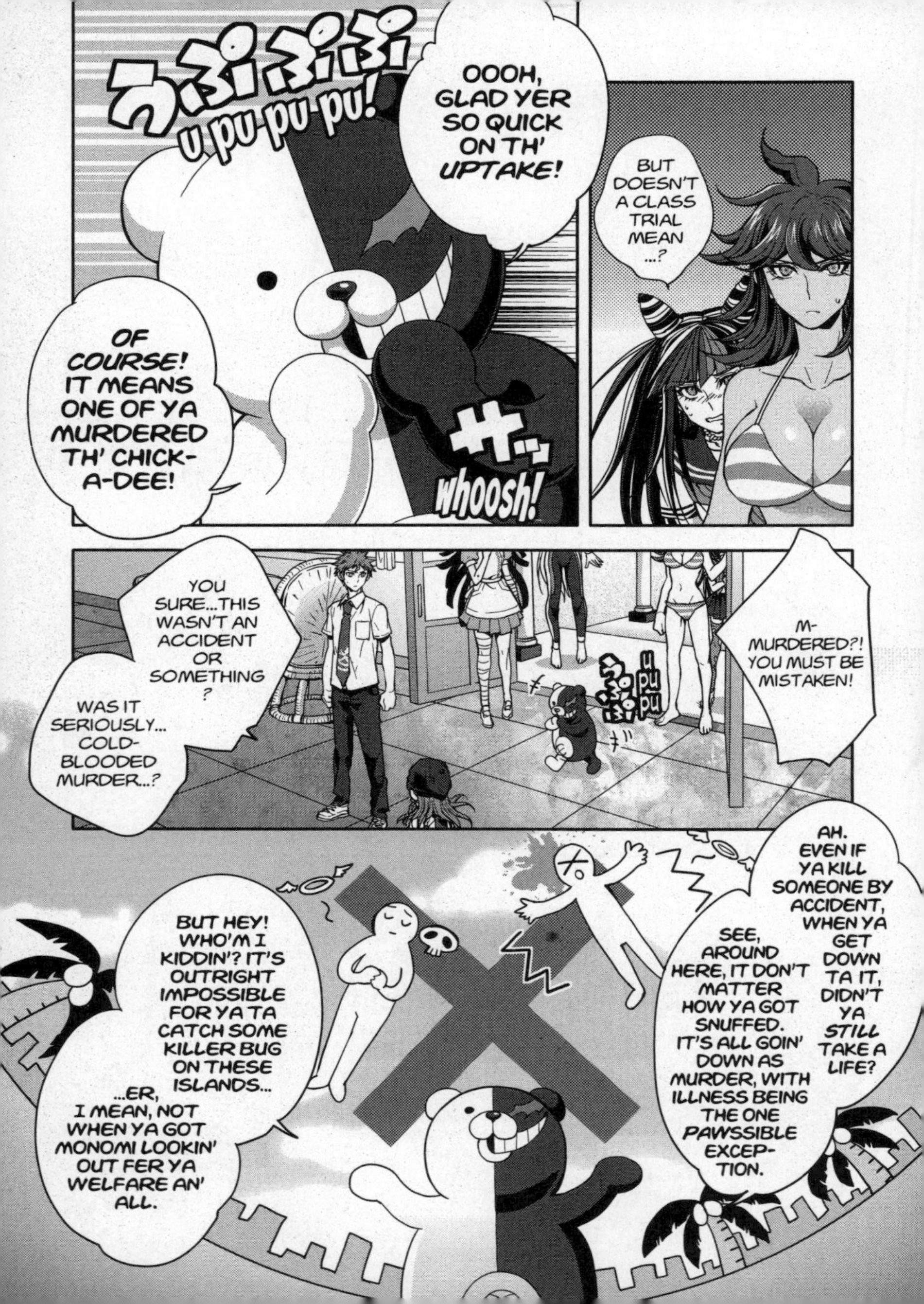
BUT DOESN'T A CLASS TRIAL MEAN ...?
うぷぷぷ
u pu pu pu!
OOOH, GLAD YER SO QUICK ON TH' UPTAKE!
OF COURSE! IT MEANS ONE OF YA MURDERED TH' CHICK-A-DEE!
サッ
whoosh!
M-MURDERED?! YOU MUST BE MISTAKEN!
うぷぷ
u pu pu
YOU SURE...THIS WASN'T AN ACCIDENT OR SOMETHING ?
WAS IT SERIOUSLY... COLD-BLOODED MURDER...?
AH. EVEN IF YA KILL SOMEONE BY ACCIDENT, WHEN YA GET DOWN TA IT, DIDN'T YA STILL TAKE A LIFE?
SEE, AROUND HERE, IT DON'T MATTER HOW YA GOT SNUFFED. IT'S ALL GOIN' DOWN AS MURDER, WITH ILLNESS BEING THE ONE PAWSSIBLE EXCEP-TION.
BUT HEY! WHO'M I KIDDIN'? IT'S OUTRIGHT IMPOSSIBLE FOR YA TA CATCH SOME KILLER BUG ON THESE ISLANDS...
...ER, I MEAN, NOT WHEN YA GOT MONOMI LOOKIN' OUT FER YA WELFARE AN' ALL.

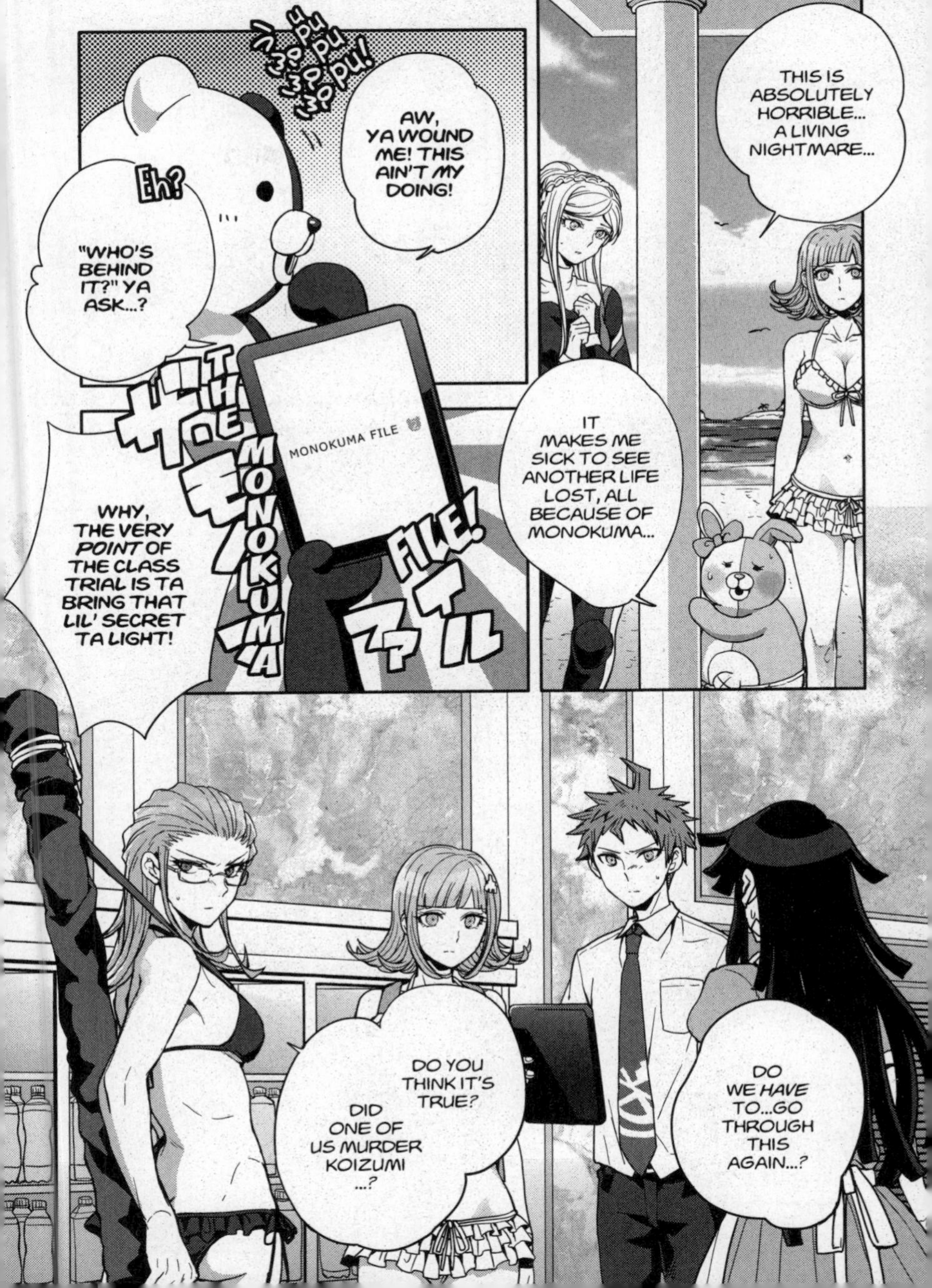
THIS IS ABSOLUTELY HORRIBLE... A LIVING NIGHTMARE...
IT MAKES ME SICK TO SEE ANOTHER LIFE LOST, ALL BECAUSE OF MONOKUMA...
u pu pu pu!
AW, YA WOUND ME! THIS AIN'T MY DOING!
Eh?
"WHO'S BEHIND IT?" YA ASK...?
THE MONOKUMA FILE!
MONOKUMA FILE
WHY, THE VERY *POINT* OF THE CLASS TRIAL IS TA BRING THAT LIL' SECRET TA LIGHT!
DO WE *HAVE* TO...GO THROUGH THIS AGAIN...?
DO YOU THINK IT'S TRUE?
DID ONE OF US MURDER KOIZUMI ...?

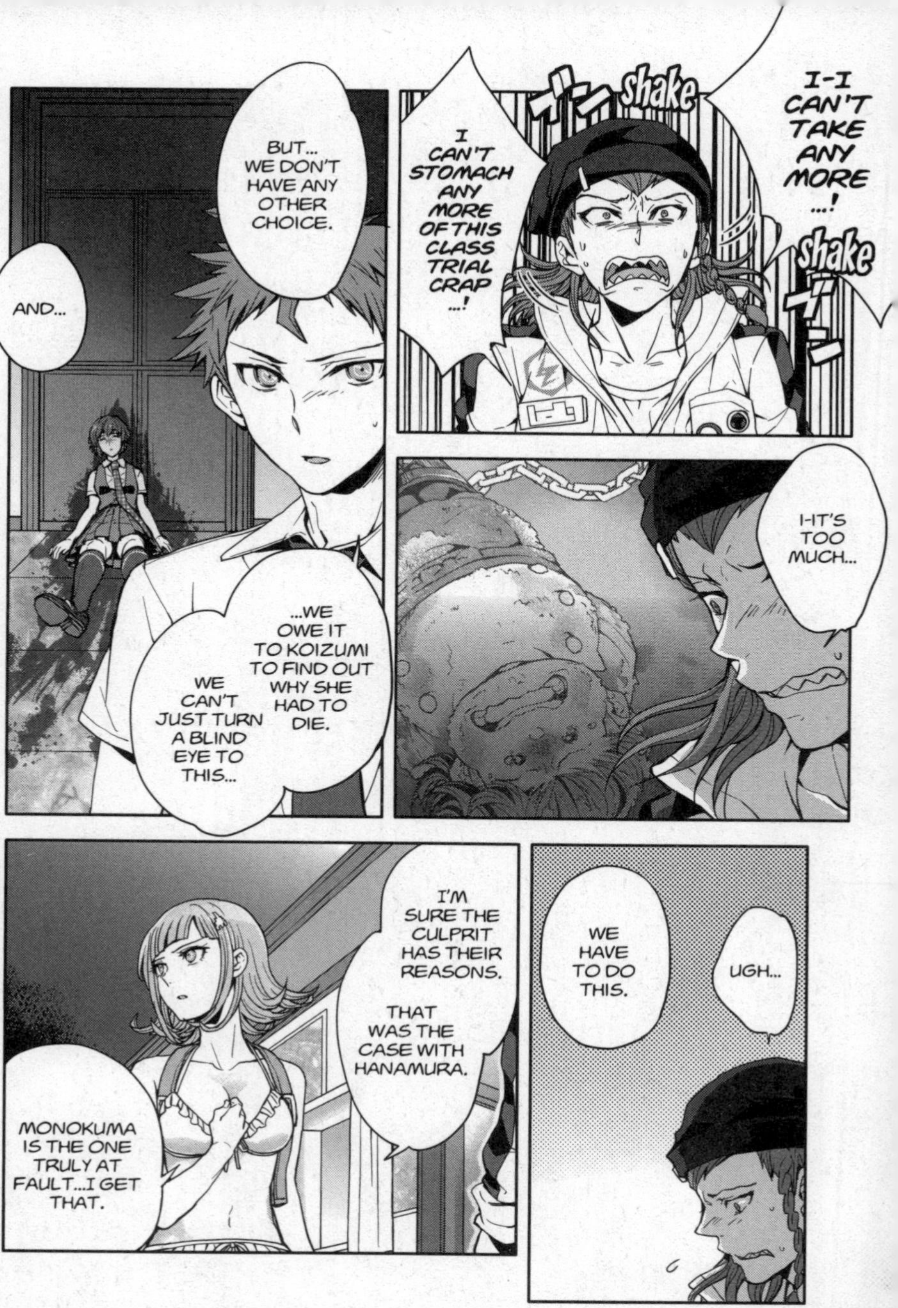
shake
I CAN'T STOMACH ANY MORE OF THIS CLASS TRIAL CRAP ...!
I-I CAN'T TAKE ANY MORE ...!
shake
I-IT'S TOO MUCH...
BUT... WE DON'T HAVE ANY OTHER CHOICE.
AND...
...WE OWE IT TO KOIZUMI TO FIND OUT WHY SHE HAD TO DIE.
WE CAN'T JUST TURN A BLIND EYE TO THIS...
UGH...
WE HAVE TO DO THIS.
I'M SURE THE CULPRIT HAS THEIR REASONS.
THAT WAS THE CASE WITH HANAMURA.
MONOKUMA IS THE ONE TRULY AT FAULT...I GET THAT.

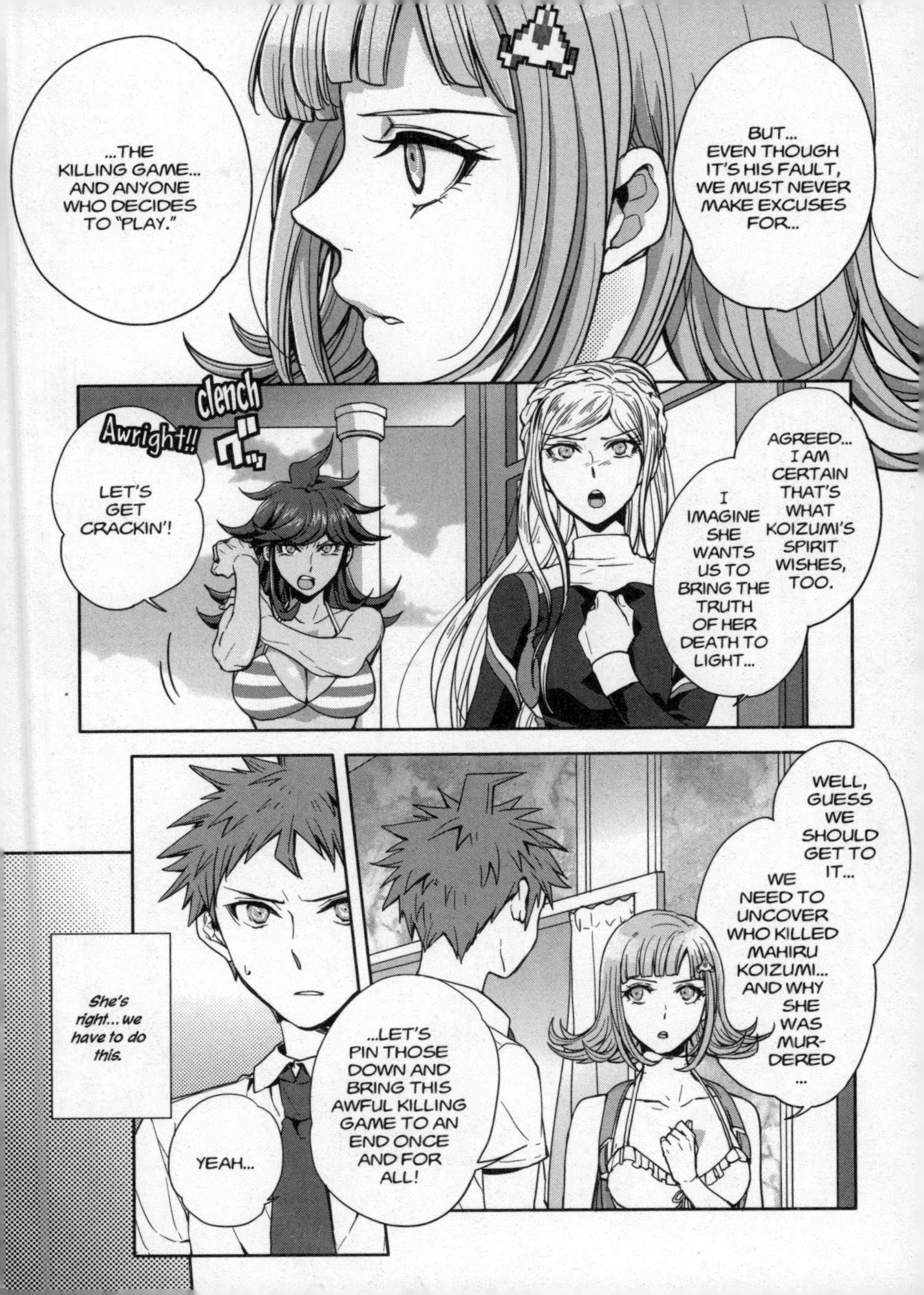
BUT... EVEN THOUGH IT'S HIS FAULT, WE MUST NEVER MAKE EXCUSES FOR...
...THE KILLING GAME... AND ANYONE WHO DECIDES TO "PLAY."
AGREED... I AM CERTAIN THAT'S WHAT KOIZUMI'S SPIRIT WISHES, TOO.
I IMAGINE SHE WANTS US TO BRING THE TRUTH OF HER DEATH TO LIGHT...
clench
Awright!!
LET'S GET CRACKIN'!
WELL, GUESS WE SHOULD GET TO IT...
WE NEED TO UNCOVER WHO KILLED MAHIRU KOIZUMI... AND WHY SHE WAS MUR-DERED ...
...LET'S PIN THOSE DOWN AND BRING THIS AWFUL KILLING GAME TO AN END ONCE AND FOR ALL!
She's right... we have to do this.
YEAH...

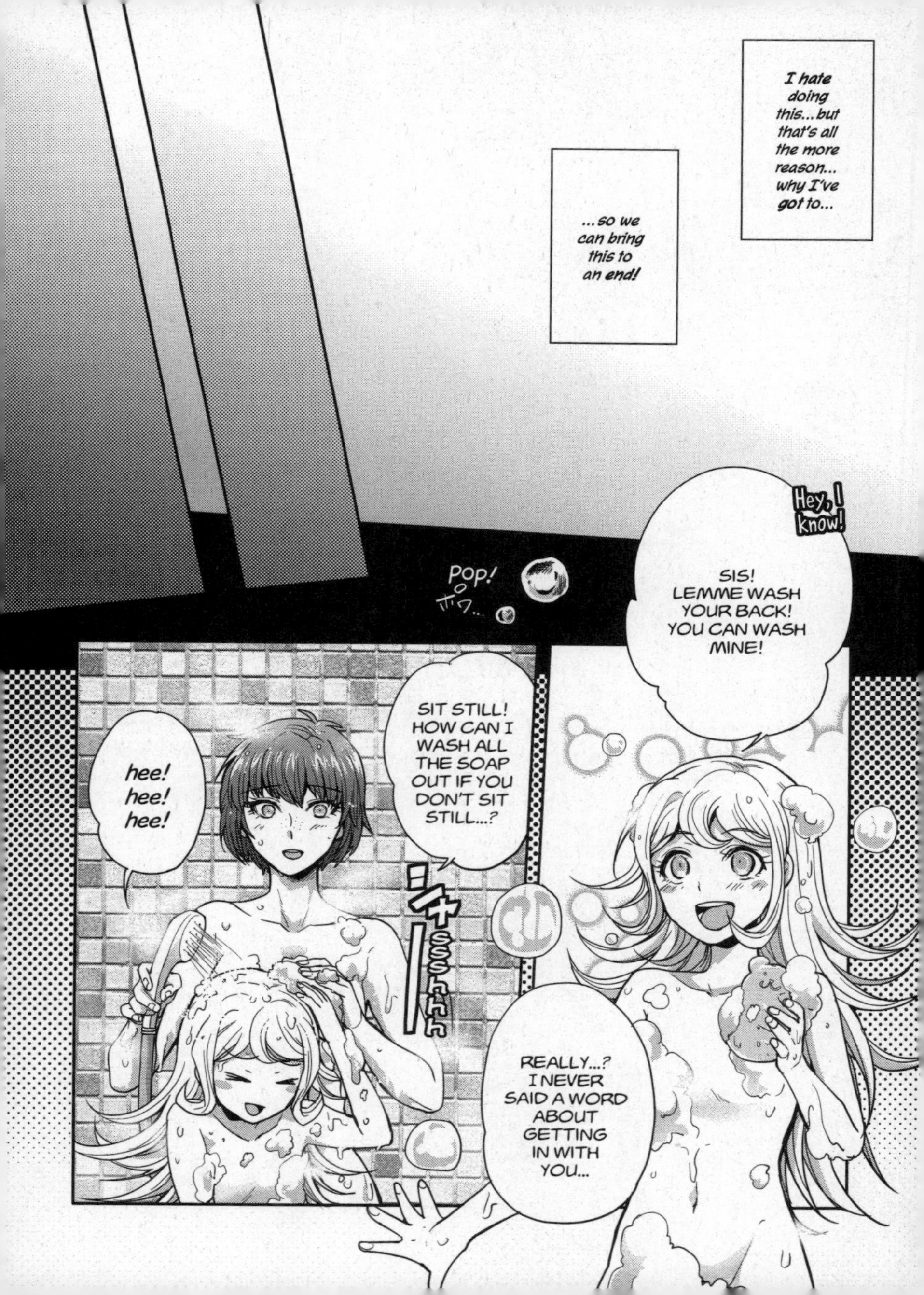
I hate doing this... but that's all the more reason... why I've got to...
...so we can bring this to an end!
POP!
Hey, I know!
SIS! LEMME WASH YOUR BACK! YOU CAN WASH MINE!
REALLY...? I NEVER SAID A WORD ABOUT GETTING IN WITH YOU...
SIT STILL! HOW CAN I WASH ALL THE SOAP OUT IF YOU DON'T SIT STILL...?
hee! hee! hee!
シャSSShhhh

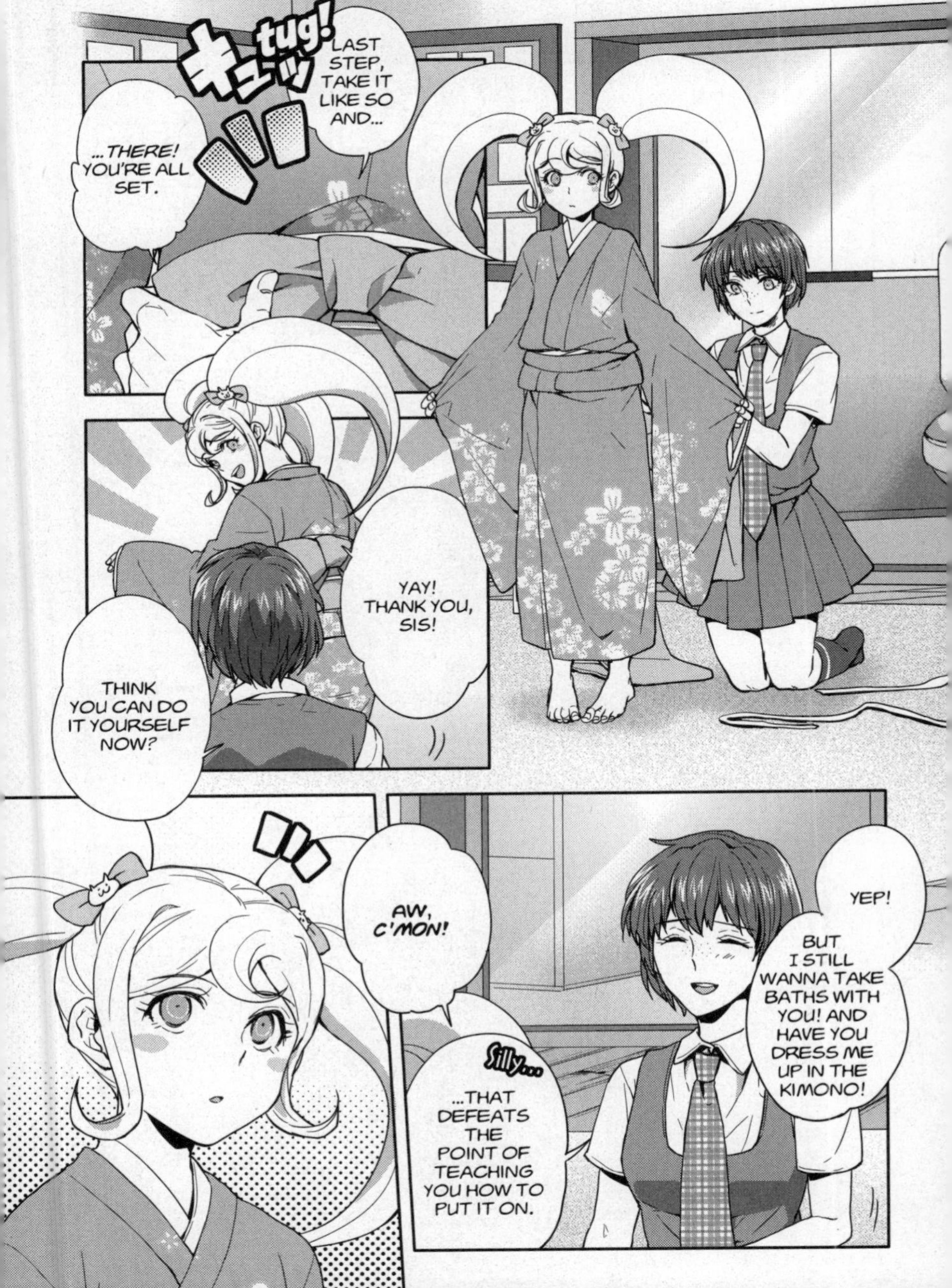

LAST STEP, TAKE IT LIKE SO AND...
キュッ tug!
...THERE! YOU'RE ALL SET.
YAY! THANK YOU, SIS!
THINK YOU CAN DO IT YOURSELF NOW?
YEP!
BUT I STILL WANNA TAKE BATHS WITH YOU! AND HAVE YOU DRESS ME UP IN THE KIMONO!
Silly...
...THAT DEFEATS THE POINT OF TEACHING YOU HOW TO PUT IT ON.
AW, C'MON!

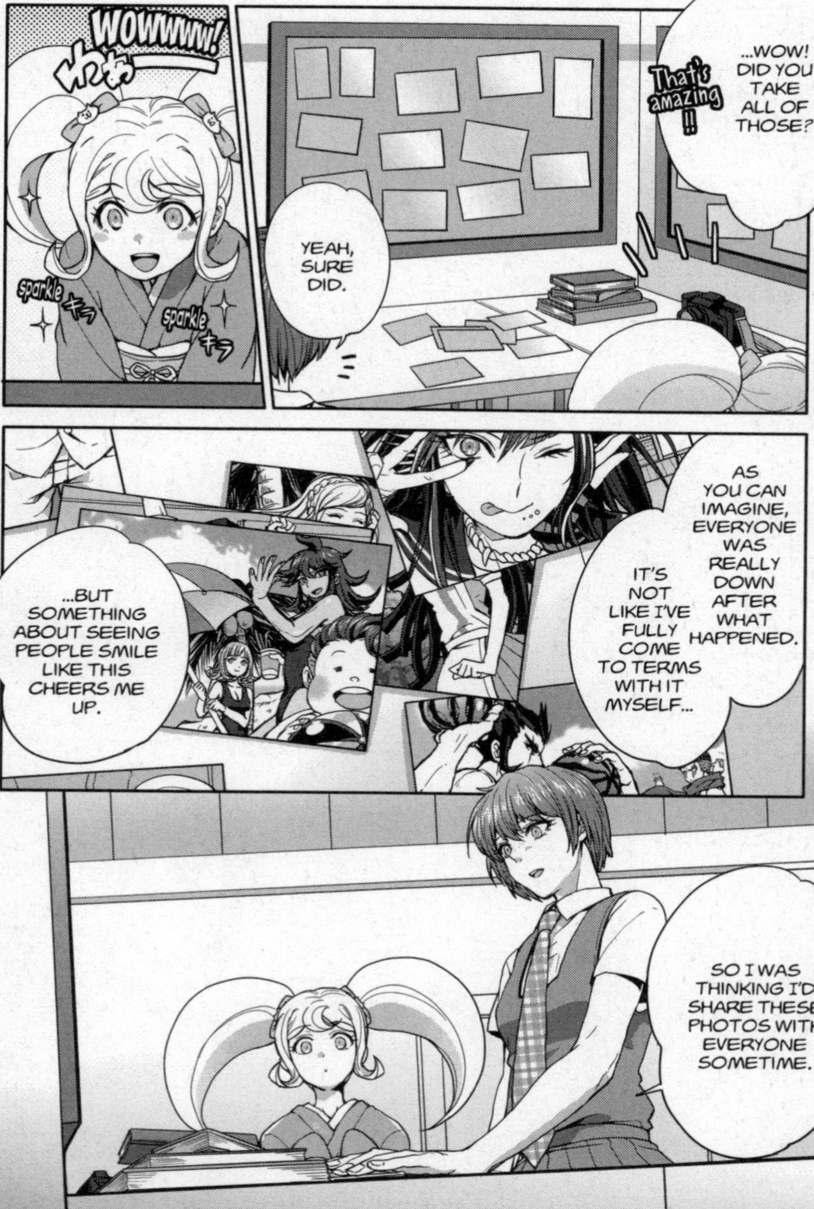
...WOW! DID YOU TAKE ALL OF THOSE?
That's amazing!!
YEAH, SURE DID.
WOWWWW!
わぁ——
sparkle キラ
sparkle キラ
AS YOU CAN IMAGINE, EVERYONE WAS REALLY DOWN AFTER WHAT HAPPENED.
IT'S NOT LIKE I'VE FULLY COME TO TERMS WITH IT MYSELF...
...BUT SOMETHING ABOUT SEEING PEOPLE SMILE LIKE THIS CHEERS ME UP.
SO I WAS THINKING I'D SHARE THESE PHOTOS WITH EVERYONE SOMETIME.

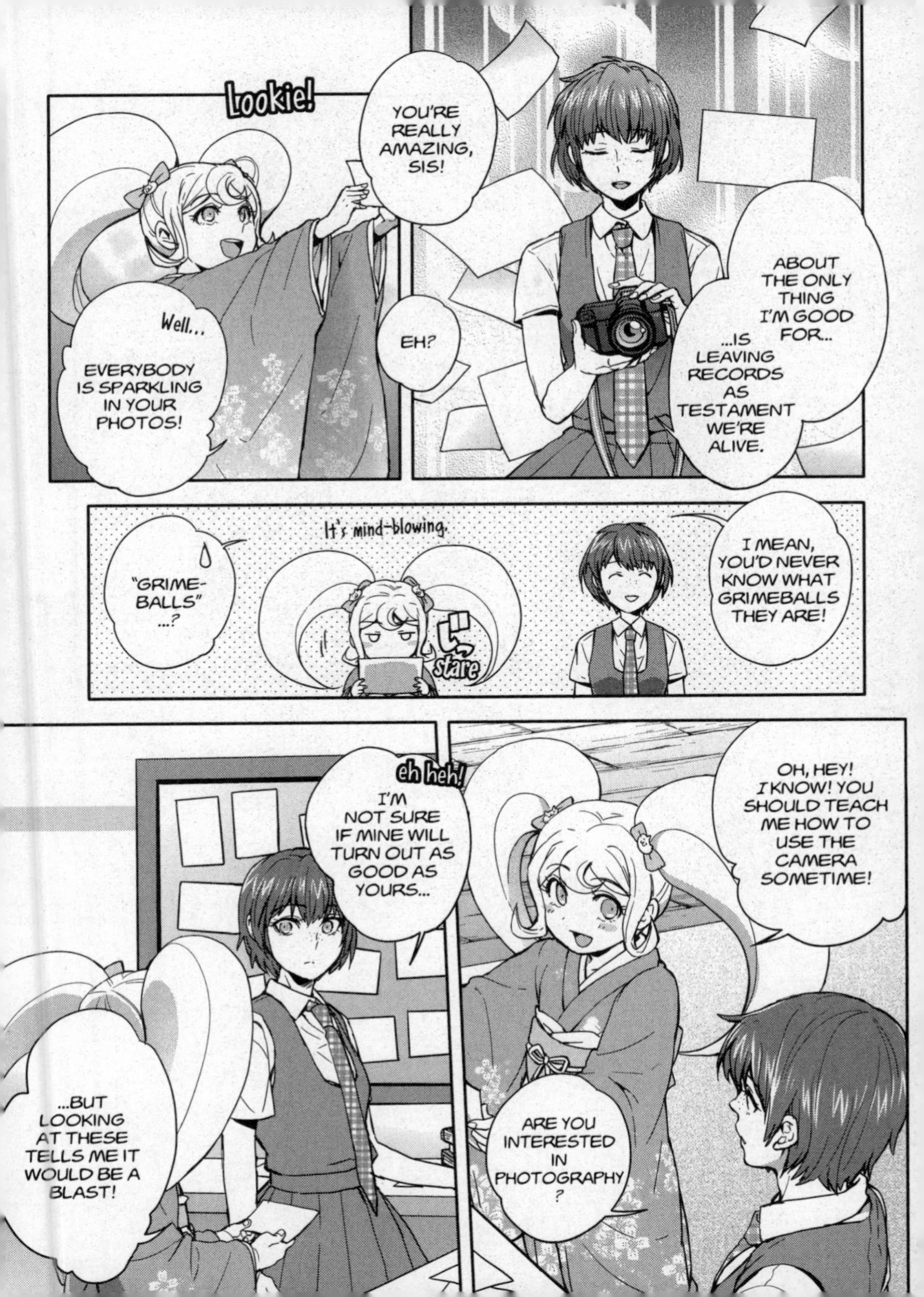
YOU'RE REALLY AMAZING, SIS!
EH?
ABOUT THE ONLY THING I'M GOOD FOR..
...IS LEAVING RECORDS AS TESTAMENT WE'RE ALIVE.
Lookie!
Well...
EVERYBODY IS SPARKLING IN YOUR PHOTOS!
I MEAN, YOU'D NEVER KNOW WHAT GRIMEBALLS THEY ARE!
It's mind-blowing.
"GRIME-BALLS" ...?
stare
OH, HEY! I KNOW! YOU SHOULD TEACH ME HOW TO USE THE CAMERA SOMETIME!
ARE YOU INTERESTED IN PHOTOGRAPHY?
eh heh!
I'M NOT SURE IF MINE WILL TURN OUT AS GOOD AS YOURS...
...BUT LOOKING AT THESE TELLS ME IT WOULD BE A BLAST!

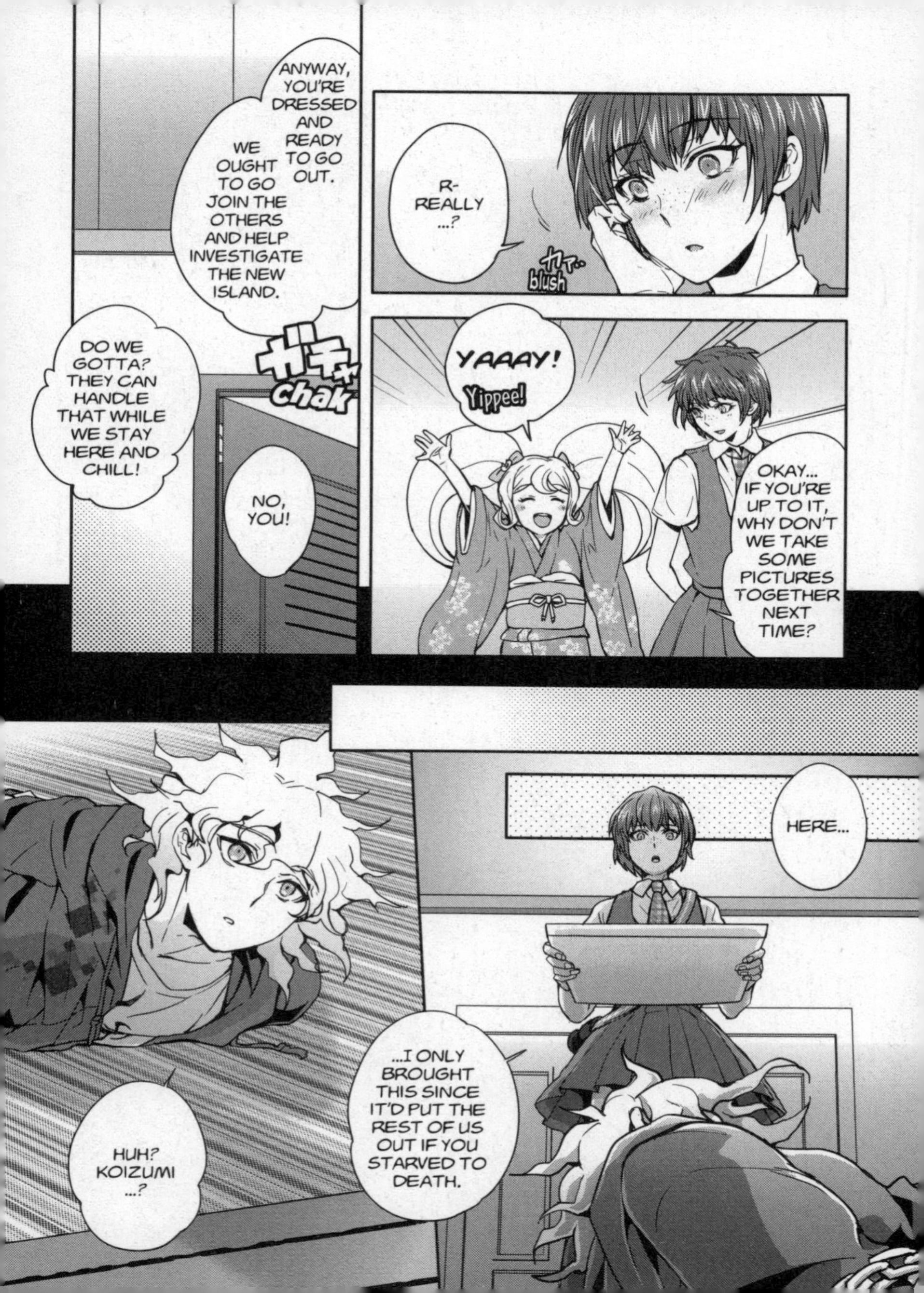

R-REALLY ...?
blush
YAAAY!
Yippee!
OKAY... IF YOU'RE UP TO IT, WHY DON'T WE TAKE SOME PICTURES TOGETHER NEXT TIME?
ANYWAY, YOU'RE DRESSED AND READY TO GO OUT.
WE OUGHT TO GO JOIN THE OTHERS AND HELP INVESTIGATE THE NEW ISLAND.
Chak
DO WE GOTTA? THEY CAN HANDLE THAT WHILE WE STAY HERE AND CHILL!
NO, YOU!
HERE...
...I ONLY BROUGHT THIS SINCE IT'D PUT THE REST OF US OUT IF YOU STARVED TO DEATH.
HUH? KOIZUMI ...?

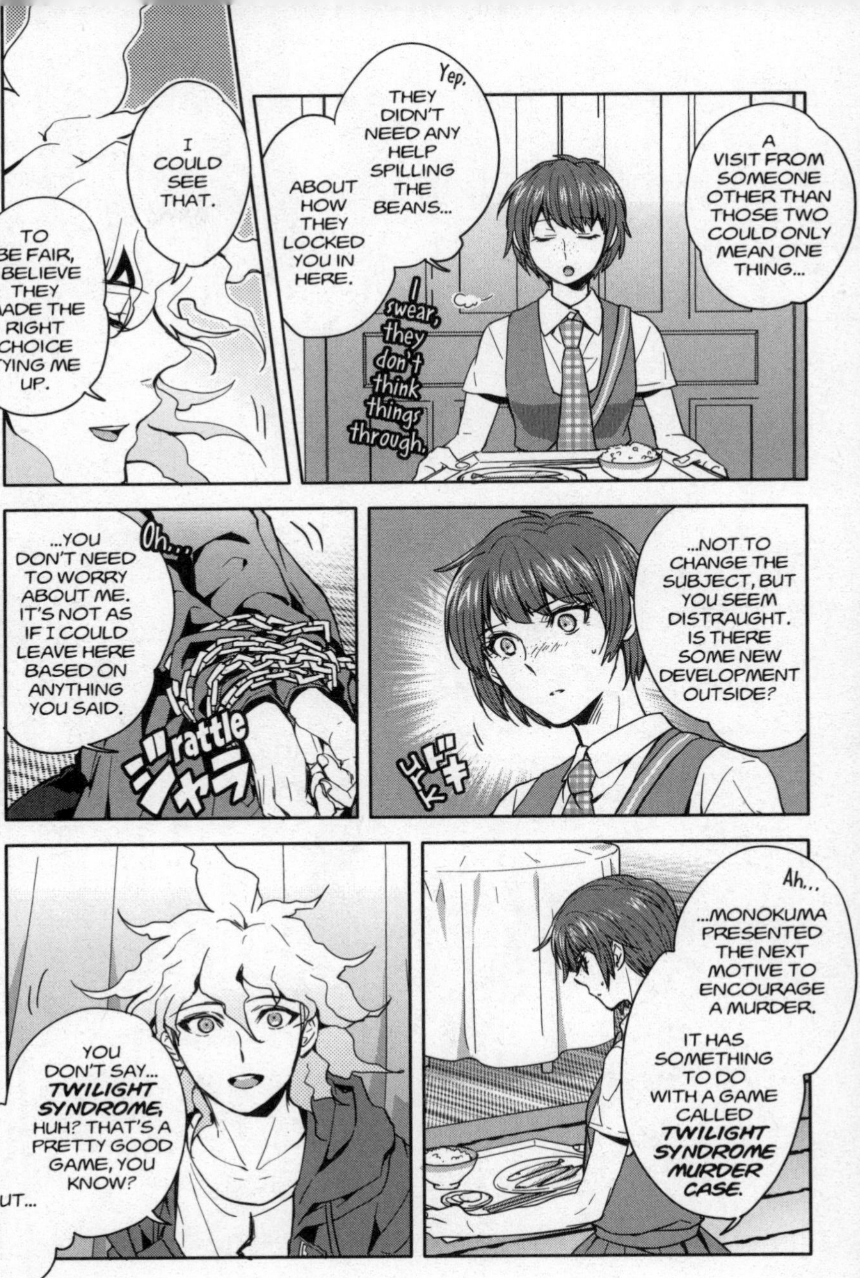
A VISIT FROM SOMEONE OTHER THAN THOSE TWO COULD ONLY MEAN ONE THING...
Yep.
THEY DIDN'T NEED ANY HELP SPILLING THE BEANS... ABOUT HOW THEY LOCKED YOU IN HERE.
I swear, they don't think things through.
I COULD SEE THAT.
TO BE FAIR, I BELIEVE THEY MADE THE RIGHT CHOICE TYING ME UP.
...NOT TO CHANGE THE SUBJECT, BUT YOU SEEM DISTRAUGHT. IS THERE SOME NEW DEVELOPMENT OUTSIDE?
ドキ
Oh...
...YOU DON'T NEED TO WORRY ABOUT ME. IT'S NOT AS IF I COULD LEAVE HERE BASED ON ANYTHING YOU SAID.
rattle
ジャラ
Ah...
...MONOKUMA PRESENTED THE NEXT MOTIVE TO ENCOURAGE A MURDER.
IT HAS SOMETHING TO DO WITH A GAME CALLED ***TWILIGHT SYNDROME MURDER CASE.***
YOU DON'T SAY... ***TWILIGHT SYNDROME,*** HUH? THAT'S A PRETTY GOOD GAME, YOU KNOW?
BUT...

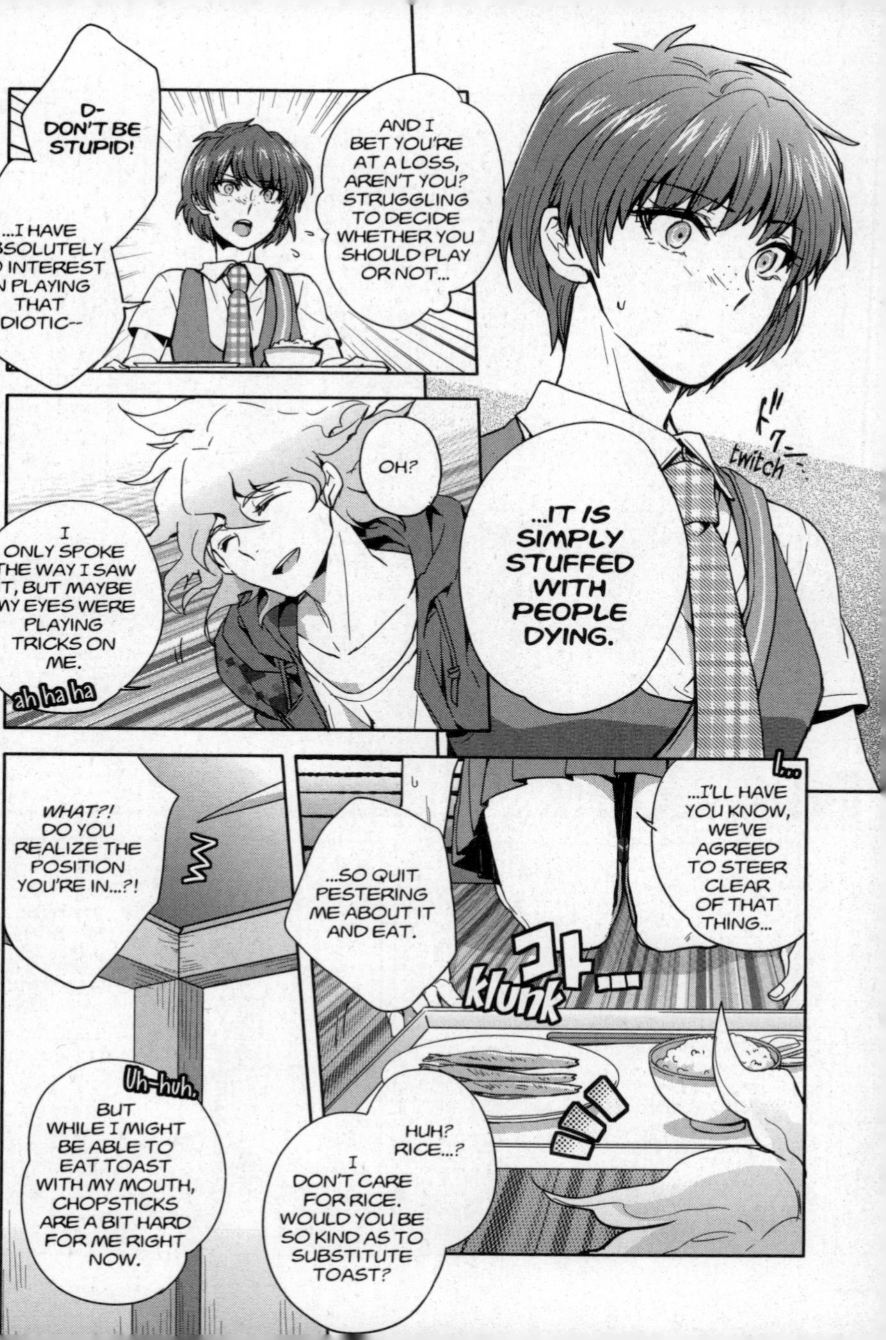
ドク
twitch
...IT IS SIMPLY STUFFED WITH PEOPLE DYING.
AND I BET YOU'RE AT A LOSS, AREN'T YOU? STRUGGLING TO DECIDE WHETHER YOU SHOULD PLAY OR NOT...
D- DON'T BE STUPID!
...I HAVE ABSOLUTELY NO INTEREST IN PLAYING THAT IDIOTIC--
OH?
I ONLY SPOKE THE WAY I SAW IT, BUT MAYBE MY EYES WERE PLAYING TRICKS ON ME.
ah ha ha
I...
...I'LL HAVE YOU KNOW, WE'VE AGREED TO STEER CLEAR OF THAT THING...
...SO QUIT PESTERING ME ABOUT IT AND EAT.
コト...
klunk
WHAT?! DO YOU REALIZE THE POSITION YOU'RE IN...?!
HUH? RICE...?
I DON'T CARE FOR RICE. WOULD YOU BE SO KIND AS TO SUBSTITUTE TOAST?
Uh-huh.
BUT WHILE I MIGHT BE ABLE TO EAT TOAST WITH MY MOUTH, CHOPSTICKS ARE A BIT HARD FOR ME RIGHT NOW.

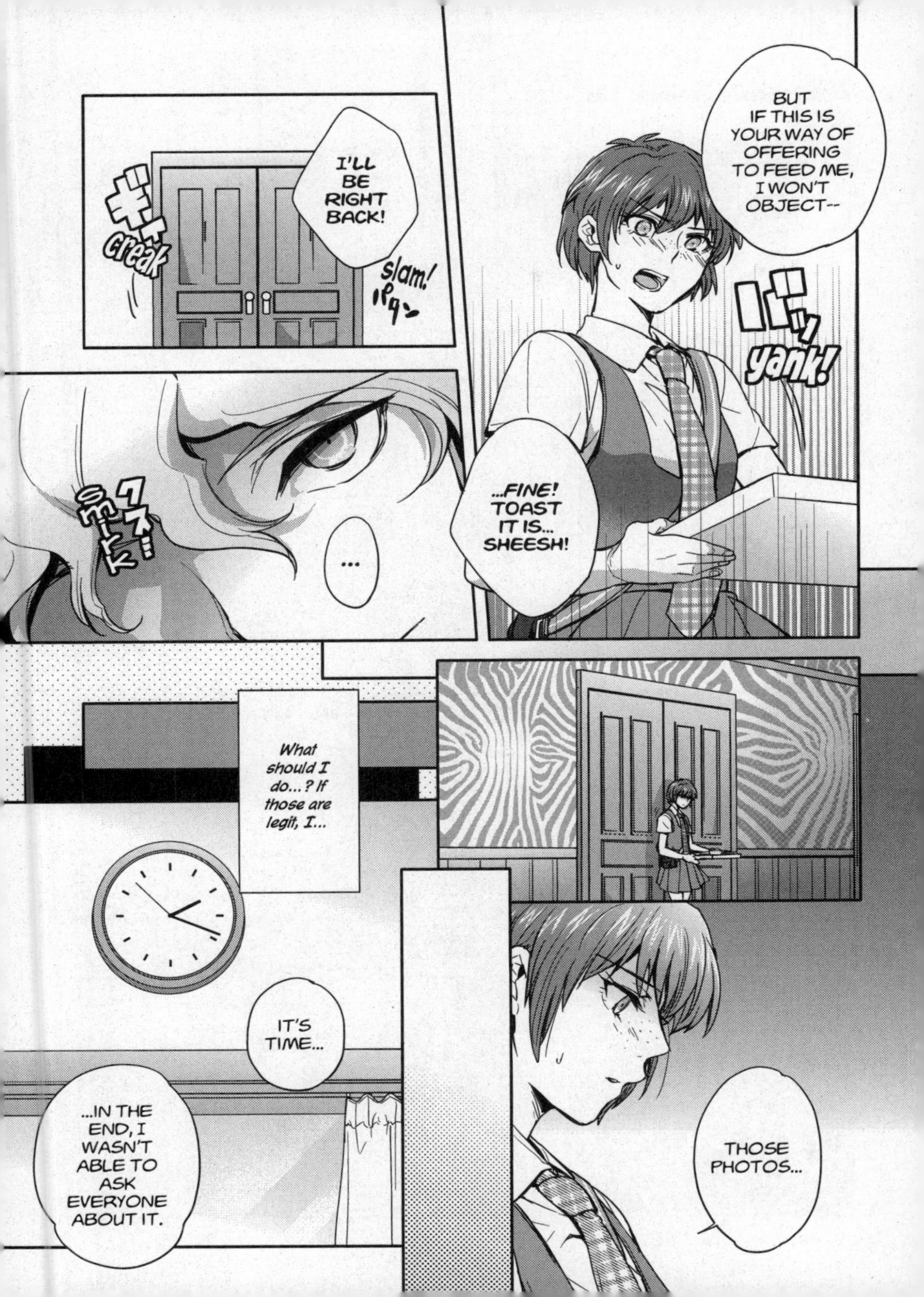
BUT IF THIS IS YOUR WAY OF OFFERING TO FEED ME, I WON'T OBJECT--
yank!
...FINE! TOAST IT IS... SHEESH!
I'LL BE RIGHT BACK!
creak
slam!
smirk
...
What should I do...? If those are legit, I...
THOSE PHOTOS...
IT'S TIME...
...IN THE END, I WASN'T ABLE TO ASK EVERYONE ABOUT IT.

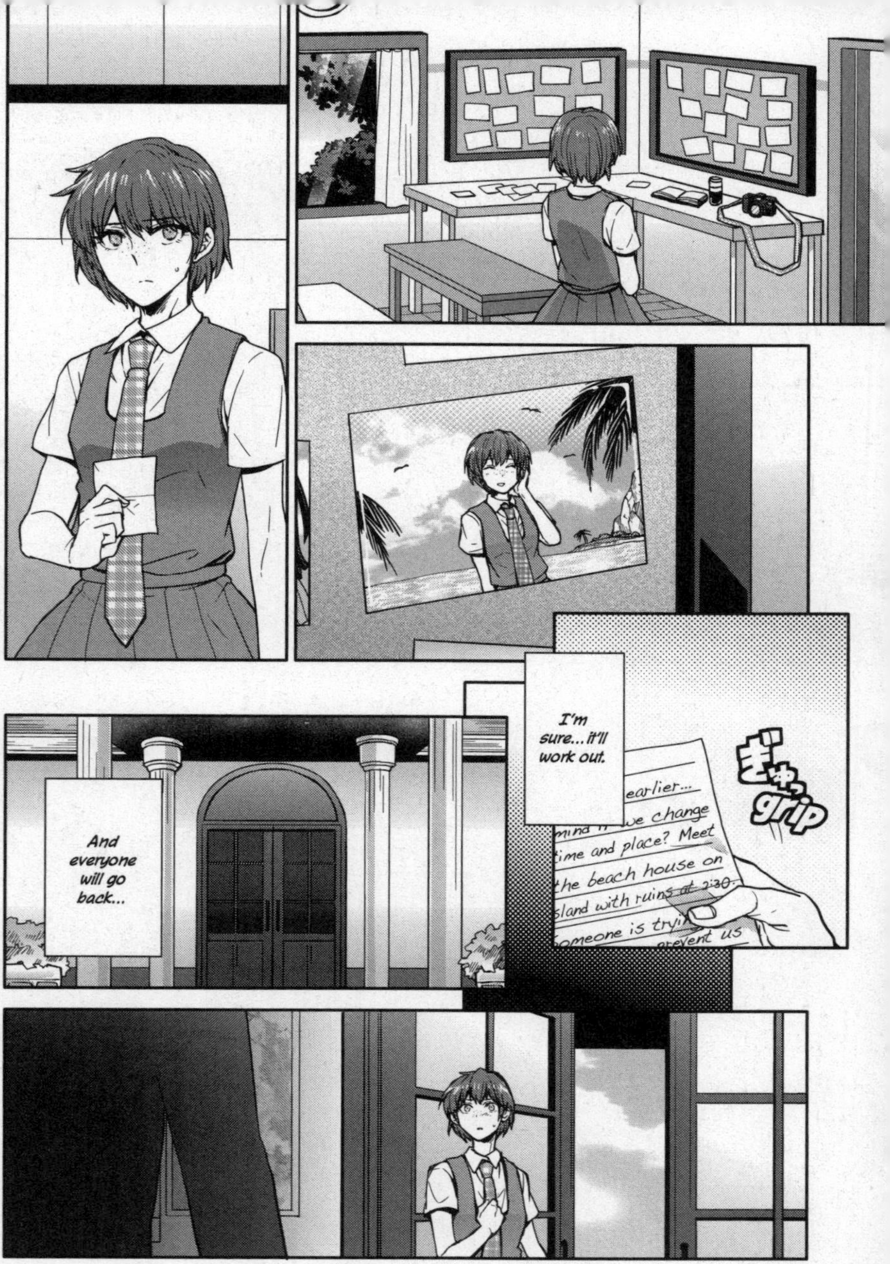
ぎゅっ
grip
I'm sure... it'll work out.
earlier...
mind if we change
time and place? Meet
the beach house on
sland with ruins at 2:30.
Someone is tryi
prevent us
And everyone will go back...

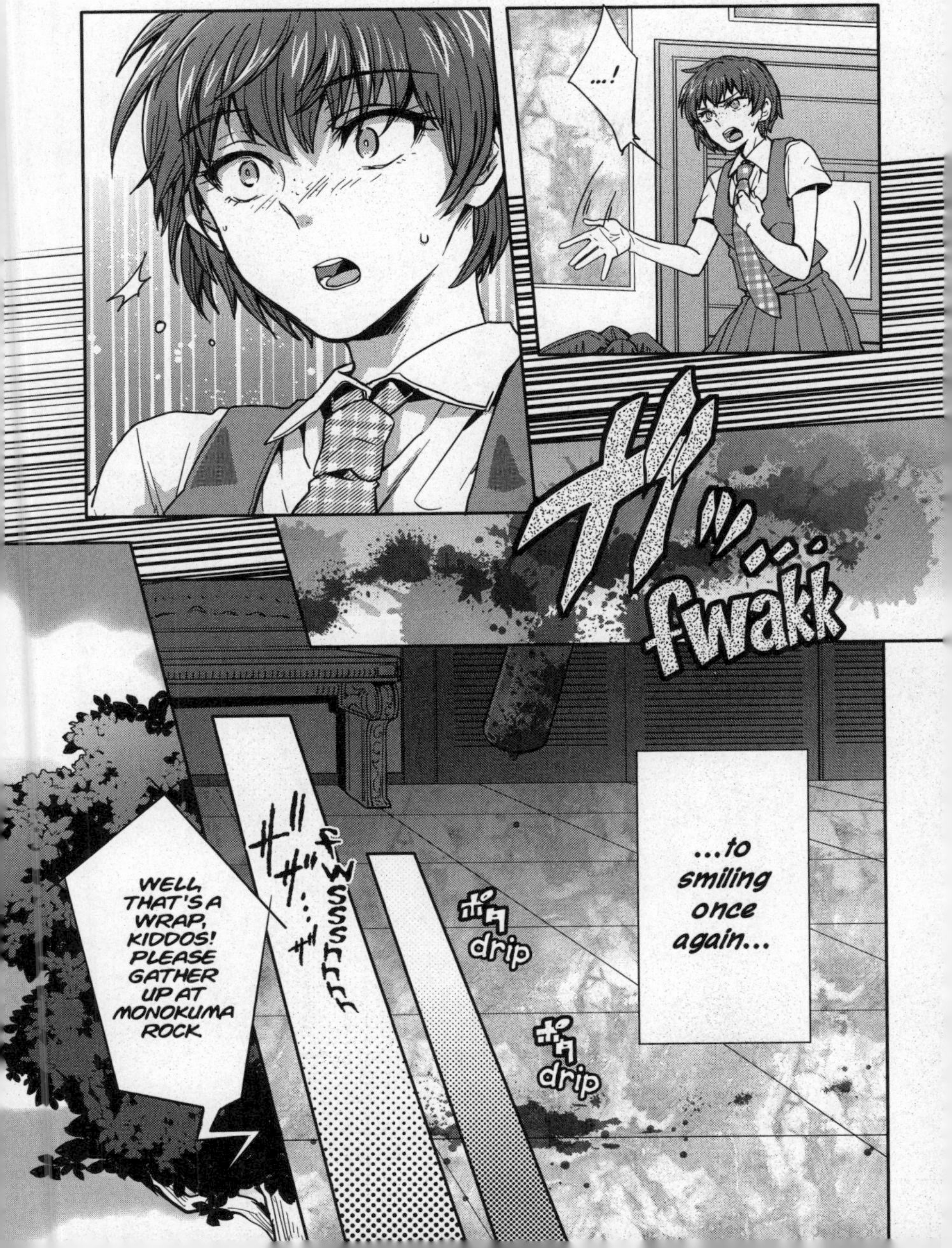
...!
fwakk
...to smiling once again...
drip
drip
fwsssrrrr
WELL, THAT'S A WRAP, KIDDOS! PLEASE GATHER UP AT MONOKUMA ROCK.

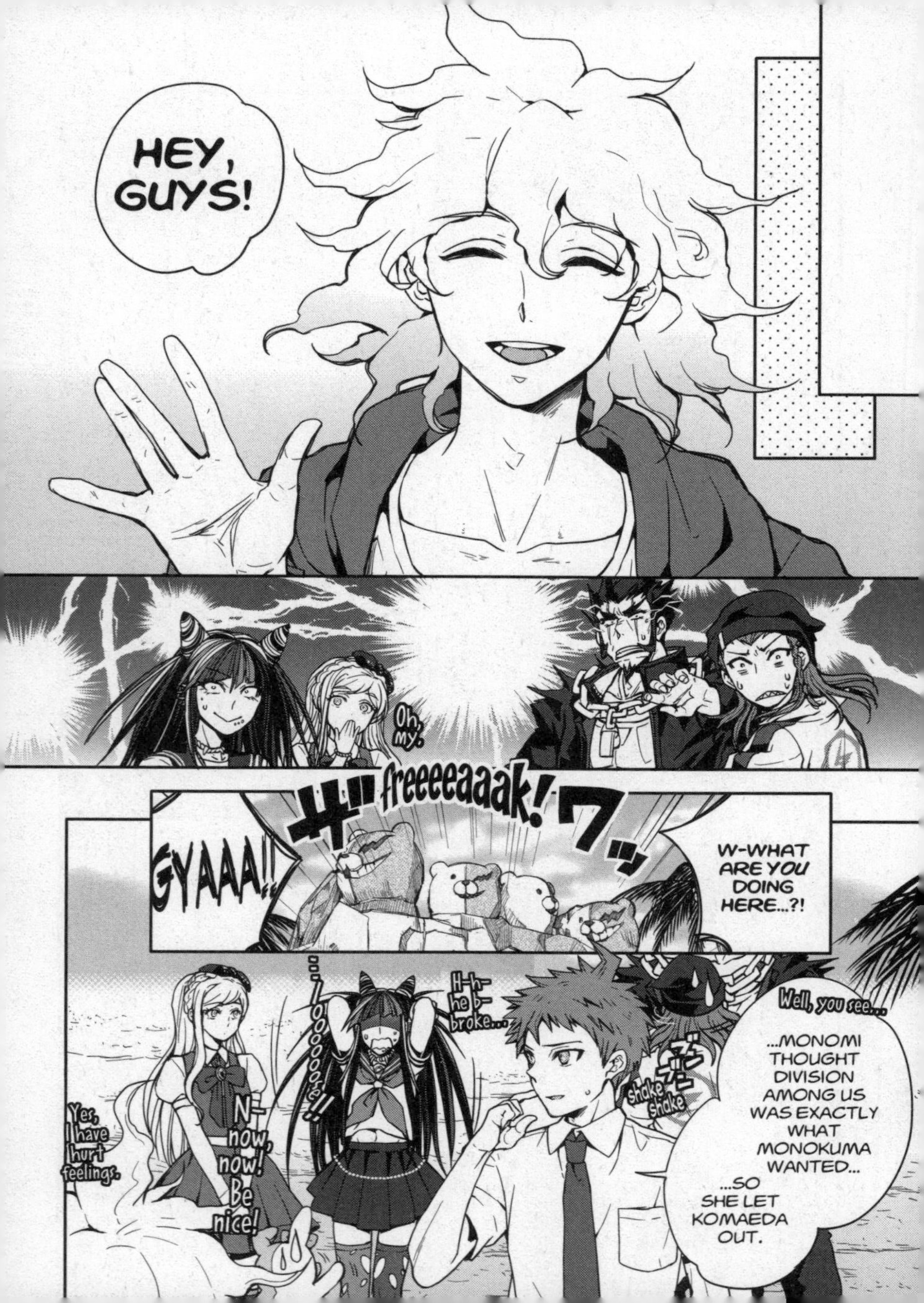
HEY, GUYS!
Oh, my.
W-WHAT ARE YOU DOING HERE...?!
freeeeaaak!
GYAAA!!
Well, you see...
...MONOMI THOUGHT DIVISION AMONG US WAS EXACTLY WHAT MONOKUMA WANTED...
...SO SHE LET KOMAEDA OUT.
shake shake
H-h-he b-broke...
...Looooooore!!
N-now, now! Be nice!
Yes, I have hurt feelings.

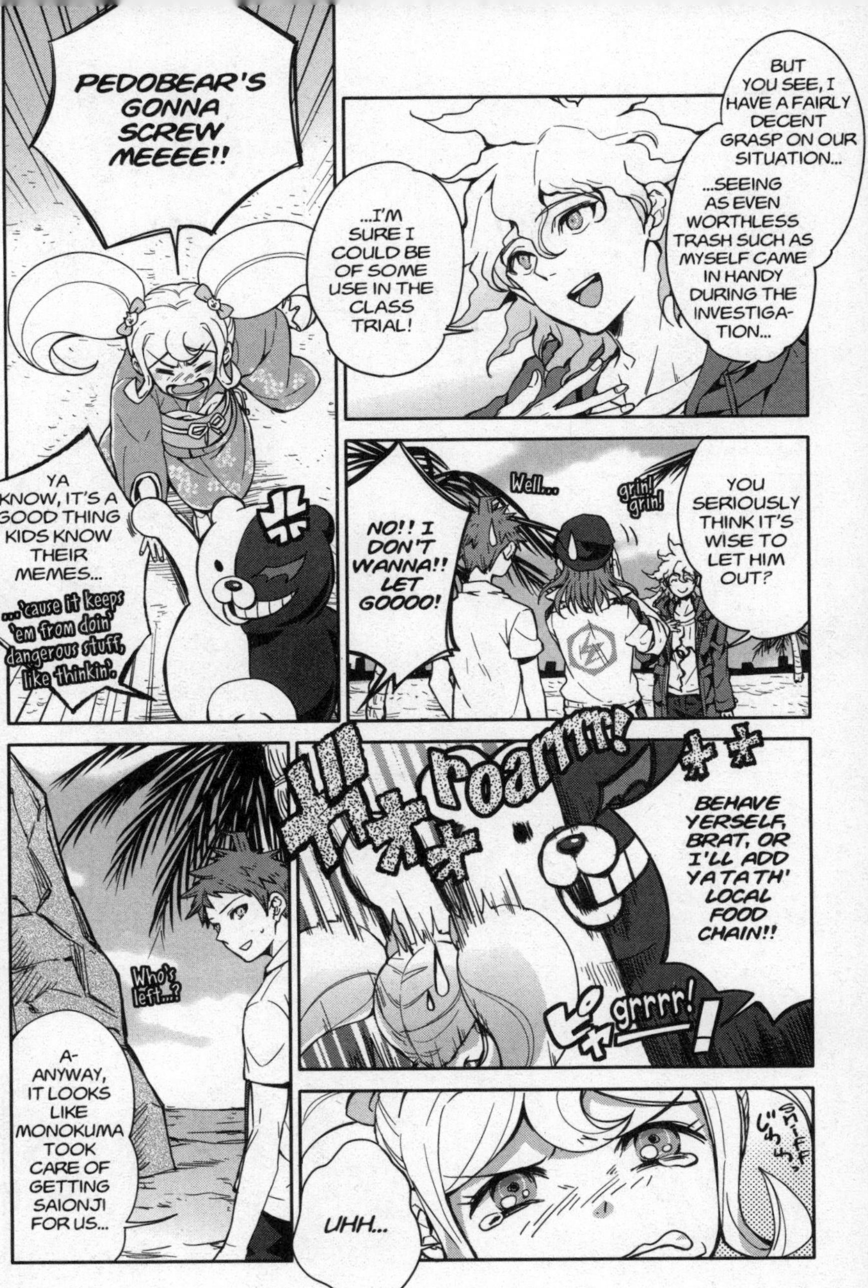
BUT YOU SEE, I HAVE A FAIRLY DECENT GRASP ON OUR SITUATION...
...SEEING AS EVEN WORTHLESS TRASH SUCH AS MYSELF CAME IN HANDY DURING THE INVESTIGA-TION...
...I'M SURE I COULD BE OF SOME USE IN THE CLASS TRIAL!
YOU SERIOUSLY THINK IT'S WISE TO LET HIM OUT?
grin! grin!
Well...
NO!! I DON'T WANNA!! LET GOOOO!
PEDOBEAR'S GONNA SCREW MEEEE!!
YA KNOW, IT'S A GOOD THING KIDS KNOW THEIR MEMES...
...'cause it keeps 'em from doin' dangerous stuff, like thinkin'.
roarrrr!
BEHAVE YERSELF, BRAT, OR I'LL ADD YA TA TH' LOCAL FOOD CHAIN!!
grrrr!
SNIFF
UHH...
Who's left...?
A-ANYWAY, IT LOOKS LIKE MONOKUMA TOOK CARE OF GETTING SAIONJI FOR US...

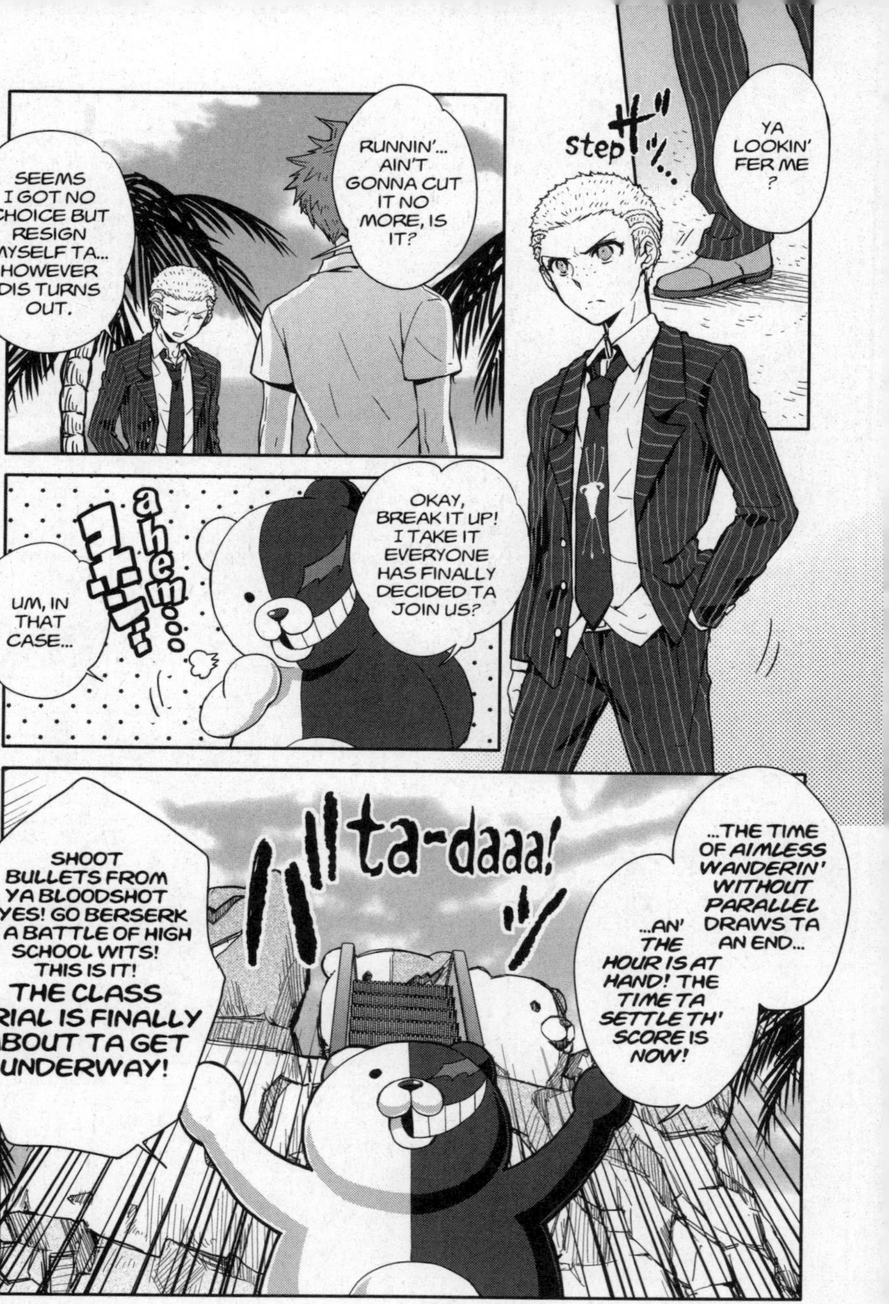
step
YA LOOKIN' FER ME?
RUNNIN'... AIN'T GONNA CUT IT NO MORE, IS IT?
SEEMS I GOT NO CHOICE BUT RESIGN MYSELF TA... HOWEVER DIS TURNS OUT.
OKAY, BREAK IT UP! I TAKE IT EVERYONE HAS FINALLY DECIDED TA JOIN US?
ahem...
UM, IN THAT CASE...
...THE TIME OF AIMLESS WANDERIN' WITHOUT PARALLEL DRAWS TA AN END...
...AN' THE HOUR IS AT HAND! THE TIME TA SETTLE TH' SCORE IS NOW!
ta-daaa!
SHOOT BULLETS FROM YA BLOODSHOT EYES! GO BERSERK IN A BATTLE OF HIGH SCHOOL WITS! THIS IS IT! THE CLASS TRIAL IS FINALLY ABOUT TA GET UNDERWAY!

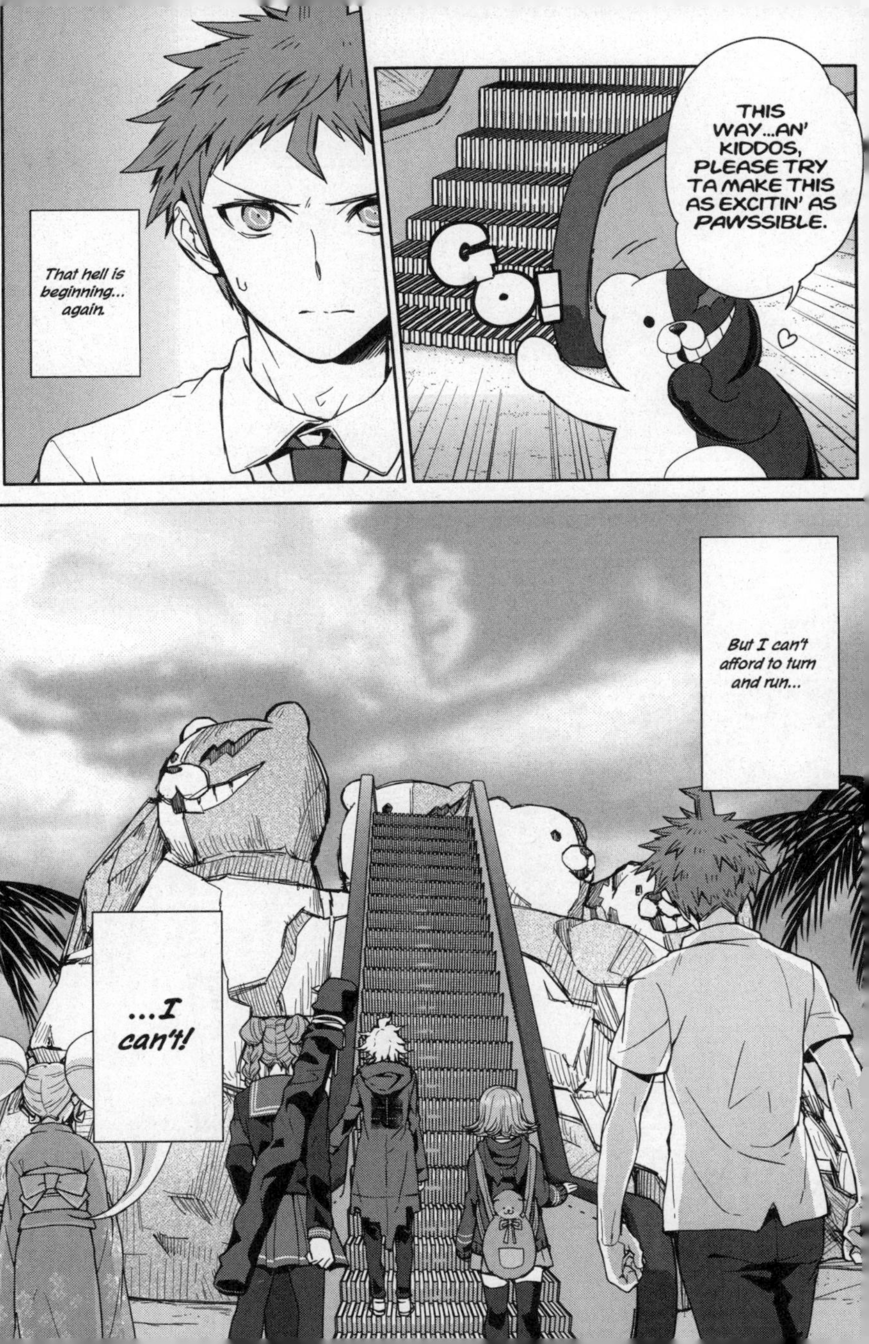
THIS WAY...AN' KIDDOS, PLEASE TRY TA MAKE THIS AS EXCITIN' AS PAWSSIBLE.
GO!
That hell is beginning... again.
But I can't afford to turn and run...
...I can't!

DR2

CHAPTER 11: THE CLASS TRIAL IS NOW IN SESSION! [PART ONE]

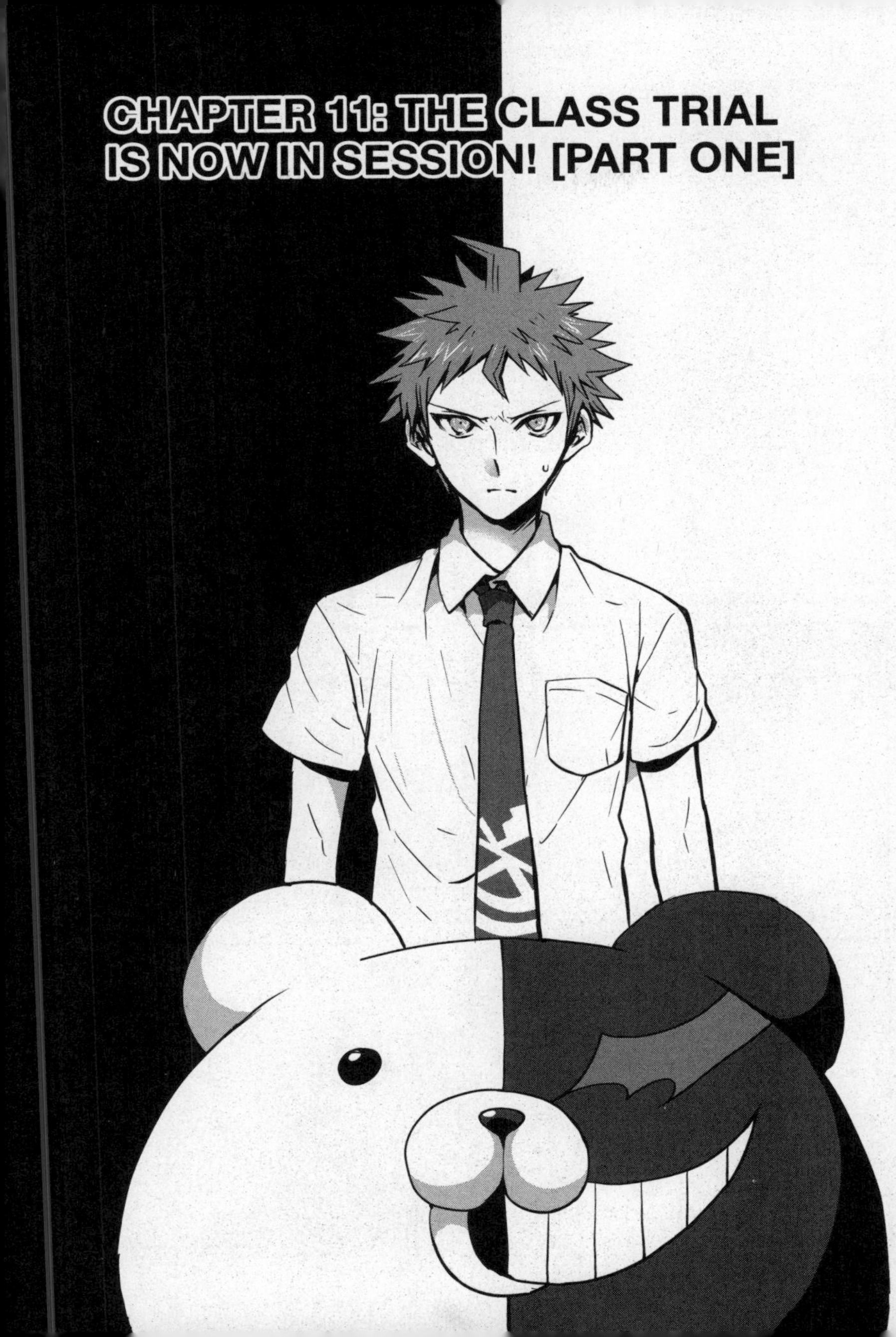

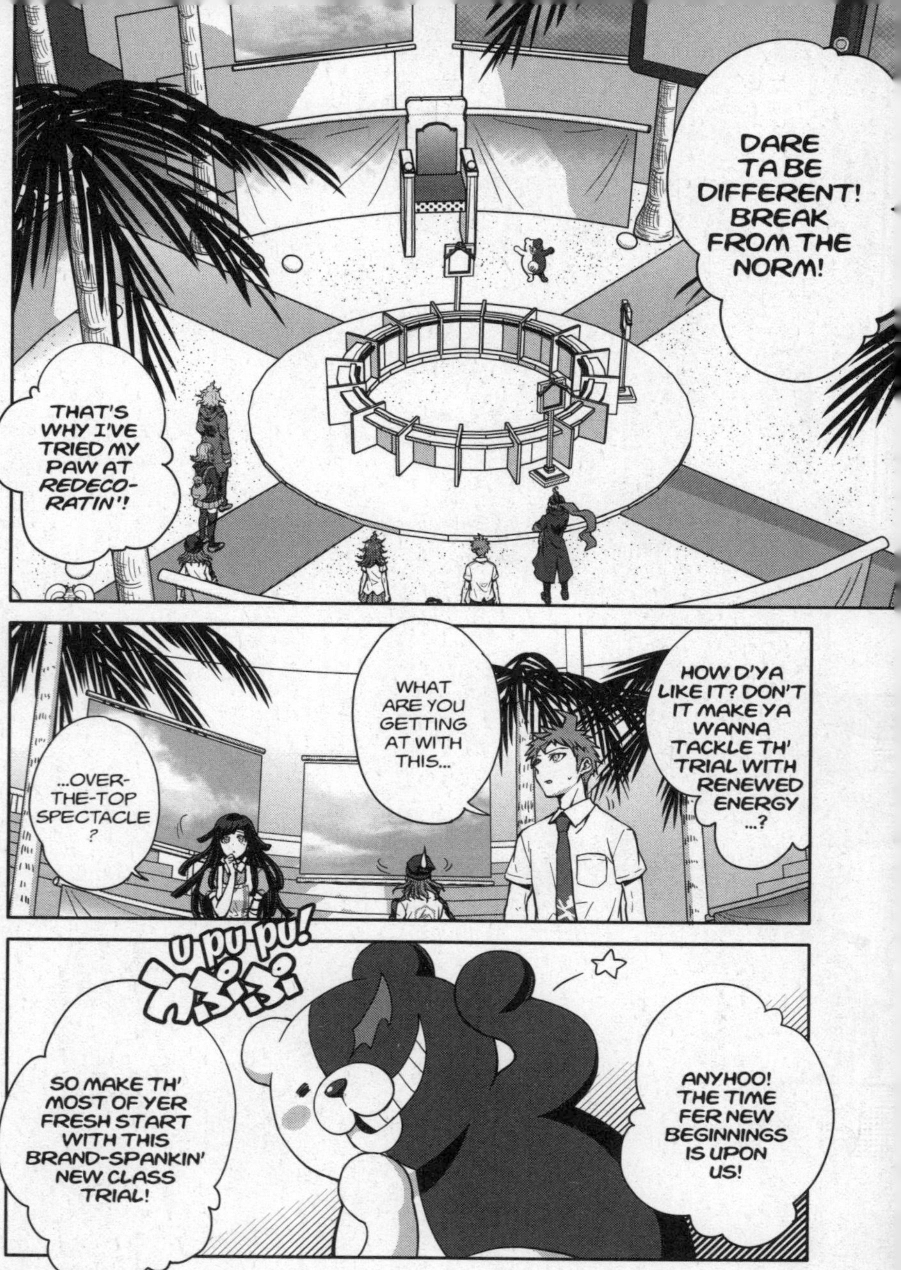
DARE TA BE DIFFERENT! BREAK FROM THE NORM!
THAT'S WHY I'VE TRIED MY PAW AT REDECO-RATIN'!
HOW D'YA LIKE IT? DON'T IT MAKE YA WANNA TACKLE TH' TRIAL WITH RENEWED ENERGY ...?
WHAT ARE YOU GETTING AT WITH THIS...
...OVER-THE-TOP SPECTACLE ?
U PU PU!
うぷぷ
ANYHOO! THE TIME FER NEW BEGINNINGS IS UPON US!
SO MAKE TH' MOST OF YER FRESH START WITH THIS BRAND-SPANKIN' NEW CLASS TRIAL!

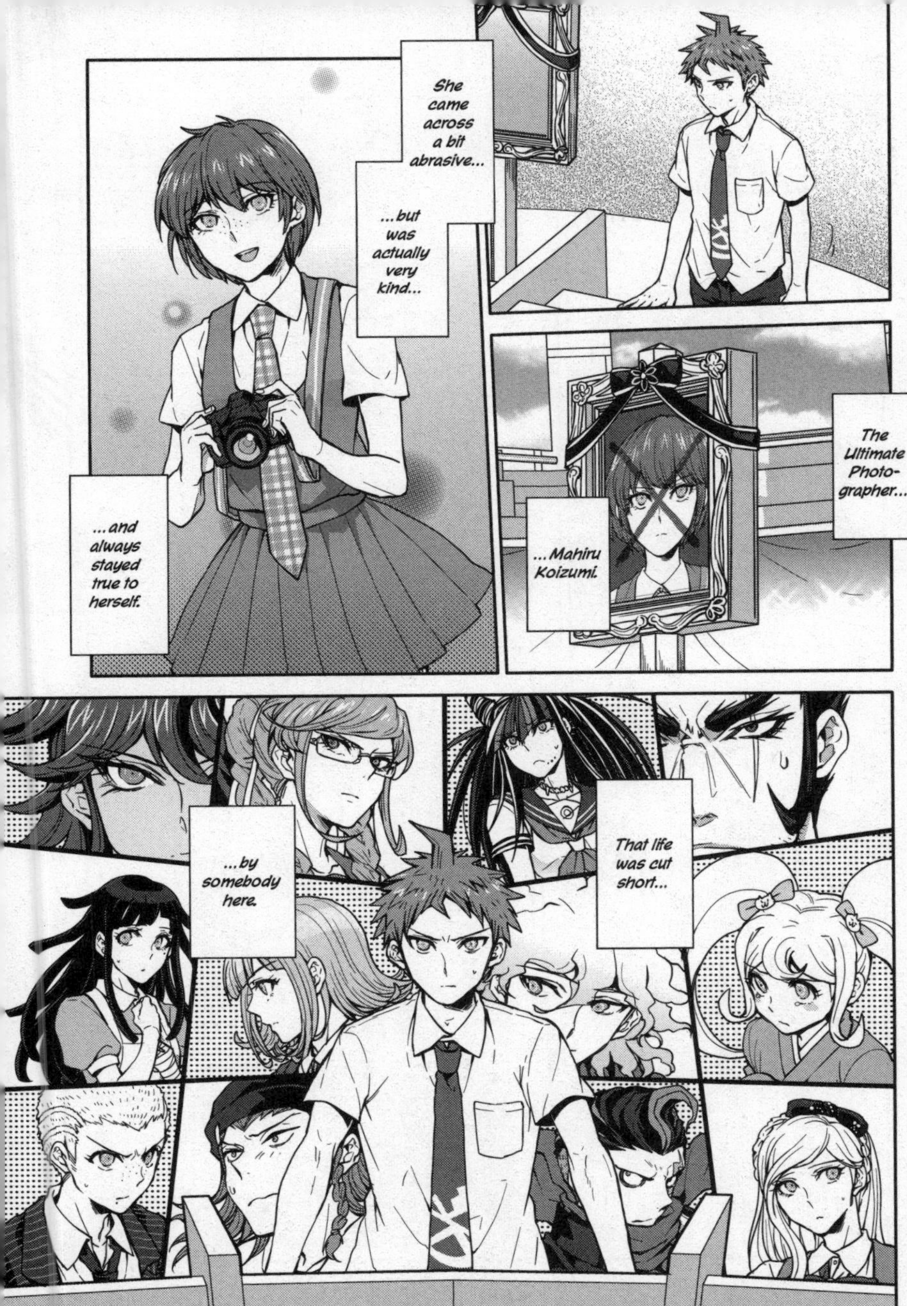
The Ultimate Photo-grapher...
...Mahiru Koizumi.
She came across a bit abrasive...
...but was actually very kind...
...and always stayed true to herself.
That life was cut short...
...by somebody here.

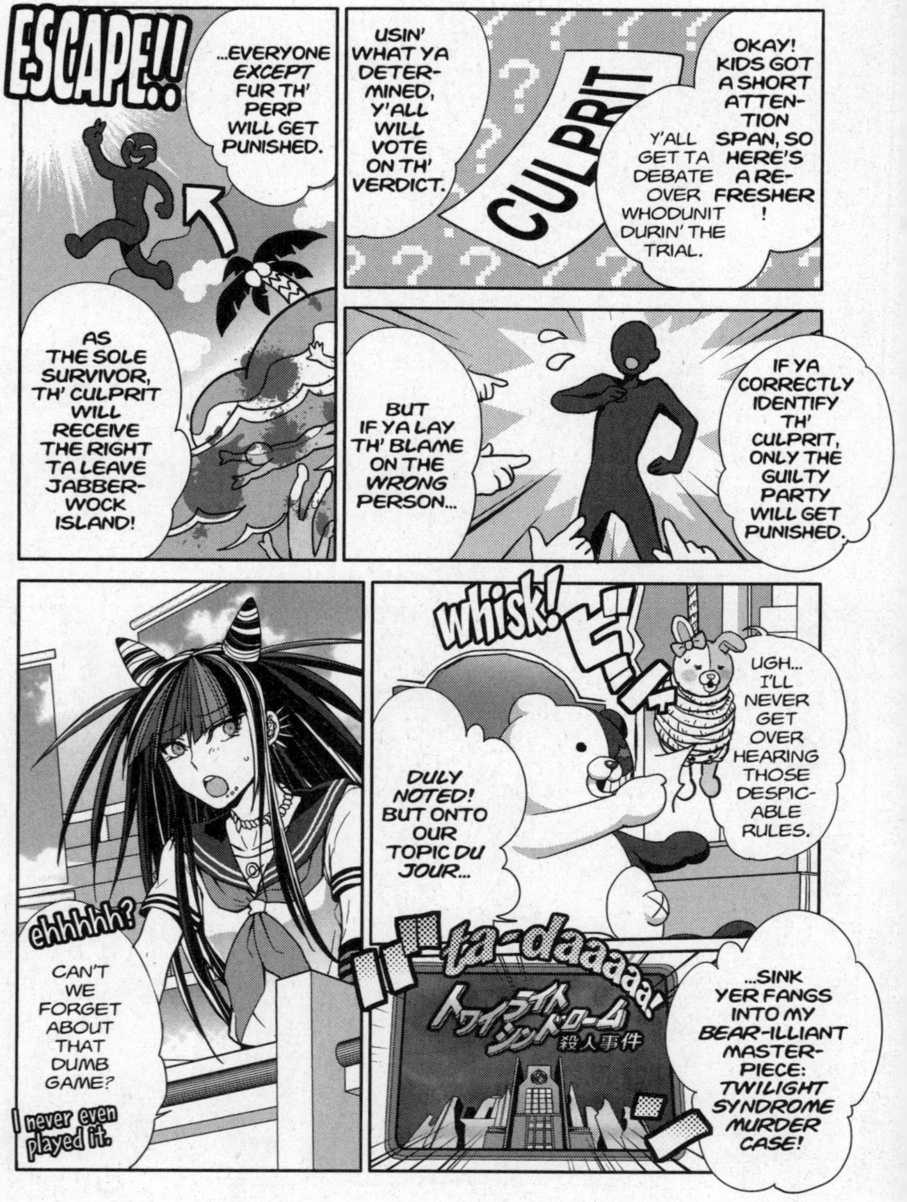
OKAY! KIDS GOT A SHORT ATTENTION SPAN, SO HERE'S A REFRESHER!
Y'ALL GET TA DEBATE OVER WHODUNIT DURIN' THE TRIAL.
CULPRIT
USIN' WHAT YA DETERMINED, Y'ALL WILL VOTE ON TH' VERDICT.
IF YA CORRECTLY IDENTIFY TH' CULPRIT, ONLY THE GUILTY PARTY WILL GET PUNISHED.
BUT IF YA LAY TH' BLAME ON THE WRONG PERSON...
...EVERYONE EXCEPT FUR TH' PERP WILL GET PUNISHED.
ESCAPE!!
AS THE SOLE SURVIVOR, TH' CULPRIT WILL RECEIVE THE RIGHT TA LEAVE JABBERWOCK ISLAND!
whisk!
UGH... I'LL NEVER GET OVER HEARING THOSE DESPICABLE RULES.
DULY NOTED! BUT ONTO OUR TOPIC DU JOUR...
ta-daaaaaa!
トワイライトシンドローム殺人事件
...SINK YER FANGS INTO MY BEAR-ILLIANT MASTERPIECE: TWILIGHT SYNDROME MURDER CASE!
ehhhhh?
CAN'T WE FORGET ABOUT THAT DUMB GAME?
I never even played it.

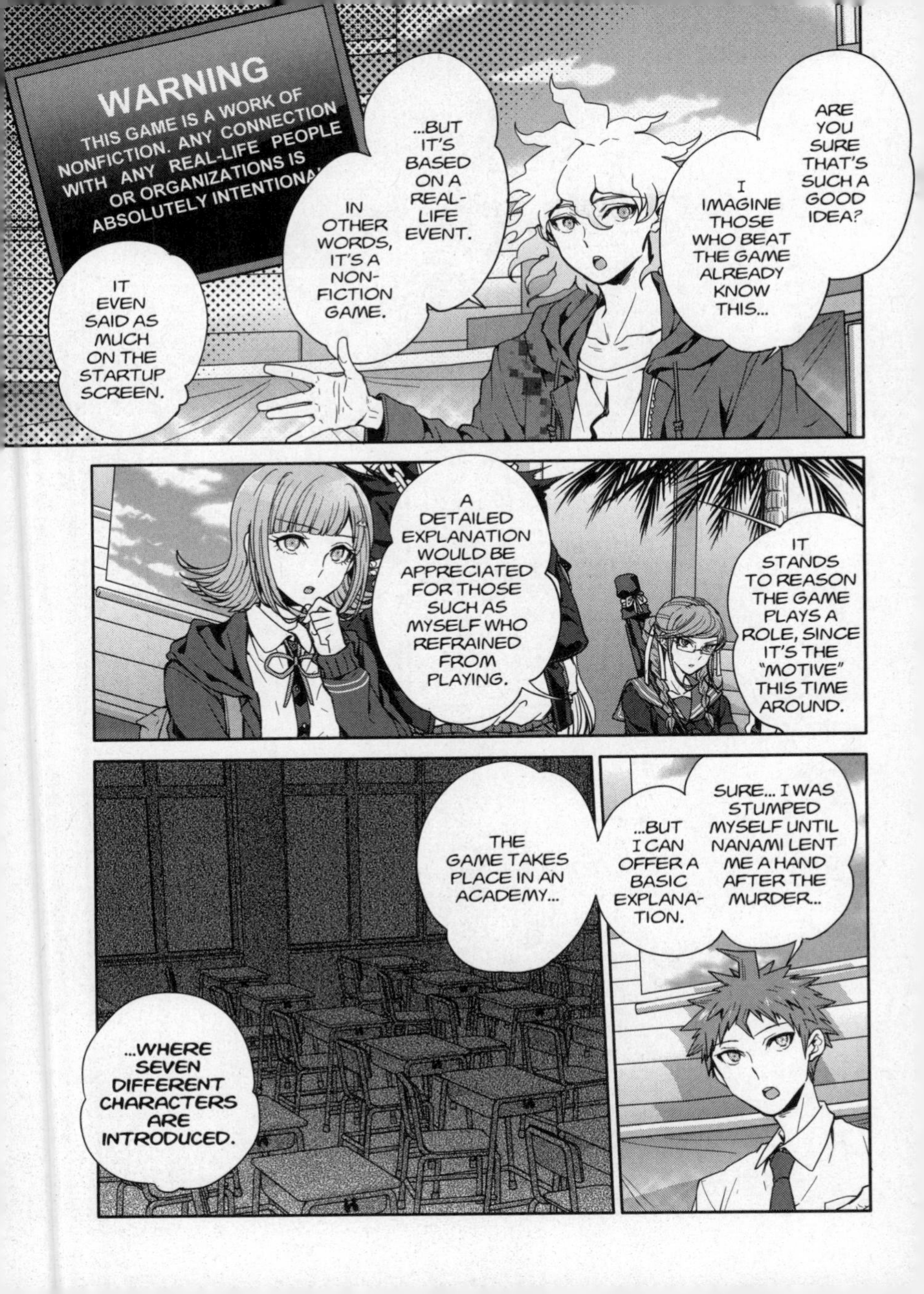
ARE YOU SURE THAT'S SUCH A GOOD IDEA?
I IMAGINE THOSE WHO BEAT THE GAME ALREADY KNOW THIS...
...BUT IT'S BASED ON A REAL-LIFE EVENT.
IN OTHER WORDS, IT'S A NON-FICTION GAME.
IT EVEN SAID AS MUCH ON THE STARTUP SCREEN.
WARNING
THIS GAME IS A WORK OF NONFICTION. ANY CONNECTION WITH ANY REAL-LIFE PEOPLE OR ORGANIZATIONS IS ABSOLUTELY INTENTIONAL
IT STANDS TO REASON THE GAME PLAYS A ROLE, SINCE IT'S THE "MOTIVE" THIS TIME AROUND.
A DETAILED EXPLANATION WOULD BE APPRECIATED FOR THOSE SUCH AS MYSELF WHO REFRAINED FROM PLAYING.
SURE... I WAS STUMPED MYSELF UNTIL NANAMI LENT ME A HAND AFTER THE MURDER...
...BUT I CAN OFFER A BASIC EXPLANA-TION.
THE GAME TAKES PLACE IN AN ACADEMY...
...WHERE SEVEN DIFFERENT CHARACTERS ARE INTRODUCED.

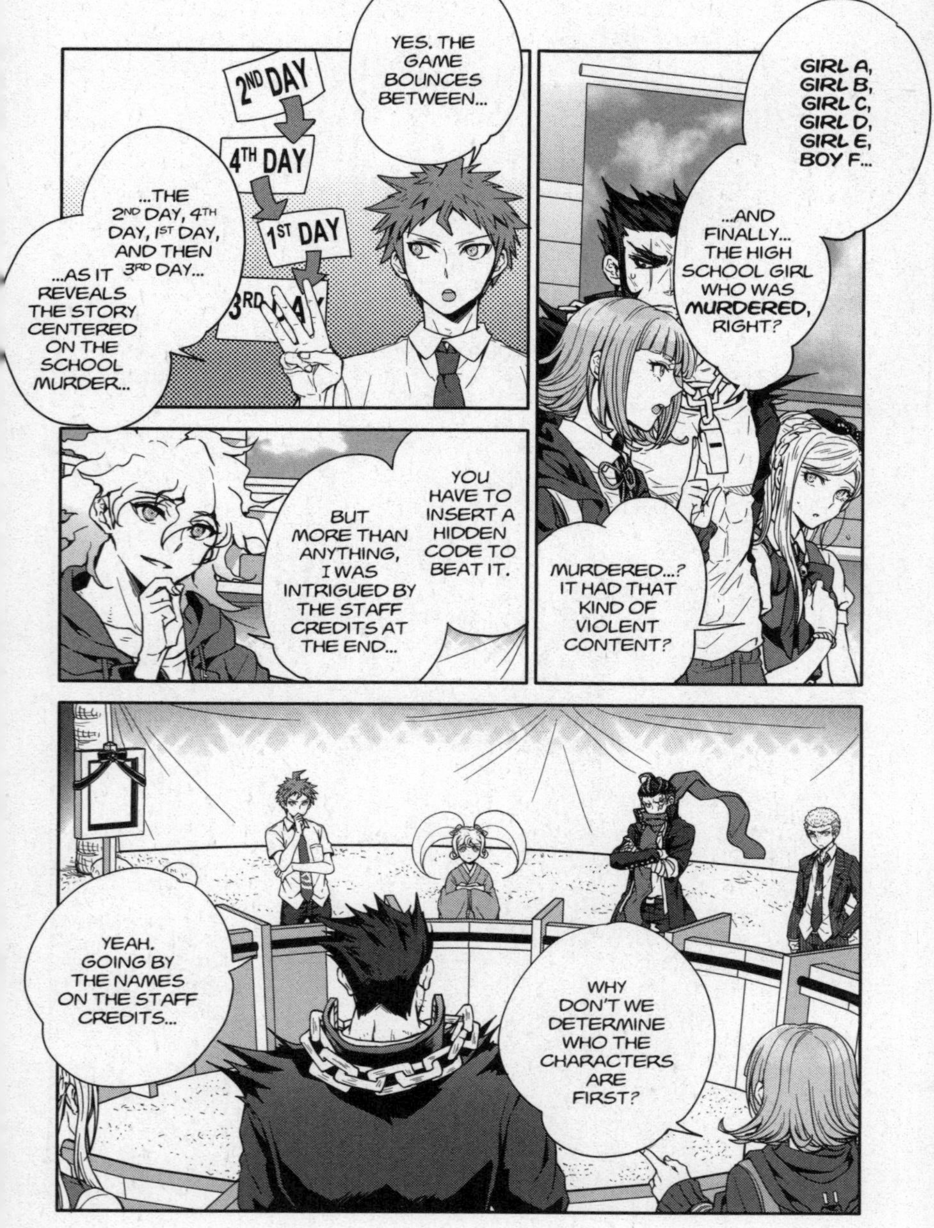
GIRL A, GIRL B, GIRL C, GIRL D, GIRL E, BOY F...
...AND FINALLY... THE HIGH SCHOOL GIRL WHO WAS **MURDERED**, RIGHT?
MURDERED...? IT HAD THAT KIND OF VIOLENT CONTENT?
YES. THE GAME BOUNCES BETWEEN...
2ND DAY
4TH DAY
1ST DAY
3RD DAY
...THE 2ND DAY, 4TH DAY, 1ST DAY, AND THEN 3RD DAY...
...AS IT REVEALS THE STORY CENTERED ON THE SCHOOL MURDER...
YOU HAVE TO INSERT A HIDDEN CODE TO BEAT IT.
BUT MORE THAN ANYTHING, I WAS INTRIGUED BY THE STAFF CREDITS AT THE END...
WHY DON'T WE DETERMINE WHO THE CHARACTERS ARE FIRST?
YEAH. GOING BY THE NAMES ON THE STAFF CREDITS...

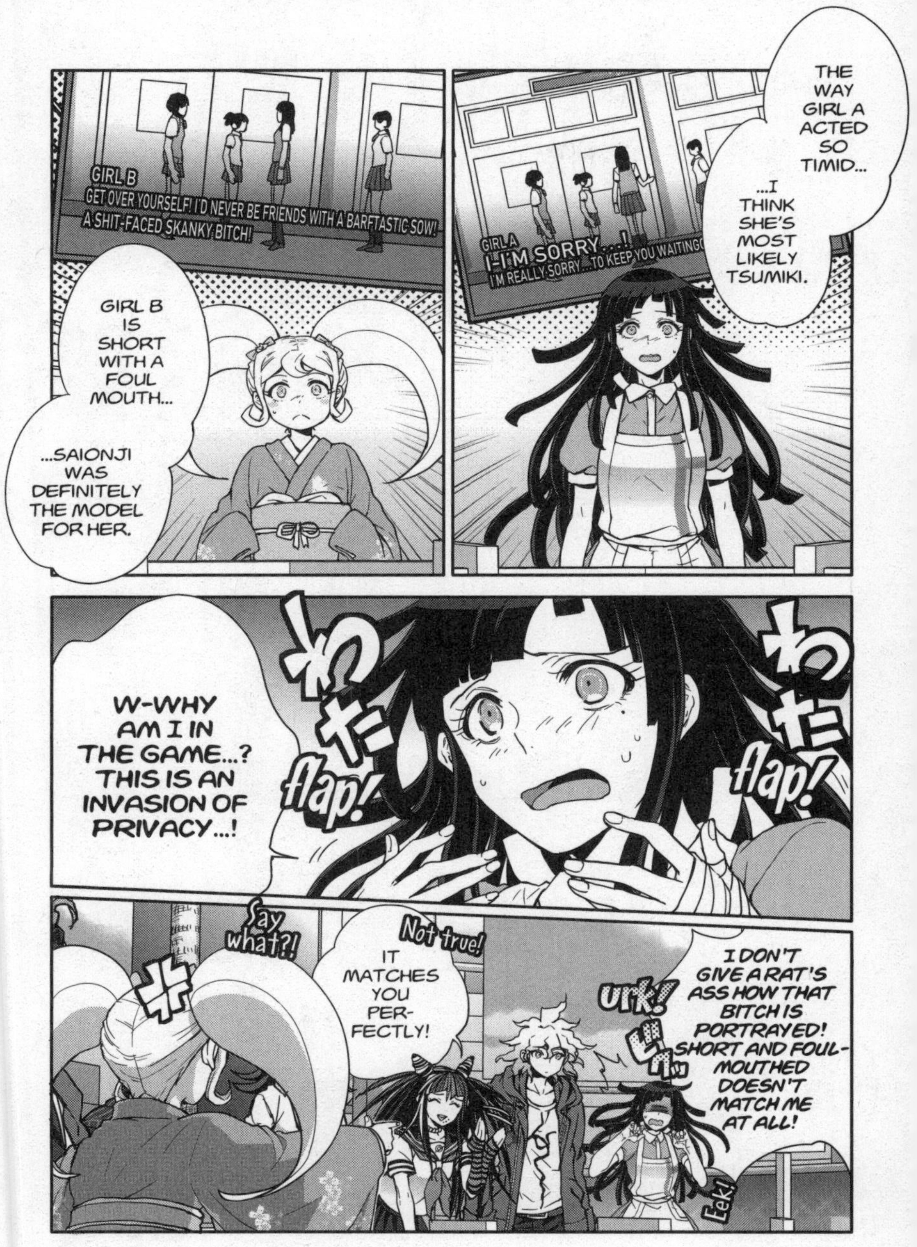
THE WAY GIRL A ACTED SO TIMID...
...I THINK SHE'S MOST LIKELY TSUMIKI.
GIRL A
I-I'M SORRY...!
I'M REALLY SORRY... TO KEEP YOU WAITING
GIRL B
GET OVER YOURSELF! I'D NEVER BE FRIENDS WITH A BARFTASTIC SOW!
A SHIT-FACED SKANKY BITCH!
GIRL B IS SHORT WITH A FOUL MOUTH...
...SAIONJI WAS DEFINITELY THE MODEL FOR HER.
flap!
flap!
W-WHY AM I IN THE GAME...? THIS IS AN INVASION OF PRIVACY...!
I DON'T GIVE A RAT'S ASS HOW THAT BITCH IS PORTRAYED! SHORT AND FOUL-MOUTHED DOESN'T MATCH ME AT ALL!
urk!
Eek!
Not true!
IT MATCHES YOU PER-FECTLY!
Say what?!

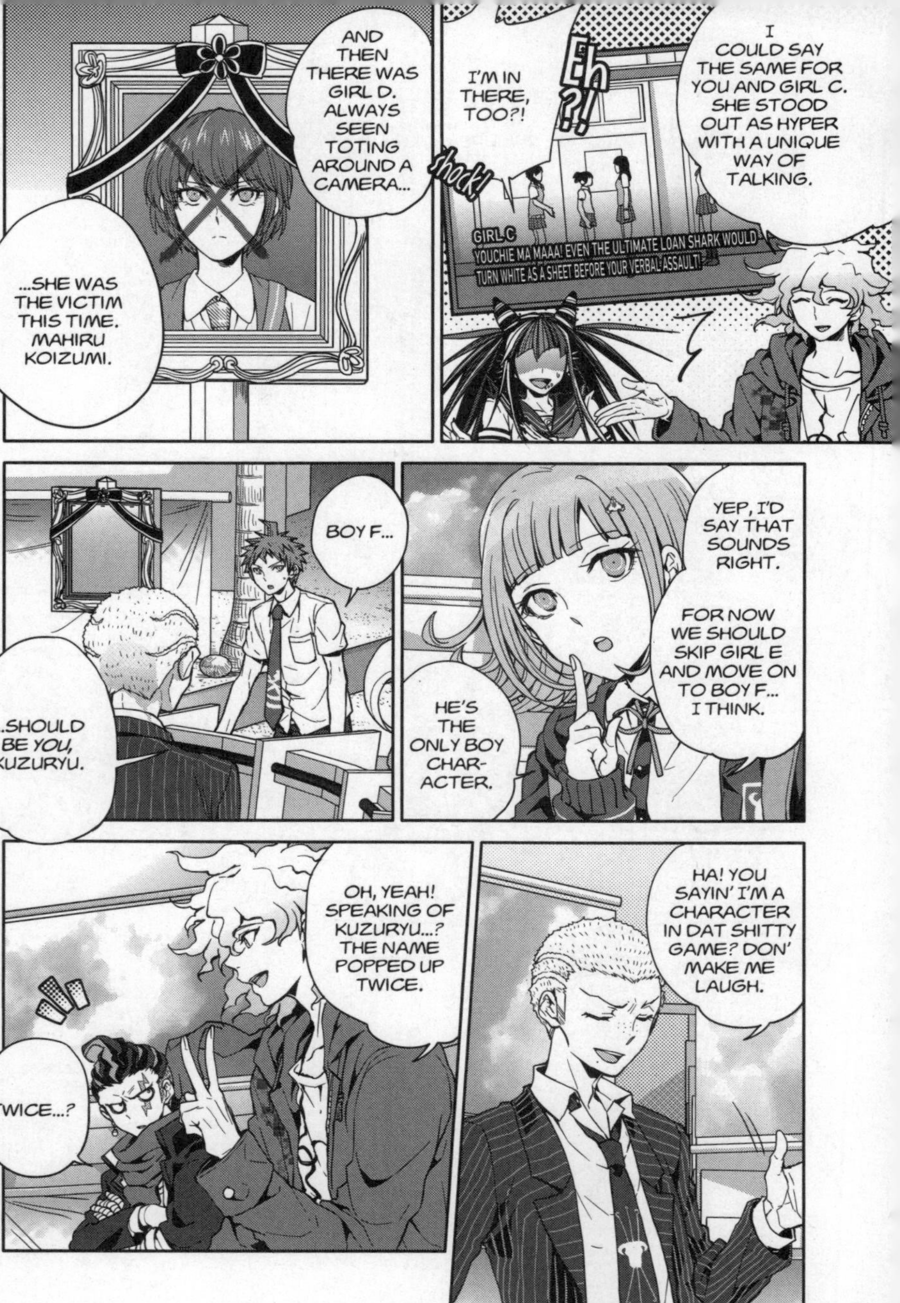
I COULD SAY THE SAME FOR YOU AND GIRL C. SHE STOOD OUT AS HYPER WITH A UNIQUE WAY OF TALKING.
Eh?!
I'M IN THERE, TOO?!
shock!
GIRL C
YOUCHIE MA MAAA! EVEN THE ULTIMATE LOAN SHARK WOULD TURN WHITE AS A SHEET BEFORE YOUR VERBAL ASSAULT!
AND THEN THERE WAS GIRL D. ALWAYS SEEN TOTING AROUND A CAMERA...
...SHE WAS THE VICTIM THIS TIME. MAHIRU KOIZUMI.
YEP, I'D SAY THAT SOUNDS RIGHT.
FOR NOW WE SHOULD SKIP GIRL E AND MOVE ON TO BOY F... I THINK.
HE'S THE ONLY BOY CHARACTER.
BOY F...
...SHOULD BE *YOU*, KUZURYU.
HA! YOU SAYIN' I'M A CHARACTER IN DAT SHITTY GAME? DON' MAKE ME LAUGH.
OH, YEAH! SPEAKING OF KUZURYU...? THE NAME POPPED UP TWICE.
TWICE...?

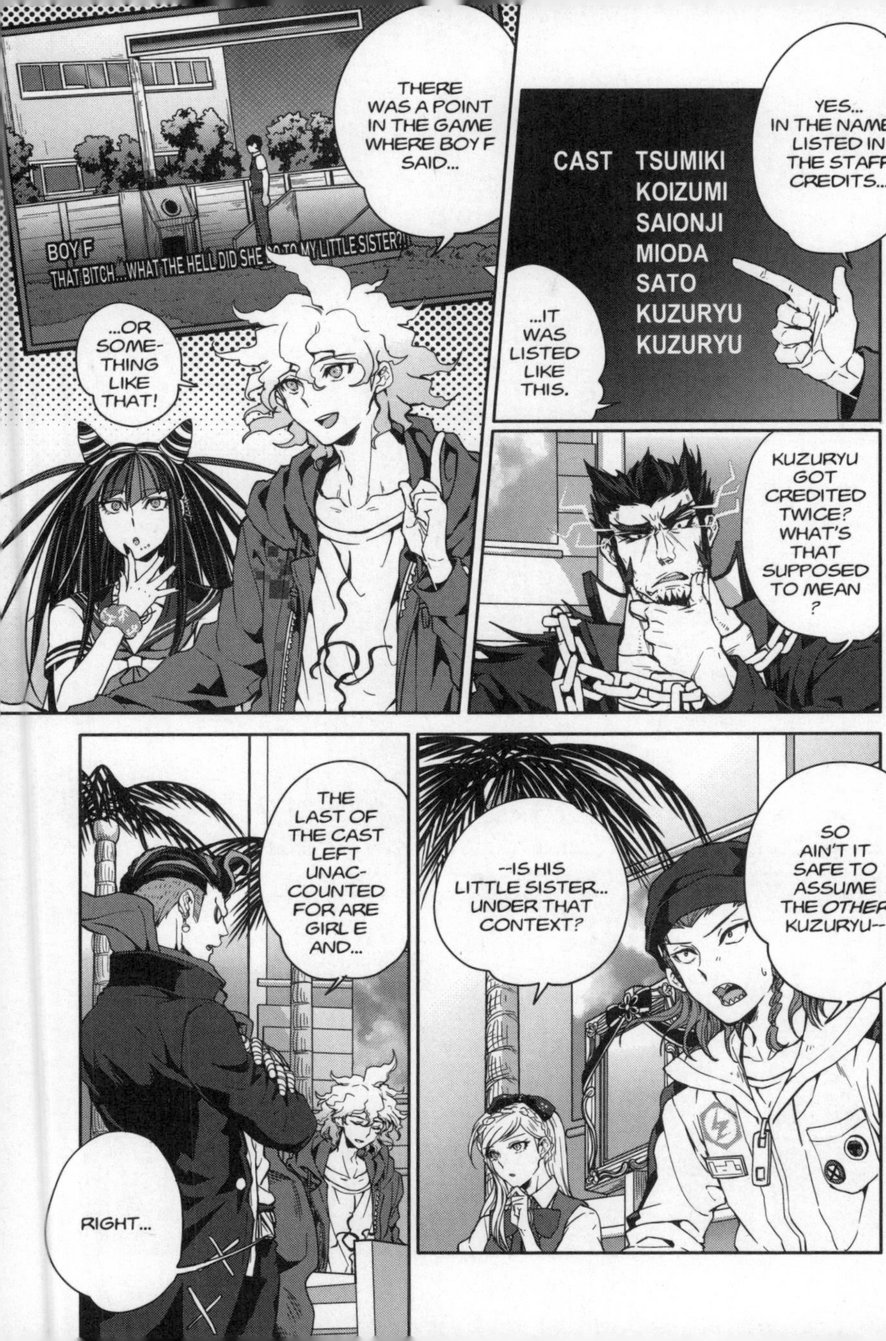
YES... IN THE NAMES LISTED IN THE STAFF CREDITS...
CAST TSUMIKI KOIZUMI SAIONJI MIODA SATO KUZURYU KUZURYU
...IT WAS LISTED LIKE THIS.
KUZURYU GOT CREDITED TWICE? WHAT'S THAT SUPPOSED TO MEAN?
THERE WAS A POINT IN THE GAME WHERE BOY F SAID...
BOY F
THAT BITCH... WHAT THE HELL DID SHE DO TO MY LITTLE SISTER?!
...OR SOMETHING LIKE THAT!
SO AIN'T IT SAFE TO ASSUME THE *OTHER* KUZURYU--
--IS HIS LITTLE SISTER... UNDER THAT CONTEXT?
THE LAST OF THE CAST LEFT UNACCOUNTED FOR ARE GIRL E AND...
RIGHT...

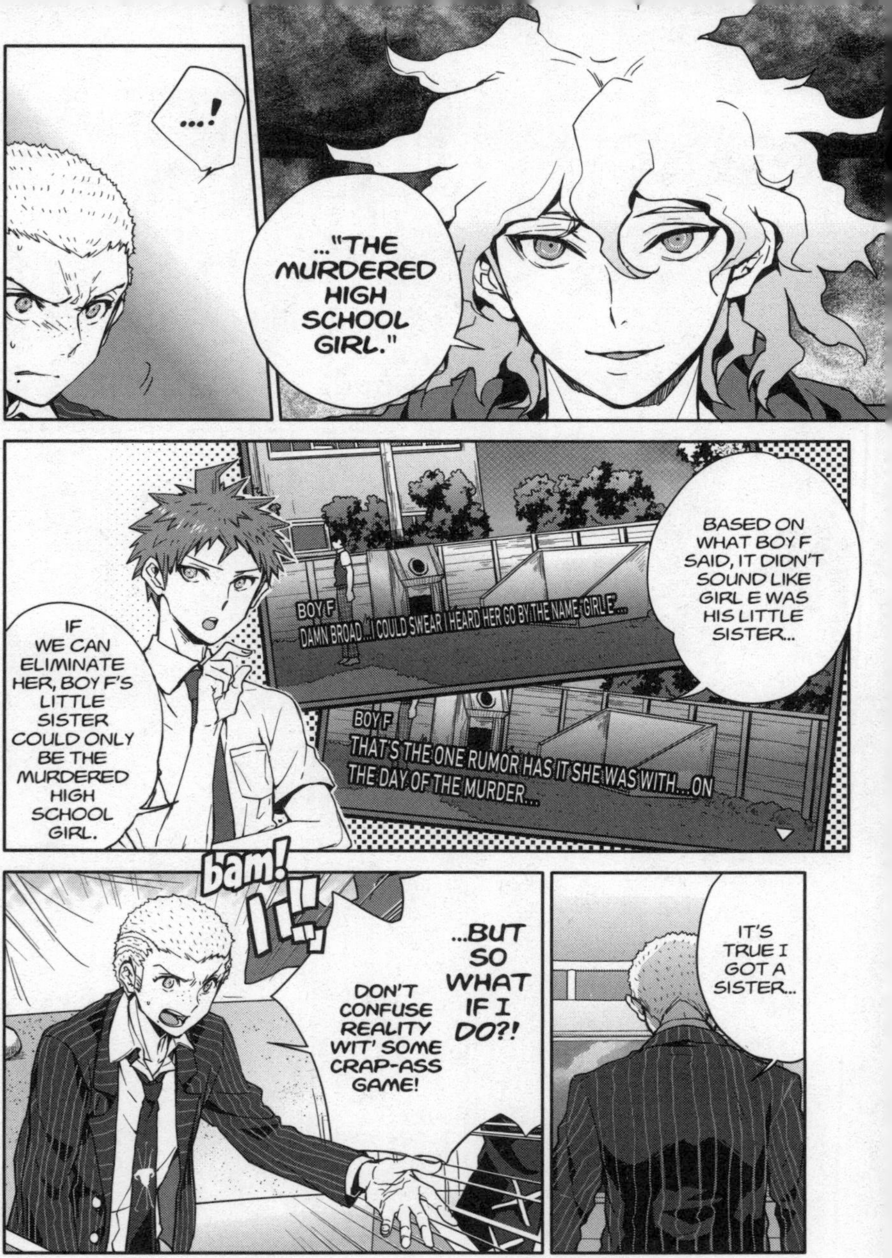
..."THE MURDERED HIGH SCHOOL GIRL."
...!
BASED ON WHAT BOY F SAID, IT DIDN'T SOUND LIKE GIRL E WAS HIS LITTLE SISTER...
BOY F
DAMN BROAD...I COULD SWEAR I HEARD HER GO BY THE NAME "GIRL E"...
BOY F
THAT'S THE ONE RUMOR HAS IT SHE WAS WITH...ON THE DAY OF THE MURDER...
IF WE CAN ELIMINATE HER, BOY F'S LITTLE SISTER COULD ONLY BE THE MURDERED HIGH SCHOOL GIRL.
IT'S TRUE I GOT A SISTER...
bam!
...BUT SO WHAT IF I DO?!
DON'T CONFUSE REALITY WIT' SOME CRAP-ASS GAME!

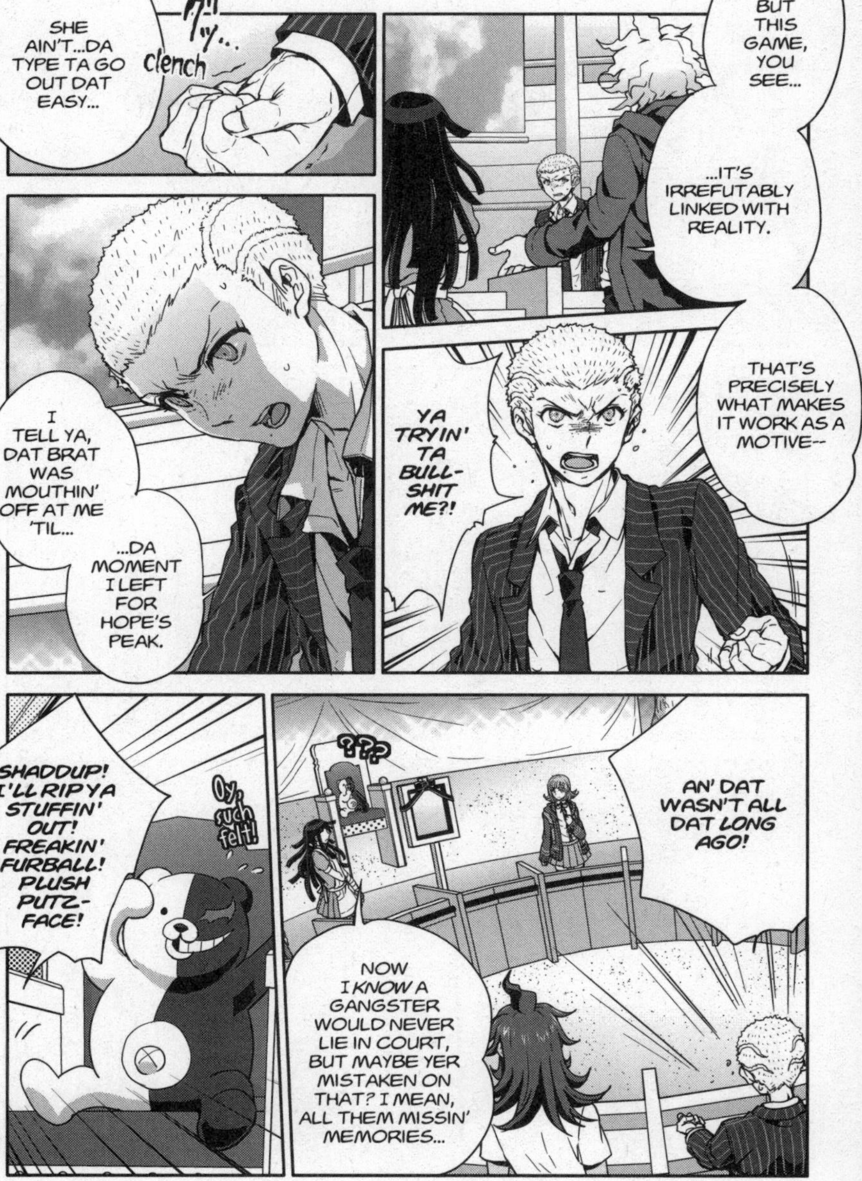
AH, BUT THIS GAME, YOU SEE...
...IT'S IRREFUTABLY LINKED WITH REALITY.
SHE AIN'T...DA TYPE TA GO OUT DAT EASY...
clench
THAT'S PRECISELY WHAT MAKES IT WORK AS A MOTIVE--
YA TRYIN' TA BULL-SHIT ME?!
I TELL YA, DAT BRAT WAS MOUTHIN' OFF AT ME 'TIL...
...DA MOMENT I LEFT FOR HOPE'S PEAK.
AN' DAT WASN'T ALL DAT LONG AGO!
???
NOW I KNOW A GANGSTER WOULD NEVER LIE IN COURT, BUT MAYBE YER MISTAKEN ON THAT? I MEAN, ALL THEM MISSIN' MEMORIES...
SHADDUP! I'LL RIP YA STUFFIN' OUT! FREAKIN' FURBALL! PLUSH PUTZ-FACE!
Oy, such felt!

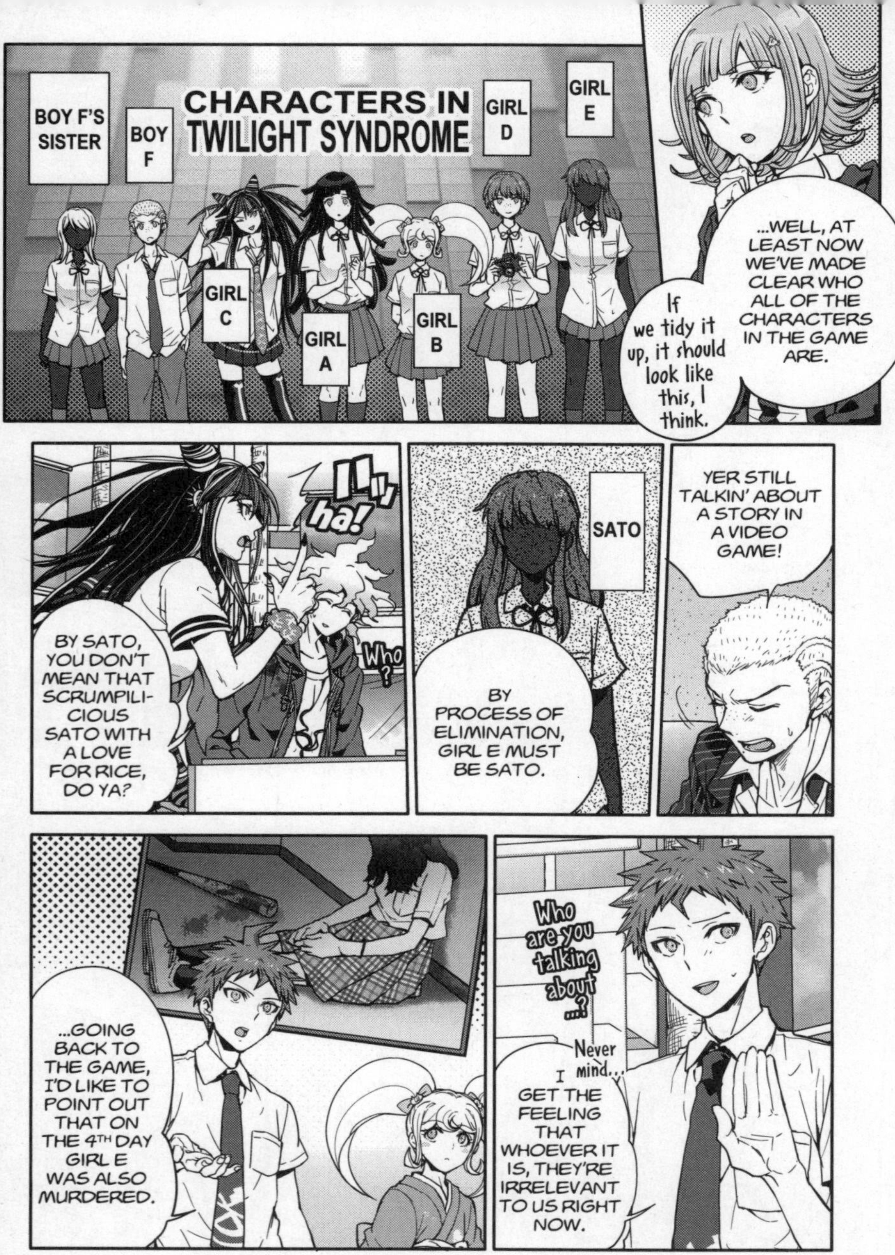
...WELL, AT LEAST NOW WE'VE MADE CLEAR WHO ALL OF THE CHARACTERS IN THE GAME ARE.
If we tidy it up, it should look like this, I think.
GIRL E
GIRL D
CHARACTERS IN TWILIGHT SYNDROME
BOY F
BOY F'S SISTER
GIRL B
GIRL C
GIRL A
YER STILL TALKIN' ABOUT A STORY IN A VIDEO GAME!
SATO
BY PROCESS OF ELIMINATION, GIRL E MUST BE SATO.
ha!
BY SATO, YOU DON'T MEAN THAT SCRUMPILI-CIOUS SATO WITH A LOVE FOR RICE, DO YA?
Who?
Who are you talking about...?
Never mind...
I GET THE FEELING THAT WHOEVER IT IS, THEY'RE IRRELEVANT TO US RIGHT NOW.
...GOING BACK TO THE GAME, I'D LIKE TO POINT OUT THAT ON THE 4TH DAY GIRL E WAS ALSO MURDERED.

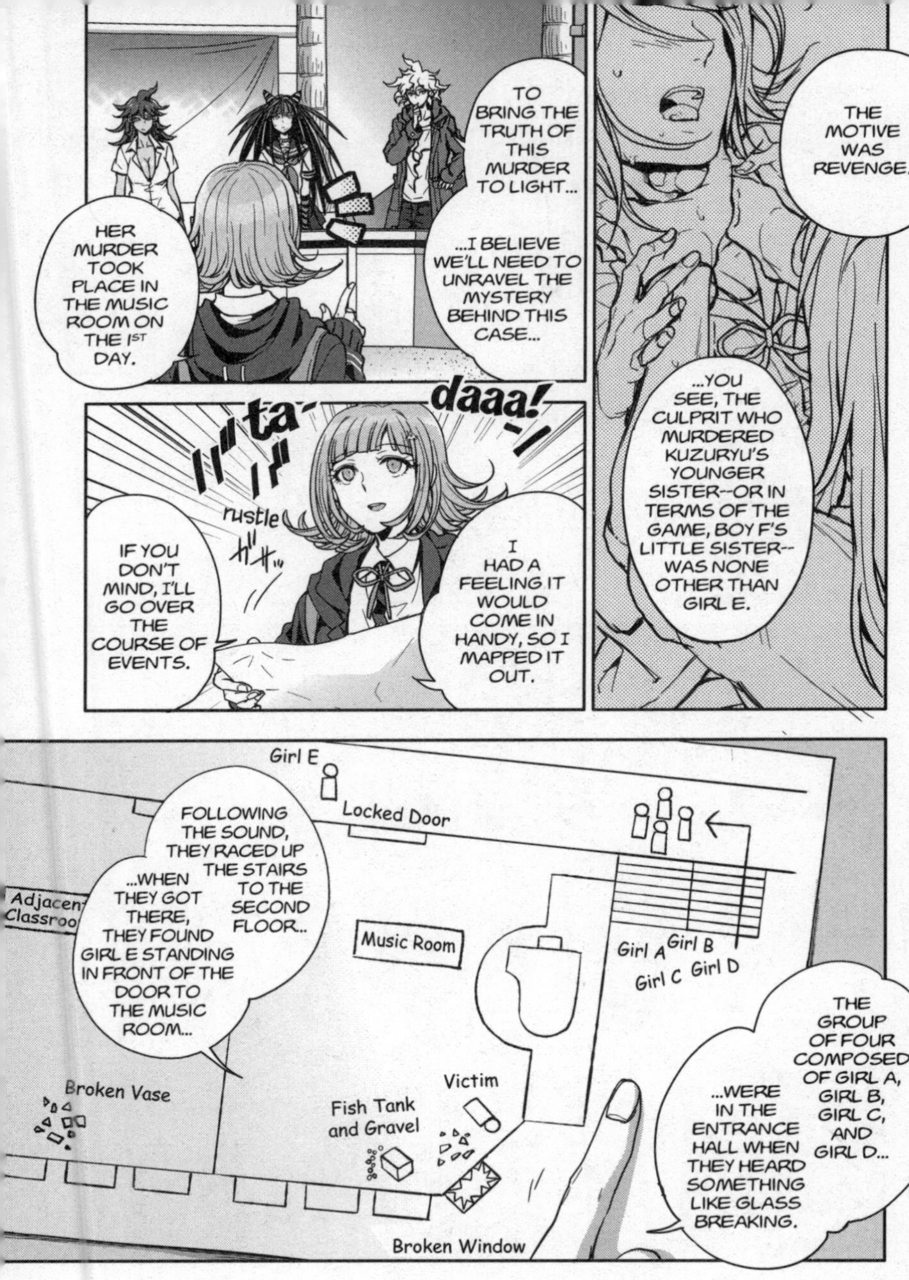
THE MOTIVE WAS REVENGE.
...YOU SEE, THE CULPRIT WHO MURDERED KUZURYU'S YOUNGER SISTER--OR IN TERMS OF THE GAME, BOY F'S LITTLE SISTER--WAS NONE OTHER THAN GIRL E.
TO BRING THE TRUTH OF THIS MURDER TO LIGHT...
...I BELIEVE WE'LL NEED TO UNRAVEL THE MYSTERY BEHIND THIS CASE...
HER MURDER TOOK PLACE IN THE MUSIC ROOM ON THE 1ST DAY.
ta-daaa!
I HAD A FEELING IT WOULD COME IN HANDY, SO I MAPPED IT OUT.
rustle
IF YOU DON'T MIND, I'LL GO OVER THE COURSE OF EVENTS.
THE GROUP OF FOUR COMPOSED OF GIRL A, GIRL B, GIRL C, AND GIRL D...
...WERE IN THE ENTRANCE HALL WHEN THEY HEARD SOMETHING LIKE GLASS BREAKING.
Girl E
Locked Door
Girl A
Girl B
Girl C
Girl D
Music Room
Adjacen
Classroo
FOLLOWING THE SOUND, THEY RACED UP THE STAIRS TO THE SECOND FLOOR...
...WHEN THEY GOT THERE, THEY FOUND GIRL E STANDING IN FRONT OF THE DOOR TO THE MUSIC ROOM...
Victim
Fish Tank and Gravel
Broken Vase
Broken Window

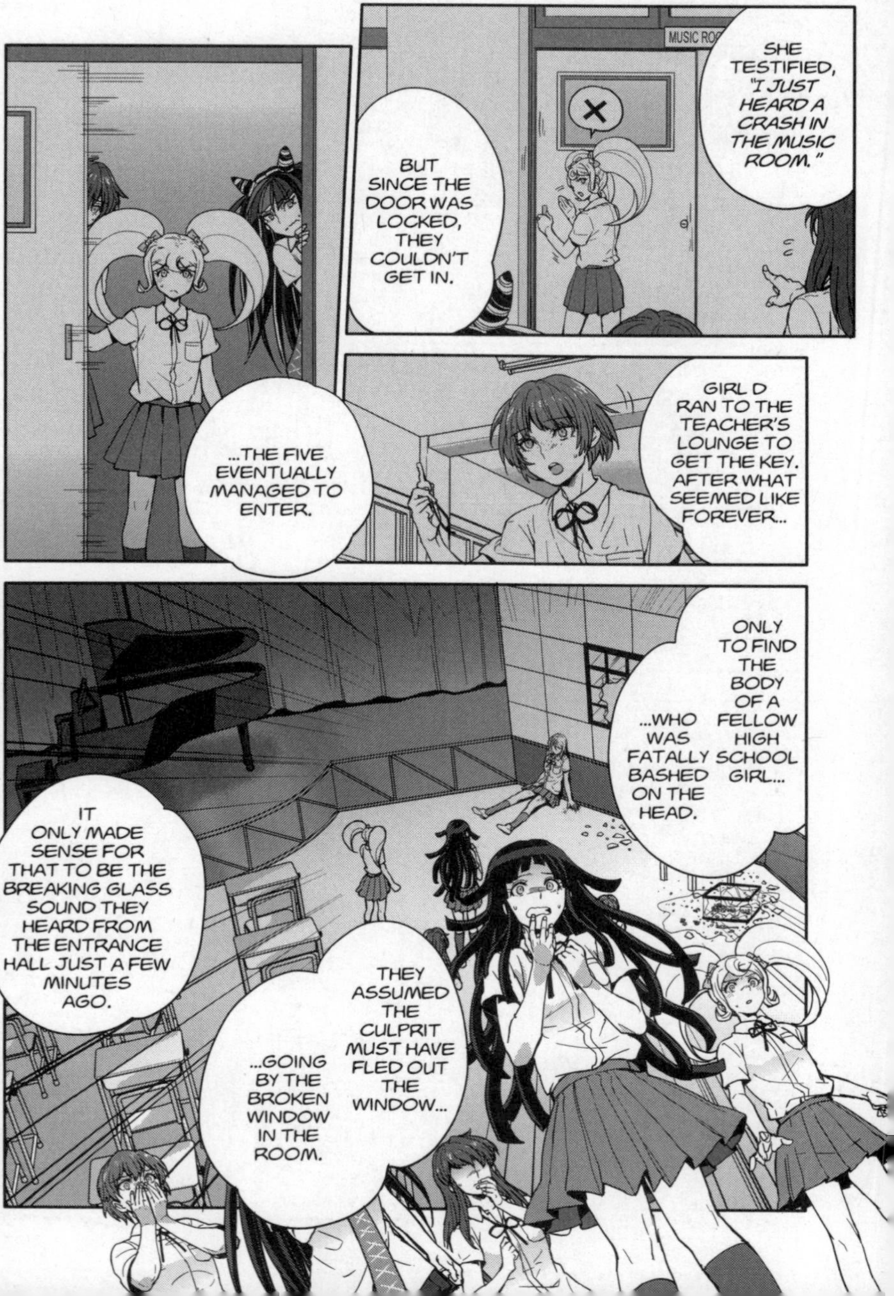
SHE TESTIFIED, "I JUST HEARD A CRASH IN THE MUSIC ROOM."
BUT SINCE THE DOOR WAS LOCKED, THEY COULDN'T GET IN.
GIRL D RAN TO THE TEACHER'S LOUNGE TO GET THE KEY. AFTER WHAT SEEMED LIKE FOREVER...
...THE FIVE EVENTUALLY MANAGED TO ENTER.
ONLY TO FIND THE BODY OF A FELLOW HIGH SCHOOL GIRL...
...WHO WAS FATALLY BASHED ON THE HEAD.
IT ONLY MADE SENSE FOR THAT TO BE THE BREAKING GLASS SOUND THEY HEARD FROM THE ENTRANCE HALL JUST A FEW MINUTES AGO.
THEY ASSUMED THE CULPRIT MUST HAVE FLED OUT THE WINDOW...
...GOING BY THE BROKEN WINDOW IN THE ROOM.

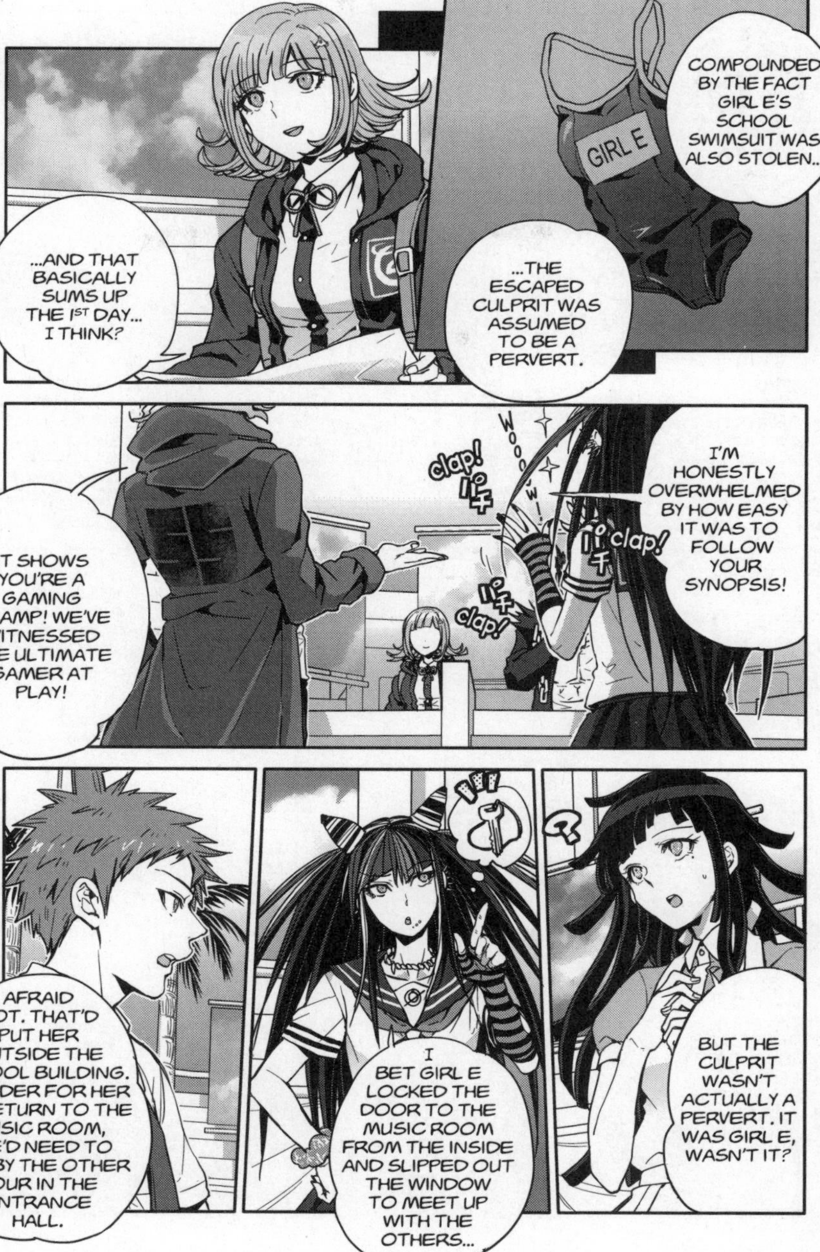
COMPOUNDED BY THE FACT GIRL E'S SCHOOL SWIMSUIT WAS ALSO STOLEN...
GIRL E
...THE ESCAPED CULPRIT WAS ASSUMED TO BE A PERVERT.
...AND THAT BASICALLY SUMS UP THE 1ST DAY... I THINK?
I'M HONESTLY OVERWHELMED BY HOW EASY IT WAS TO FOLLOW YOUR SYNOPSIS!
WOOOOOW!
clap! パチ
clap! パチ
パチ clap!
IT SHOWS YOU'RE A GAMING CHAMP! WE'VE WITNESSED THE ULTIMATE GAMER AT PLAY!
BUT THE CULPRIT WASN'T ACTUALLY A PERVERT. IT WAS GIRL E, WASN'T IT?
I BET GIRL E LOCKED THE DOOR TO THE MUSIC ROOM FROM THE INSIDE AND SLIPPED OUT THE WINDOW TO MEET UP WITH THE OTHERS...
AFRAID NOT. THAT'D PUT HER OUTSIDE THE SCHOOL BUILDING. IN ORDER FOR HER TO RETURN TO THE MUSIC ROOM, SHE'D NEED TO SLIP BY THE OTHER FOUR IN THE ENTRANCE HALL.

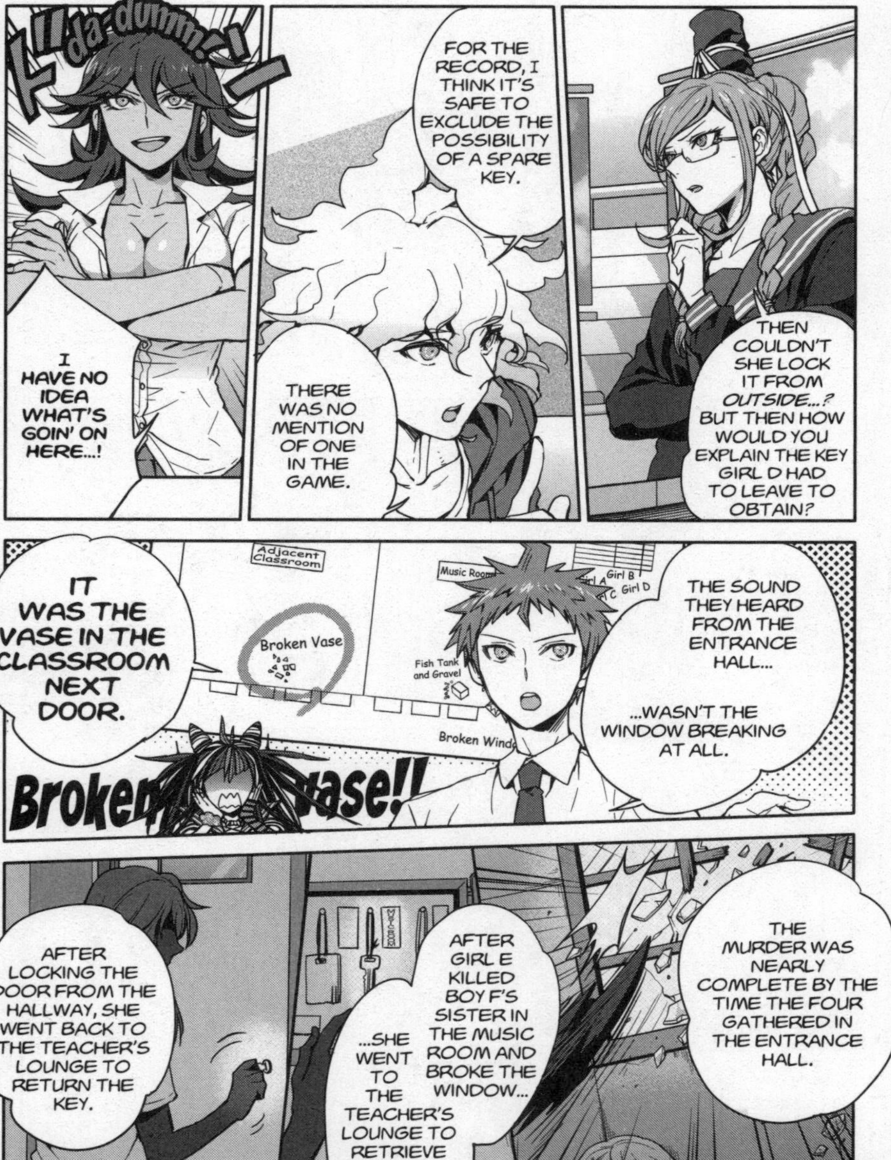
THEN COULDN'T SHE LOCK IT FROM *OUTSIDE*...? BUT THEN HOW WOULD YOU EXPLAIN THE KEY GIRL D HAD TO LEAVE TO OBTAIN?
FOR THE RECORD, I THINK IT'S SAFE TO EXCLUDE THE POSSIBILITY OF A SPARE KEY.
THERE WAS NO MENTION OF ONE IN THE GAME.
da-dumm
I HAVE NO IDEA WHAT'S GOIN' ON HERE...!
THE SOUND THEY HEARD FROM THE ENTRANCE HALL...
...WASN'T THE WINDOW BREAKING AT ALL.
Adjacent Classroom
Girl B
Girl D
Broken Vase
Fish Tank and Gravel
IT WAS THE VASE IN THE CLASSROOM NEXT DOOR.
Broken
vase!!
THE MURDER WAS NEARLY COMPLETE BY THE TIME THE FOUR GATHERED IN THE ENTRANCE HALL.
AFTER GIRL E KILLED BOY F'S SISTER IN THE MUSIC ROOM AND BROKE THE WINDOW...
...SHE WENT TO THE TEACHER'S LOUNGE TO RETRIEVE THE MUSIC ROOM'S KEY...
AFTER LOCKING THE DOOR FROM THE HALLWAY, SHE WENT BACK TO THE TEACHER'S LOUNGE TO RETURN THE KEY.

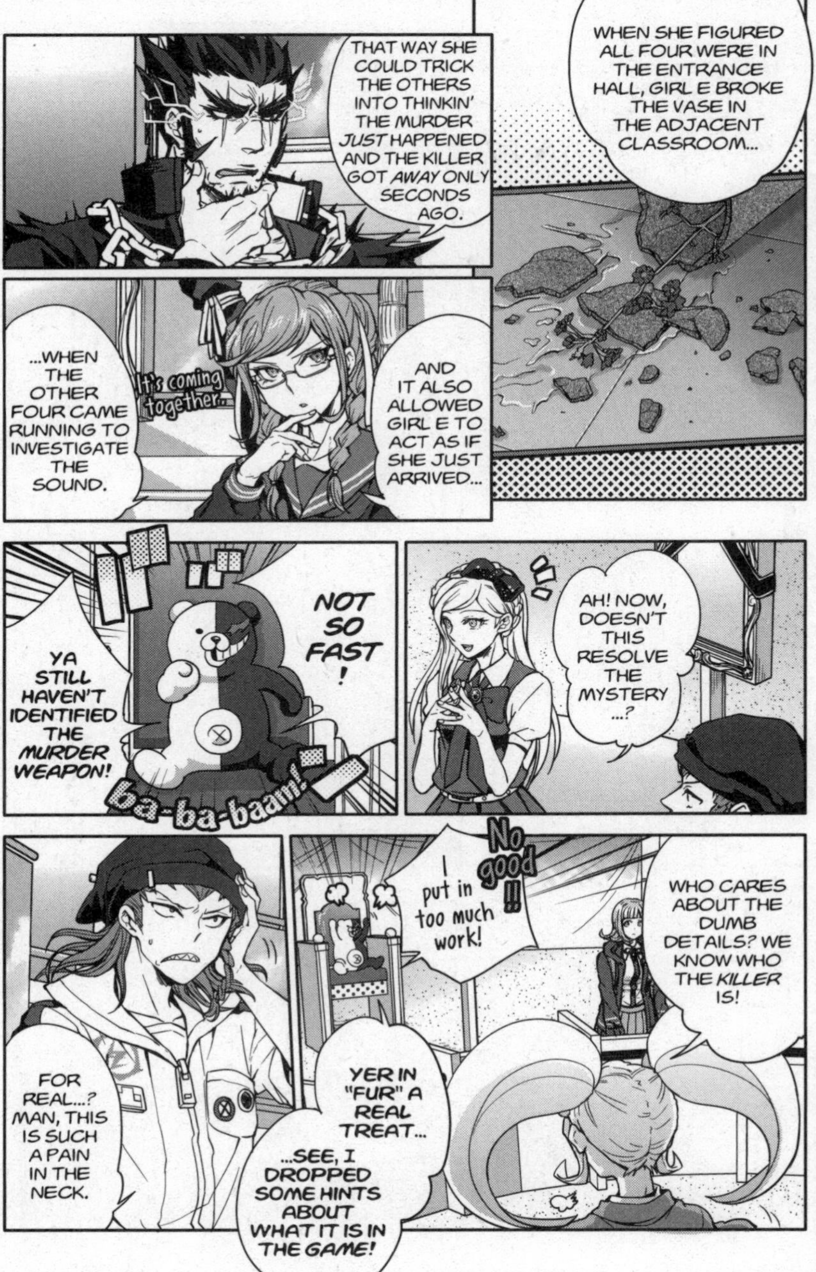
WHEN SHE FIGURED ALL FOUR WERE IN THE ENTRANCE HALL, GIRL E BROKE THE VASE IN THE ADJACENT CLASSROOM...
THAT WAY SHE COULD TRICK THE OTHERS INTO THINKIN' THE MURDER JUST HAPPENED AND THE KILLER GOT AWAY ONLY SECONDS AGO.
AND IT ALSO ALLOWED GIRL E TO ACT AS IF SHE JUST ARRIVED...
It's coming together.
...WHEN THE OTHER FOUR CAME RUNNING TO INVESTIGATE THE SOUND.
AH! NOW, DOESN'T THIS RESOLVE THE MYSTERY ...?
NOT SO FAST!
YA STILL HAVEN'T IDENTIFIED THE MURDER WEAPON!
ba-ba-baam!
WHO CARES ABOUT THE DUMB DETAILS? WE KNOW WHO THE KILLER IS!
No good!!
I put in too much work!
YER IN "FUR" A REAL TREAT...
...SEE, I DROPPED SOME HINTS ABOUT WHAT IT IS IN THE GAME!
FOR REAL...? MAN, THIS IS SUCH A PAIN IN THE NECK.

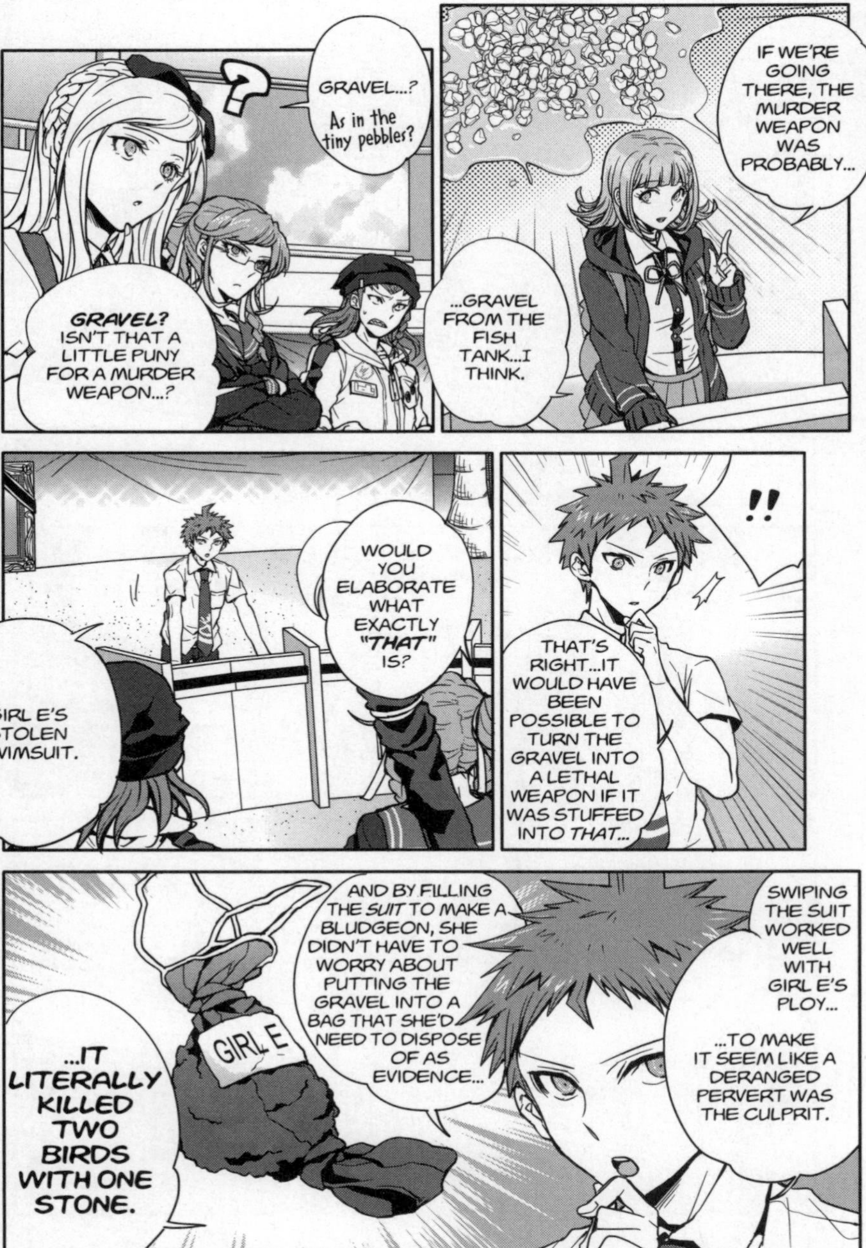
IF WE'RE GOING THERE, THE MURDER WEAPON WAS PROBABLY...
...GRAVEL FROM THE FISH TANK...I THINK.
GRAVEL...? As in the tiny pebbles?
?
GRAVEL? ISN'T THAT A LITTLE PUNY FOR A MURDER WEAPON...?
!!
THAT'S RIGHT...IT WOULD HAVE BEEN POSSIBLE TO TURN THE GRAVEL INTO A LETHAL WEAPON IF IT WAS STUFFED INTO THAT...
WOULD YOU ELABORATE WHAT EXACTLY "THAT" IS?
GIRL E'S STOLEN SWIMSUIT.
SWIPING THE SUIT WORKED WELL WITH GIRL E'S PLOY...
...TO MAKE IT SEEM LIKE A DERANGED PERVERT WAS THE CULPRIT.
AND BY FILLING THE SUIT TO MAKE A BLUDGEON, SHE DIDN'T HAVE TO WORRY ABOUT PUTTING THE GRAVEL INTO A BAG THAT SHE'D NEED TO DISPOSE OF AS EVIDENCE...
GIRL E
...IT LITERALLY KILLED TWO BIRDS WITH ONE STONE.

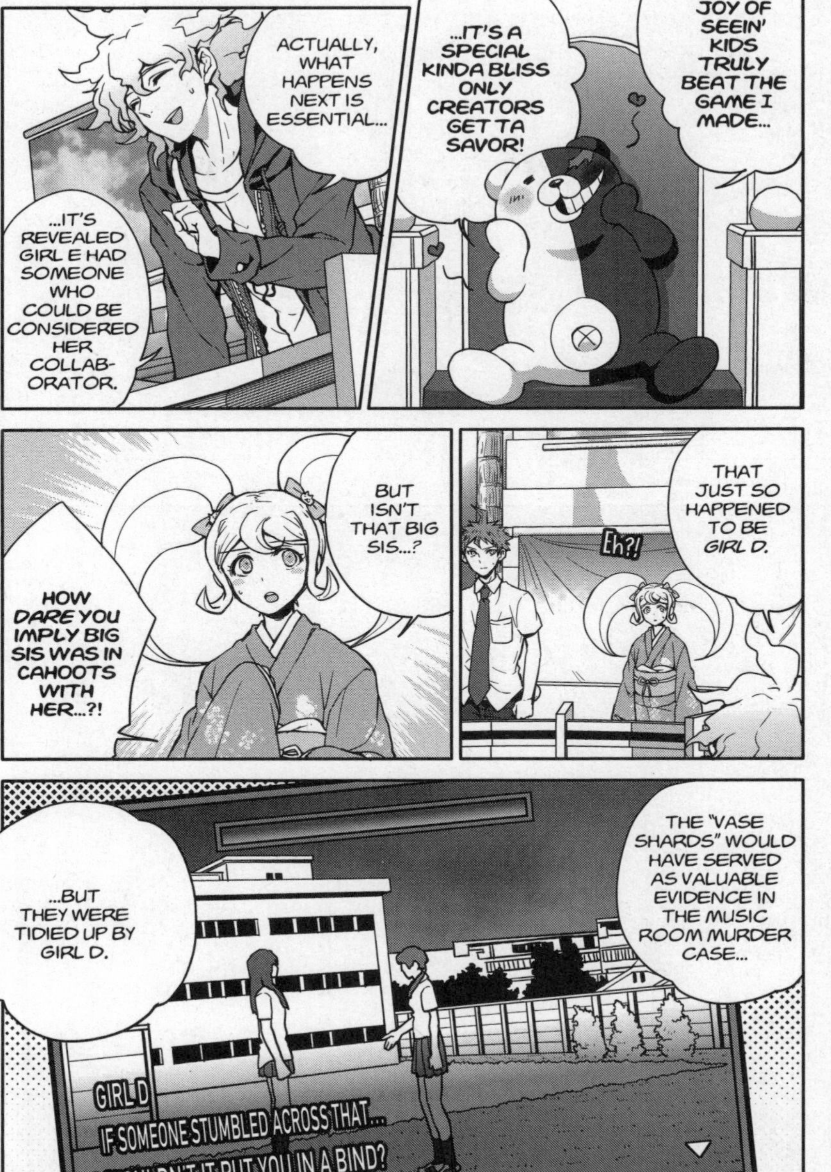
AH, THE JOY OF SEEIN' KIDS TRULY BEAT THE GAME I MADE...
...IT'S A SPECIAL KINDA BLISS ONLY CREATORS GET TA SAVOR!
ACTUALLY, WHAT HAPPENS NEXT IS ESSENTIAL...
...IT'S REVEALED GIRL E HAD SOMEONE WHO COULD BE CONSIDERED HER COLLAB-ORATOR.
THAT JUST SO HAPPENED TO BE GIRL D.
Eh?!
BUT ISN'T THAT BIG SIS...?
HOW DARE YOU IMPLY BIG SIS WAS IN CAHOOTS WITH HER...?!
THE "VASE SHARDS" WOULD HAVE SERVED AS VALUABLE EVIDENCE IN THE MUSIC ROOM MURDER CASE...
...BUT THEY WERE TIDIED UP BY GIRL D.
GIRL D
IF SOMEONE STUMBLED ACROSS THAT...
WOULDN'T IT PUT YOU IN A BIND?

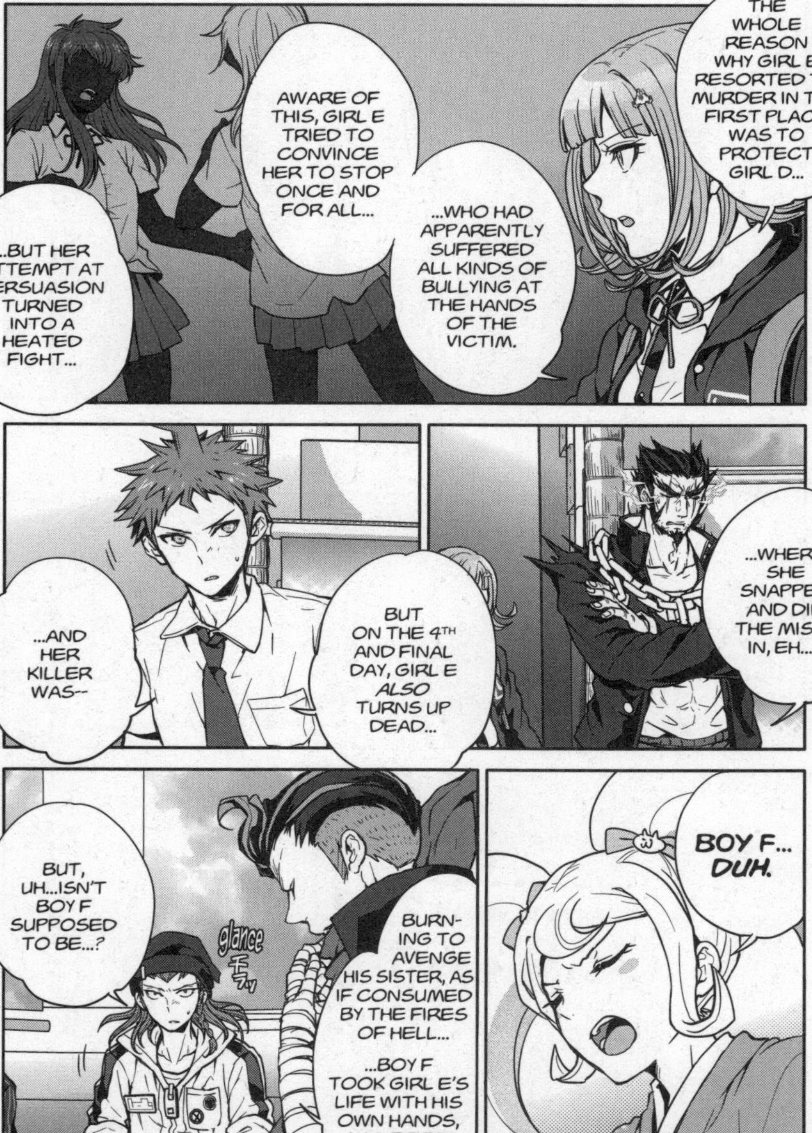
THE WHOLE REASON WHY GIRL E RESORTED TO MURDER IN THE FIRST PLACE WAS TO PROTECT GIRL D...
...WHO HAD APPARENTLY SUFFERED ALL KINDS OF BULLYING AT THE HANDS OF THE VICTIM.
AWARE OF THIS, GIRL E TRIED TO CONVINCE HER TO STOP ONCE AND FOR ALL...
...BUT HER ATTEMPT AT PERSUASION TURNED INTO A HEATED FIGHT...
...WHERE SHE SNAPPED AND DID THE MISSY IN, EH...?
BUT ON THE 4TH AND FINAL DAY, GIRL E *ALSO* TURNS UP DEAD...
...AND HER KILLER WAS--
BOY F... *DUH.*
BUT, UH...ISN'T BOY F SUPPOSED TO BE...?
glance
BURN-ING TO AVENGE HIS SISTER, AS IF CONSUMED BY THE FIRES OF HELL...
...BOY F TOOK GIRL E'S LIFE WITH HIS OWN HANDS, IN A TRIED AND TRUE CLICHÉ.

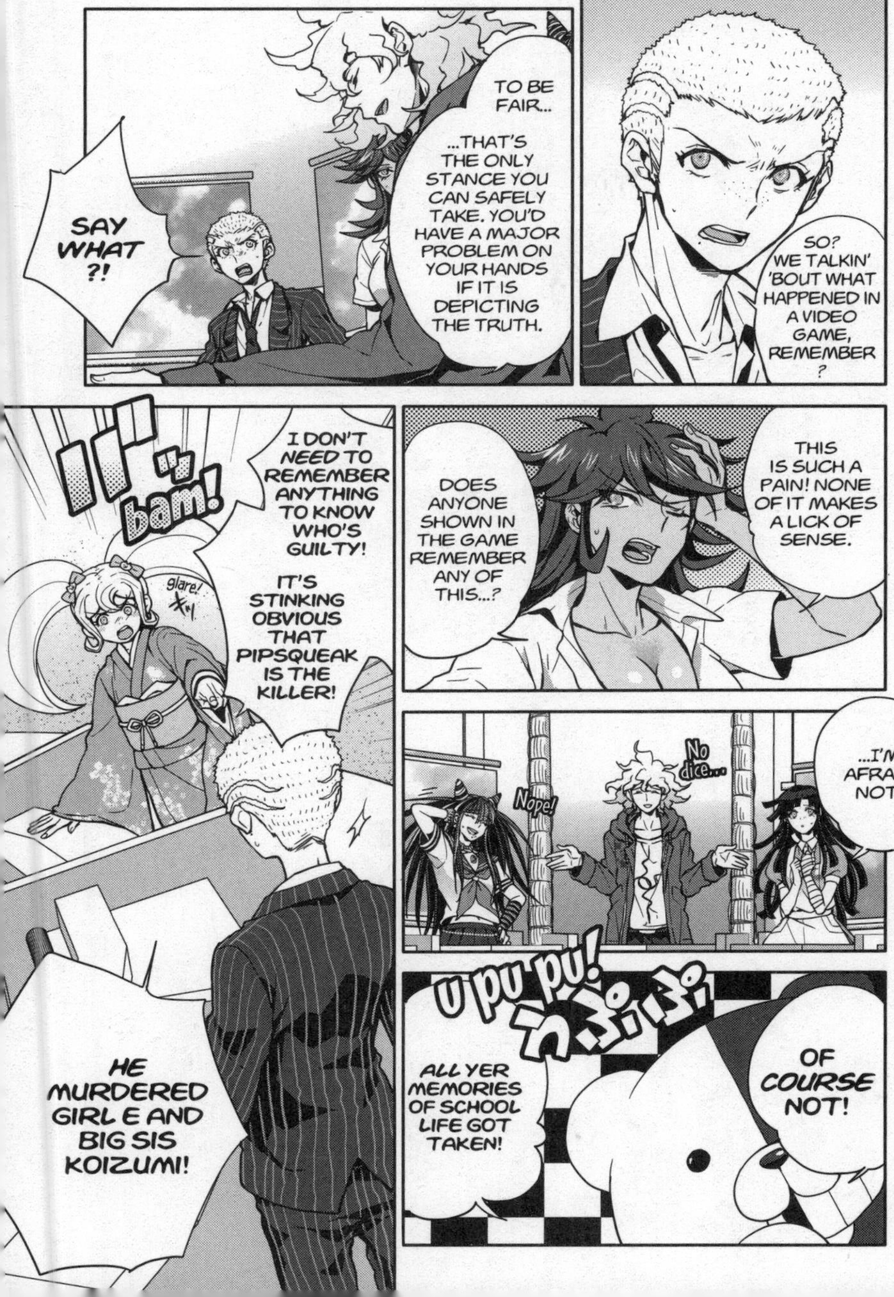
SO? WE TALKIN' 'BOUT WHAT HAPPENED IN A VIDEO GAME, REMEMBER?
TO BE FAIR...
...THAT'S THE ONLY STANCE YOU CAN SAFELY TAKE. YOU'D HAVE A MAJOR PROBLEM ON YOUR HANDS IF IT IS DEPICTING THE TRUTH.
SAY WHAT?!
THIS IS SUCH A PAIN! NONE OF IT MAKES A LICK OF SENSE.
DOES ANYONE SHOWN IN THE GAME REMEMBER ANY OF THIS...?
...I'M AFRAID NOT.
No dice...
Nope!
U PU PU!
うぷぷ
OF COURSE NOT!
ALL YER MEMORIES OF SCHOOL LIFE GOT TAKEN!
I DON'T NEED TO REMEMBER ANYTHING TO KNOW WHO'S GUILTY!
bam!
IT'S STINKING OBVIOUS THAT PIPSQUEAK IS THE KILLER!
glare!
HE MURDERED GIRL E AND BIG SIS KOIZUMI!

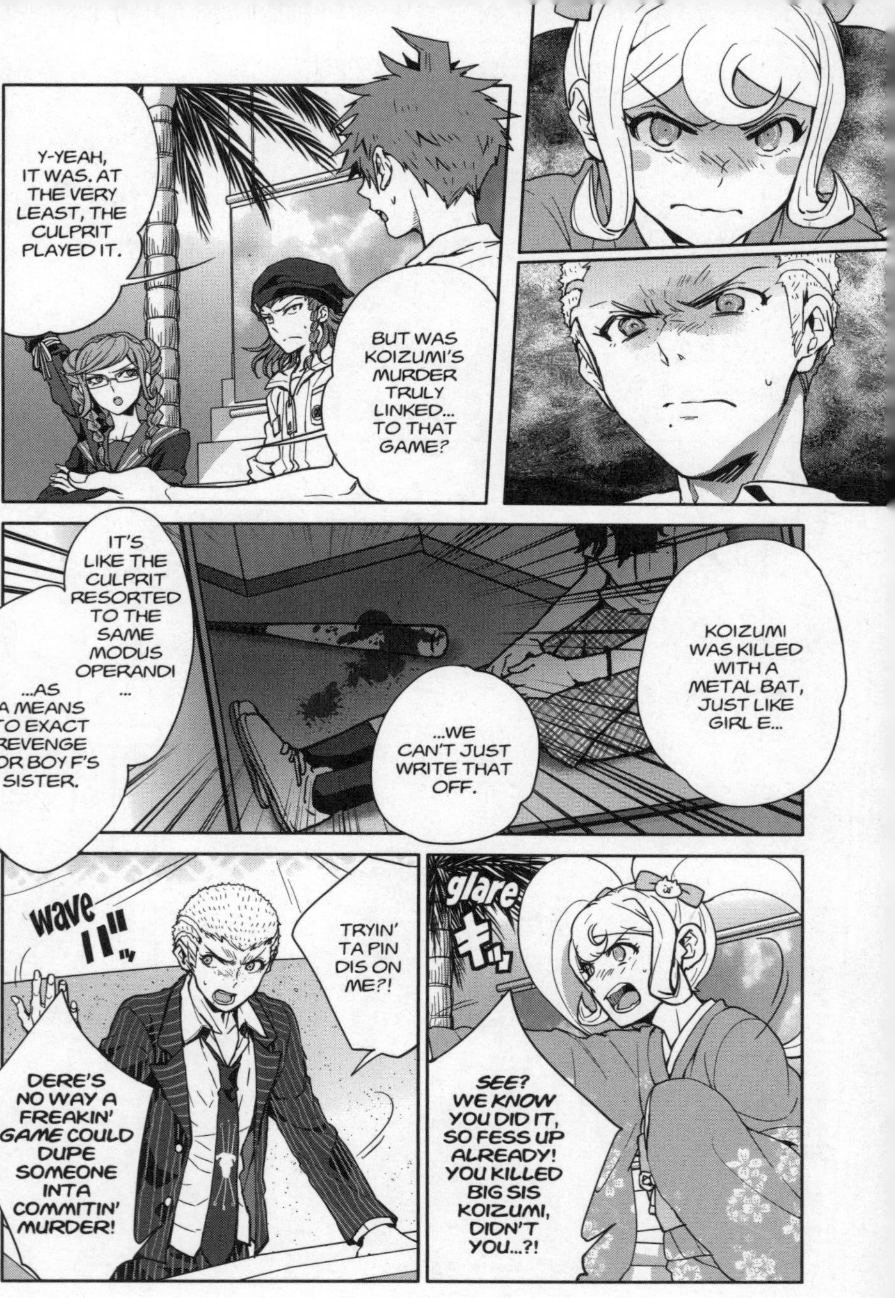
Y-YEAH, IT WAS. AT THE VERY LEAST, THE CULPRIT PLAYED IT.
BUT WAS KOIZUMI'S MURDER TRULY LINKED... TO THAT GAME?
KOIZUMI WAS KILLED WITH A METAL BAT, JUST LIKE GIRL E...
...WE CAN'T JUST WRITE THAT OFF.
IT'S LIKE THE CULPRIT RESORTED TO THE SAME MODUS OPERANDI...
...AS A MEANS TO EXACT REVENGE FOR BOY F'S SISTER.
glare
SEE? WE KNOW YOU DID IT, SO FESS UP ALREADY! YOU KILLED BIG SIS KOIZUMI, DIDN'T YOU...?!
wave
TRYIN' TA PIN DIS ON ME?!
DERE'S NO WAY A FREAKIN' GAME COULD DUPE SOMEONE INTA COMMITIN' MURDER!

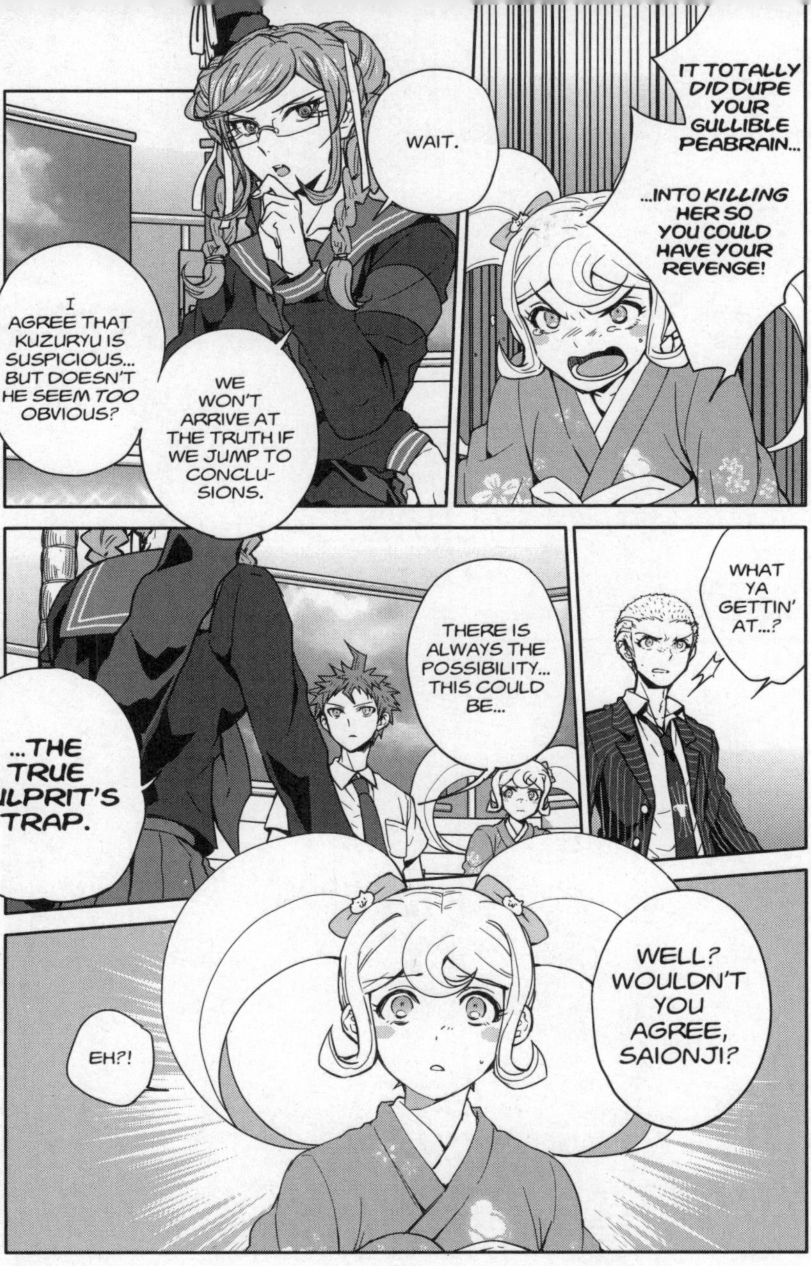
IT TOTALLY DID DUPE YOUR GULLIBLE PEABRAIN...
...INTO KILLING HER SO YOU COULD HAVE YOUR REVENGE!
WAIT.
I AGREE THAT KUZURYU IS SUSPICIOUS... BUT DOESN'T HE SEEM TOO OBVIOUS?
WE WON'T ARRIVE AT THE TRUTH IF WE JUMP TO CONCLUSIONS.
WHAT YA GETTIN' AT...?
THERE IS ALWAYS THE POSSIBILITY... THIS COULD BE...
...THE TRUE CULPRIT'S TRAP.
WELL? WOULDN'T YOU AGREE, SAIONJI?
EH?!

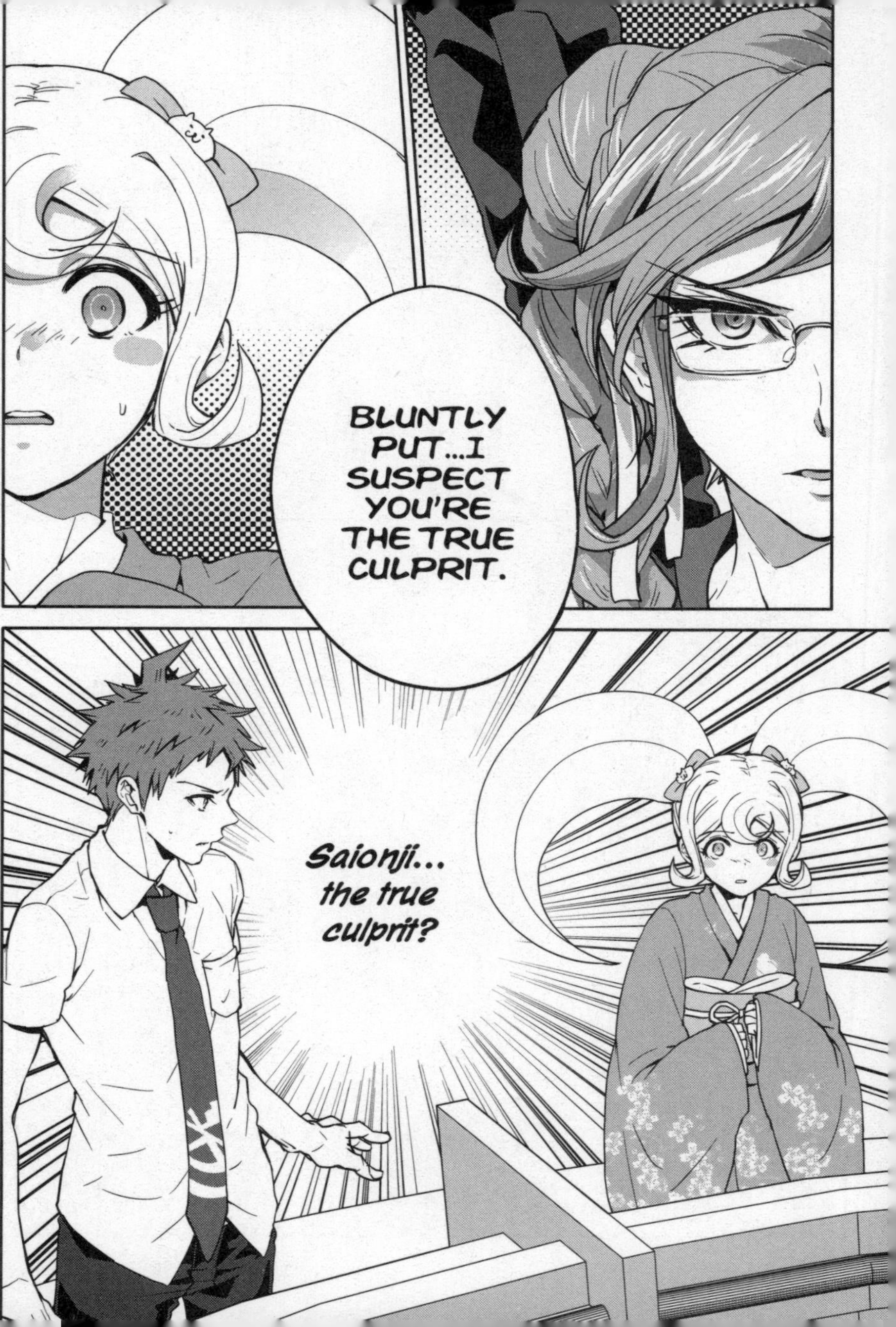
BLUNTLY PUT...I SUSPECT YOU'RE THE TRUE CULPRIT.
Saionji... the true culprit?

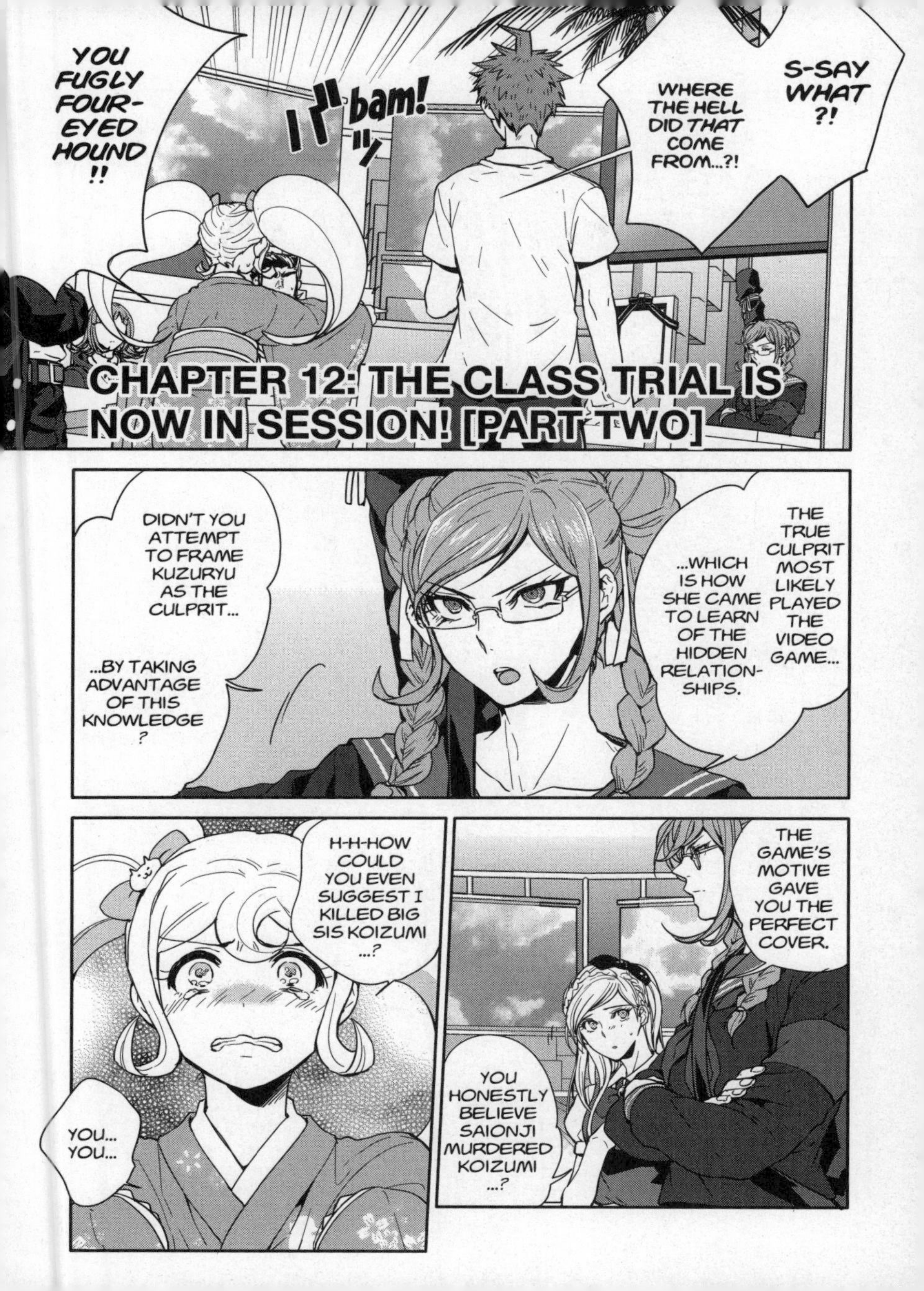
S-SAY WHAT?!
WHERE THE HELL DID THAT COME FROM...?!
bam!
YOU FUGLY FOUR-EYED HOUND!!
CHAPTER 12: THE CLASS TRIAL IS NOW IN SESSION! [PART TWO]
THE TRUE CULPRIT MOST LIKELY PLAYED THE VIDEO GAME...
...WHICH IS HOW SHE CAME TO LEARN OF THE HIDDEN RELATIONSHIPS.
DIDN'T YOU ATTEMPT TO FRAME KUZURYU AS THE CULPRIT...
...BY TAKING ADVANTAGE OF THIS KNOWLEDGE?
THE GAME'S MOTIVE GAVE YOU THE PERFECT COVER.
YOU HONESTLY BELIEVE SAIONJI MURDERED KOIZUMI...?
H-H-HOW COULD YOU EVEN SUGGEST I KILLED BIG SIS KOIZUMI...?
YOU... YOU...

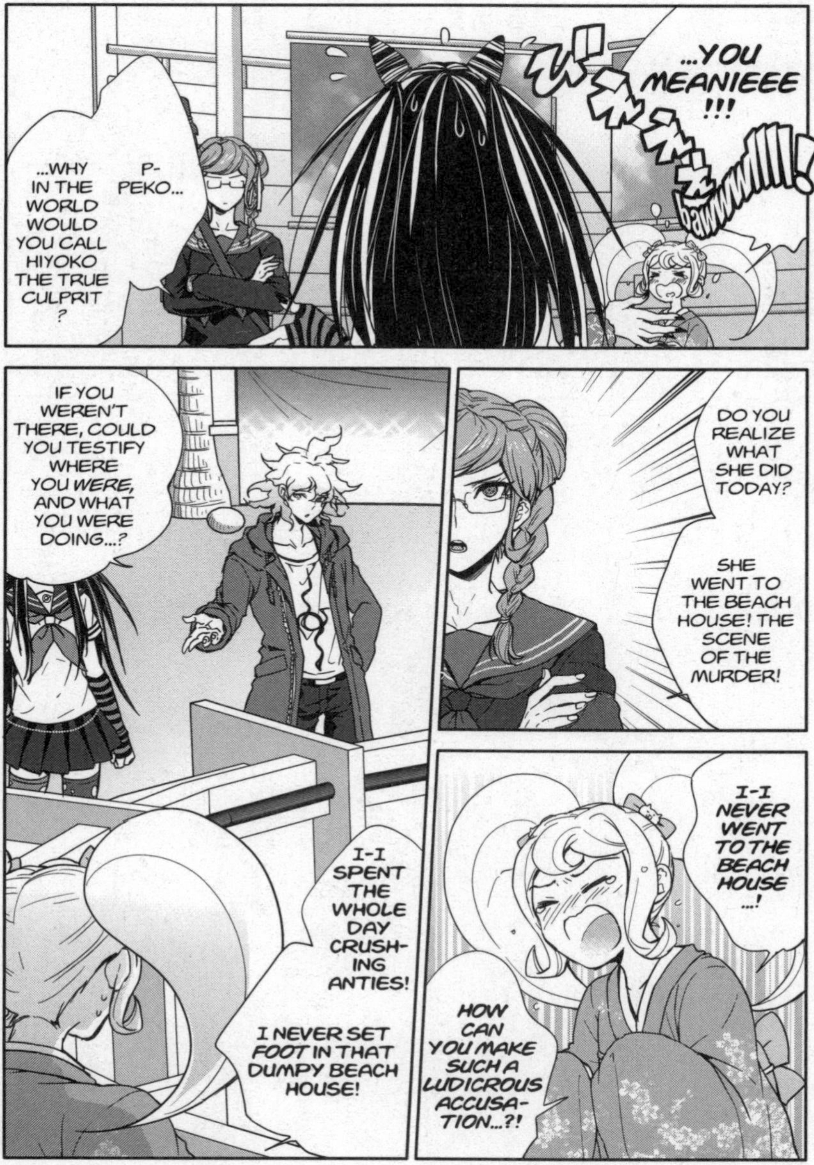
...YOU MEANIEEE!!!
bawwwllll!
P-PEKO...
...WHY IN THE WORLD WOULD YOU CALL HIYOKO THE TRUE CULPRIT?
DO YOU REALIZE WHAT SHE DID TODAY?
SHE WENT TO THE BEACH HOUSE! THE SCENE OF THE MURDER!
I-I NEVER WENT TO THE BEACH HOUSE...!
HOW CAN YOU MAKE SUCH A LUDICROUS ACCUSATION...?!
IF YOU WEREN'T THERE, COULD YOU TESTIFY WHERE YOU WERE, AND WHAT YOU WERE DOING...?
I-I SPENT THE WHOLE DAY CRUSHING ANTIES!
I NEVER SET FOOT IN THAT DUMPY BEACH HOUSE!

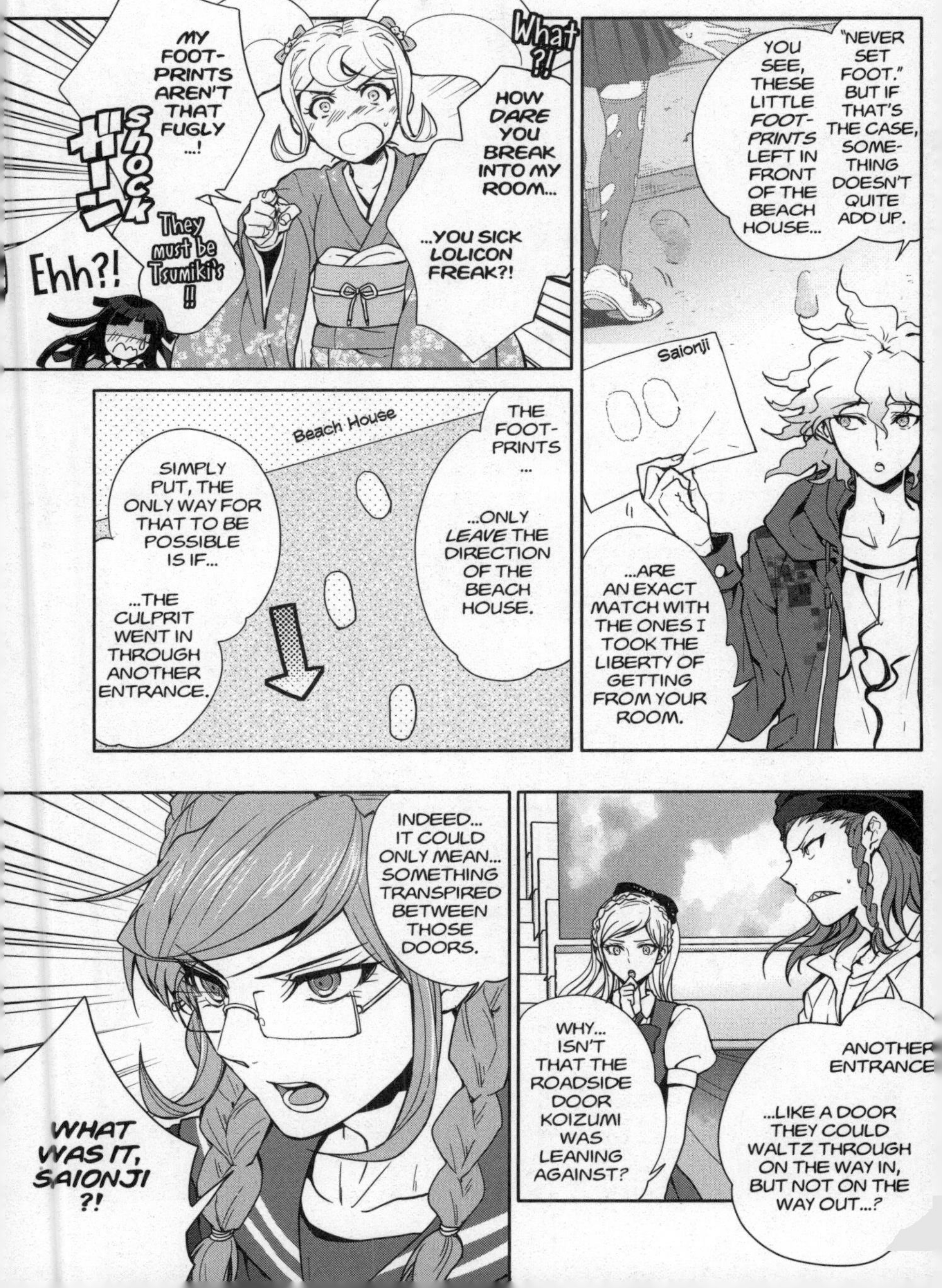
"NEVER SET FOOT." BUT IF THAT'S THE CASE, SOMETHING DOESN'T QUITE ADD UP.
YOU SEE, THESE LITTLE FOOTPRINTS LEFT IN FRONT OF THE BEACH HOUSE...
Saionji
...ARE AN EXACT MATCH WITH THE ONES I TOOK THE LIBERTY OF GETTING FROM YOUR ROOM.
What?!
HOW DARE YOU BREAK INTO MY ROOM...
...YOU SICK LOLICON FREAK?!
MY FOOTPRINTS AREN'T THAT FUGLY...!
Shock
They must be Tsumiki's!!
Ehh?!
Beach House
THE FOOTPRINTS...
...ONLY LEAVE THE DIRECTION OF THE BEACH HOUSE.
SIMPLY PUT, THE ONLY WAY FOR THAT TO BE POSSIBLE IS IF...
...THE CULPRIT WENT IN THROUGH ANOTHER ENTRANCE.
ANOTHER ENTRANCE
...LIKE A DOOR THEY COULD WALTZ THROUGH ON THE WAY IN, BUT NOT ON THE WAY OUT...?
WHY... ISN'T THAT THE ROADSIDE DOOR KOIZUMI WAS LEANING AGAINST?
INDEED... IT COULD ONLY MEAN... SOMETHING TRANSPIRED BETWEEN THOSE DOORS.
WHAT WAS IT, SAIONJI?!

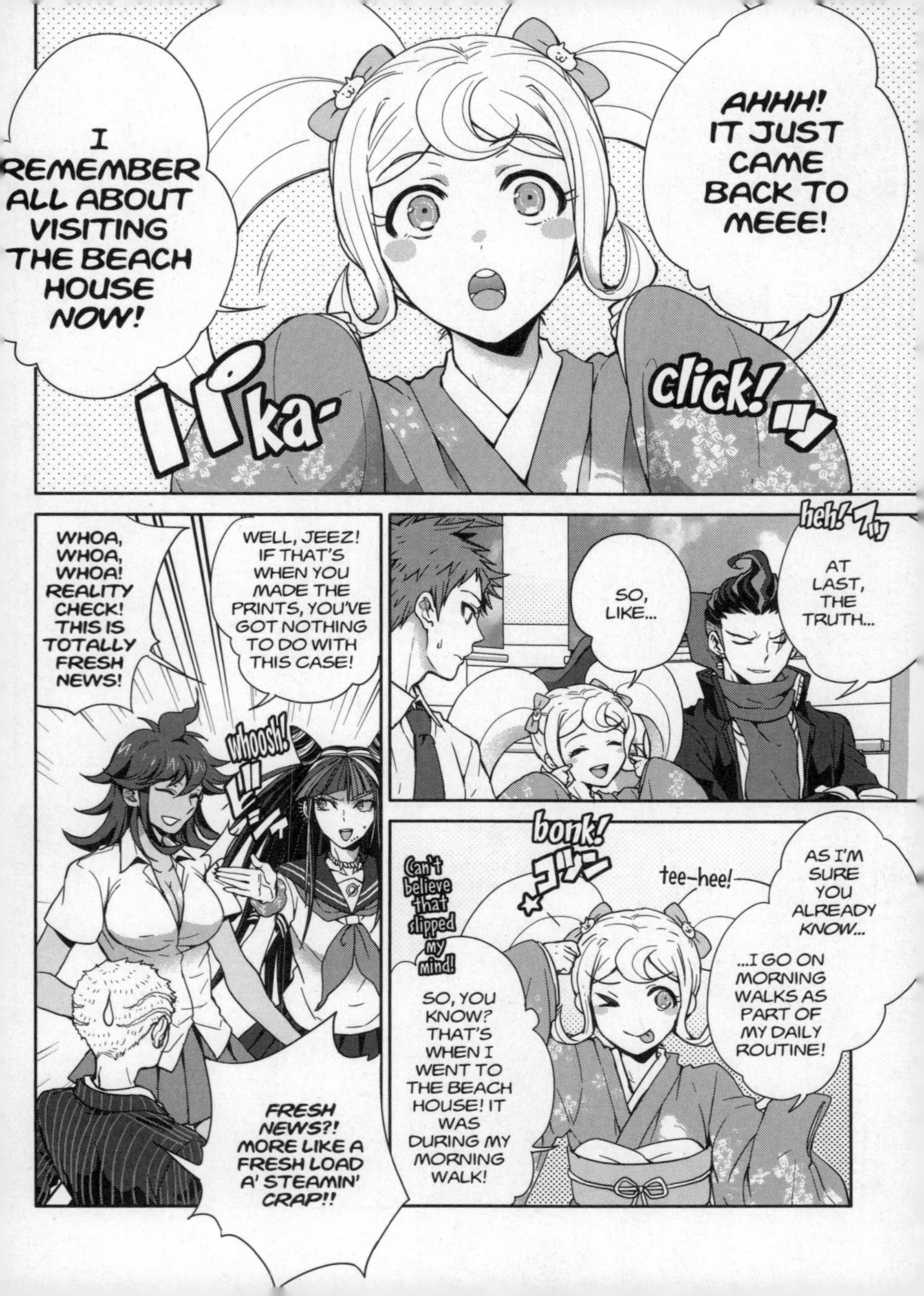
AHHH! IT JUST CAME BACK TO MEEE!
I REMEMBER ALL ABOUT VISITING THE BEACH HOUSE NOW!
ka-click!
heh!
AT LAST, THE TRUTH...
SO, LIKE...
bonk!
AS I'M SURE YOU ALREADY KNOW...
...I GO ON MORNING WALKS AS PART OF MY DAILY ROUTINE!
tee-hee!
Can't believe that slipped my mind!
SO, YOU KNOW? THAT'S WHEN I WENT TO THE BEACH HOUSE! IT WAS DURING MY MORNING WALK!
WELL, JEEZ! IF THAT'S WHEN YOU MADE THE PRINTS, YOU'VE GOT NOTHING TO DO WITH THIS CASE!
WHOA, WHOA, WHOA! REALITY CHECK! THIS IS TOTALLY FRESH NEWS!
whoosh!
FRESH NEWS?! MORE LIKE A FRESH LOAD A' STEAMIN' CRAP!!

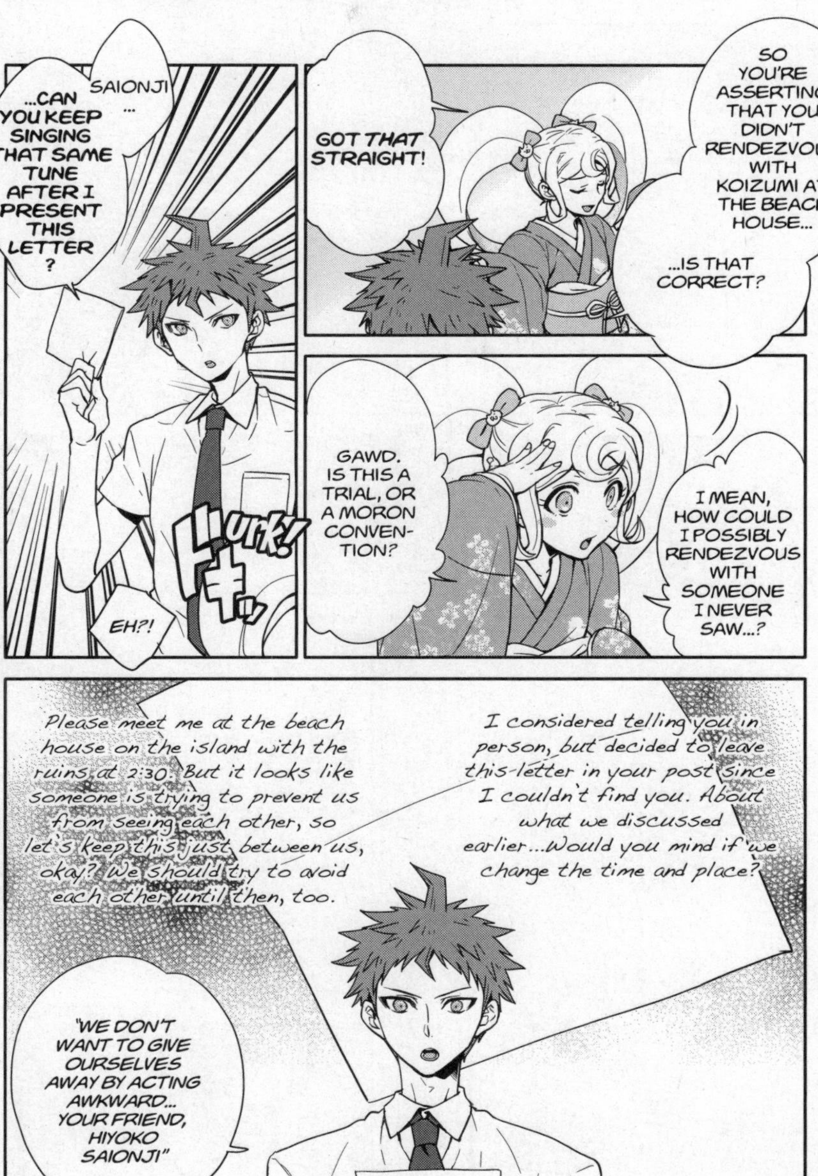
SO YOU'RE ASSERTING THAT YOU DIDN'T RENDEZVOUS WITH KOIZUMI AT THE BEACH HOUSE...
...IS THAT CORRECT?
GOT THAT STRAIGHT!
I MEAN, HOW COULD I POSSIBLY RENDEZVOUS WITH SOMEONE I NEVER SAW...?
GAWD. IS THIS A TRIAL, OR A MORON CONVEN-TION?
SAIONJI...
...CAN YOU KEEP SINGING THAT SAME TUNE AFTER I PRESENT THIS LETTER?
Hurk!
EH?!
I considered telling you in person, but decided to leave this letter in your post since I couldn't find you. About what we discussed earlier...Would you mind if we change the time and place?
Please meet me at the beach house on the island with the ruins at 2:30. But it looks like someone is trying to prevent us from seeing each other, so let's keep this just between us, okay? We should try to avoid each other until then, too.
"WE DON'T WANT TO GIVE OURSELVES AWAY BY ACTING AWKWARD... YOUR FRIEND, HIYOKO SAIONJI"

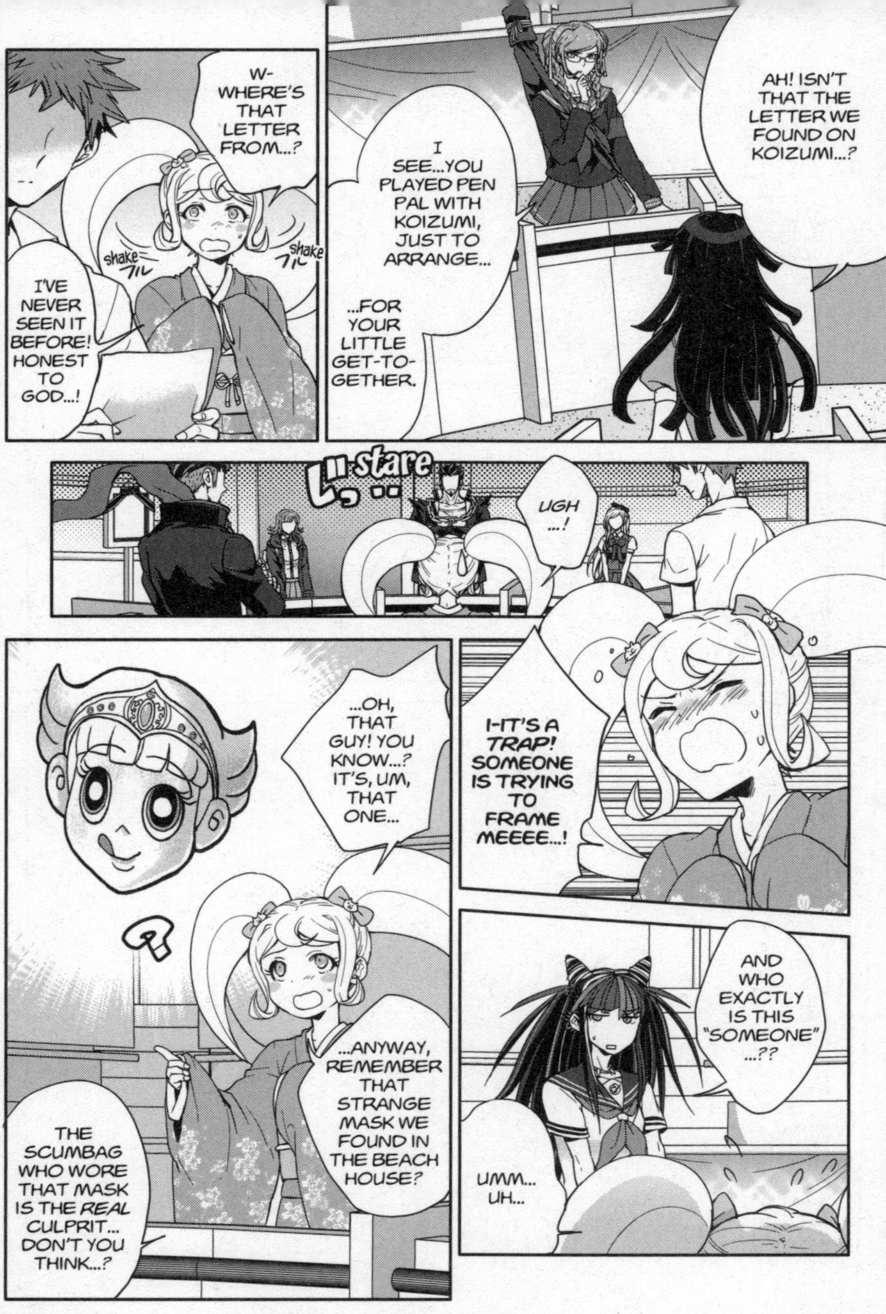
AH! ISN'T THAT THE LETTER WE FOUND ON KOIZUMI...?
I SEE...YOU PLAYED PEN PAL WITH KOIZUMI, JUST TO ARRANGE...
...FOR YOUR LITTLE GET-TO-GETHER.
W-WHERE'S THAT LETTER FROM...?
shake フル
shake フル
I'VE NEVER SEEN IT BEFORE! HONEST TO GOD...!
stare
UGH ...!
I-IT'S A *TRAP!* SOMEONE IS TRYING TO FRAME MEEEE...!
AND WHO EXACTLY IS THIS "SOMEONE" ...??
UMM... UH...
...OH, THAT GUY! YOU KNOW...? IT'S, UM, THAT ONE...
...ANYWAY, REMEMBER THAT STRANGE MASK WE FOUND IN THE BEACH HOUSE?
THE SCUMBAG WHO WORE THAT MASK IS THE *REAL* CULPRIT... DON'T YOU THINK...?

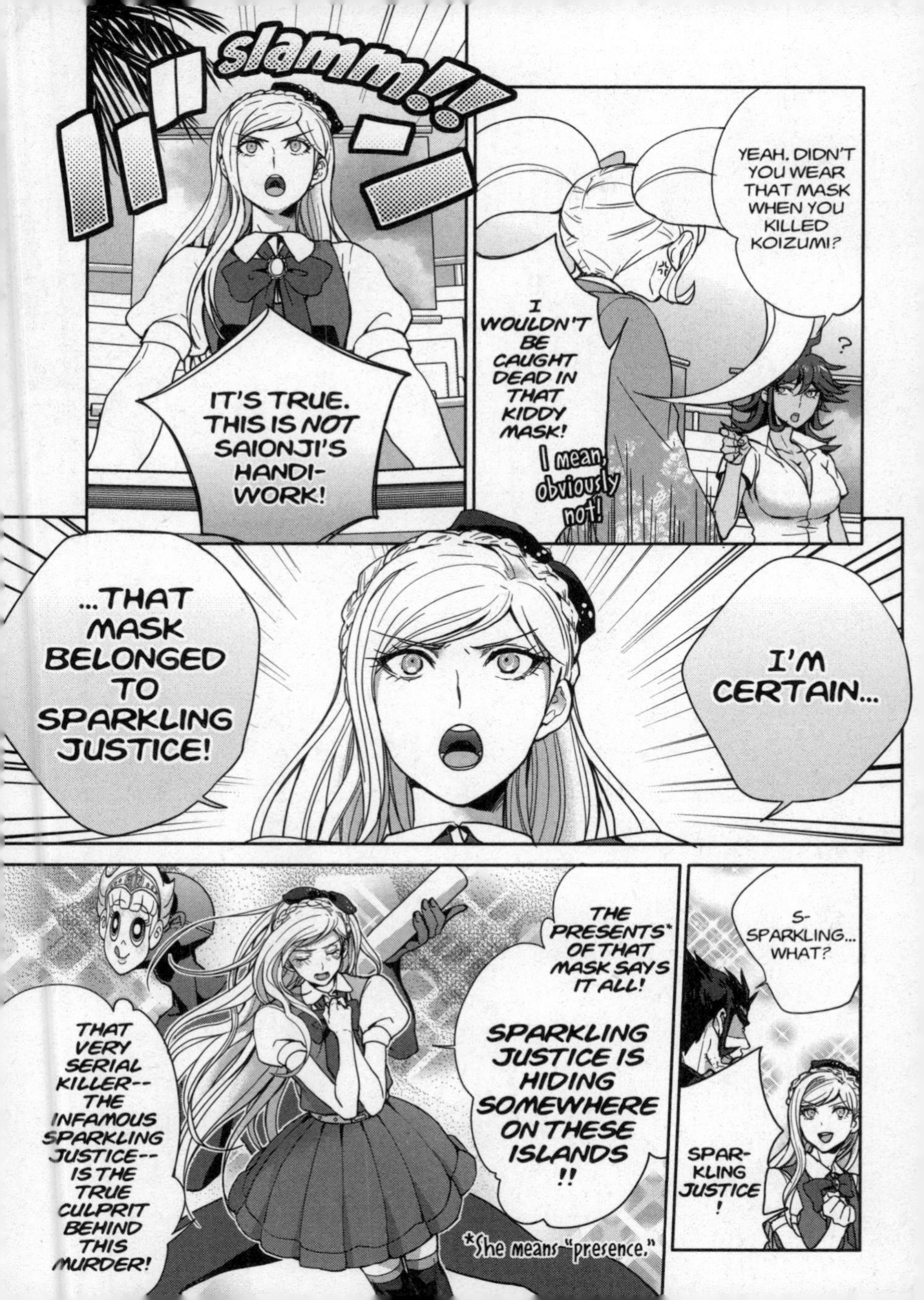
YEAH. DIDN'T YOU WEAR THAT MASK WHEN YOU KILLED KOIZUMI?
I WOULDN'T BE CAUGHT DEAD IN THAT KIDDY MASK!
I mean, obviously not!
?
slamm!!
IT'S TRUE. THIS IS NOT SAIONJI'S HANDI-WORK!
I'M CERTAIN...
...THAT MASK BELONGED TO SPARKLING JUSTICE!
S-SPARKLING... WHAT?
SPAR-KLING JUSTICE!
THE PRESENTS* OF THAT MASK SAYS IT ALL!
SPARKLING JUSTICE IS HIDING SOMEWHERE ON THESE ISLANDS!!
THAT VERY SERIAL KILLER--THE INFAMOUS SPARKLING JUSTICE--IS THE TRUE CULPRIT BEHIND THIS MURDER!
*She means "presence."

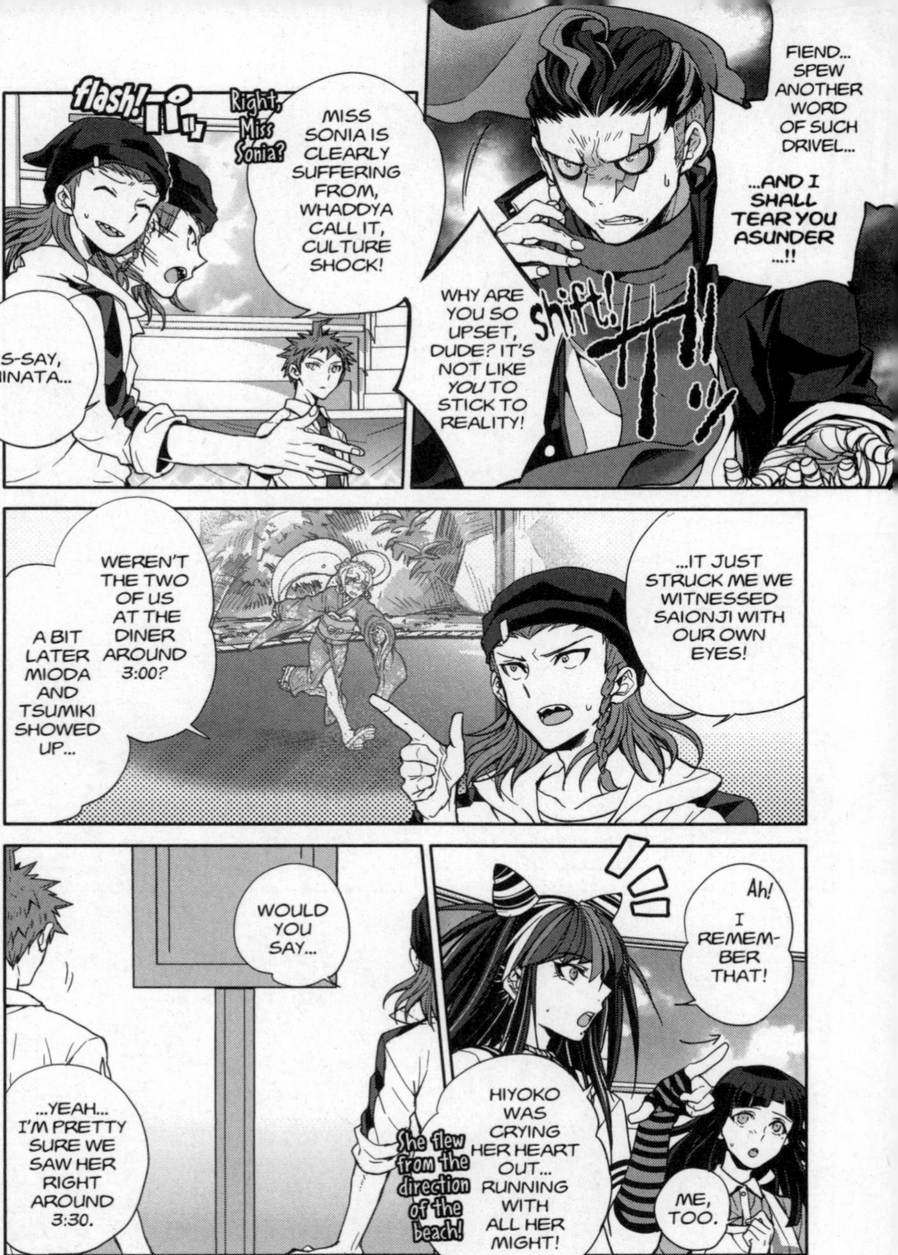
FIEND... SPEW ANOTHER WORD OF SUCH DRIVEL...
...AND I SHALL TEAR YOU ASUNDER ...!!
shift!
WHY ARE YOU SO UPSET, DUDE? IT'S NOT LIKE YOU TO STICK TO REALITY!
MISS SONIA IS CLEARLY SUFFERING FROM, WHADDYA CALL IT, CULTURE SHOCK!
Right, Miss Sonia?
flash!
S-SAY, HINATA...
...IT JUST STRUCK ME WE WITNESSED SAIONJI WITH OUR OWN EYES!
WEREN'T THE TWO OF US AT THE DINER AROUND 3:00?
A BIT LATER MIODA AND TSUMIKI SHOWED UP...
Ah!
I REMEMBER THAT!
HIYOKO WAS CRYING HER HEART OUT... RUNNING WITH ALL HER MIGHT!
She flew from the direction of the beach!
ME, TOO.
WOULD YOU SAY...
...YEAH... I'M PRETTY SURE WE SAW HER RIGHT AROUND 3:30.

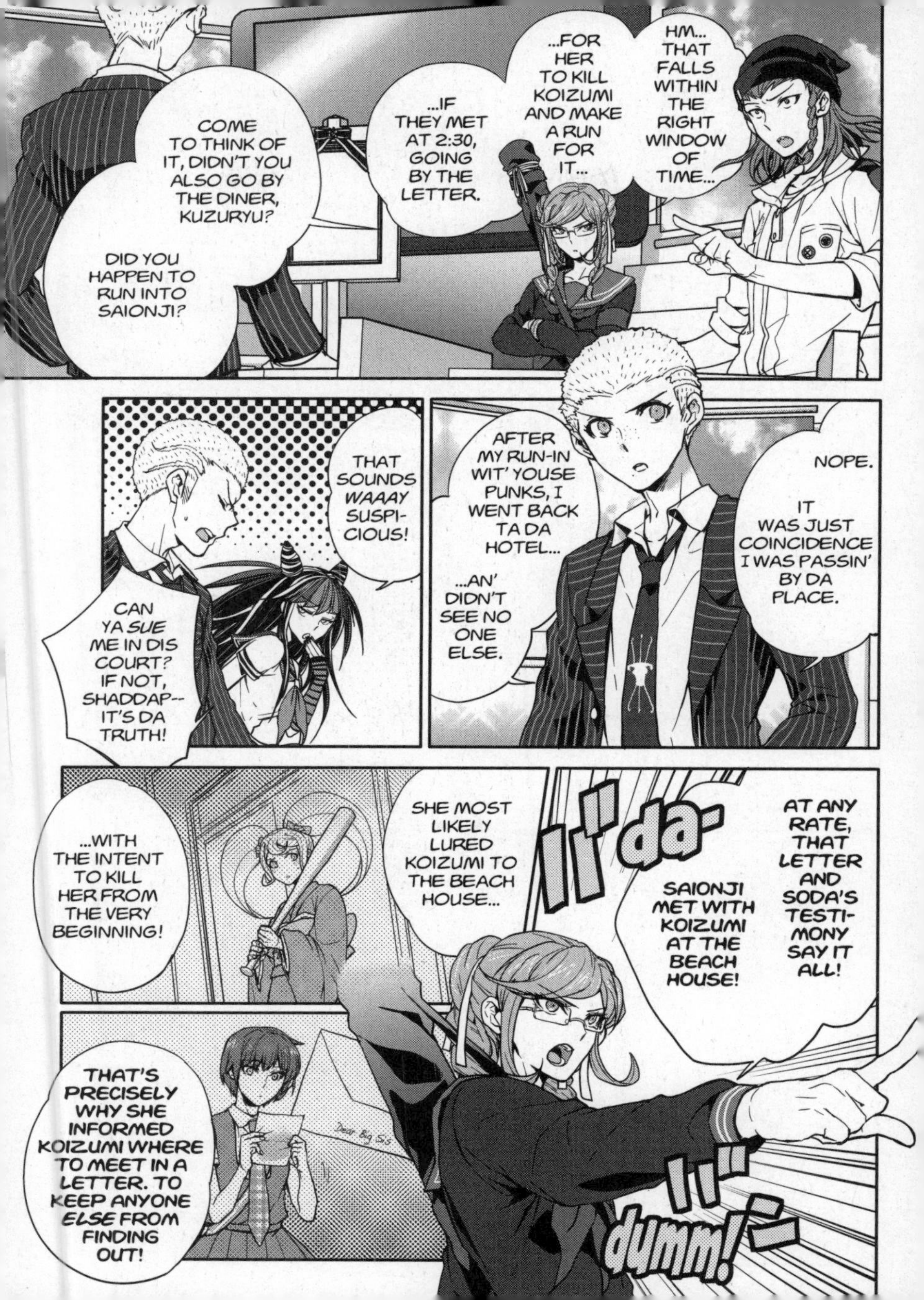
HM... THAT FALLS WITHIN THE RIGHT WINDOW OF TIME...
...FOR HER TO KILL KOIZUMI AND MAKE A RUN FOR IT...
...IF THEY MET AT 2:30, GOING BY THE LETTER.
COME TO THINK OF IT, DIDN'T YOU ALSO GO BY THE DINER, KUZURYU?
DID YOU HAPPEN TO RUN INTO SAIONJI?
NOPE.
IT WAS JUST COINCIDENCE I WAS PASSIN' BY DA PLACE.
AFTER MY RUN-IN WIT' YOUSE PUNKS, I WENT BACK TA DA HOTEL...
...AN' DIDN'T SEE NO ONE ELSE.
THAT SOUNDS *WAAAY* SUSPICIOUS!
CAN YA *SUE* ME IN DIS COURT? IF NOT, SHADDAP-- IT'S DA TRUTH!
AT ANY RATE, THAT LETTER AND SODA'S TESTIMONY SAY IT ALL!
SAIONJI MET WITH KOIZUMI AT THE BEACH HOUSE!
da-
dumm!
SHE MOST LIKELY LURED KOIZUMI TO THE BEACH HOUSE...
...WITH THE INTENT TO KILL HER FROM THE VERY BEGINNING!
Dear Big Sis
THAT'S PRECISELY WHY SHE INFORMED KOIZUMI WHERE TO MEET IN A LETTER. TO KEEP ANYONE *ELSE* FROM FINDING OUT!

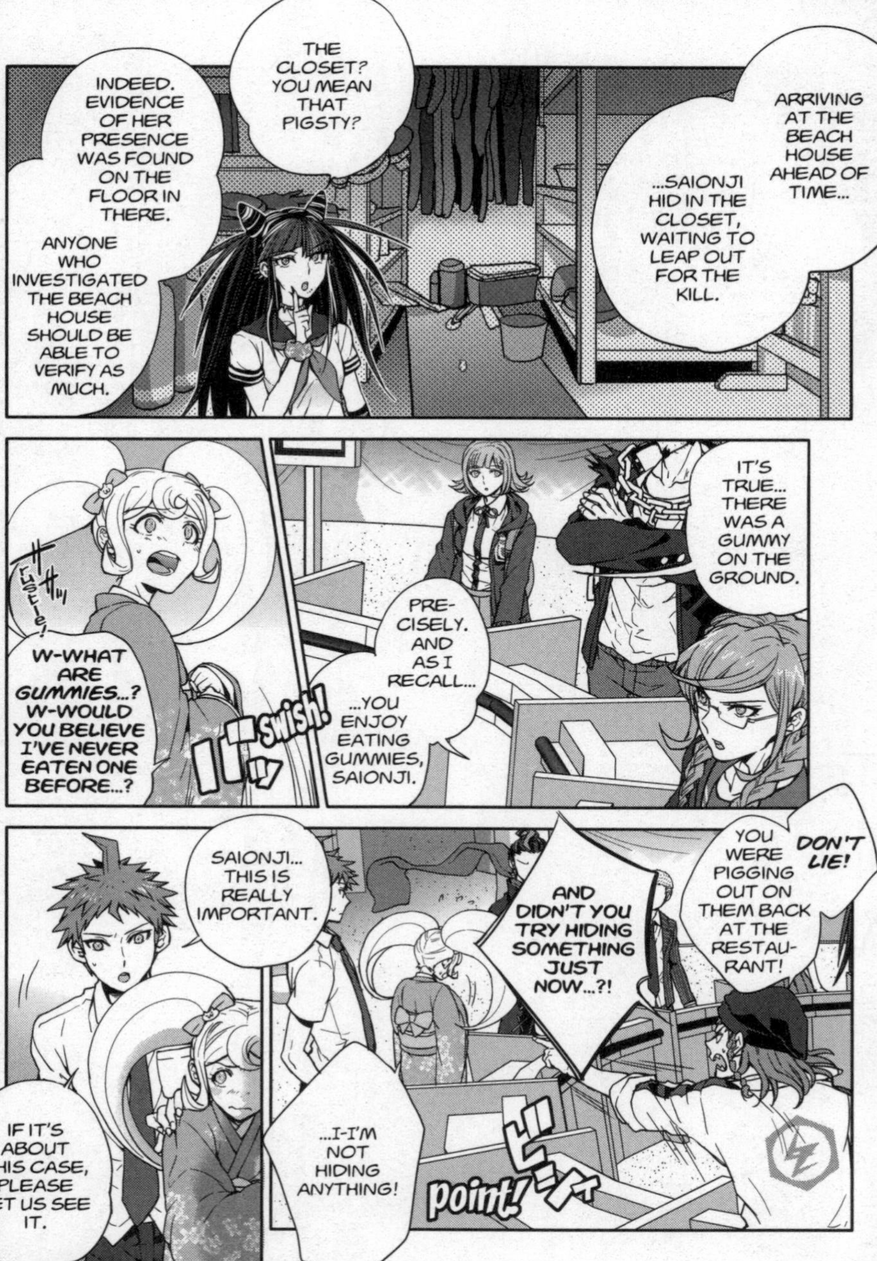
ARRIVING AT THE BEACH HOUSE AHEAD OF TIME...
...SAIONJI HID IN THE CLOSET, WAITING TO LEAP OUT FOR THE KILL.
THE CLOSET? YOU MEAN THAT PIGSTY?
INDEED. EVIDENCE OF HER PRESENCE WAS FOUND ON THE FLOOR IN THERE.
ANYONE WHO INVESTIGATED THE BEACH HOUSE SHOULD BE ABLE TO VERIFY AS MUCH.
IT'S TRUE... THERE WAS A GUMMY ON THE GROUND.
PRE-CISELY. AND AS I RECALL...
...YOU ENJOY EATING GUMMIES, SAIONJI.
swish!
rustle!
W-WHAT ARE GUMMIES...? W-WOULD YOU BELIEVE I'VE NEVER EATEN ONE BEFORE...?
DON'T LIE!
YOU WERE PIGGING OUT ON THEM BACK AT THE RESTAU-RANT!
AND DIDN'T YOU TRY HIDING SOMETHING JUST NOW...?!
...I-I'M NOT HIDING ANYTHING!
point!
SAIONJI... THIS IS REALLY IMPORTANT.
IF IT'S ABOUT THIS CASE, PLEASE LET US SEE IT.

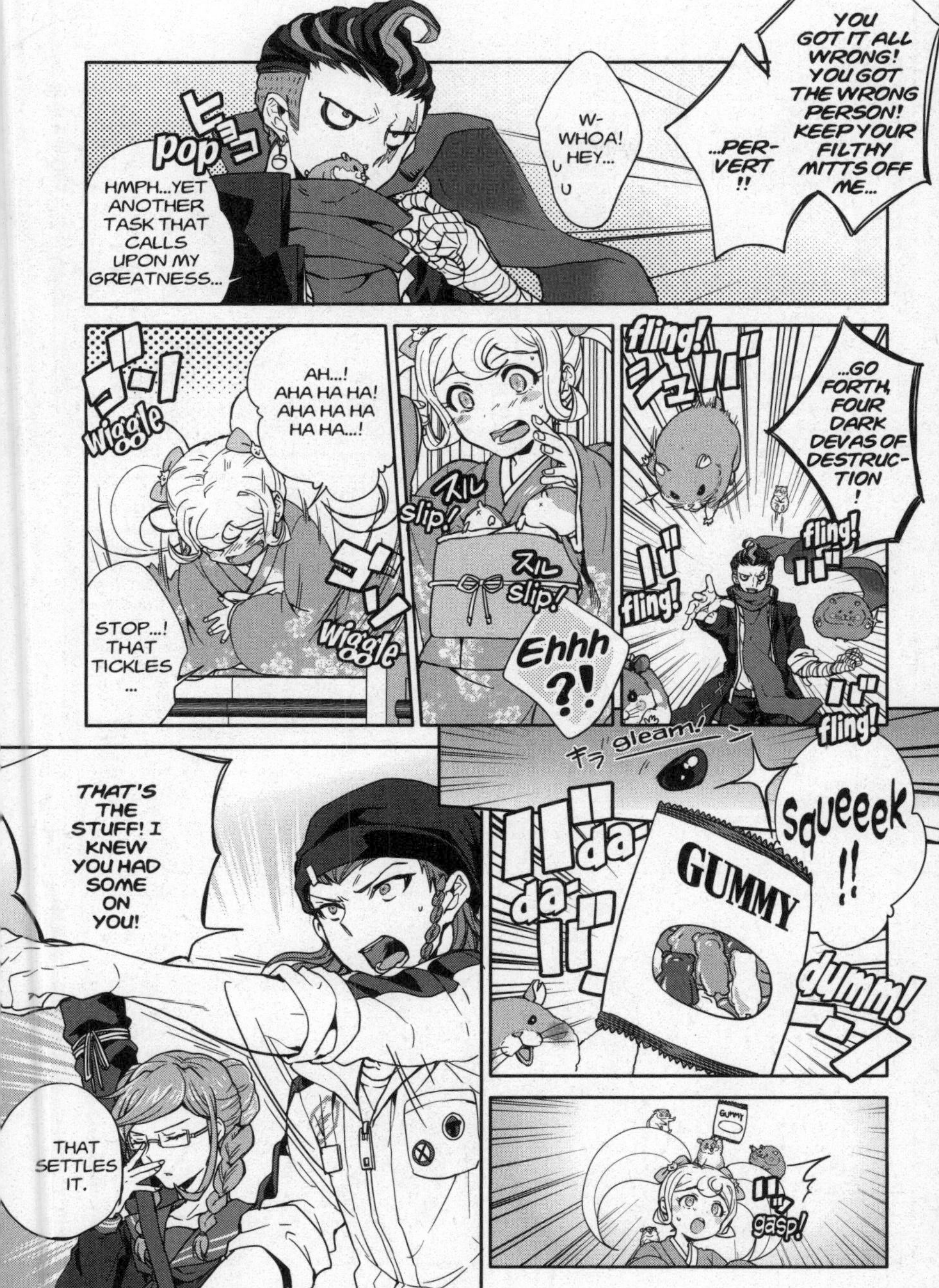
YOU GOT IT ALL WRONG! YOU GOT THE WRONG PERSON! KEEP YOUR FILTHY MITTS OFF ME...
...PER-VERT!!
W-WHOA! HEY...
ヒョコ
pop
HMPH...YET ANOTHER TASK THAT CALLS UPON MY GREATNESS...
fling!
シュ
...GO FORTH, FOUR DARK DEVAS OF DESTRUCTION!
fling!
fling!
fling!
スル
slip!
スル
slip!
Ehhh?!
AH...! AHA HA HA! AHA HA HA HA HA...!
wiggle
wiggle
STOP...! THAT TICKLES...
キラ
gleam!
Squeeek!!
da
da
GUMMY
dumm!
GUMMY
gasp!
THAT'S THE STUFF! I KNEW YOU HAD SOME ON YOU!
THAT SETTLES IT.

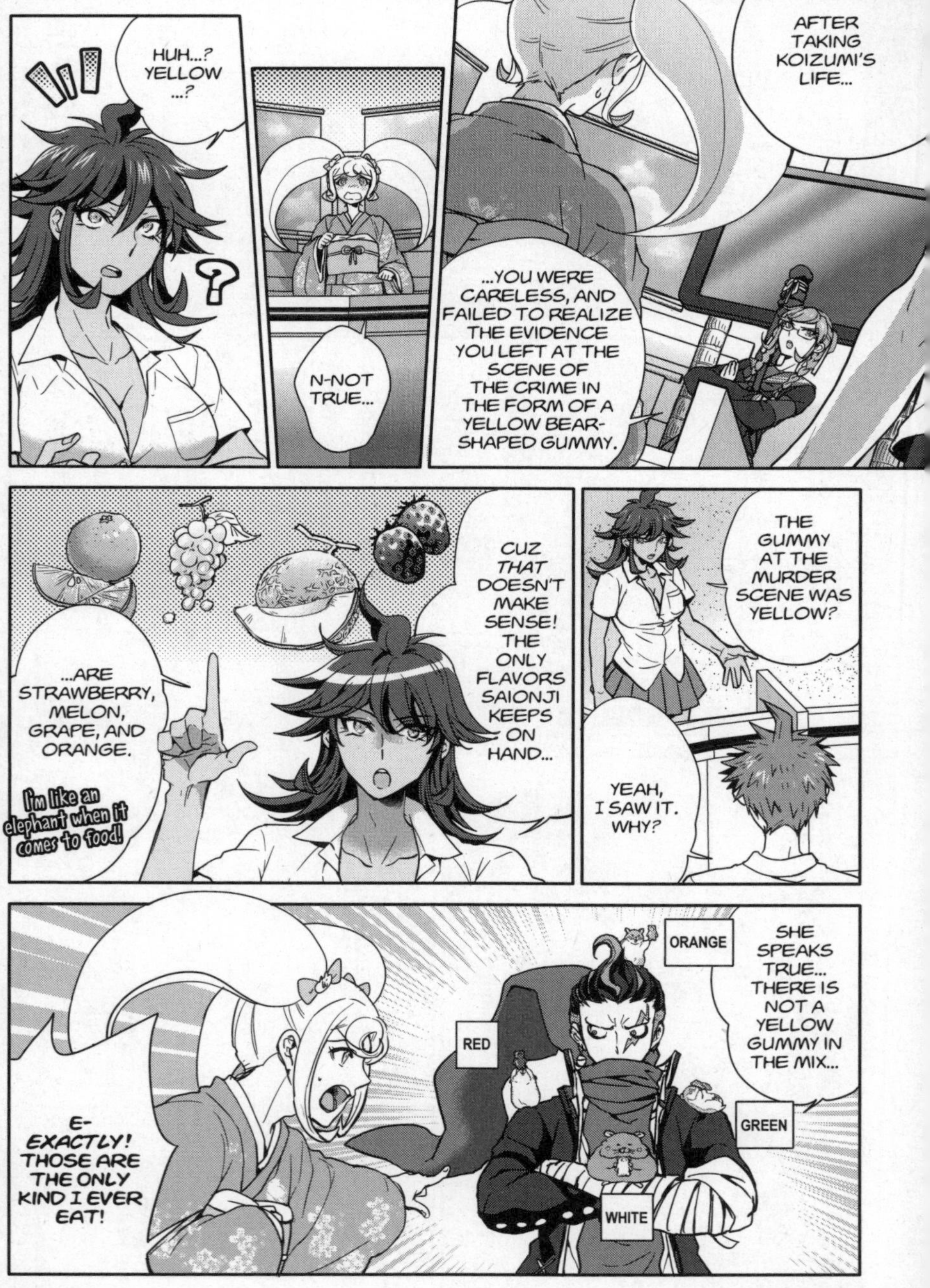
AFTER TAKING KOIZUMI'S LIFE...
...YOU WERE CARELESS, AND FAILED TO REALIZE THE EVIDENCE YOU LEFT AT THE SCENE OF THE CRIME IN THE FORM OF A YELLOW BEAR-SHAPED GUMMY.
N-NOT TRUE...
HUH...? YELLOW ...?
THE GUMMY AT THE MURDER SCENE WAS YELLOW?
YEAH, I SAW IT. WHY?
CUZ *THAT* DOESN'T MAKE SENSE! THE ONLY FLAVORS SAIONJI KEEPS ON HAND...
...ARE STRAWBERRY, MELON, GRAPE, AND ORANGE.
I'm like an elephant when it comes to food!
SHE SPEAKS TRUE... THERE IS NOT A YELLOW GUMMY IN THE MIX...
ORANGE
RED
GREEN
WHITE
E-*EXACTLY!* THOSE ARE THE ONLY KIND I EVER EAT!

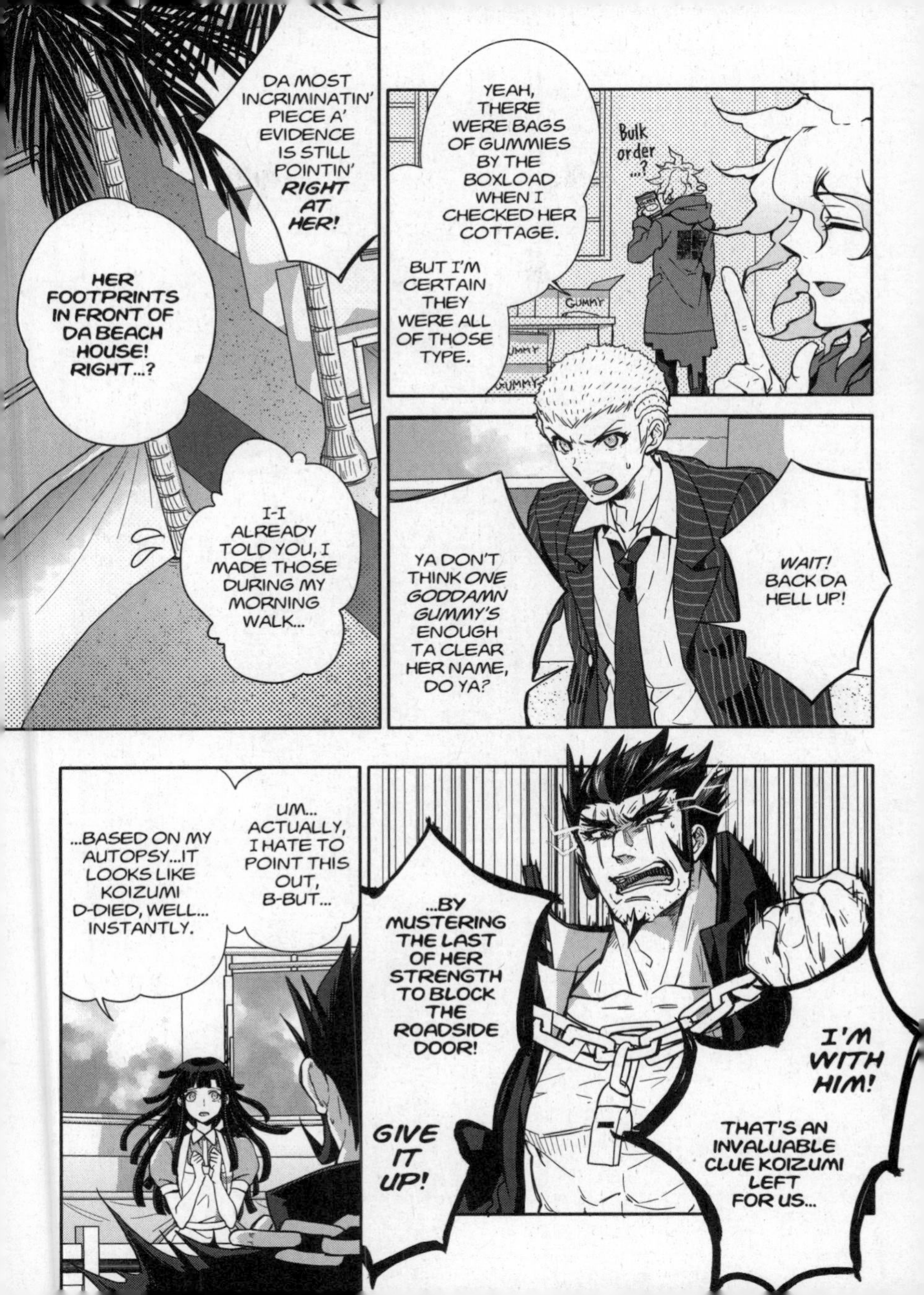
YEAH, THERE WERE BAGS OF GUMMIES BY THE BOXLOAD WHEN I CHECKED HER COTTAGE.
Bulk order ...?
BUT I'M CERTAIN THEY WERE ALL OF THOSE TYPE.
GUMMY
GUMMY
GUMMY
WAIT! BACK DA HELL UP!
YA DON'T THINK *ONE GODDAMN GUMMY'S* ENOUGH TA CLEAR HER NAME, DO YA?
DA MOST INCRIMINATIN' PIECE A' EVIDENCE IS STILL POINTIN' ***RIGHT AT HER!***
HER FOOTPRINTS IN FRONT OF DA BEACH HOUSE! RIGHT...?
I-I ALREADY TOLD YOU, I MADE THOSE DURING MY MORNING WALK...
...BY MUSTERING THE LAST OF HER STRENGTH TO BLOCK THE ROADSIDE DOOR!
I'M WITH HIM!
THAT'S AN INVALUABLE CLUE KOIZUMI LEFT FOR US...
GIVE IT UP!
UM... ACTUALLY, I HATE TO POINT THIS OUT, B-BUT...
...BASED ON MY AUTOPSY...IT LOOKS LIKE KOIZUMI D-DIED, WELL... INSTANTLY.

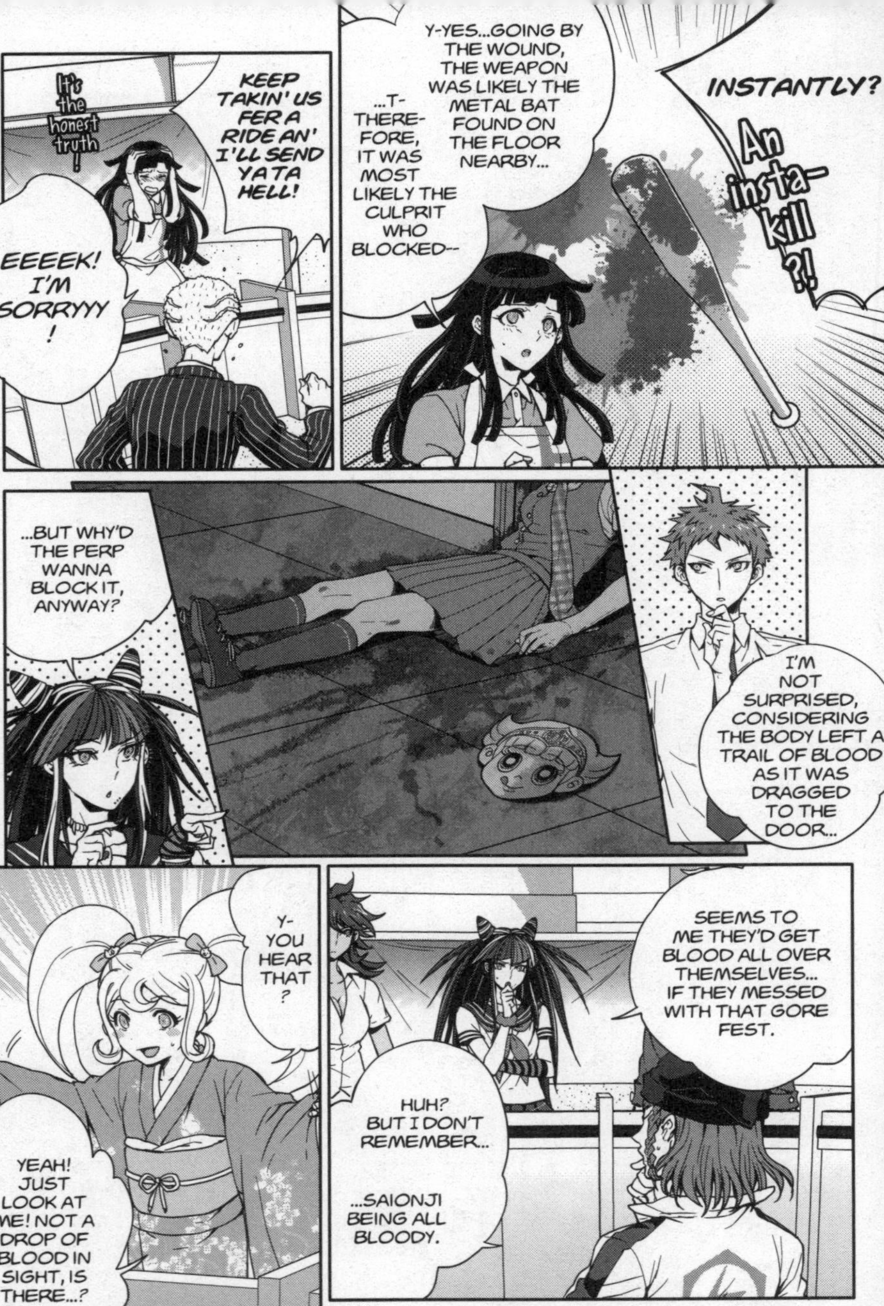
INSTANTLY?
An insta-kill?!
Y-YES...GOING BY THE WOUND, THE WEAPON WAS LIKELY THE METAL BAT FOUND ON THE FLOOR NEARBY...
...T-THEREFORE, IT WAS MOST LIKELY THE CULPRIT WHO BLOCKED--
KEEP TAKIN' US FER A RIDE AN' I'LL SEND YA TA HELL!
It's the honest truth!
EEEEK! I'M SORRYYY!
I'M NOT SURPRISED, CONSIDERING THE BODY LEFT A TRAIL OF BLOOD AS IT WAS DRAGGED TO THE DOOR...
...BUT WHY'D THE PERP WANNA BLOCK IT, ANYWAY?
SEEMS TO ME THEY'D GET BLOOD ALL OVER THEMSELVES... IF THEY MESSED WITH THAT GORE FEST.
HUH? BUT I DON'T REMEMBER...
...SAIONJI BEING ALL BLOODY.
Y-YOU HEAR THAT?
YEAH! JUST LOOK AT ME! NOT A DROP OF BLOOD IN SIGHT, IS THERE...?

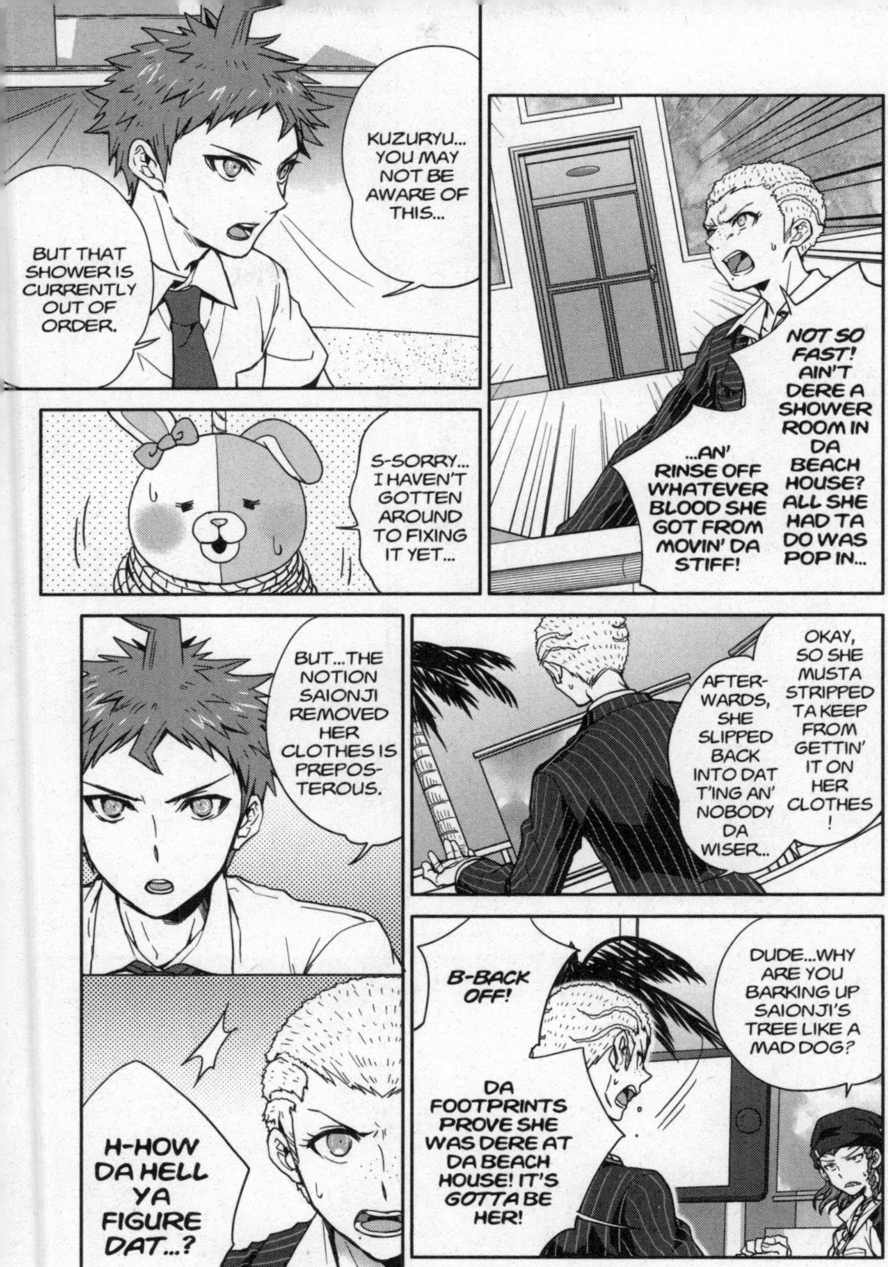
NOT SO FAST! AIN'T DERE A SHOWER ROOM IN DA BEACH HOUSE? ALL SHE HAD TA DO WAS POP IN...
...AN' RINSE OFF WHATEVER BLOOD SHE GOT FROM MOVIN' DA STIFF!
KUZURYU... YOU MAY NOT BE AWARE OF THIS...
BUT THAT SHOWER IS CURRENTLY OUT OF ORDER.
S-SORRY... I HAVEN'T GOTTEN AROUND TO FIXING IT YET...
OKAY, SO SHE MUSTA STRIPPED TA KEEP FROM GETTIN' IT ON HER CLOTHES!
AFTER-WARDS, SHE SLIPPED BACK INTO DAT T'ING AN' NOBODY DA WISER...
BUT...THE NOTION SAIONJI REMOVED HER CLOTHES IS PREPOS-TEROUS.
H-HOW DA HELL YA FIGURE DAT...?
DUDE...WHY ARE YOU BARKING UP SAIONJI'S TREE LIKE A MAD DOG?
B-BACK OFF!
DA FOOTPRINTS PROVE SHE WAS DERE AT DA BEACH HOUSE! IT'S GOTTA BE HER!

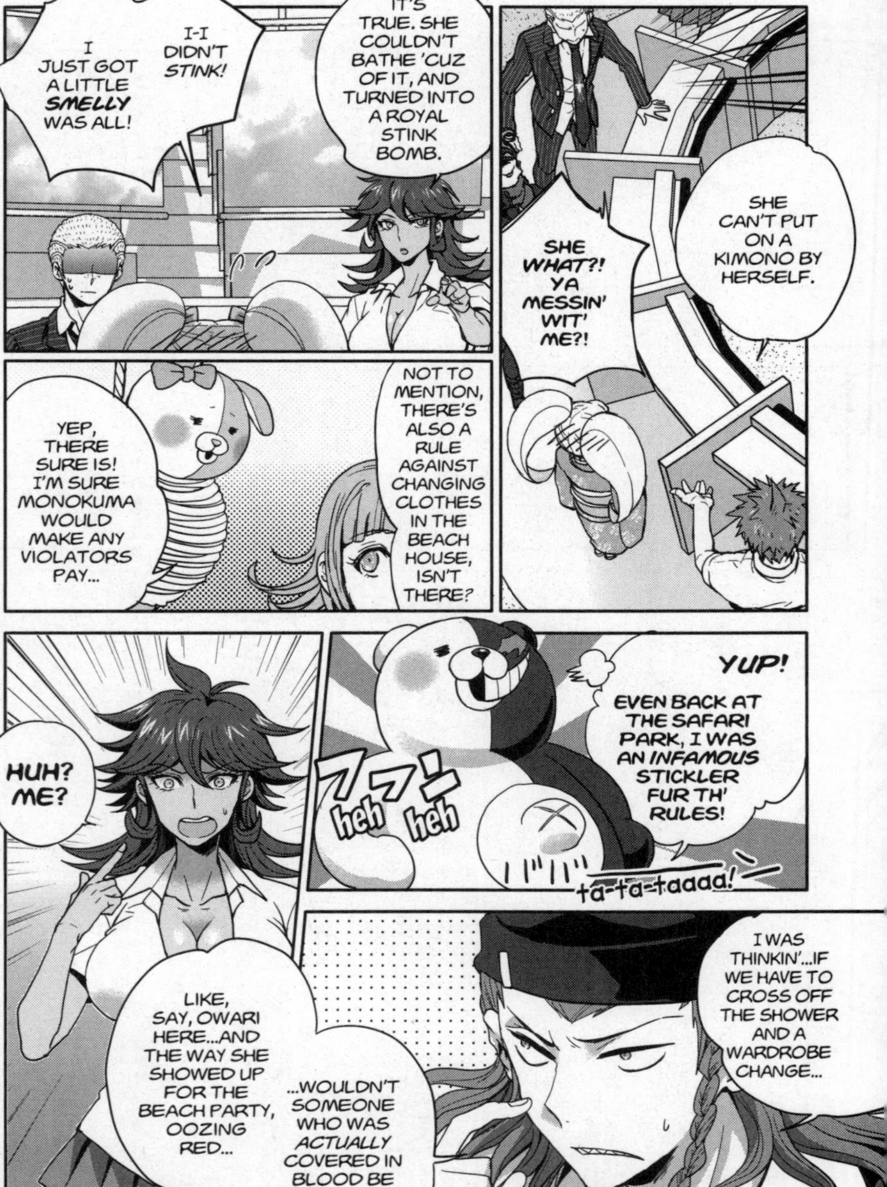
SHE CAN'T PUT ON A KIMONO BY HERSELF.
SHE *WHAT?!* YA MESSIN' WIT' ME?!
IT'S TRUE. SHE COULDN'T BATHE 'CUZ OF IT, AND TURNED INTO A ROYAL STINK BOMB.
I-I DIDN'T *STINK!*
I JUST GOT A LITTLE ***SMELLY*** WAS ALL!
NOT TO MENTION, THERE'S ALSO A RULE AGAINST CHANGING CLOTHES IN THE BEACH HOUSE, ISN'T THERE?
YEP, THERE SURE IS! I'M SURE MONOKUMA WOULD MAKE ANY VIOLATORS PAY...
YUP!
EVEN BACK AT THE SAFARI PARK, I WAS AN *INFAMOUS* STICKLER FUR TH' RULES!
heh heh
ta-ta-taaaa!
I WAS THINKIN'...IF WE HAVE TO CROSS OFF THE SHOWER AND A WARDROBE CHANGE...
LIKE, SAY, OWARI HERE...AND THE WAY SHE SHOWED UP FOR THE BEACH PARTY, OOZING RED...
...WOULDN'T SOMEONE WHO WAS *ACTUALLY* COVERED IN BLOOD BE THE MOST SUSPICIOUS?
HUH? ME?

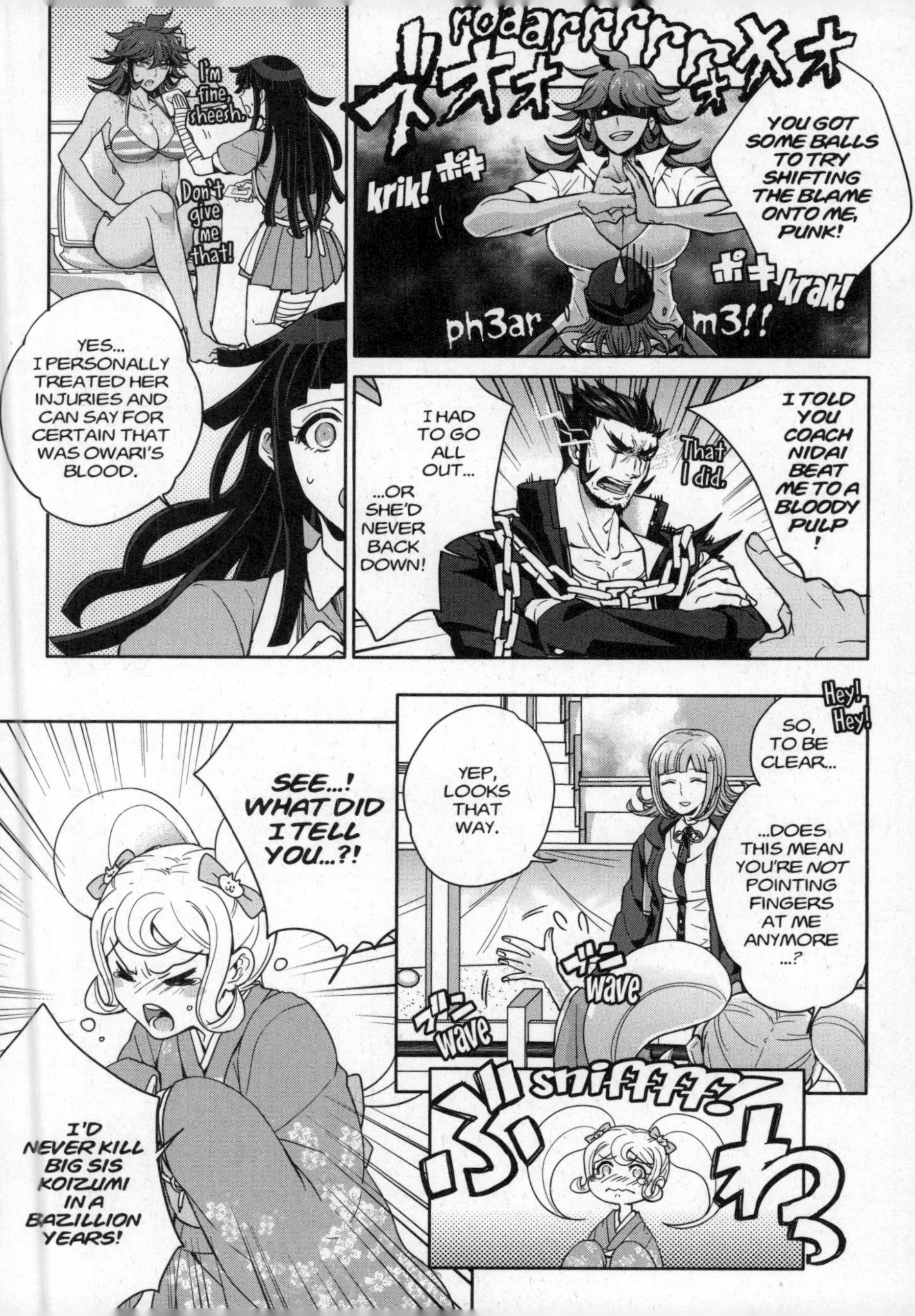
roaarrrrrrr
YOU GOT SOME BALLS TO TRY SHIFTING THE BLAME ONTO ME, PUNK!
krik! ポキ
ポキ krak!
ph3ar m3!!
I'm fine, sheesh.
Don't give me that!
I TOLD YOU COACH NIDAI BEAT ME TO A BLOODY PULP!
That I did.
I HAD TO GO ALL OUT...
...OR SHE'D NEVER BACK DOWN!
YES... I PERSONALLY TREATED HER INJURIES AND CAN SAY FOR CERTAIN THAT WAS OWARI'S BLOOD.
Hey! Hey!
SO, TO BE CLEAR...
YEP, LOOKS THAT WAY.
...DOES THIS MEAN YOU'RE NOT POINTING FINGERS AT ME ANYMORE...?
wave
wave
sniffff!
SEE...! WHAT DID I TELL YOU...?!
I'D NEVER KILL BIG SIS KOIZUMI IN A BAZILLION YEARS!

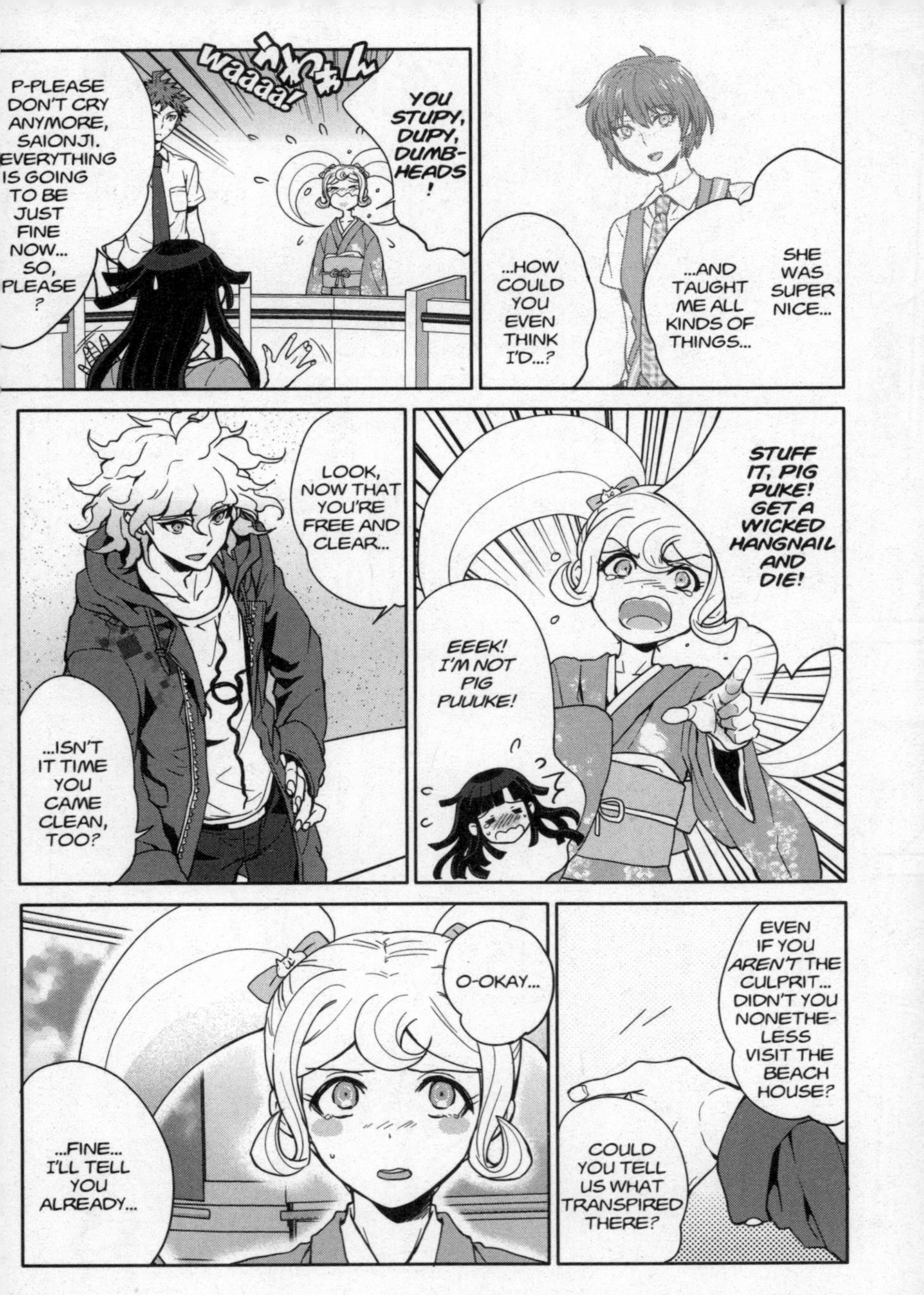
SHE WAS SUPER NICE...
...AND TAUGHT ME ALL KINDS OF THINGS...
...HOW COULD YOU EVEN THINK I'D...?
waaaa!
YOU STUPY, DUPY, DUMB-HEADS!
P-PLEASE DON'T CRY ANYMORE, SAIONJI. EVERYTHING IS GOING TO BE JUST FINE NOW... SO, PLEASE?
STUFF IT, PIG PUKE! GET A WICKED HANGNAIL AND DIE!
EEEK! I'M NOT PIG PUUUKE!
LOOK, NOW THAT YOU'RE FREE AND CLEAR...
...ISN'T IT TIME YOU CAME CLEAN, TOO?
EVEN IF YOU *AREN'T* THE CULPRIT... DIDN'T YOU NONETHELESS VISIT THE BEACH HOUSE?
COULD YOU TELL US WHAT TRANSPIRED THERE?
O-OKAY...
...FINE... I'LL TELL YOU ALREADY...

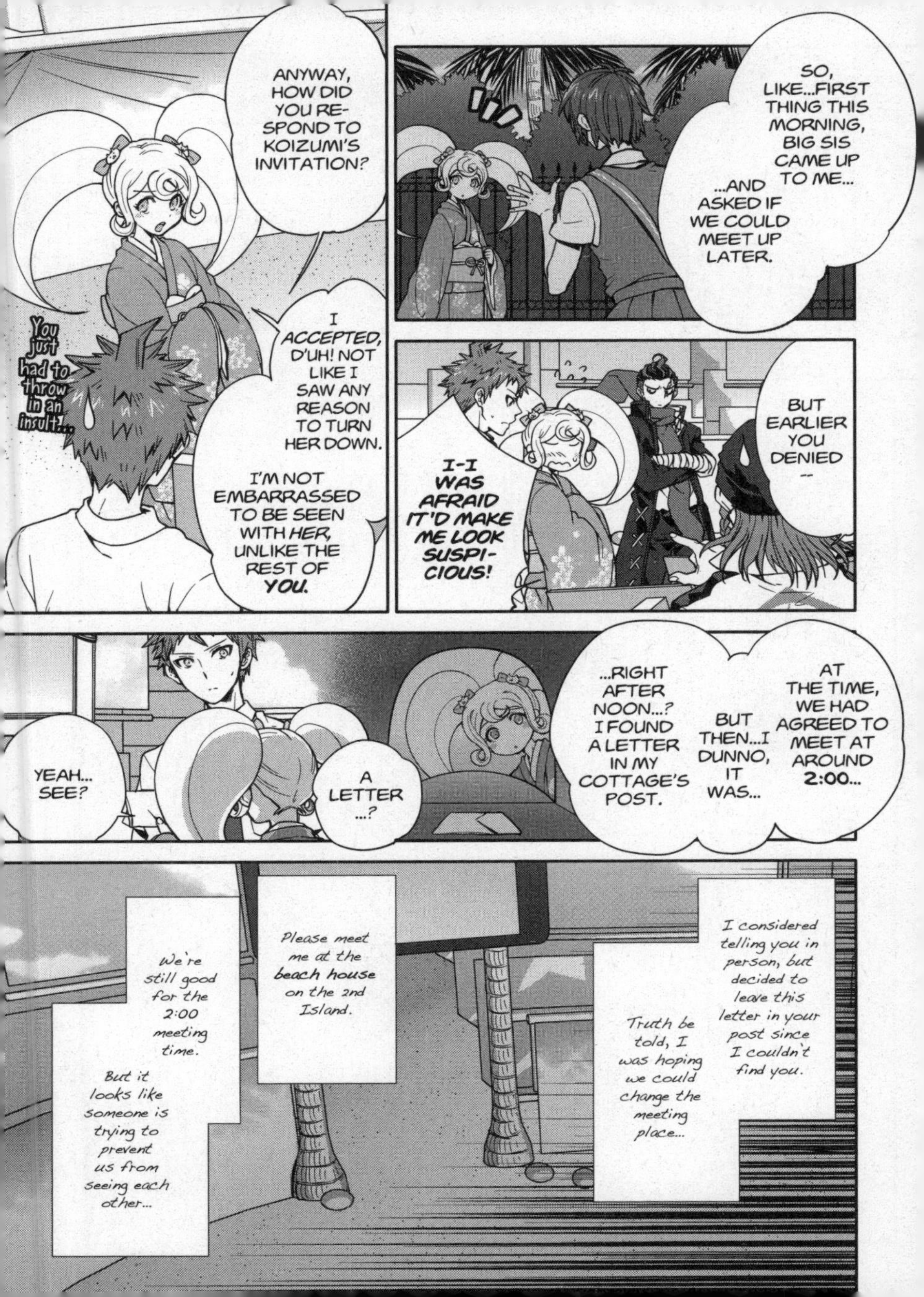
SO, LIKE...FIRST THING THIS MORNING, BIG SIS CAME UP TO ME...
...AND ASKED IF WE COULD MEET UP LATER.
BUT EARLIER YOU DENIED --
I-I WAS AFRAID IT'D MAKE ME LOOK SUSPICIOUS!
ANYWAY, HOW DID YOU RESPOND TO KOIZUMI'S INVITATION?
I ACCEPTED, D'UH! NOT LIKE I SAW ANY REASON TO TURN HER DOWN.
I'M NOT EMBARRASSED TO BE SEEN WITH HER, UNLIKE THE REST OF YOU.
You just had to throw in an insult...
AT THE TIME, WE HAD AGREED TO MEET AT AROUND 2:00...
BUT THEN...I DUNNO, IT WAS...
...RIGHT AFTER NOON...? I FOUND A LETTER IN MY COTTAGE'S POST.
A LETTER ...?
YEAH... SEE?
I considered telling you in person, but decided to leave this letter in your post since I couldn't find you.
Truth be told, I was hoping we could change the meeting place...
Please meet me at the beach house on the 2nd Island.
We're still good for the 2:00 meeting time.
But it looks like someone is trying to prevent us from seeing each other...

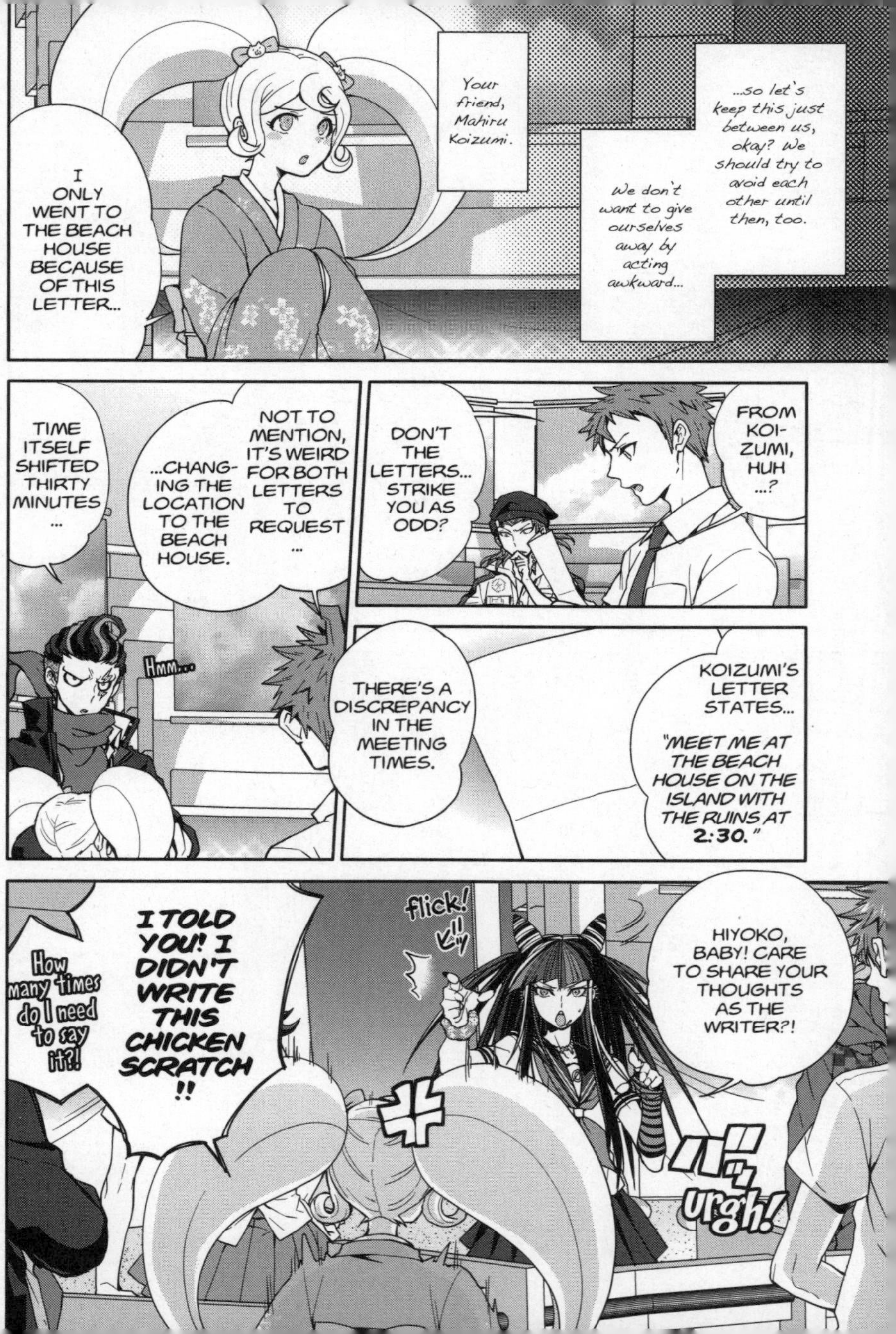
We don't want to give ourselves away by acting awkward...
...so let's keep this just between us, okay? We should try to avoid each other until then, too.
Your friend, Mahiru Koizumi.
I ONLY WENT TO THE BEACH HOUSE BECAUSE OF THIS LETTER...
FROM KOIZUMI, HUH...?
DON'T THE LETTERS... STRIKE YOU AS ODD?
KOIZUMI'S LETTER STATES... "MEET ME AT THE BEACH HOUSE ON THE ISLAND WITH THE RUINS AT 2:30."
THERE'S A DISCREPANCY IN THE MEETING TIMES.
NOT TO MENTION, IT'S WEIRD FOR BOTH LETTERS TO REQUEST...
...CHANGING THE LOCATION TO THE BEACH HOUSE.
TIME ITSELF SHIFTED THIRTY MINUTES...
Hmm...
HIYOKO, BABY! CARE TO SHARE YOUR THOUGHTS AS THE WRITER?!
flick!
ビッ
I TOLD YOU! I DIDN'T WRITE THIS CHICKEN SCRATCH!!
How many times do I need to say it?!
ハッ
urgh!

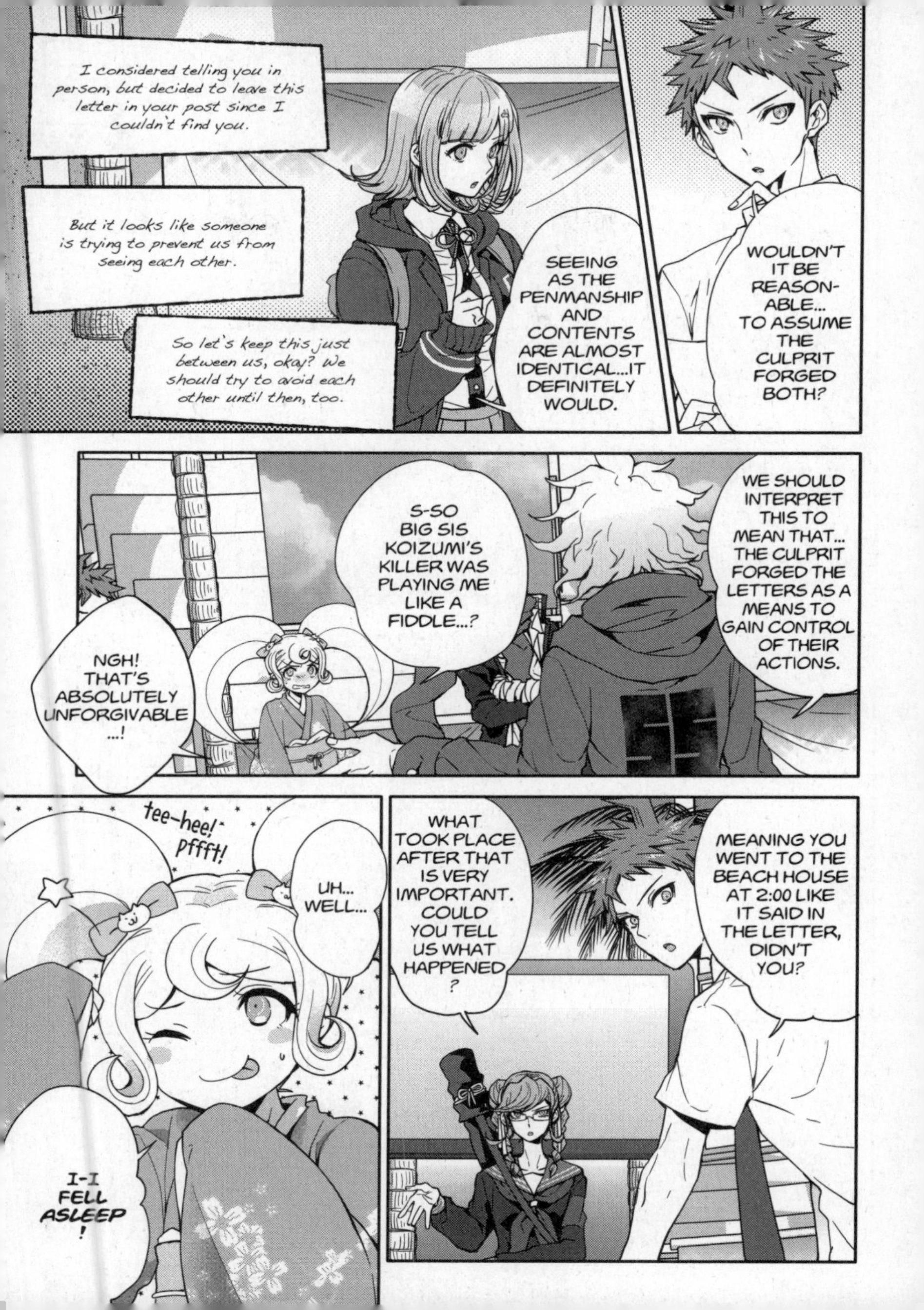
WOULDN'T IT BE REASONABLE... TO ASSUME THE CULPRIT FORGED BOTH?
SEEING AS THE PENMANSHIP AND CONTENTS ARE ALMOST IDENTICAL...IT DEFINITELY WOULD.
I considered telling you in person, but decided to leave this letter in your post since I couldn't find you.
But it looks like someone is trying to prevent us from seeing each other.
So let's keep this just between us, okay? We should try to avoid each other until then, too.
WE SHOULD INTERPRET THIS TO MEAN THAT... THE CULPRIT FORGED THE LETTERS AS A MEANS TO GAIN CONTROL OF THEIR ACTIONS.
S-SO BIG SIS KOIZUMI'S KILLER WAS PLAYING ME LIKE A FIDDLE...?
NGH! THAT'S ABSOLUTELY UNFORGIVABLE...!
MEANING YOU WENT TO THE BEACH HOUSE AT 2:00 LIKE IT SAID IN THE LETTER, DIDN'T YOU?
WHAT TOOK PLACE AFTER THAT IS VERY IMPORTANT. COULD YOU TELL US WHAT HAPPENED?
UH... WELL...
tee-hee! pffft!
I-I FELL ASLEEP!

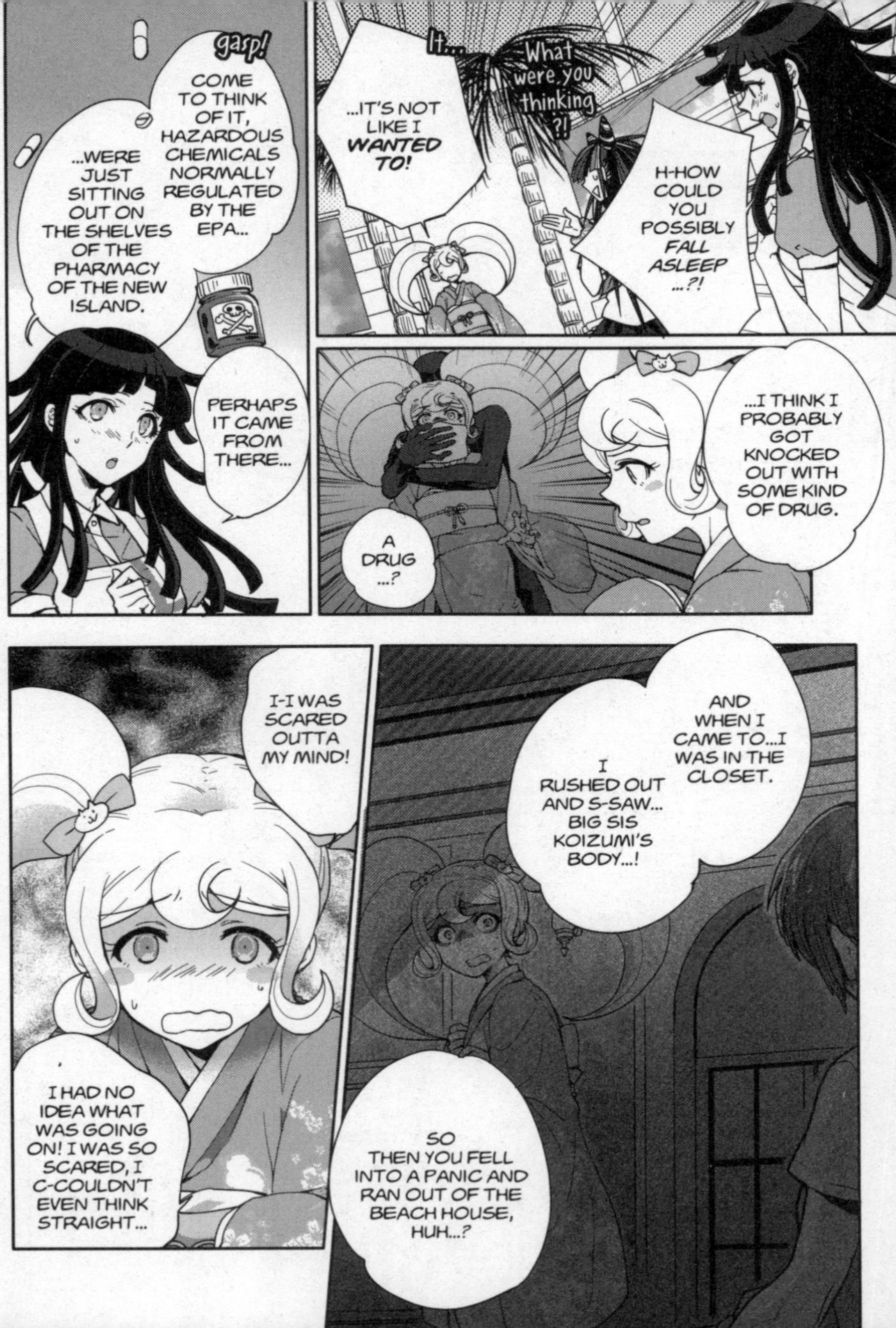

What were you thinking?!
H-HOW COULD YOU POSSIBLY FALL ASLEEP ...?!
It...
...IT'S NOT LIKE I WANTED TO!
...I THINK I PROBABLY GOT KNOCKED OUT WITH SOME KIND OF DRUG.
A DRUG ...?
gasp!
COME TO THINK OF IT, HAZARDOUS CHEMICALS NORMALLY REGULATED BY THE EPA...
...WERE JUST SITTING OUT ON THE SHELVES OF THE PHARMACY OF THE NEW ISLAND.
PERHAPS IT CAME FROM THERE...
AND WHEN I CAME TO...I WAS IN THE CLOSET.
I RUSHED OUT AND S-SAW... BIG SIS KOIZUMI'S BODY...!
SO THEN YOU FELL INTO A PANIC AND RAN OUT OF THE BEACH HOUSE, HUH...?
I-I WAS SCARED OUTTA MY MIND!
I HAD NO IDEA WHAT WAS GOING ON! I WAS SO SCARED, I C-COULDN'T EVEN THINK STRAIGHT...

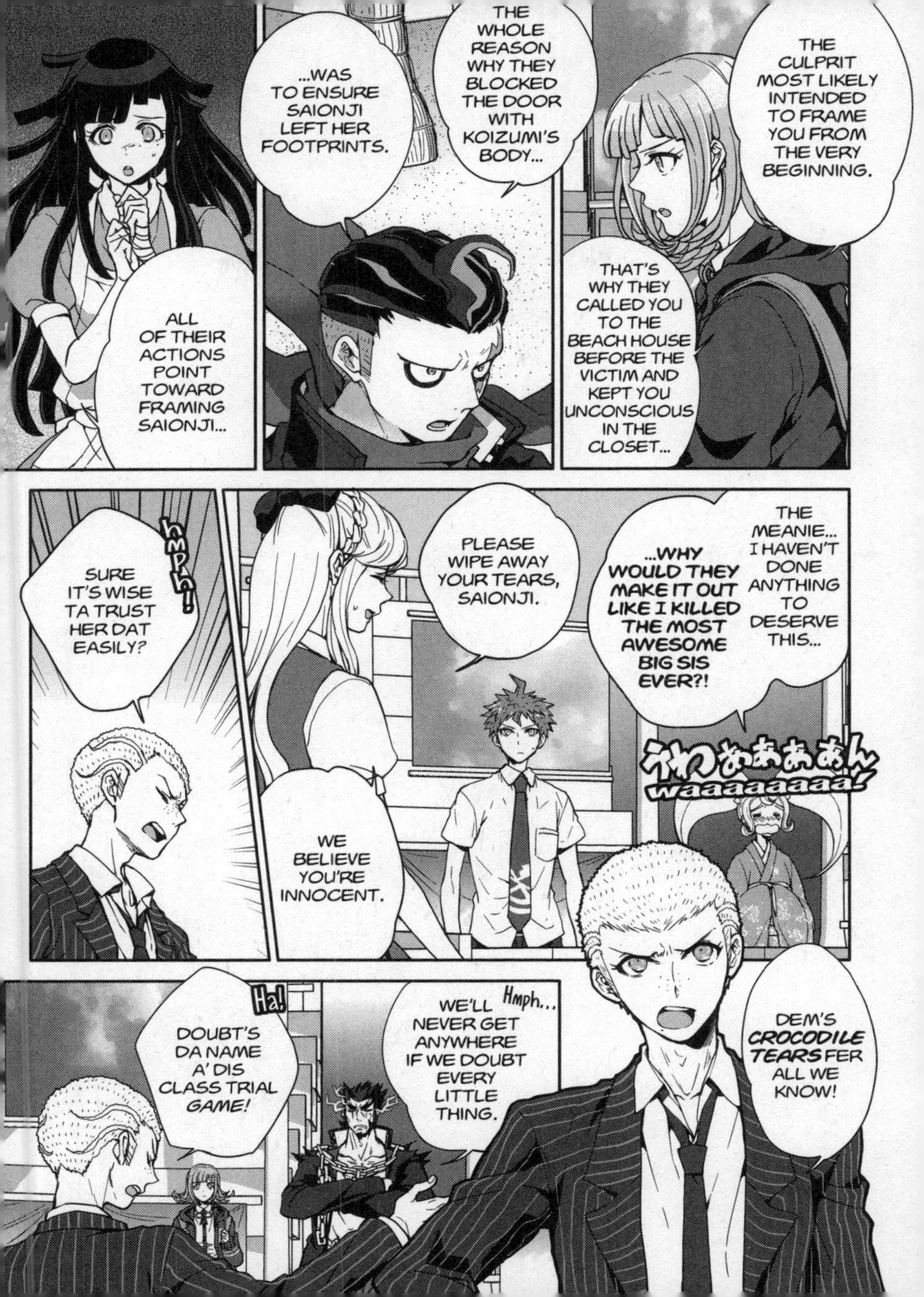
THE CULPRIT MOST LIKELY INTENDED TO FRAME YOU FROM THE VERY BEGINNING.
THAT'S WHY THEY CALLED YOU TO THE BEACH HOUSE BEFORE THE VICTIM AND KEPT YOU UNCONSCIOUS IN THE CLOSET...
THE WHOLE REASON WHY THEY BLOCKED THE DOOR WITH KOIZUMI'S BODY...
...WAS TO ENSURE SAIONJI LEFT HER FOOTPRINTS.
ALL OF THEIR ACTIONS POINT TOWARD FRAMING SAIONJI...
THE MEANIE... I HAVEN'T DONE ANYTHING TO DESERVE THIS...
...WHY WOULD THEY MAKE IT OUT LIKE I KILLED THE MOST AWESOME BIG SIS EVER?!
waaaaaaaaa!
PLEASE WIPE AWAY YOUR TEARS, SAIONJI.
WE BELIEVE YOU'RE INNOCENT.
hmph!
SURE IT'S WISE TA TRUST HER DAT EASILY?
DEM'S *CROCODILE TEARS* FER ALL WE KNOW!
Hmph...
WE'LL NEVER GET ANYWHERE IF WE DOUBT EVERY LITTLE THING.
Ha!
DOUBT'S DA NAME A' DIS CLASS TRIAL *GAME!*

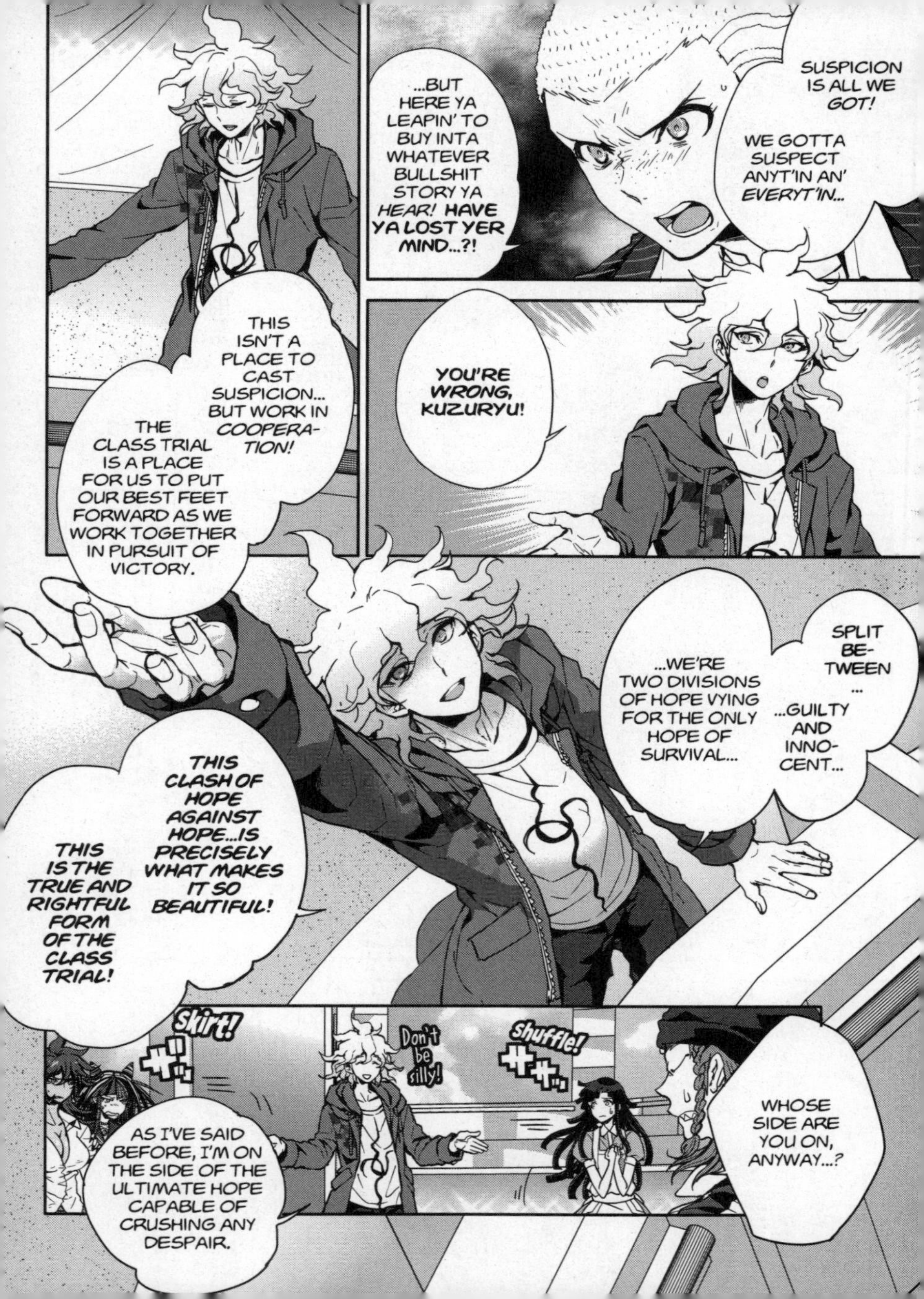
SUSPICION IS ALL WE GOT!
WE GOTTA SUSPECT ANYT'IN AN' EVERYT'IN...
...BUT HERE YA LEAPIN' TO BUY INTA WHATEVER BULLSHIT STORY YA HEAR! HAVE YA LOST YER MIND...?!
YOU'RE WRONG, KUZURYU!
THIS ISN'T A PLACE TO CAST SUSPICION... BUT WORK IN COOPERATION!
THE CLASS TRIAL IS A PLACE FOR US TO PUT OUR BEST FEET FORWARD AS WE WORK TOGETHER IN PURSUIT OF VICTORY.
SPLIT BETWEEN... ...GUILTY AND INNOCENT...
...WE'RE TWO DIVISIONS OF HOPE VYING FOR THE ONLY HOPE OF SURVIVAL...
THIS CLASH OF HOPE AGAINST HOPE...IS PRECISELY WHAT MAKES IT SO BEAUTIFUL!
THIS IS THE TRUE AND RIGHTFUL FORM OF THE CLASS TRIAL!
Shuffle!
WHOSE SIDE ARE YOU ON, ANYWAY...?
Don't be silly!
Skirt!
AS I'VE SAID BEFORE, I'M ON THE SIDE OF THE ULTIMATE HOPE CAPABLE OF CRUSHING ANY DESPAIR.

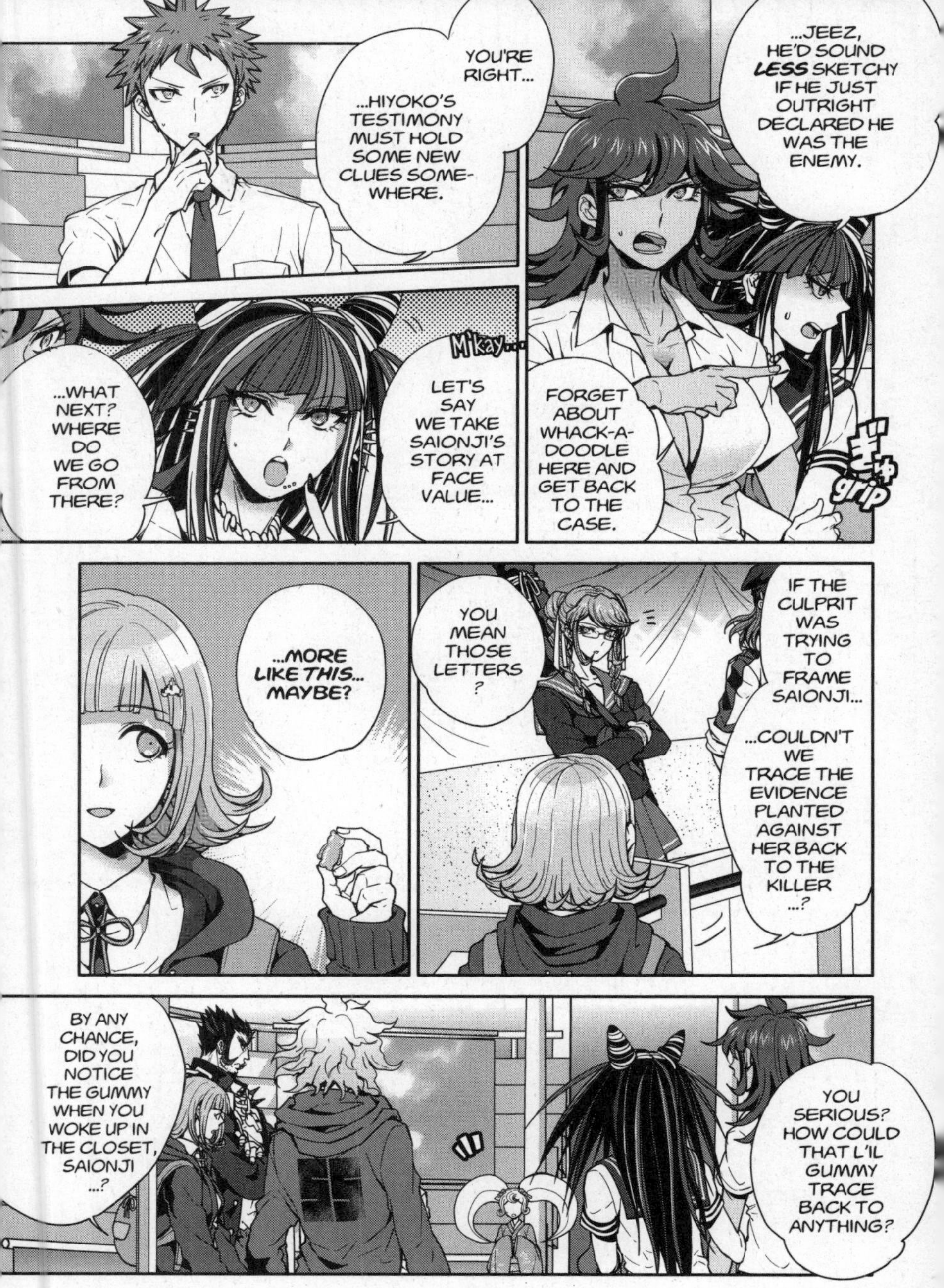
...JEEZ, HE'D SOUND LESS SKETCHY IF HE JUST OUTRIGHT DECLARED HE WAS THE ENEMY.
YOU'RE RIGHT...
...HIYOKO'S TESTIMONY MUST HOLD SOME NEW CLUES SOME-WHERE.
FORGET ABOUT WHACK-A-DOODLE HERE AND GET BACK TO THE CASE.
grip
M'kay...
LET'S SAY WE TAKE SAIONJI'S STORY AT FACE VALUE...
...WHAT NEXT? WHERE DO WE GO FROM THERE?
IF THE CULPRIT WAS TRYING TO FRAME SAIONJI...
...COULDN'T WE TRACE THE EVIDENCE PLANTED AGAINST HER BACK TO THE KILLER ...?
YOU MEAN THOSE LETTERS ?
...MORE LIKE THIS... MAYBE?
YOU SERIOUS? HOW COULD THAT L'IL GUMMY TRACE BACK TO ANYTHING?
BY ANY CHANCE, DID YOU NOTICE THE GUMMY WHEN YOU WOKE UP IN THE CLOSET, SAIONJI ...?

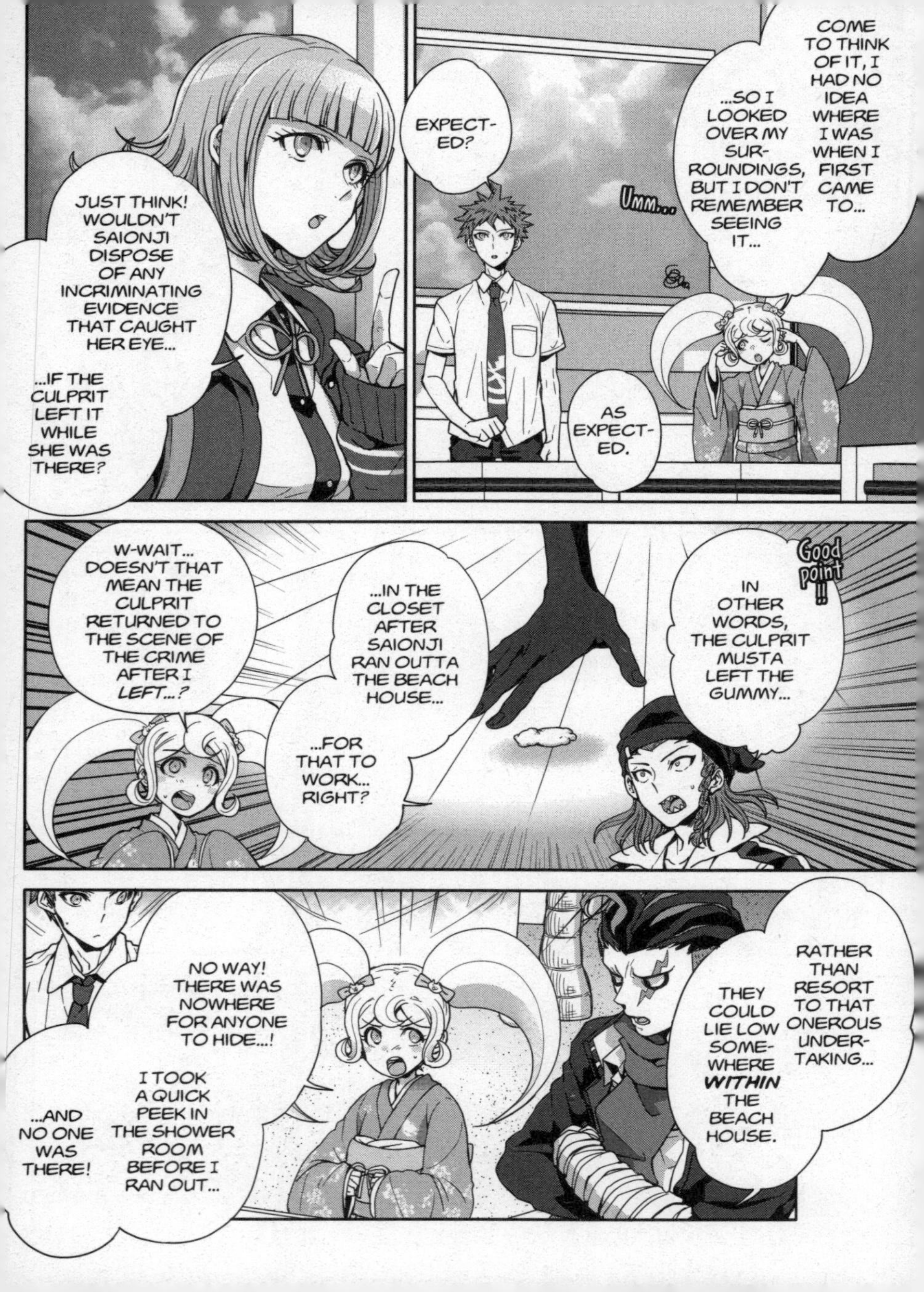
COME TO THINK OF IT, I HAD NO IDEA WHERE I WAS WHEN I FIRST CAME TO...
...SO I LOOKED OVER MY SUR-ROUNDINGS, BUT I DON'T REMEMBER SEEING IT...
EXPECT-ED?
UMM...
AS EXPECT-ED.
JUST THINK! WOULDN'T SAIONJI DISPOSE OF ANY INCRIMINATING EVIDENCE THAT CAUGHT HER EYE...
...IF THE CULPRIT LEFT IT WHILE SHE WAS THERE?
Good point!!
IN OTHER WORDS, THE CULPRIT MUSTA LEFT THE GUMMY...
...IN THE CLOSET AFTER SAIONJI RAN OUTTA THE BEACH HOUSE...
...FOR THAT TO WORK... RIGHT?
W-WAIT... DOESN'T THAT MEAN THE CULPRIT RETURNED TO THE SCENE OF THE CRIME AFTER I *LEFT*...?
RATHER THAN RESORT TO THAT ONEROUS UNDER-TAKING...
THEY COULD LIE LOW SOME-WHERE ***WITHIN*** THE BEACH HOUSE.
NO WAY! THERE WAS NOWHERE FOR ANYONE TO HIDE...!
I TOOK A QUICK PEEK IN THE SHOWER ROOM BEFORE I RAN OUT...
...AND NO ONE WAS THERE!

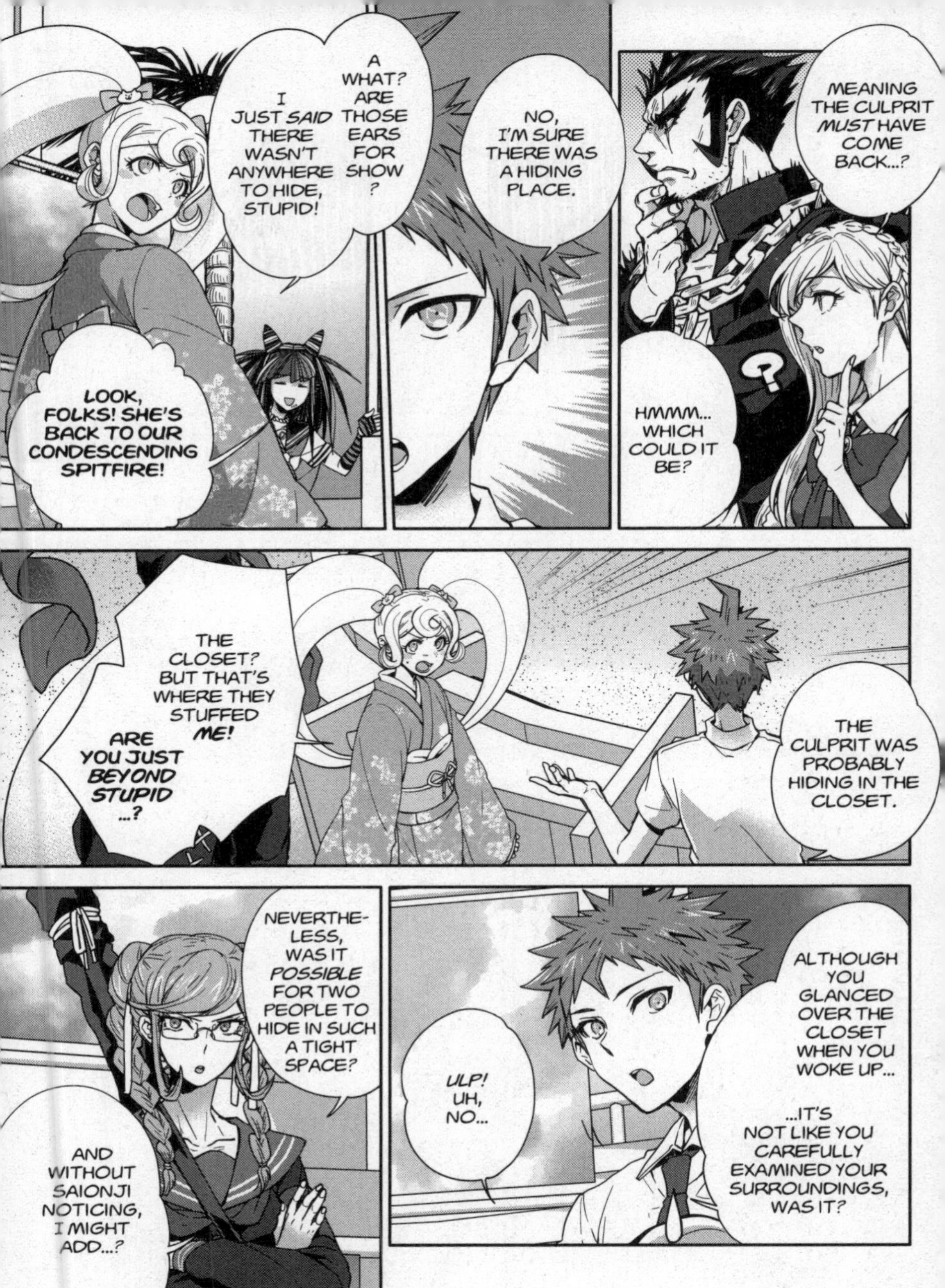
MEANING THE CULPRIT *MUST* HAVE COME BACK...?
HMMM... WHICH COULD IT BE?
NO, I'M SURE THERE WAS A HIDING PLACE.
A WHAT? ARE THOSE EARS FOR SHOW?
I JUST *SAID* THERE WASN'T ANYWHERE TO HIDE, STUPID!
LOOK, FOLKS! SHE'S BACK TO OUR CONDESCENDING SPITFIRE!
THE CULPRIT WAS PROBABLY HIDING IN THE CLOSET.
THE CLOSET? BUT THAT'S WHERE THEY STUFFED *ME!*
ARE YOU JUST *BEYOND STUPID* ...?
ALTHOUGH YOU GLANCED OVER THE CLOSET WHEN YOU WOKE UP...
ULP! UH, NO...
...IT'S NOT LIKE YOU CAREFULLY EXAMINED YOUR SURROUNDINGS, WAS IT?
NEVERTHE-LESS, WAS IT *POSSIBLE* FOR TWO PEOPLE TO HIDE IN SUCH A TIGHT SPACE?
AND WITHOUT SAIONJI NOTICING, I MIGHT ADD...?

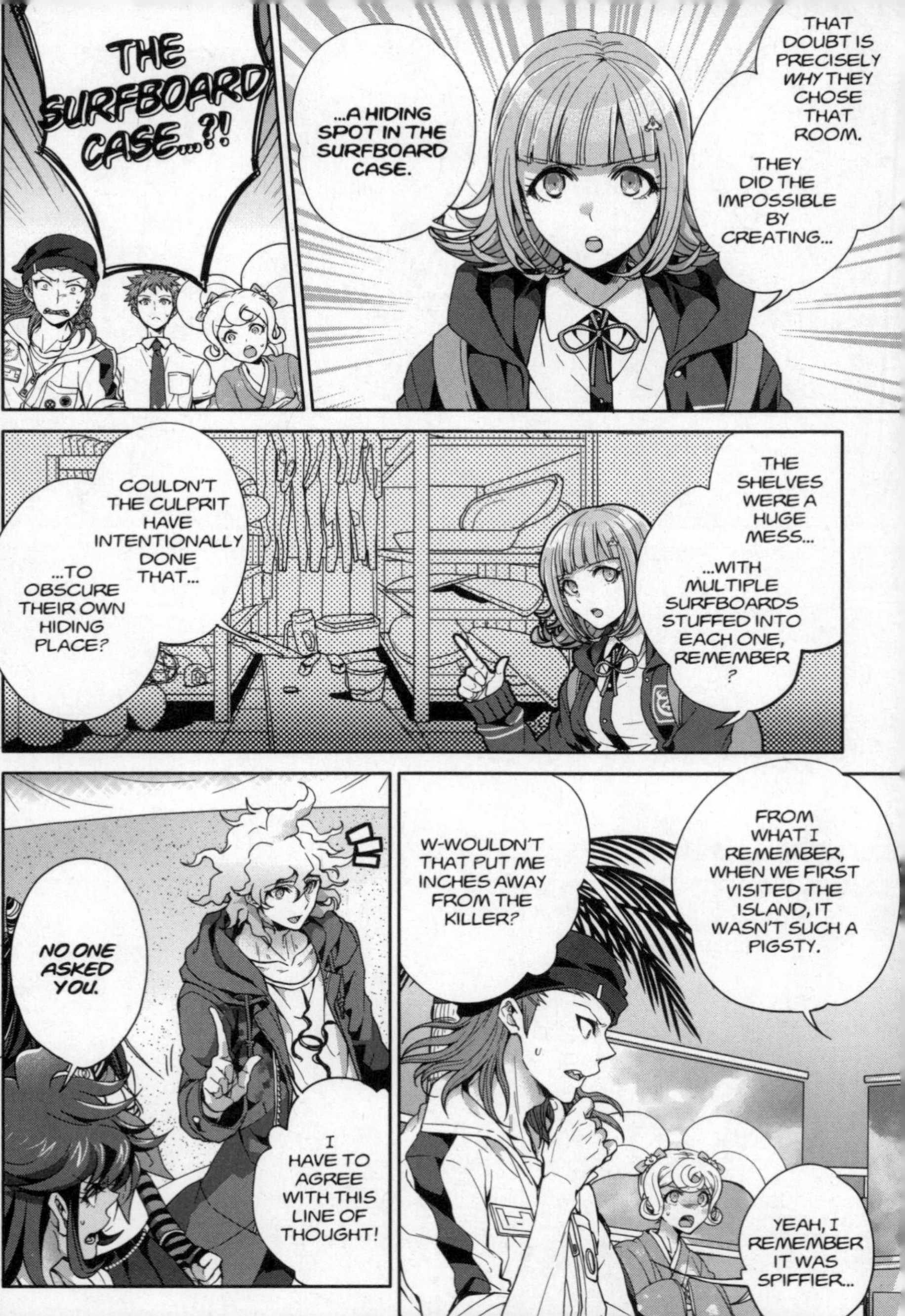
THAT DOUBT IS PRECISELY *WHY* THEY CHOSE THAT ROOM.
THEY DID THE IMPOSSIBLE BY CREATING...
...A HIDING SPOT IN THE SURFBOARD CASE.
THE SURFBOARD CASE...?!
THE SHELVES WERE A HUGE MESS...
...WITH MULTIPLE SURFBOARDS STUFFED INTO EACH ONE, REMEMBER?
COULDN'T THE CULPRIT HAVE INTENTIONALLY DONE THAT...
...TO OBSCURE THEIR OWN HIDING PLACE?
FROM WHAT I REMEMBER, WHEN WE FIRST VISITED THE ISLAND, IT WASN'T SUCH A PIGSTY.
W-WOULDN'T THAT PUT ME INCHES AWAY FROM THE KILLER?
YEAH, I REMEMBER IT WAS SPIFFIER...
I HAVE TO AGREE WITH THIS LINE OF THOUGHT!
NO ONE ASKED YOU.

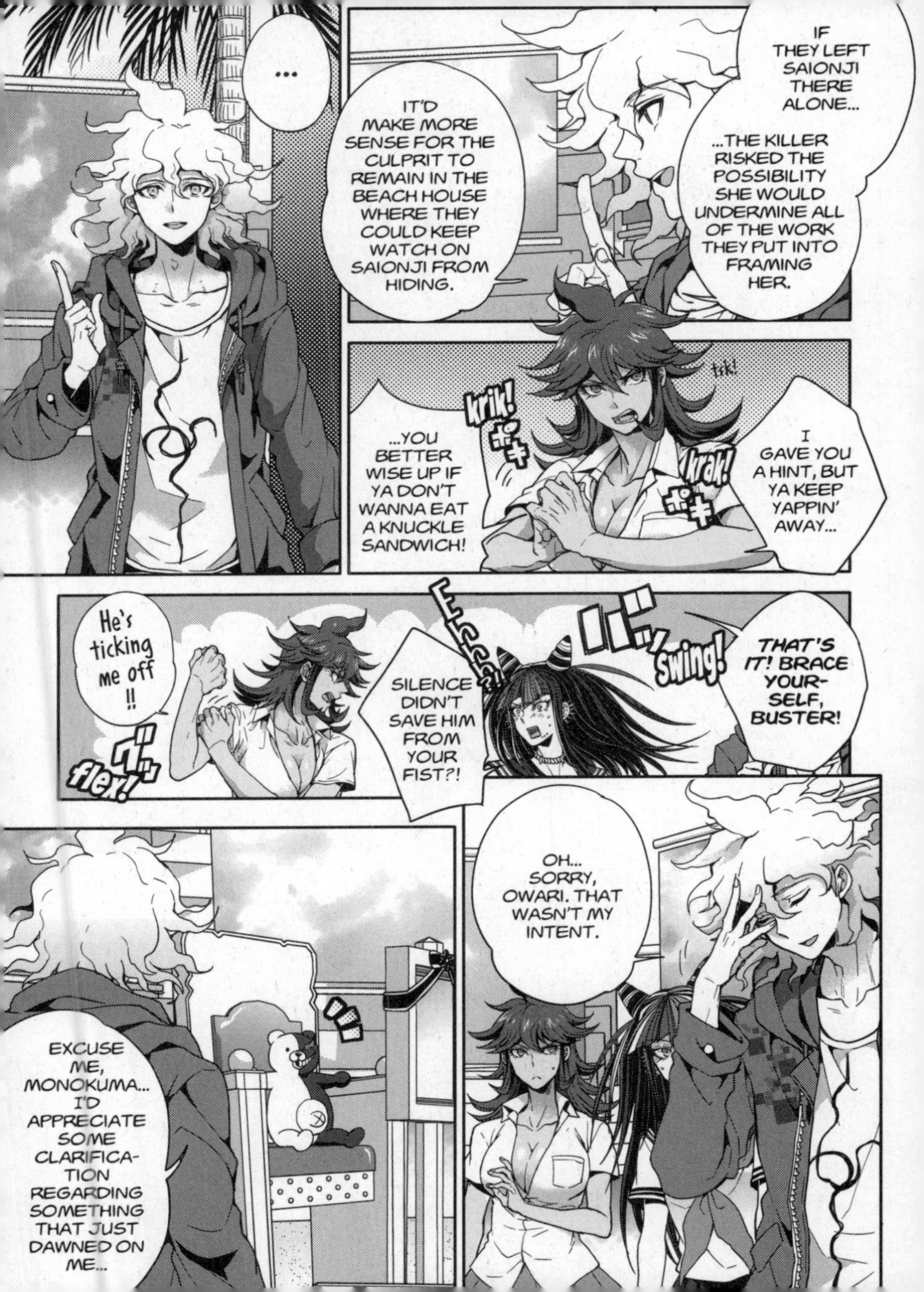
IF THEY LEFT SAIONJI THERE ALONE...
...THE KILLER RISKED THE POSSIBILITY SHE WOULD UNDERMINE ALL OF THE WORK THEY PUT INTO FRAMING HER.
IT'D MAKE MORE SENSE FOR THE CULPRIT TO REMAIN IN THE BEACH HOUSE WHERE THEY COULD KEEP WATCH ON SAIONJI FROM HIDING.
trk!
I GAVE YOU A HINT, BUT YA KEEP YAPPIN' AWAY...
krak!
krik!
...YOU BETTER WISE UP IF YA DON'T WANNA EAT A KNUCKLE SANDWICH!
...
THAT'S IT! BRACE YOURSELF, BUSTER!
swing!
SILENCE DIDN'T SAVE HIM FROM YOUR FIST?!
He's ticking me off !!
flex!
OH... SORRY, OWARI. THAT WASN'T MY INTENT.
EXCUSE ME, MONOKUMA... I'D APPRECIATE SOME CLARIFICATION REGARDING SOMETHING THAT JUST DAWNED ON ME...

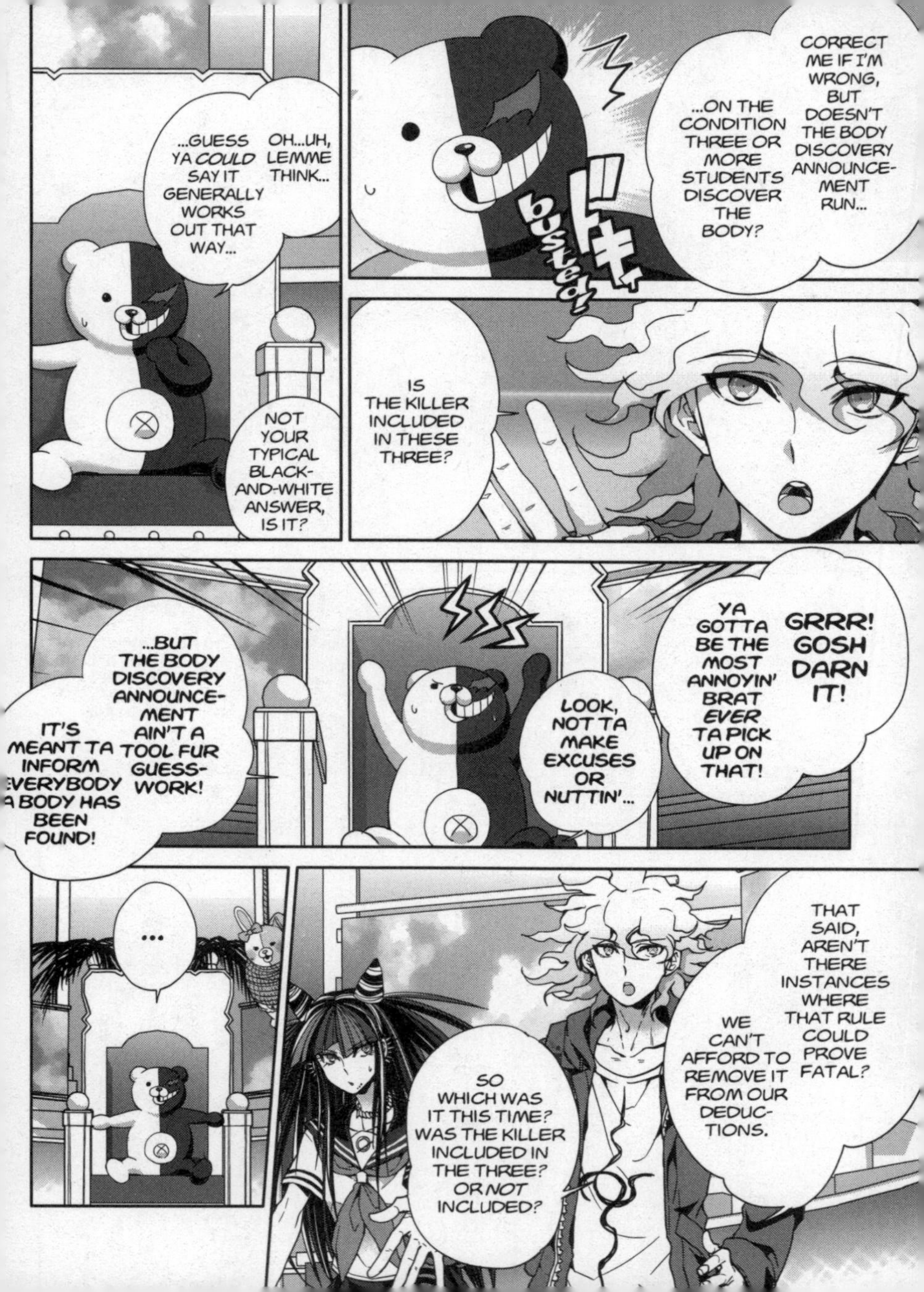
CORRECT ME IF I'M WRONG, BUT DOESN'T THE BODY DISCOVERY ANNOUNCEMENT RUN...
...ON THE CONDITION THREE OR MORE STUDENTS DISCOVER THE BODY?
busted!
IS THE KILLER INCLUDED IN THESE THREE?
OH...UH, LEMME THINK...
...GUESS YA *COULD* SAY IT GENERALLY WORKS OUT THAT WAY...
NOT YOUR TYPICAL BLACK-AND-WHITE ANSWER, IS IT?
GRRR! GOSH DARN IT!
YA GOTTA BE THE MOST ANNOYIN' BRAT *EVER* TA PICK UP ON THAT!
LOOK, NOT TA MAKE EXCUSES OR NUTTIN'...
...BUT THE BODY DISCOVERY ANNOUNCEMENT AIN'T A TOOL FUR GUESS-WORK!
IT'S MEANT TA INFORM EVERYBODY A BODY HAS BEEN FOUND!
THAT SAID, AREN'T THERE INSTANCES WHERE THAT RULE COULD PROVE FATAL?
WE CAN'T AFFORD TO REMOVE IT FROM OUR DEDUC-TIONS.
SO WHICH WAS IT THIS TIME? WAS THE KILLER INCLUDED IN THE THREE? OR *NOT* INCLUDED?
...

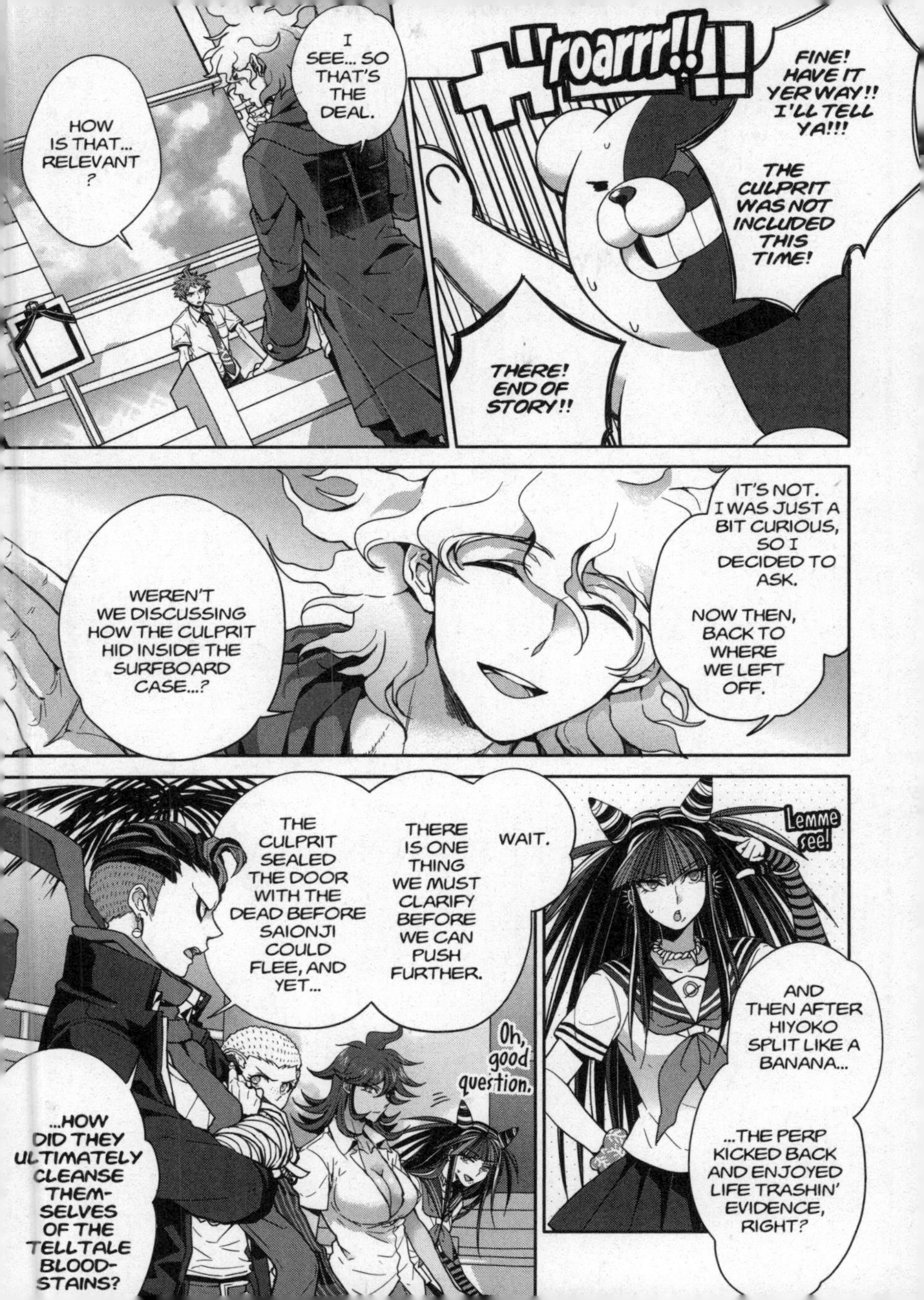
roarrr!!
FINE! HAVE IT YER WAY!! I'LL TELL YA!!!
THE CULPRIT WAS NOT INCLUDED THIS TIME!
THERE! END OF STORY!!
I SEE... SO THAT'S THE DEAL.
HOW IS THAT... RELEVANT?
IT'S NOT. I WAS JUST A BIT CURIOUS, SO I DECIDED TO ASK.
NOW THEN, BACK TO WHERE WE LEFT OFF.
WEREN'T WE DISCUSSING HOW THE CULPRIT HID INSIDE THE SURFBOARD CASE...?
Lemme see!
AND THEN AFTER HIYOKO SPLIT LIKE A BANANA...
...THE PERP KICKED BACK AND ENJOYED LIFE TRASHIN' EVIDENCE, RIGHT?
WAIT.
THERE IS ONE THING WE MUST CLARIFY BEFORE WE CAN PUSH FURTHER.
THE CULPRIT SEALED THE DOOR WITH THE DEAD BEFORE SAIONJI COULD FLEE, AND YET...
Oh, good question.
...HOW DID THEY ULTIMATELY CLEANSE THEM-SELVES OF THE TELLTALE BLOOD-STAINS?

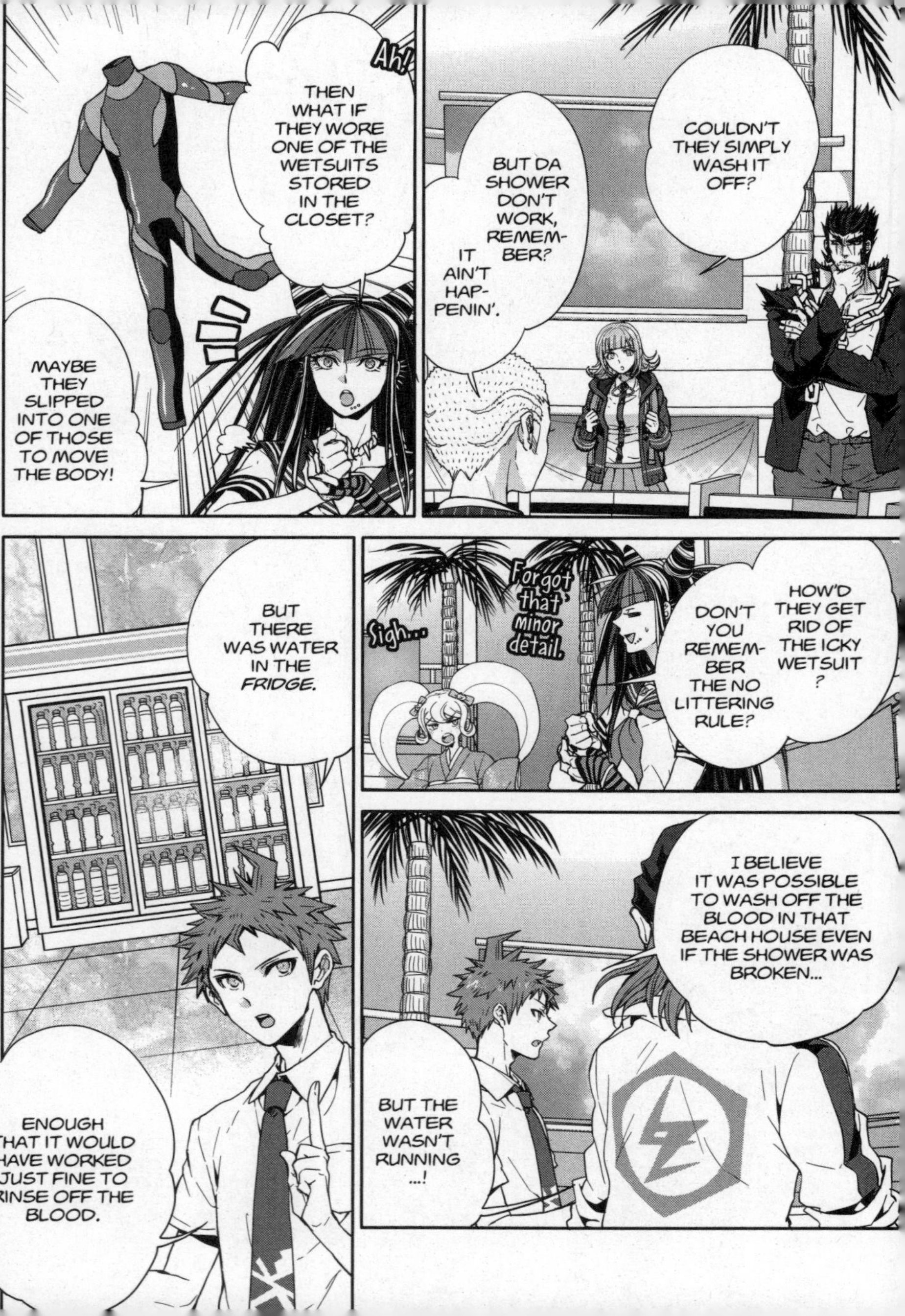
COULDN'T THEY SIMPLY WASH IT OFF?
BUT DA SHOWER DON'T WORK, REMEMBER?
IT AIN'T HAPPENIN'.
Ah!
THEN WHAT IF THEY WORE ONE OF THE WETSUITS STORED IN THE CLOSET?
MAYBE THEY SLIPPED INTO ONE OF THOSE TO MOVE THE BODY!
HOW'D THEY GET RID OF THE ICKY WETSUIT?
DON'T YOU REMEMBER THE NO LITTERING RULE?
Forgot that minor detail.
Sigh...
I BELIEVE IT WAS POSSIBLE TO WASH OFF THE BLOOD IN THAT BEACH HOUSE EVEN IF THE SHOWER WAS BROKEN...
BUT THE WATER WASN'T RUNNING...!
BUT THERE WAS WATER IN THE *FRIDGE*.
ENOUGH THAT IT WOULD HAVE WORKED JUST FINE TO RINSE OFF THE BLOOD.

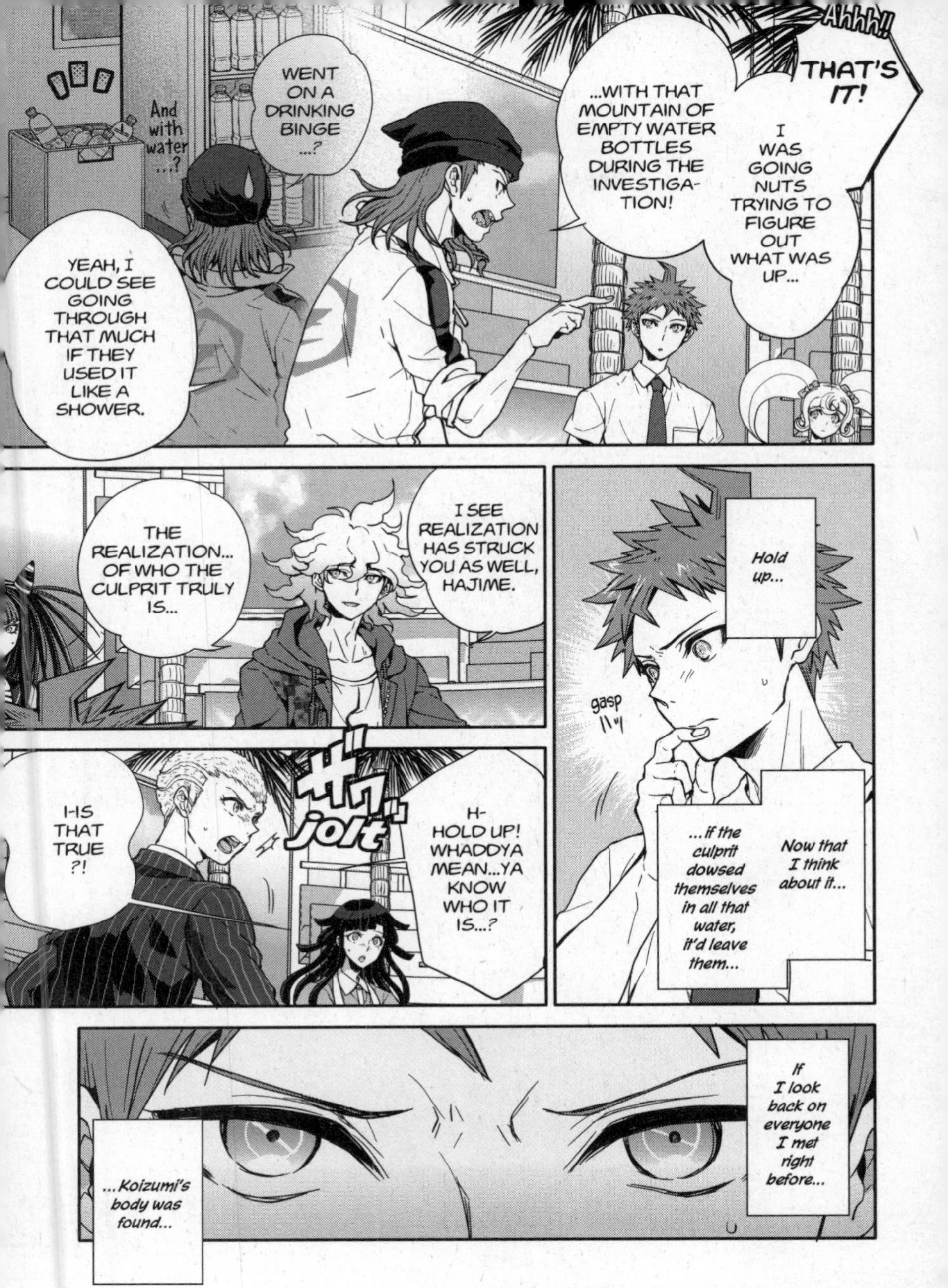
Ahhh!!
THAT'S IT!
I WAS GOING NUTS TRYING TO FIGURE OUT WHAT WAS UP...
...WITH THAT MOUNTAIN OF EMPTY WATER BOTTLES DURING THE INVESTIGA-TION!
WENT ON A DRINKING BINGE ...?
And with water ...?
YEAH, I COULD SEE GOING THROUGH THAT MUCH IF THEY USED IT LIKE A SHOWER.
Hold up...
gasp
Now that I think about it...
...if the culprit dowsed themselves in all that water, it'd leave them...
I SEE REALIZATION HAS STRUCK YOU AS WELL, HAJIME.
THE REALIZATION... OF WHO THE CULPRIT TRULY IS...
jolt
H-HOLD UP! WHADDYA MEAN...YA KNOW WHO IT IS...?
I-IS THAT TRUE ?!
If I look back on everyone I met right before...
...Koizumi's body was found...

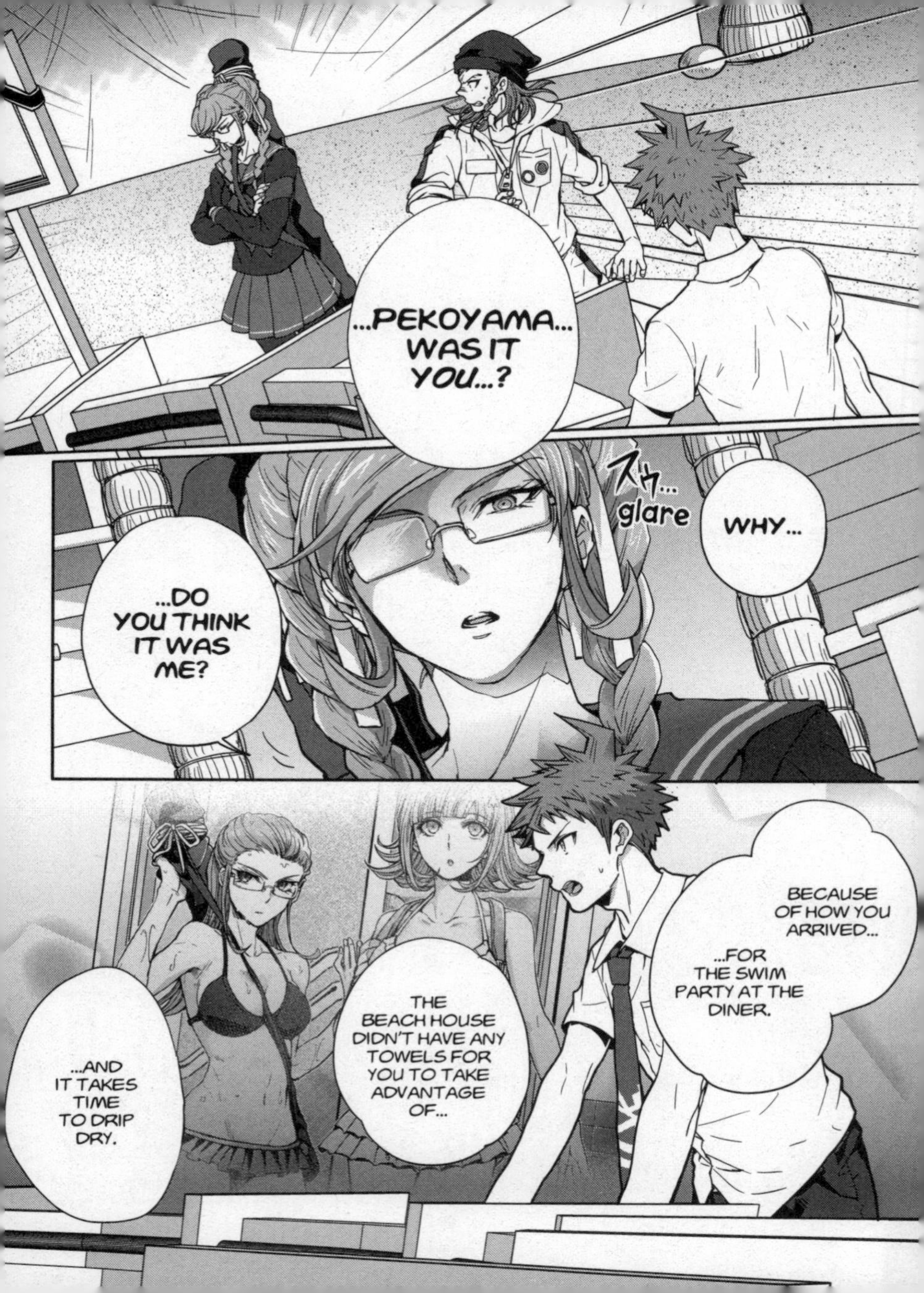
...PEKOYAMA... WAS IT YOU...?
WHY...
スゥ... glare
...DO YOU THINK IT WAS ME?
BECAUSE OF HOW YOU ARRIVED...
...FOR THE SWIM PARTY AT THE DINER.
THE BEACH HOUSE DIDN'T HAVE ANY TOWELS FOR YOU TO TAKE ADVANTAGE OF...
...AND IT TAKES TIME TO DRIP DRY.

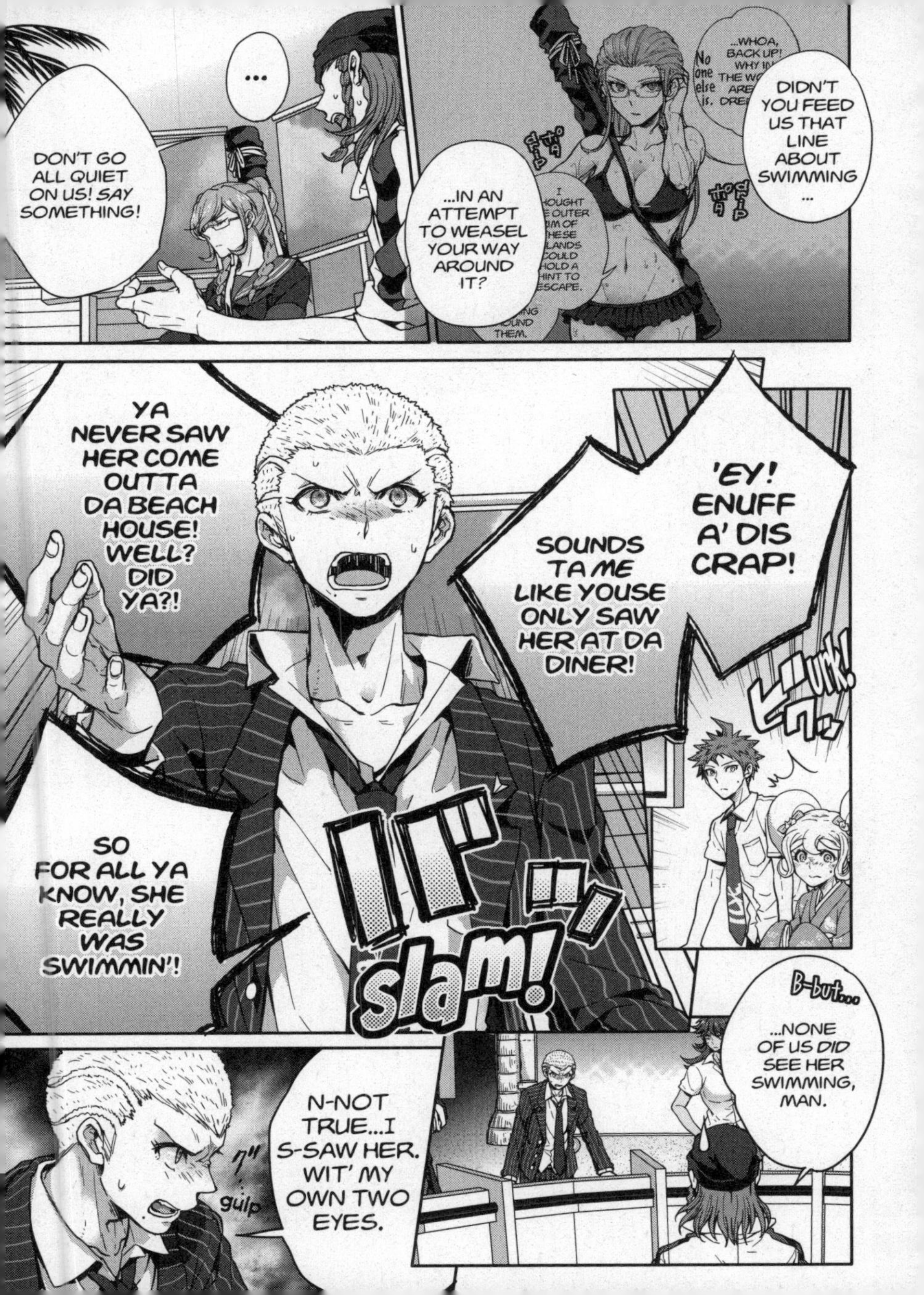
DIDN'T YOU FEED US THAT LINE ABOUT SWIMMING ...
...IN AN ATTEMPT TO WEASEL YOUR WAY AROUND IT?
...
DON'T GO ALL QUIET ON US! SAY SOMETHING!
'EY! ENUFF A' DIS CRAP!
urk!
SOUNDS TA ME LIKE YOUSE ONLY SAW HER AT DA DINER!
YA NEVER SAW HER COME OUTTA DA BEACH HOUSE! WELL? DID YA?!
SO FOR ALL YA KNOW, SHE REALLY WAS SWIMMIN'!
slam!
B-but...
...NONE OF US DID SEE HER SWIMMING, MAN.
N-NOT TRUE...I S-SAW HER. WIT' MY OWN TWO EYES.
gulp

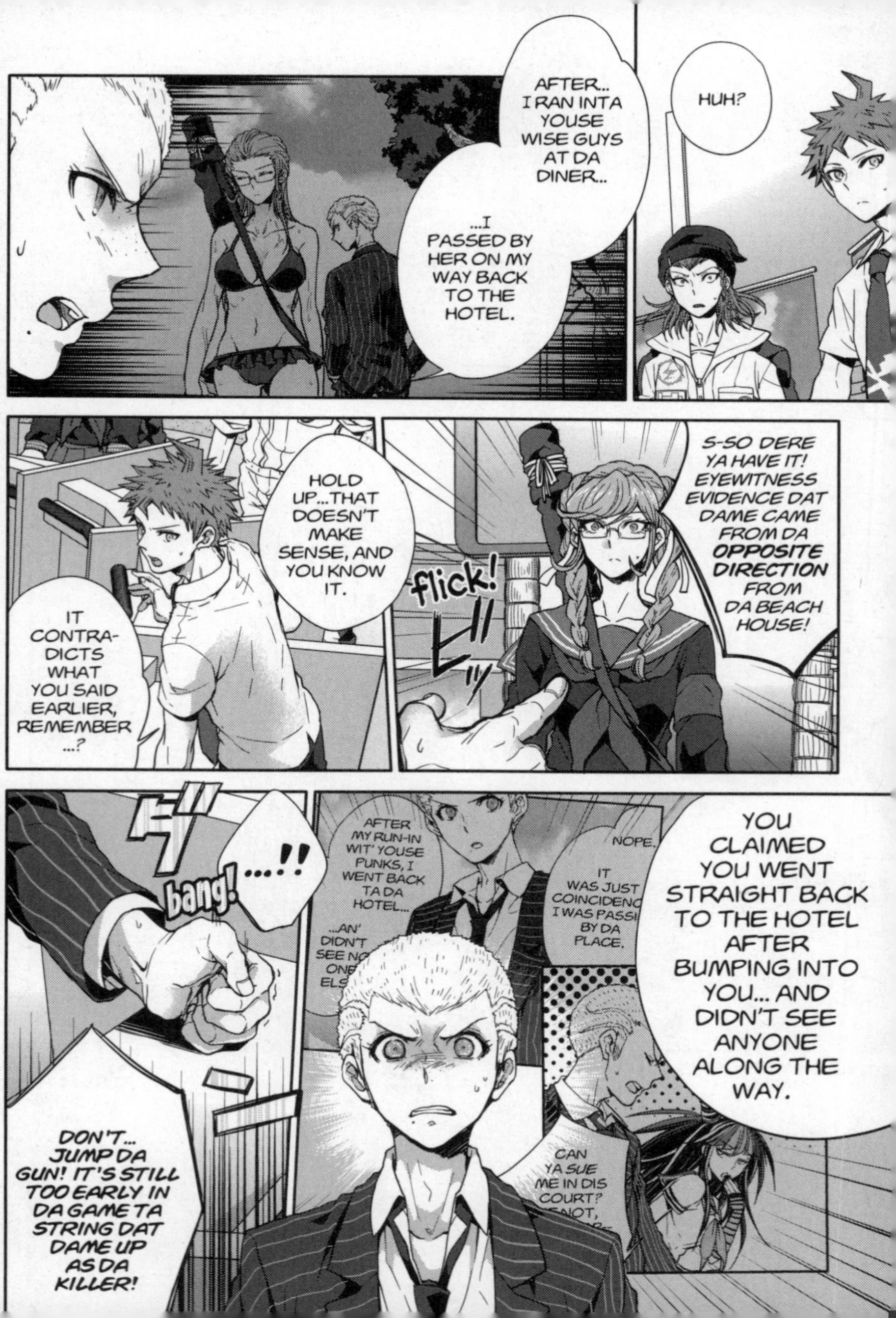
HUH?
AFTER... I RAN INTA YOUSE WISE GUYS AT DA DINER...
...I PASSED BY HER ON MY WAY BACK TO THE HOTEL.
S-SO DERE YA HAVE IT! EYEWITNESS EVIDENCE DAT DAME CAME FROM DA OPPOSITE DIRECTION FROM DA BEACH HOUSE!
flick!
HOLD UP...THAT DOESN'T MAKE SENSE, AND YOU KNOW IT.
IT CONTRA-DICTS WHAT YOU SAID EARLIER, REMEMBER ...?
YOU CLAIMED YOU WENT STRAIGHT BACK TO THE HOTEL AFTER BUMPING INTO YOU... AND DIDN'T SEE ANYONE ALONG THE WAY.
NOPE.
IT WAS JUST COINCIDENC I WAS PASSI BY DA PLACE.
AFTER MY RUN-IN WIT' YOUSE PUNKS, I WENT BACK TA DA HOTEL...
...AN' DIDN'T SEE N ONE ELS
CAN YA SUE ME IN DIS COURT?
DON'T... JUMP DA GUN! IT'S STILL TOO EARLY IN DA GAME TA STRING DAT DAME UP AS DA KILLER!
...!!
bang!

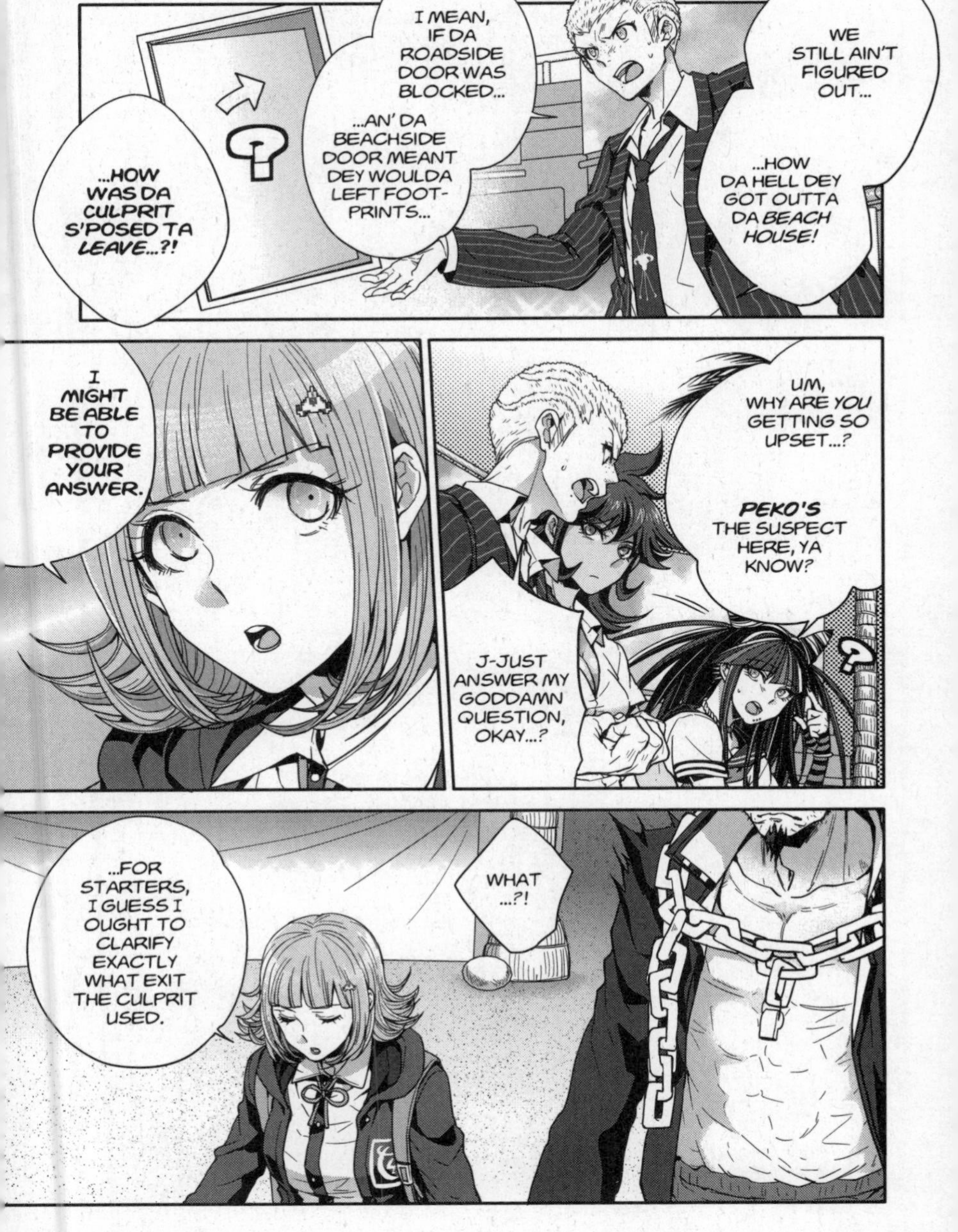
WE STILL AIN'T FIGURED OUT...
...HOW DA HELL DEY GOT OUTTA DA *BEACH HOUSE!*
I MEAN, IF DA ROADSIDE DOOR WAS BLOCKED...
...AN' DA BEACHSIDE DOOR MEANT DEY WOULDA LEFT FOOT-PRINTS...
...HOW WAS DA CULPRIT S'POSED TA *LEAVE*...?!
UM, WHY ARE *YOU* GETTING SO UPSET...?
PEKO'S THE SUSPECT HERE, YA KNOW?
J-JUST ANSWER MY GODDAMN QUESTION, OKAY...?
I MIGHT BE ABLE TO PROVIDE YOUR ANSWER.
WHAT ...?!
...FOR STARTERS, I GUESS I OUGHT TO CLARIFY EXACTLY WHAT EXIT THE CULPRIT USED.

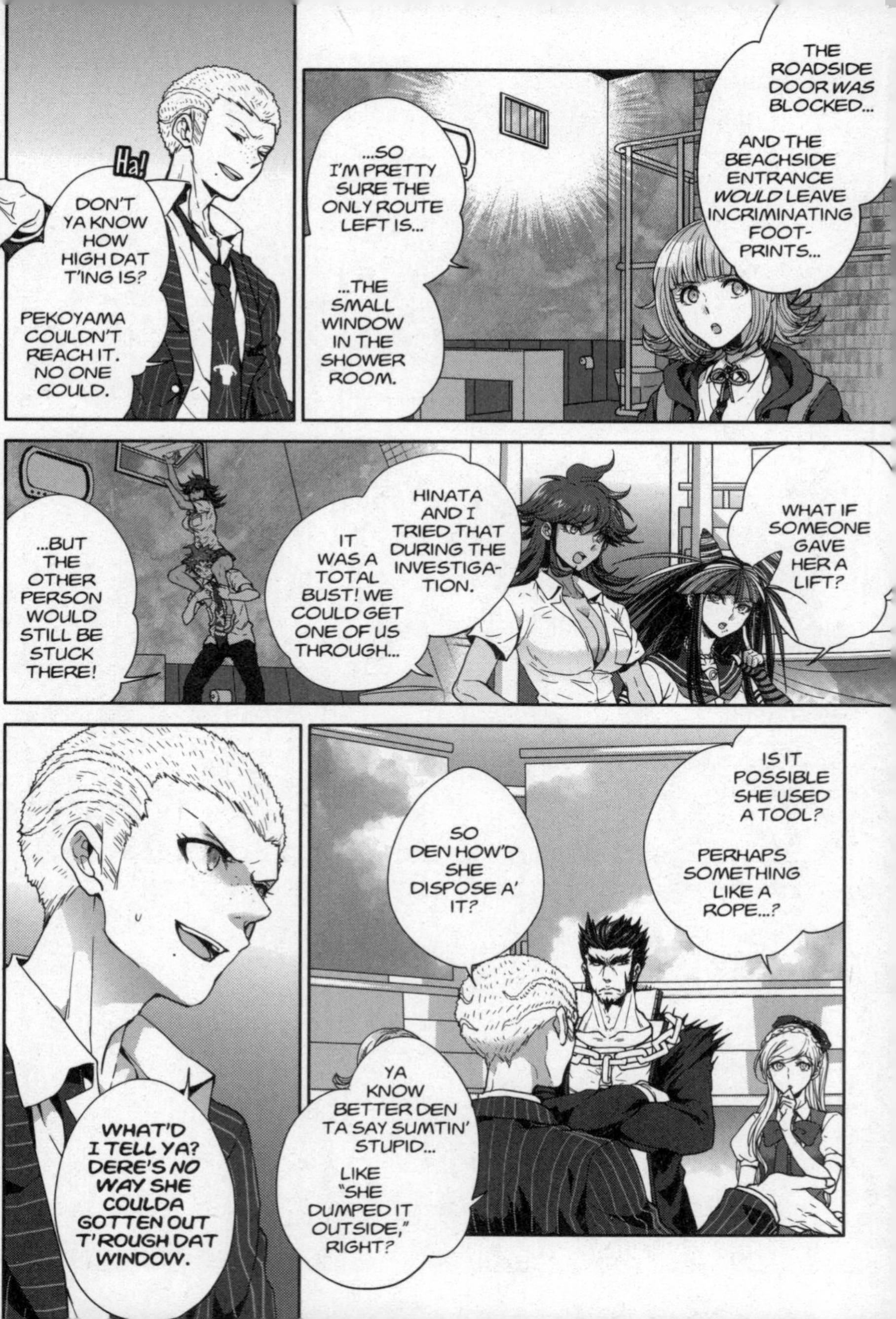
THE ROADSIDE DOOR *WAS* BLOCKED...
AND THE BEACHSIDE ENTRANCE *WOULD* LEAVE INCRIMINATING FOOT-PRINTS...
...SO I'M PRETTY SURE THE ONLY ROUTE LEFT IS...
...THE SMALL WINDOW IN THE SHOWER ROOM.
Ha!
DON'T YA KNOW HOW HIGH DAT T'ING IS?
PEKOYAMA COULDN'T REACH IT. NO ONE COULD.
WHAT IF SOMEONE GAVE HER A LIFT?
HINATA AND I TRIED THAT DURING THE INVESTIGA-TION.
IT WAS A TOTAL BUST! WE COULD GET ONE OF US THROUGH...
...BUT THE OTHER PERSON WOULD STILL BE STUCK THERE!
IS IT POSSIBLE SHE USED A TOOL?
PERHAPS SOMETHING LIKE A ROPE...?
SO DEN HOW'D SHE DISPOSE A' IT?
YA KNOW BETTER DEN TA SAY SUMTIN' STUPID...
LIKE "SHE DUMPED IT OUTSIDE," RIGHT?
WHAT'D I TELL YA? DERE'S NO WAY SHE COULDA GOTTEN OUT T'ROUGH DAT WINDOW.

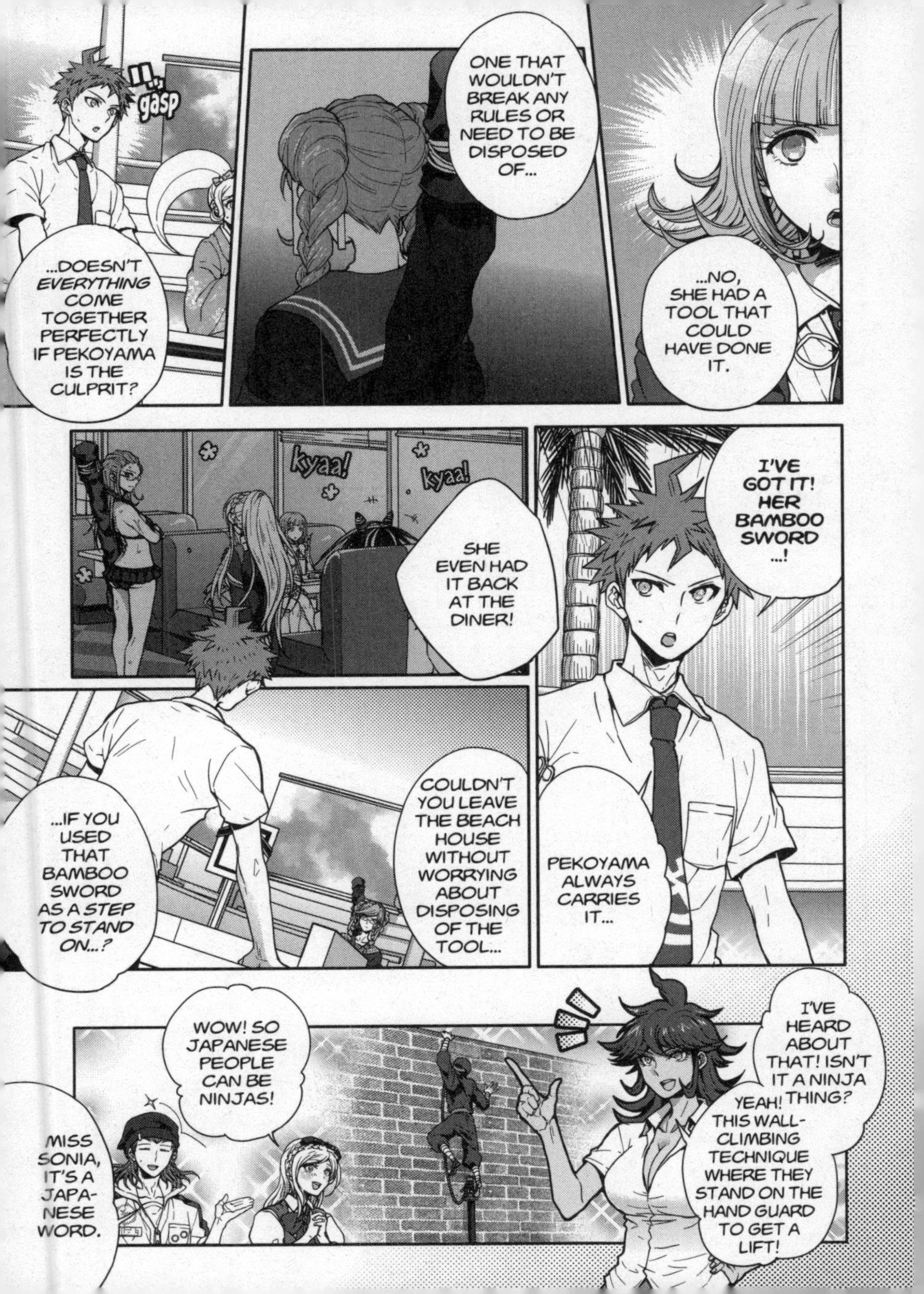
...NO, SHE HAD A TOOL THAT COULD HAVE DONE IT.
ONE THAT WOULDN'T BREAK ANY RULES OR NEED TO BE DISPOSED OF...
gasp
...DOESN'T EVERYTHING COME TOGETHER PERFECTLY IF PEKOYAMA IS THE CULPRIT?
I'VE GOT IT! HER BAMBOO SWORD ...!
PEKOYAMA ALWAYS CARRIES IT...
kyaa!
kyaa!
SHE EVEN HAD IT BACK AT THE DINER!
COULDN'T YOU LEAVE THE BEACH HOUSE WITHOUT WORRYING ABOUT DISPOSING OF THE TOOL...
...IF YOU USED THAT BAMBOO SWORD AS A STEP TO STAND ON...?
I'VE HEARD ABOUT THAT! ISN'T IT A NINJA THING?
YEAH! THIS WALL-CLIMBING TECHNIQUE WHERE THEY STAND ON THE HAND GUARD TO GET A LIFT!
WOW! SO JAPANESE PEOPLE CAN BE NINJAS!
MISS SONIA, IT'S A JAPANESE WORD.

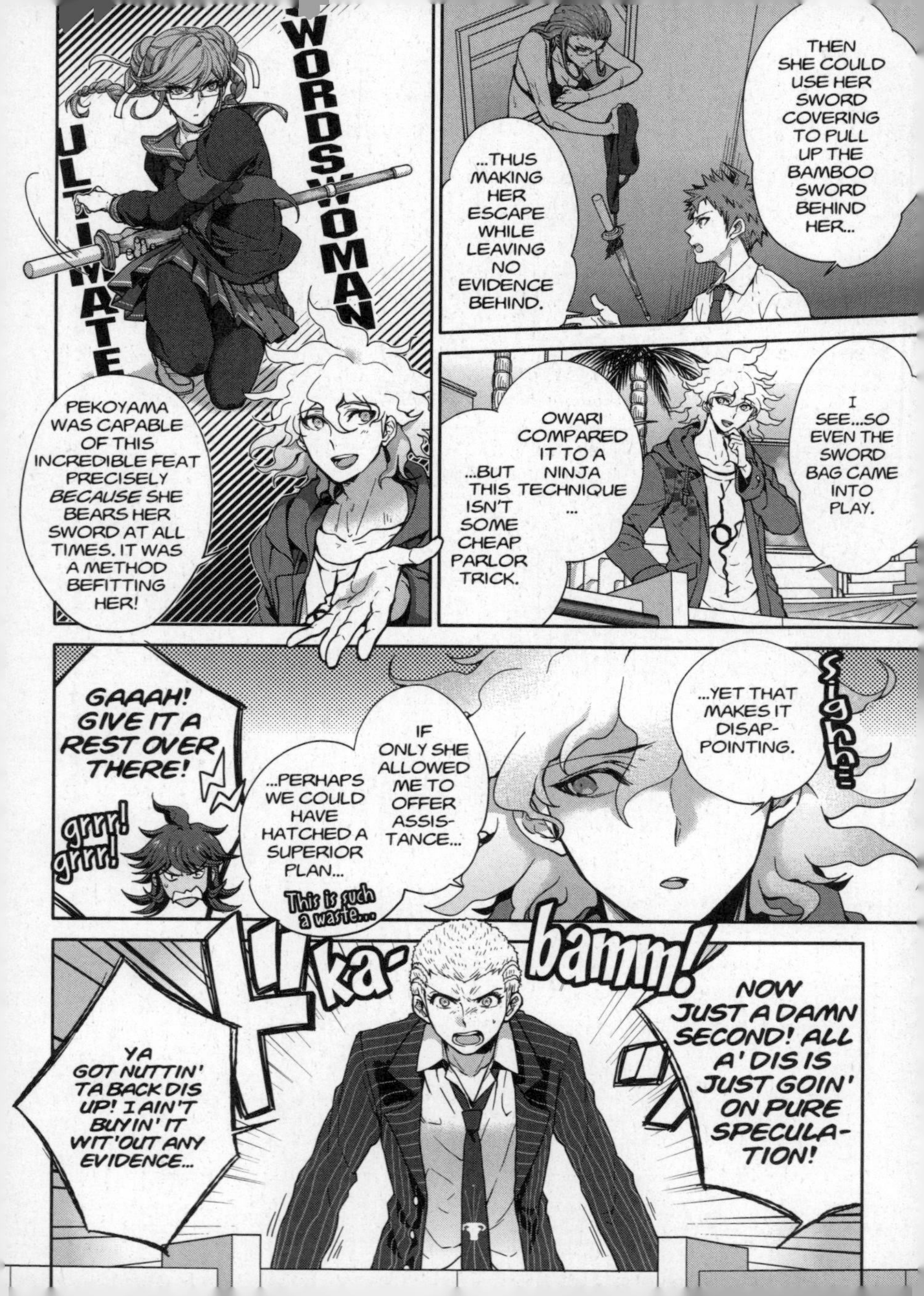
THEN SHE COULD USE HER SWORD COVERING TO PULL UP THE BAMBOO SWORD BEHIND HER...
...THUS MAKING HER ESCAPE WHILE LEAVING NO EVIDENCE BEHIND.
I SEE...SO EVEN THE SWORD BAG CAME INTO PLAY.
OWARI COMPARED IT TO A NINJA TECHNIQUE...
...BUT THIS ISN'T SOME CHEAP PARLOR TRICK.
ULTIMATE SWORDSWOMAN
PEKOYAMA WAS CAPABLE OF THIS INCREDIBLE FEAT PRECISELY *BECAUSE* SHE BEARS HER SWORD AT ALL TIMES. IT WAS A METHOD BEFITTING HER!
sigh...
...YET THAT MAKES IT DISAP-POINTING.
IF ONLY SHE ALLOWED ME TO OFFER ASSIS-TANCE...
...PERHAPS WE COULD HAVE HATCHED A SUPERIOR PLAN...
This is such a waste...
GAAAH! GIVE IT A REST OVER THERE!
grrr! grrr!
ka-bamm!
NOW JUST A DAMN SECOND! ALL A' DIS IS JUST GOIN' ON PURE SPECULA-TION!
YA GOT NUTTIN' TA BACK DIS UP! I AIN'T BUYIN' IT WIT'OUT ANY EVIDENCE...

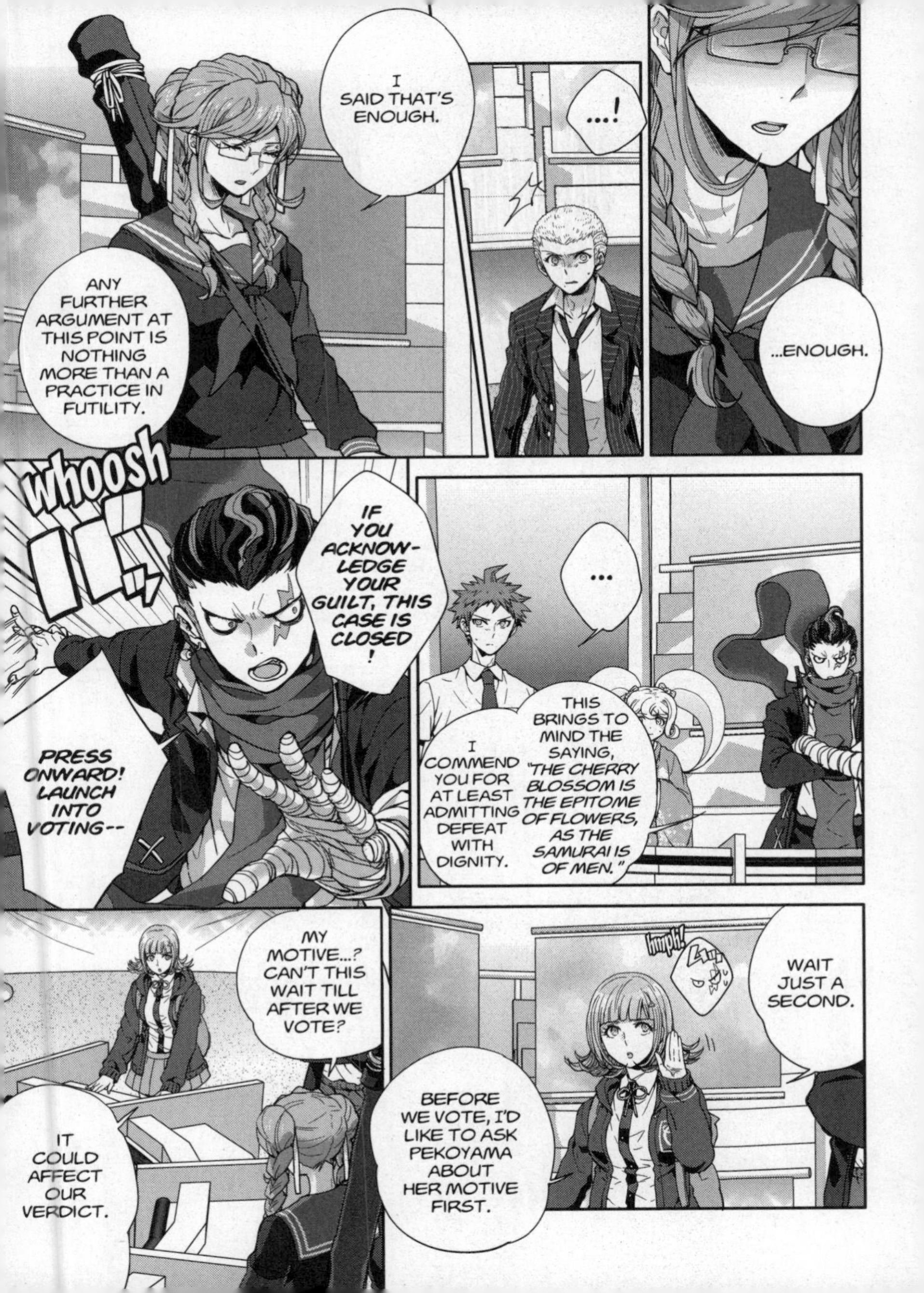
...ENOUGH.
...!
I SAID THAT'S ENOUGH.
ANY FURTHER ARGUMENT AT THIS POINT IS NOTHING MORE THAN A PRACTICE IN FUTILITY.
...
THIS BRINGS TO MIND THE SAYING, "THE CHERRY BLOSSOM IS THE EPITOME OF FLOWERS, AS THE SAMURAI IS OF MEN."
I COMMEND YOU FOR AT LEAST ADMITTING DEFEAT WITH DIGNITY.
whoosh
IF YOU ACKNOWLEDGE YOUR GUILT, THIS CASE IS CLOSED!
PRESS ONWARD! LAUNCH INTO VOTING--
hmph!
WAIT JUST A SECOND.
BEFORE WE VOTE, I'D LIKE TO ASK PEKOYAMA ABOUT HER MOTIVE FIRST.
MY MOTIVE...? CAN'T THIS WAIT TILL AFTER WE VOTE?
IT COULD AFFECT OUR VERDICT.

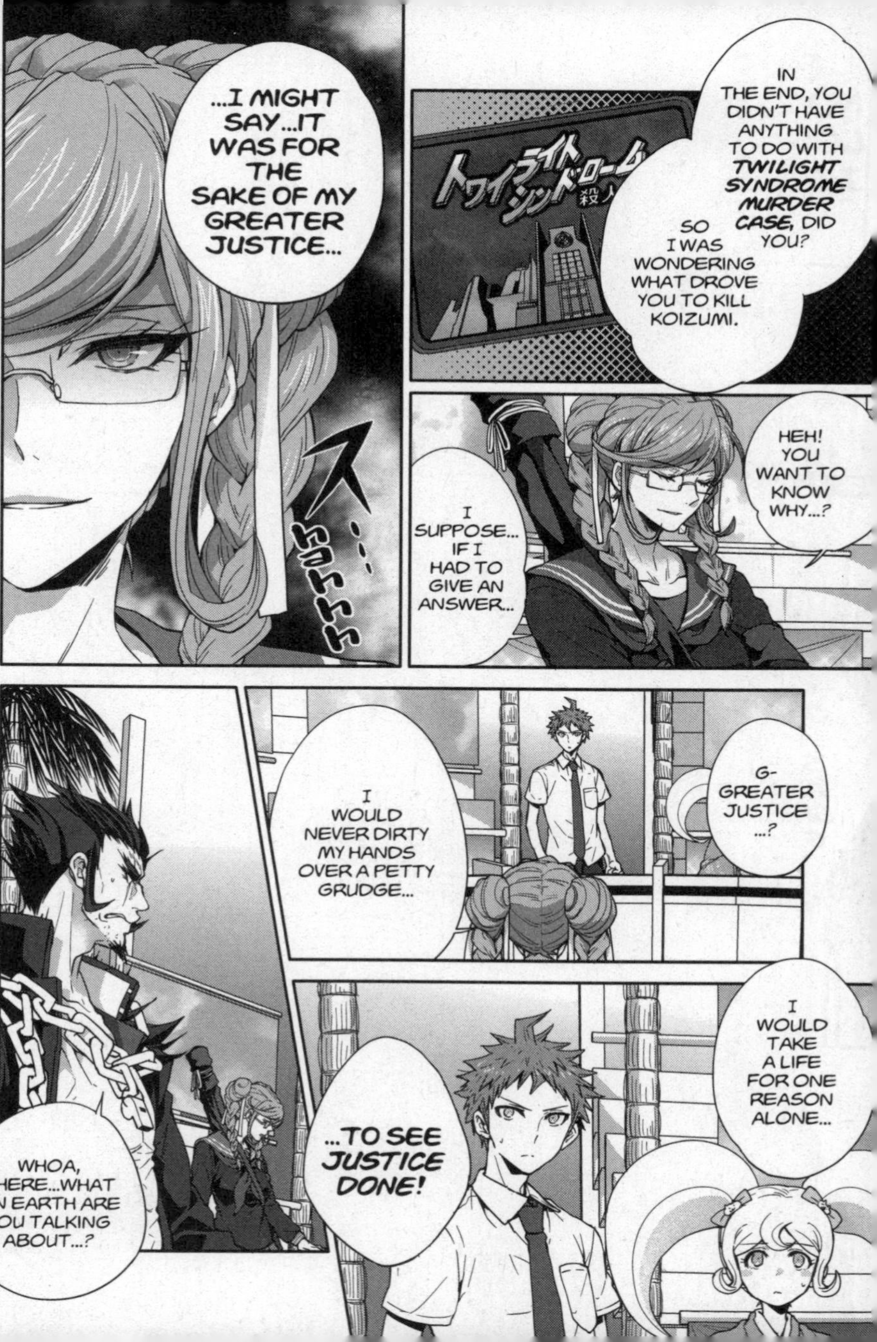
IN THE END, YOU DIDN'T HAVE ANYTHING TO DO WITH *TWILIGHT SYNDROME MURDER CASE*, DID YOU?
SO I WAS WONDERING WHAT DROVE YOU TO KILL KOIZUMI.
HEH! YOU WANT TO KNOW WHY...?
I SUPPOSE... IF I HAD TO GIVE AN ANSWER...
...I MIGHT SAY...IT WAS FOR THE SAKE OF MY GREATER JUSTICE...
G-GREATER JUSTICE...?
I WOULD NEVER DIRTY MY HANDS OVER A PETTY GRUDGE...
I WOULD TAKE A LIFE FOR ONE REASON ALONE...
...TO SEE *JUSTICE* DONE!
WHOA, THERE...WHAT ON EARTH ARE YOU TALKING ABOUT...?

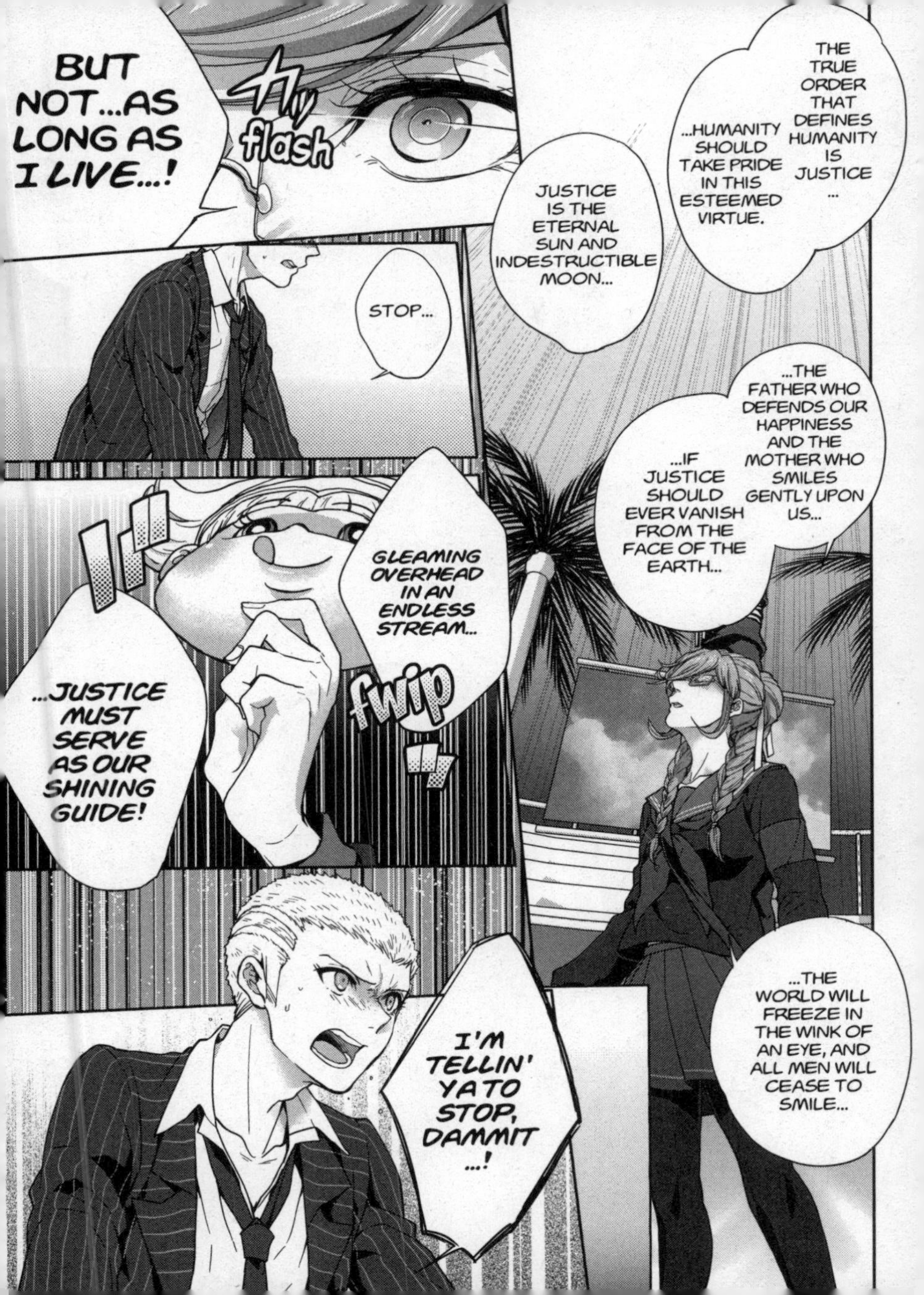
BUT NOT...AS LONG AS I LIVE...!
flash
THE TRUE ORDER THAT DEFINES HUMANITY IS JUSTICE ...
...HUMANITY SHOULD TAKE PRIDE IN THIS ESTEEMED VIRTUE.
JUSTICE IS THE ETERNAL SUN AND INDESTRUCTIBLE MOON...
STOP...
...THE FATHER WHO DEFENDS OUR HAPPINESS AND THE MOTHER WHO SMILES GENTLY UPON US...
...IF JUSTICE SHOULD EVER VANISH FROM THE FACE OF THE EARTH...
GLEAMING OVERHEAD IN AN ENDLESS STREAM...
...JUSTICE MUST SERVE AS OUR SHINING GUIDE!
fwip
...THE WORLD WILL FREEZE IN THE WINK OF AN EYE, AND ALL MEN WILL CEASE TO SMILE...
I'M TELLIN' YA TO STOP, DAMMIT ...!

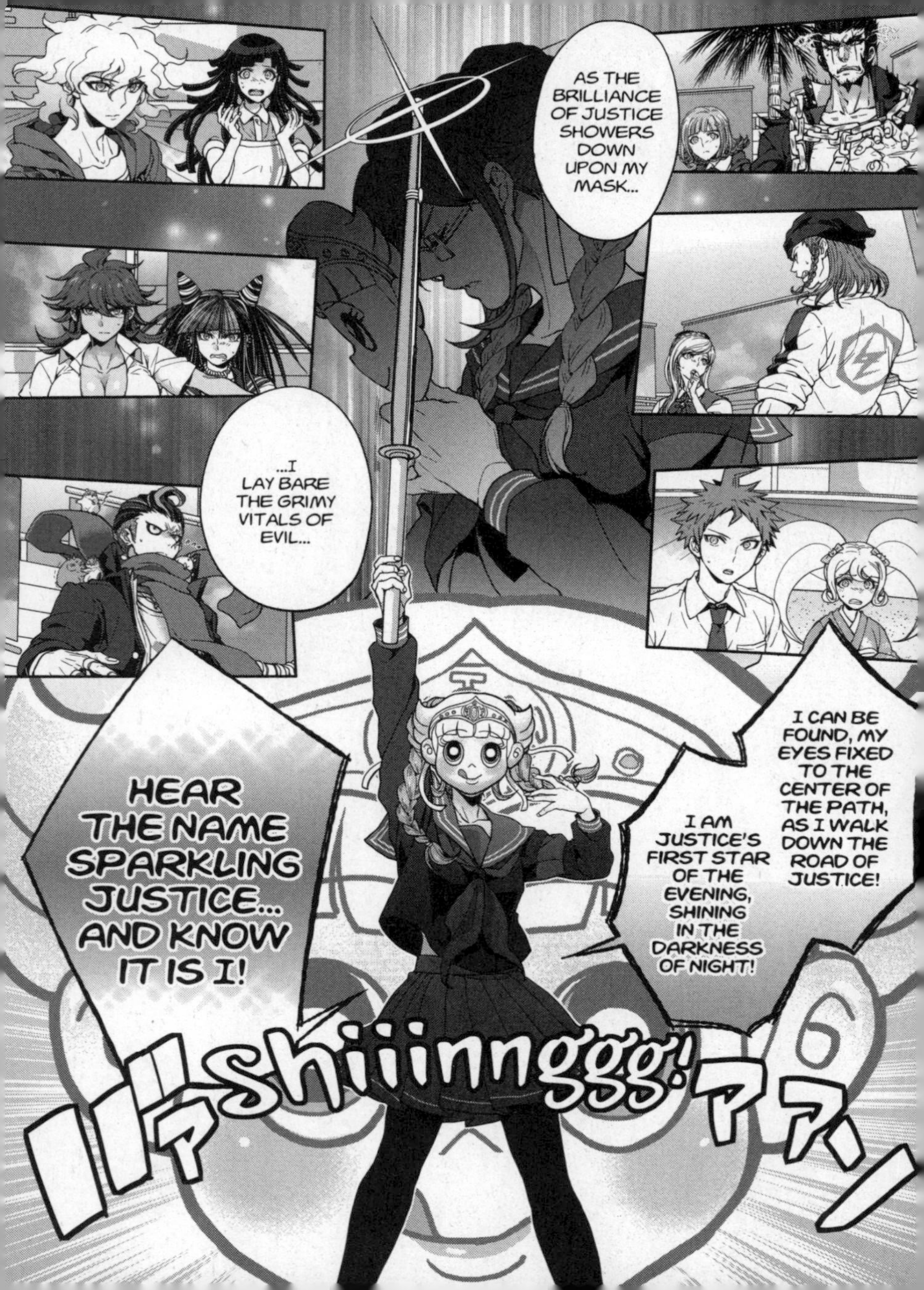
AS THE BRILLIANCE OF JUSTICE SHOWERS DOWN UPON MY MASK...
...I LAY BARE THE GRIMY VITALS OF EVIL...
I CAN BE FOUND, MY EYES FIXED TO THE CENTER OF THE PATH, AS I WALK DOWN THE ROAD OF JUSTICE!
I AM JUSTICE'S FIRST STAR OF THE EVENING, SHINING IN THE DARKNESS OF NIGHT!
HEAR THE NAME SPARKLING JUSTICE... AND KNOW IT IS I!
Shiiinnggg!

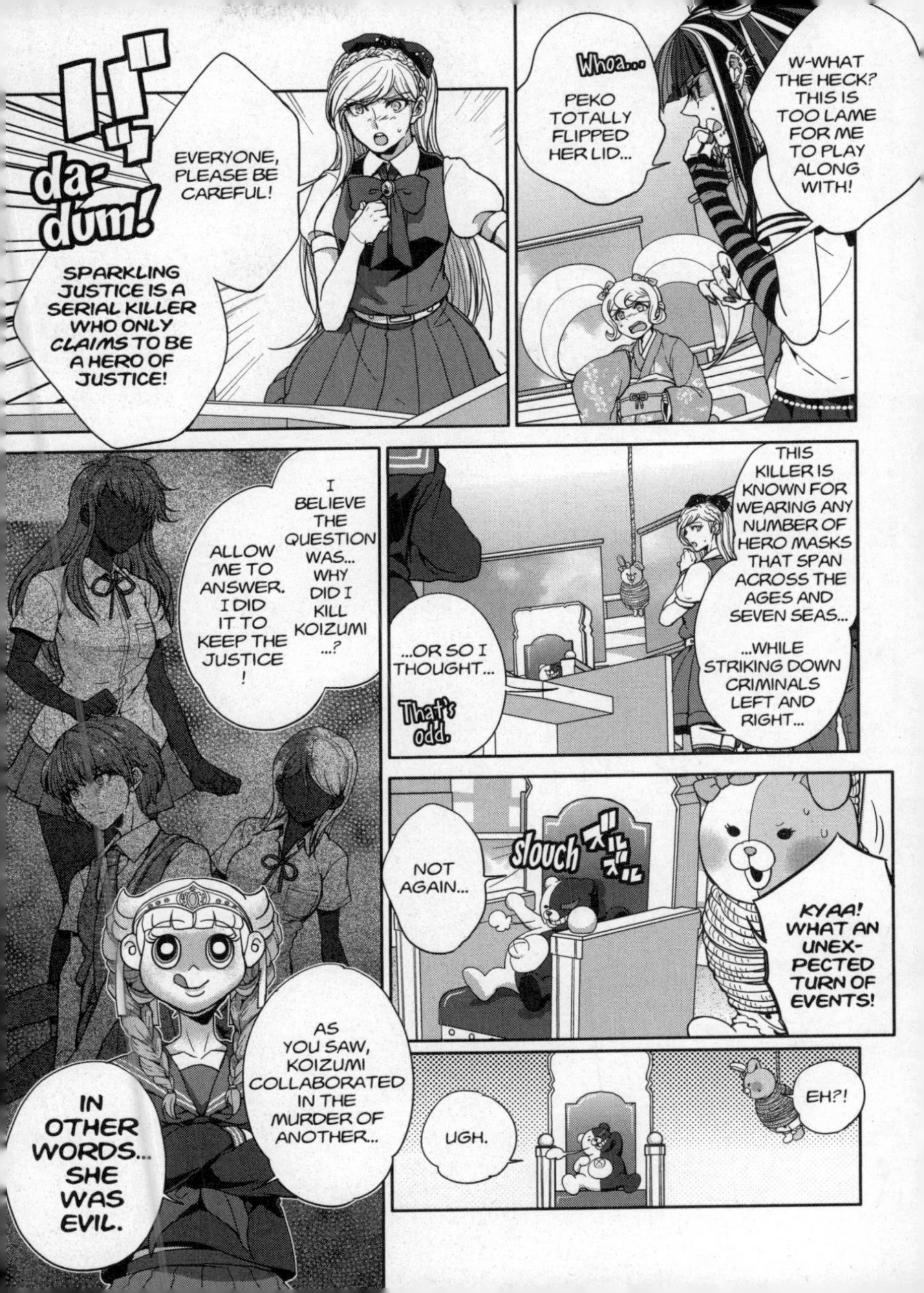
W-WHAT THE HECK? THIS IS TOO LAME FOR ME TO PLAY ALONG WITH!
Whoa...
PEKO TOTALLY FLIPPED HER LID...
EVERYONE, PLEASE BE CAREFUL!
da-dum!
SPARKLING JUSTICE IS A SERIAL KILLER WHO ONLY CLAIMS TO BE A HERO OF JUSTICE!
THIS KILLER IS KNOWN FOR WEARING ANY NUMBER OF HERO MASKS THAT SPAN ACROSS THE AGES AND SEVEN SEAS...
...WHILE STRIKING DOWN CRIMINALS LEFT AND RIGHT...
...OR SO I THOUGHT...
That's odd.
KYAA! WHAT AN UNEXPECTED TURN OF EVENTS!
slouch
NOT AGAIN...
EH?!
UGH.
I BELIEVE THE QUESTION WAS... WHY DID I KILL KOIZUMI...?
ALLOW ME TO ANSWER. I DID IT TO KEEP THE JUSTICE!
AS YOU SAW, KOIZUMI COLLABORATED IN THE MURDER OF ANOTHER...
IN OTHER WORDS... SHE WAS EVIL.

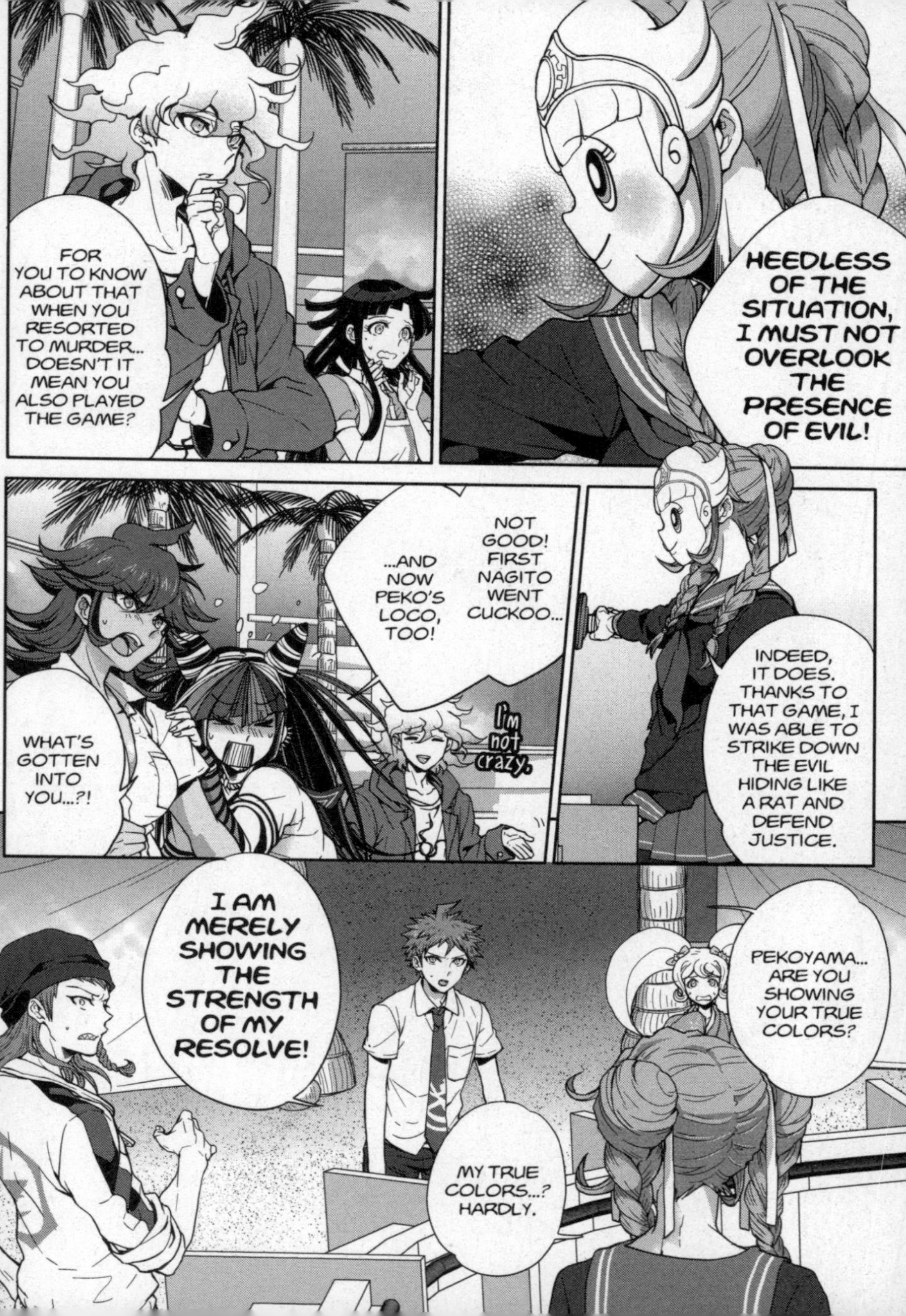
HEEDLESS OF THE SITUATION, I MUST NOT OVERLOOK THE PRESENCE OF EVIL!
FOR YOU TO KNOW ABOUT THAT WHEN YOU RESORTED TO MURDER.. DOESN'T IT MEAN YOU ALSO PLAYED THE GAME?
INDEED, IT DOES. THANKS TO THAT GAME, I WAS ABLE TO STRIKE DOWN THE EVIL HIDING LIKE A RAT AND DEFEND JUSTICE.
NOT GOOD! FIRST NAGITO WENT CUCKOO...
...AND NOW PEKO'S LOCO, TOO!
I'm not crazy.
WHAT'S GOTTEN INTO YOU...?!
PEKOYAMA... ARE YOU SHOWING YOUR TRUE COLORS?
MY TRUE COLORS...? HARDLY.
I AM MERELY SHOWING THE STRENGTH OF MY RESOLVE!

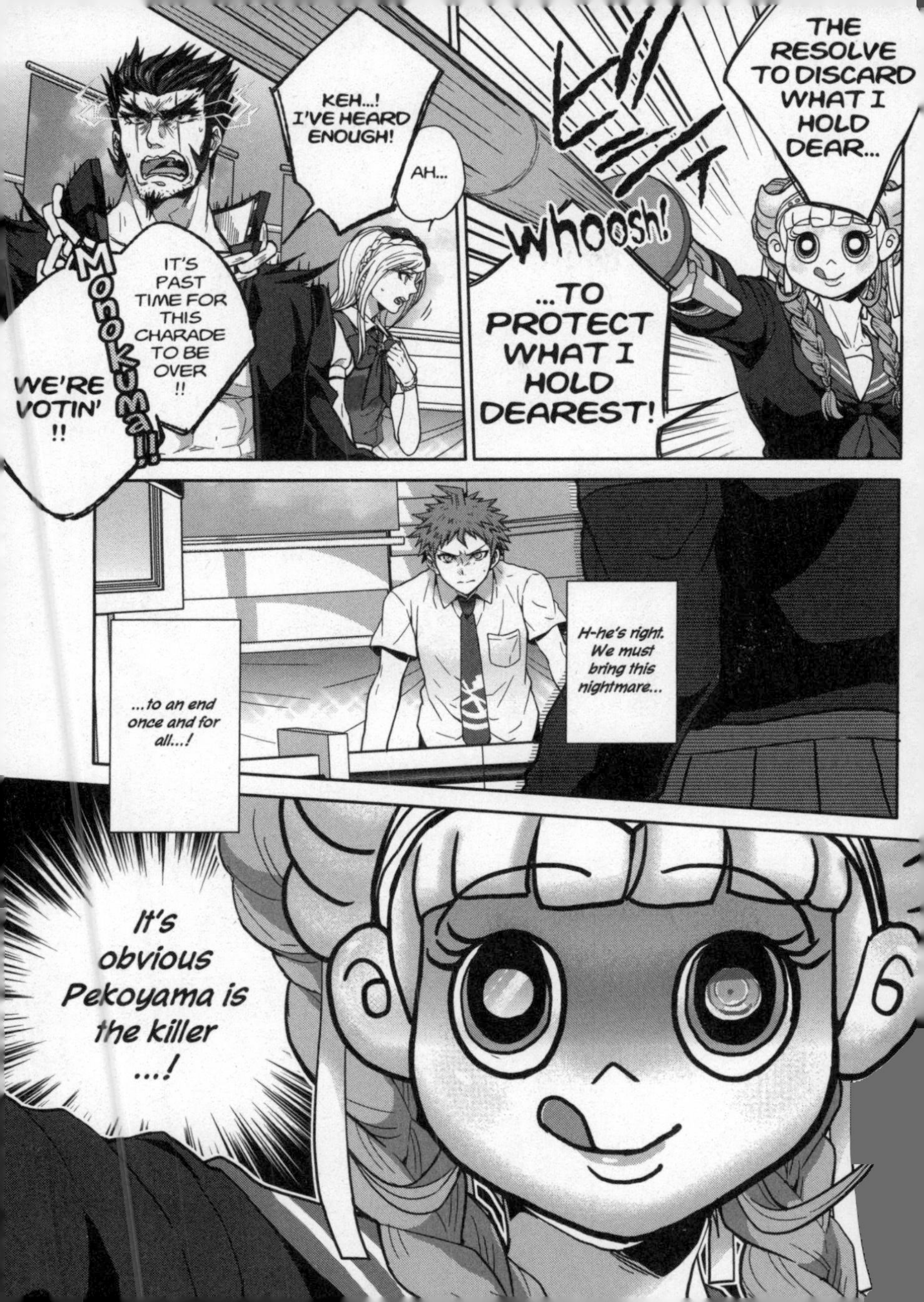
THE RESOLVE TO DISCARD WHAT I HOLD DEAR...
Whoosh!
...TO PROTECT WHAT I HOLD DEAREST!
KEH...! I'VE HEARD ENOUGH!
AH...
IT'S PAST TIME FOR THIS CHARADE TO BE OVER !!
WE'RE VOTIN' !!
Monokuma!!
H-he's right. We must bring this nightmare...
...to an end once and for all...!
It's obvious Pekoyama is the killer ...!

RONPA 2

DANGAN

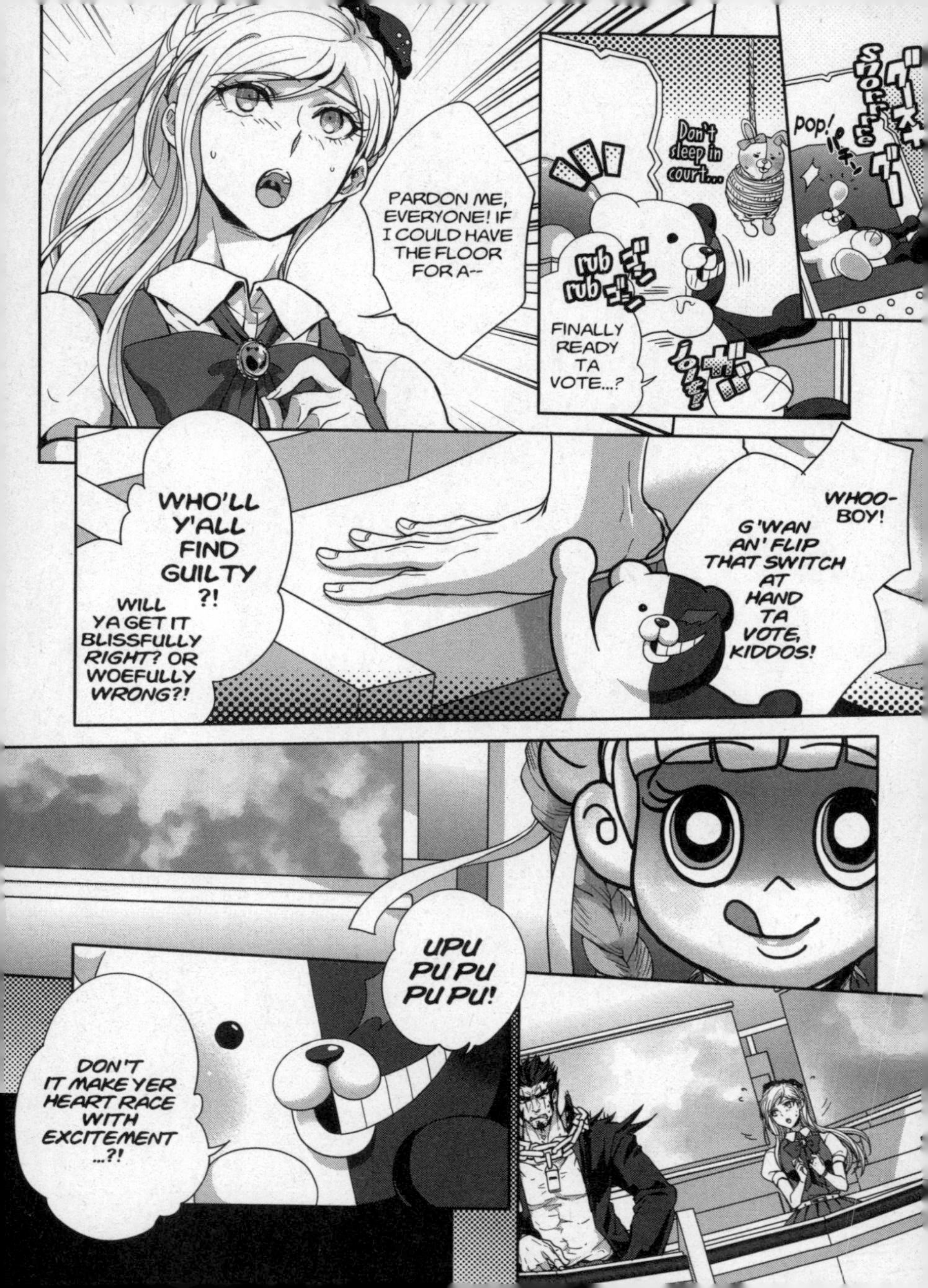
snore
pop!
Don't sleep in court...
rub rub
FINALLY READY TA VOTE...?
jolt!
PARDON ME, EVERYONE! IF I COULD HAVE THE FLOOR FOR A--
WHOO-BOY!
G'WAN AN' FLIP THAT SWITCH AT HAND TA VOTE, KIDDOS!
WHO'LL Y'ALL FIND GUILTY ?!
WILL YA GET IT BLISSFULLY RIGHT? OR WOEFULLY WRONG?!
UPU PU PU PU PU!
DON'T IT MAKE YER HEART RACE WITH EXCITEMENT ...?!

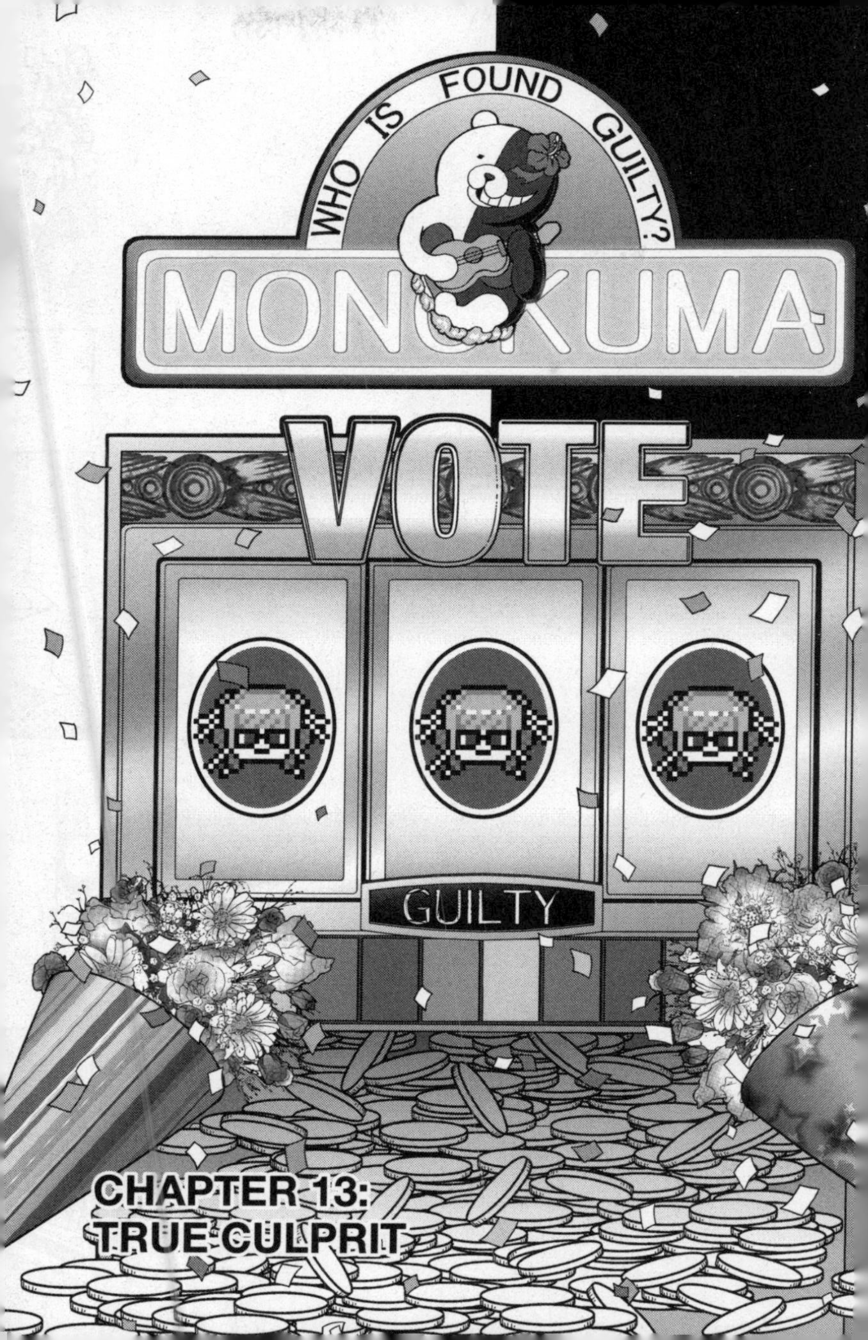
WHO IS FOUND GUILTY?
MONOKUMA
VOTE
GUILTY
CHAPTER 13:
TRUE CULPRIT

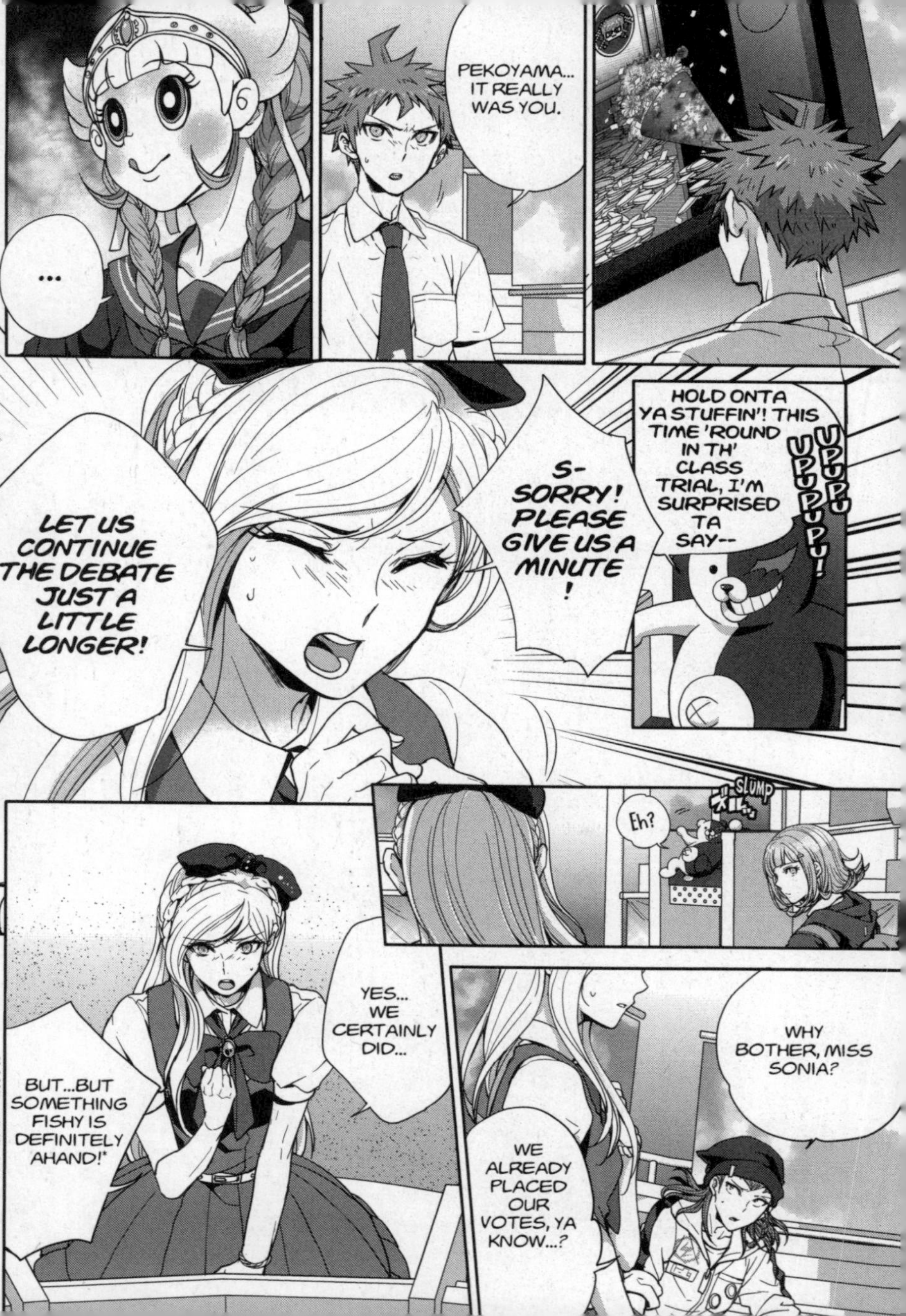
PEKOYAMA... IT REALLY WAS YOU.
...
HOLD ONTA YA STUFFIN'! THIS TIME 'ROUND IN TH' CLASS TRIAL, I'M SURPRISED TA SAY--
UPUPUPUPU UPUPUPU!
S-SORRY! PLEASE GIVE US A MINUTE!
LET US CONTINUE THE DEBATE JUST A LITTLE LONGER!
SLUMP
Eh?
WHY BOTHER, MISS SONIA?
WE ALREADY PLACED OUR VOTES, YA KNOW...?
YES... WE CERTAINLY DID...
BUT...BUT SOMETHING FISHY IS DEFINITELY AHAND!*

*She means "afoot."

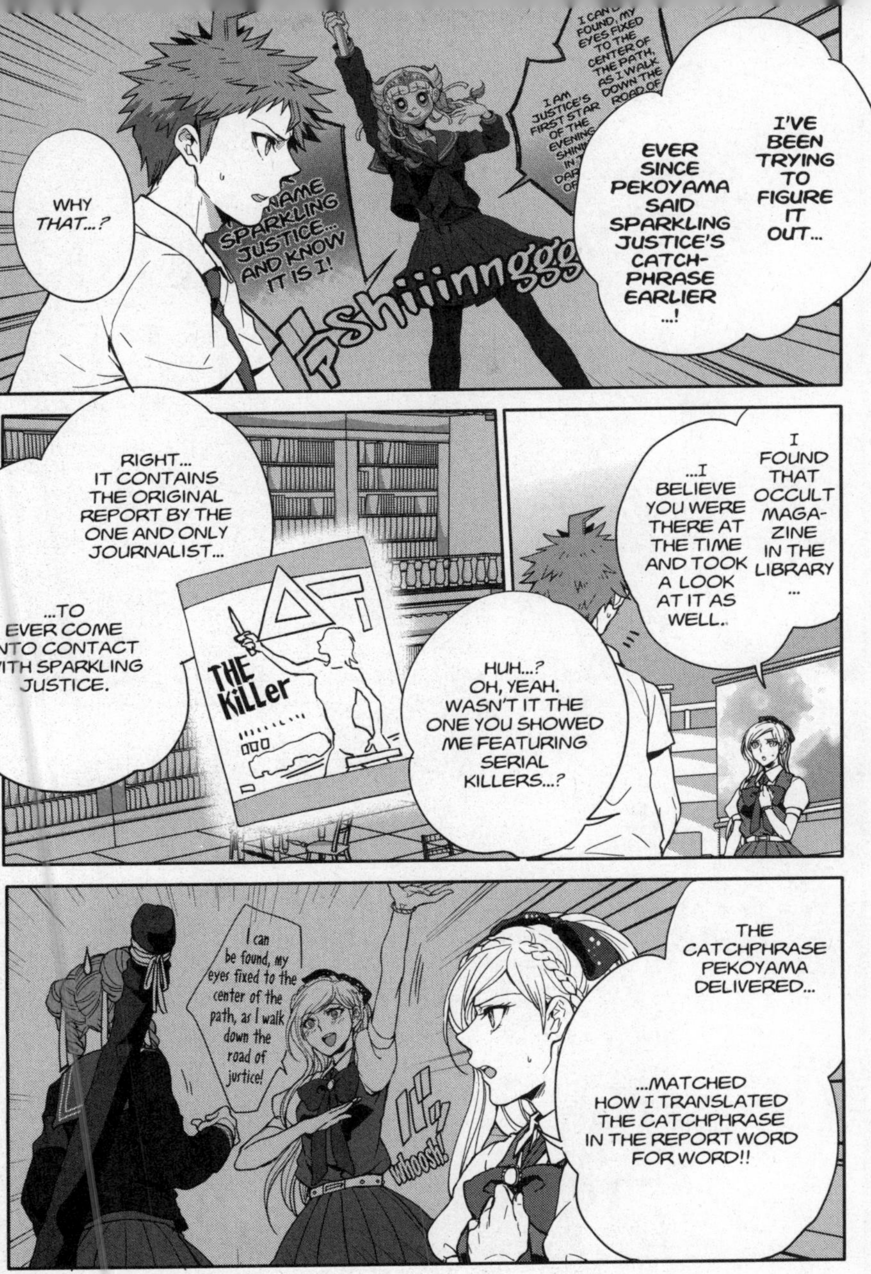
I'VE BEEN TRYING TO FIGURE IT OUT...
EVER SINCE PEKOYAMA SAID SPARKLING JUSTICE'S CATCHPHRASE EARLIER...!
I AM JUSTICE'S FIRST STAR OF THE EVENING
I CAN BE FOUND, MY EYES FIXED TO THE CENTER OF THE PATH, AS I WALK DOWN THE ROAD OF
SPARKLING JUSTICE... AND KNOW IT IS I!
shiiinnggg
WHY THAT...?
I FOUND THAT OCCULT MAGAZINE IN THE LIBRARY...
...I BELIEVE YOU WERE THERE AT THE TIME AND TOOK A LOOK AT IT AS WELL..
HUH...? OH, YEAH. WASN'T IT THE ONE YOU SHOWED ME FEATURING SERIAL KILLERS...?
RIGHT... IT CONTAINS THE ORIGINAL REPORT BY THE ONE AND ONLY JOURNALIST...
...TO EVER COME INTO CONTACT WITH SPARKLING JUSTICE.
THE KiLLer
THE CATCHPHRASE PEKOYAMA DELIVERED...
...MATCHED HOW I TRANSLATED THE CATCHPHRASE IN THE REPORT WORD FOR WORD!!
I can be found, my eyes fixed to the center of the path, as I walk down the road of justice!
whoosh!

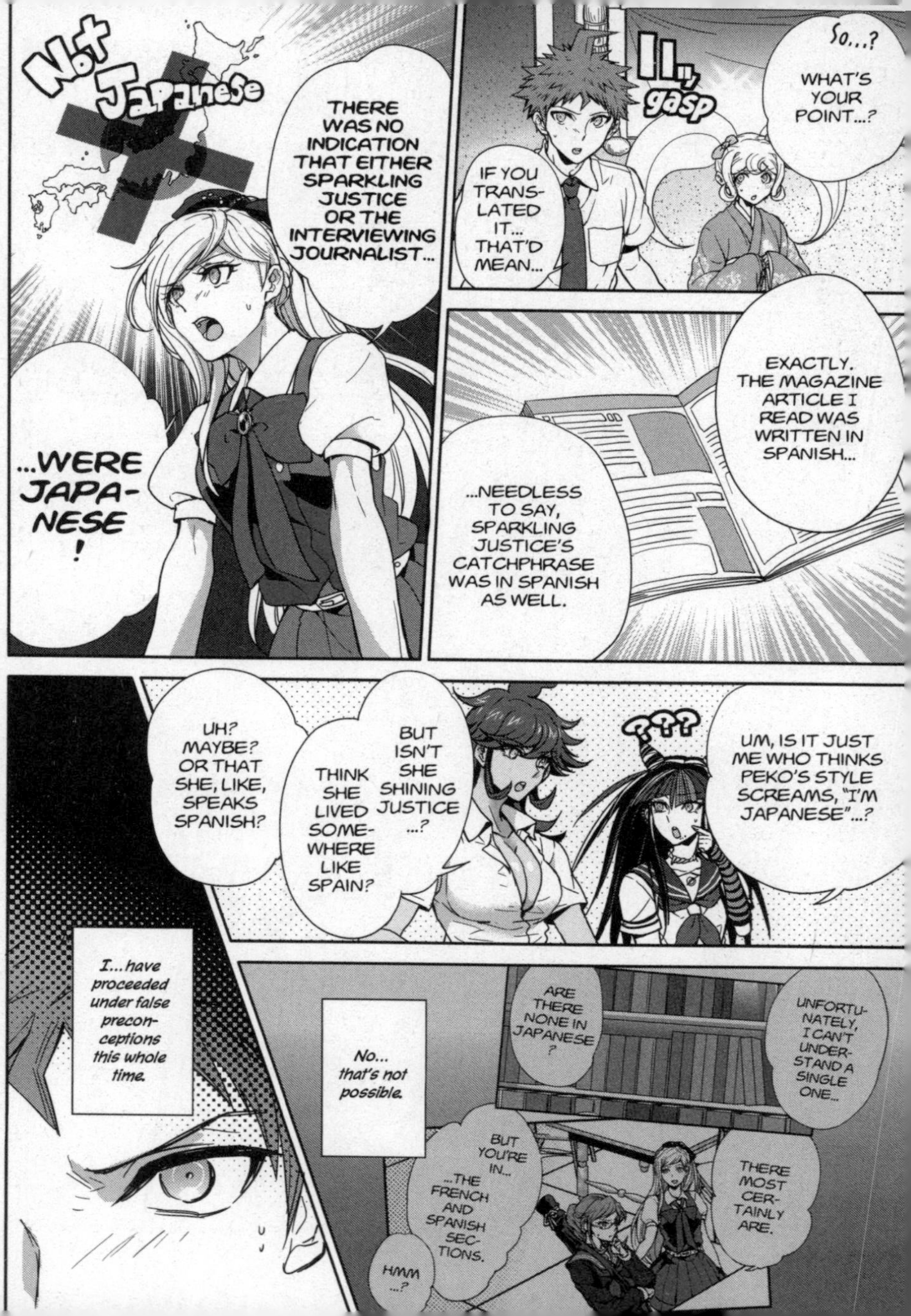
So...? WHAT'S YOUR POINT...?
IIh, gasp
IF YOU TRANSLATED IT... THAT'D MEAN...
EXACTLY. THE MAGAZINE ARTICLE I READ WAS WRITTEN IN SPANISH...
...NEEDLESS TO SAY, SPARKLING JUSTICE'S CATCHPHRASE WAS IN SPANISH AS WELL.
Not Japanese
THERE WAS NO INDICATION THAT EITHER SPARKLING JUSTICE OR THE INTERVIEWING JOURNALIST...
...WERE JAPANESE!
UM, IS IT JUST ME WHO THINKS PEKO'S STYLE SCREAMS, "I'M JAPANESE"...?
???
BUT ISN'T SHE SHINING JUSTICE...?
THINK SHE LIVED SOMEWHERE LIKE SPAIN?
UH? MAYBE? OR THAT SHE, LIKE, SPEAKS SPANISH?
UNFORTUNATELY, I CAN'T UNDERSTAND A SINGLE ONE...
ARE THERE NONE IN JAPANESE?
No... that's not possible.
THERE MOST CERTAINLY ARE.
BUT YOU'RE IN... ...THE FRENCH AND SPANISH SECTIONS.
HMM...?
I...have proceeded under false preconceptions this whole time.

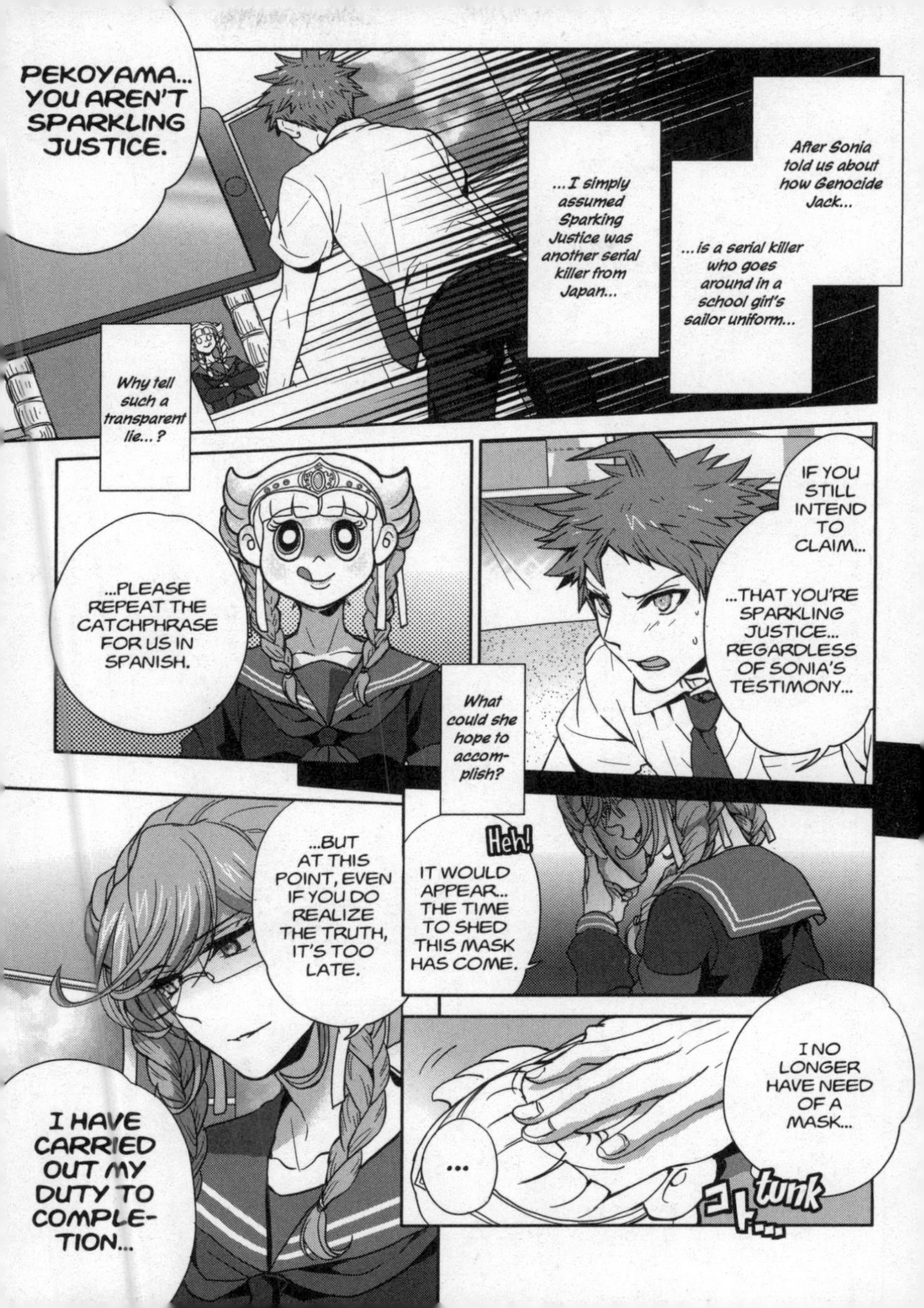
After Sonia told us about how Genocide Jack...
...is a serial killer who goes around in a school girl's sailor uniform...
...I simply assumed Sparking Justice was another serial killer from Japan...
PEKOYAMA... YOU AREN'T SPARKLING JUSTICE.
Why tell such a transparent lie...?
IF YOU STILL INTEND TO CLAIM...
...THAT YOU'RE SPARKLING JUSTICE... REGARDLESS OF SONIA'S TESTIMONY...
What could she hope to accom-plish?
...PLEASE REPEAT THE CATCHPHRASE FOR US IN SPANISH.
Heh!
IT WOULD APPEAR.. THE TIME TO SHED THIS MASK HAS COME.
I NO LONGER HAVE NEED OF A MASK...
...
tunk
...BUT AT THIS POINT, EVEN IF YOU DO REALIZE THE TRUTH, IT'S TOO LATE.
I HAVE CARRIED OUT MY DUTY TO COMPLE-TION...

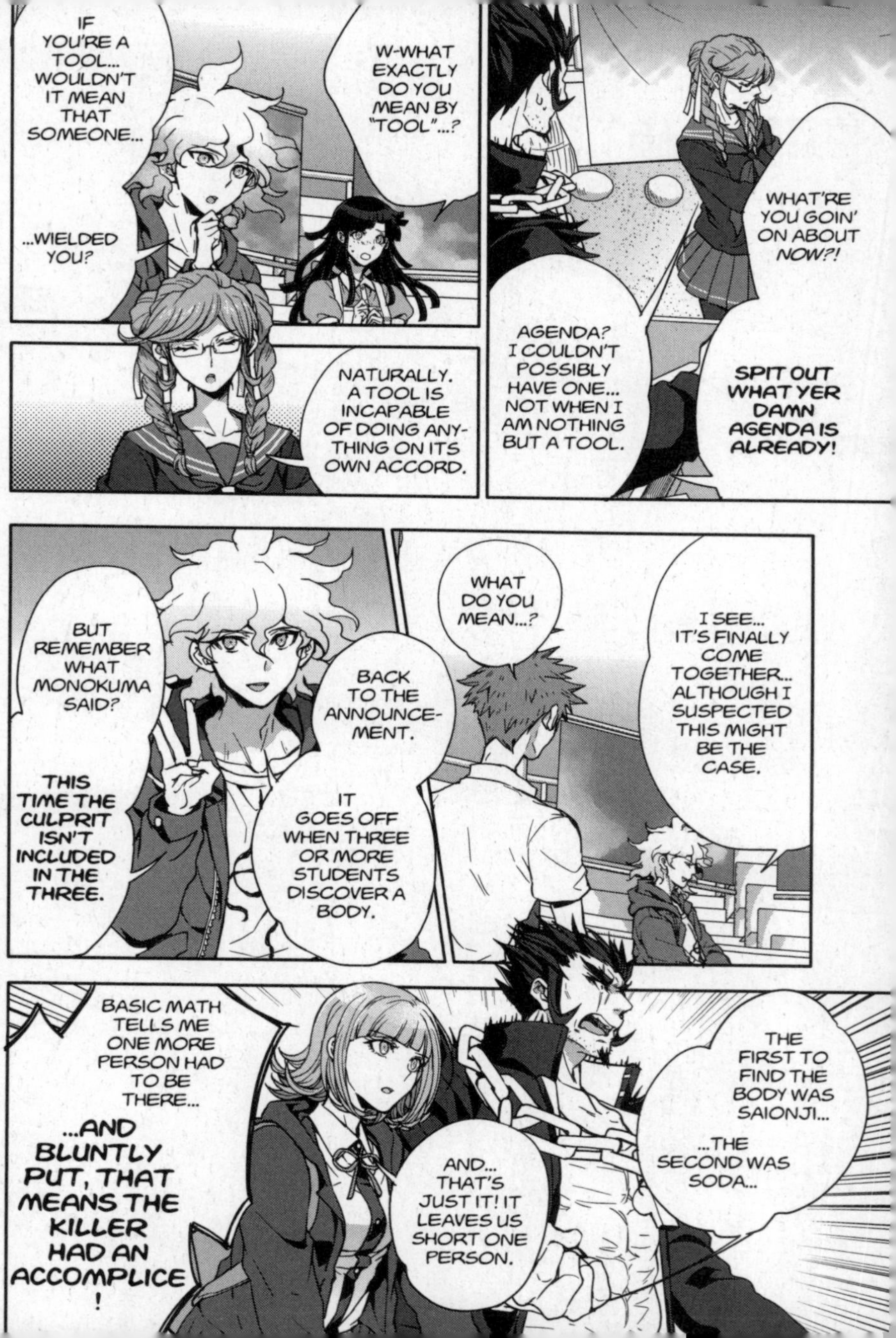
WHAT'RE YOU GOIN' ON ABOUT NOW?!
SPIT OUT WHAT YER DAMN AGENDA IS ALREADY!
AGENDA? I COULDN'T POSSIBLY HAVE ONE... NOT WHEN I AM NOTHING BUT A TOOL.
W-WHAT EXACTLY DO YOU MEAN BY "TOOL"...?
IF YOU'RE A TOOL... WOULDN'T IT MEAN THAT SOMEONE...
...WIELDED YOU?
NATURALLY. A TOOL IS INCAPABLE OF DOING ANY-THING ON ITS OWN ACCORD.
I SEE... IT'S FINALLY COME TOGETHER... ALTHOUGH I SUSPECTED THIS MIGHT BE THE CASE.
WHAT DO YOU MEAN...?
BUT REMEMBER WHAT MONOKUMA SAID?
BACK TO THE ANNOUNCE-MENT.
IT GOES OFF WHEN THREE OR MORE STUDENTS DISCOVER A BODY.
THIS TIME THE CULPRIT ISN'T INCLUDED IN THE THREE.
THE FIRST TO FIND THE BODY WAS SAIONJI...
...THE SECOND WAS SODA...
AND... THAT'S JUST IT! IT LEAVES US SHORT ONE PERSON.
BASIC MATH TELLS ME ONE MORE PERSON HAD TO BE THERE...
...AND BLUNTLY PUT, THAT MEANS THE KILLER HAD AN ACCOMPLICE!

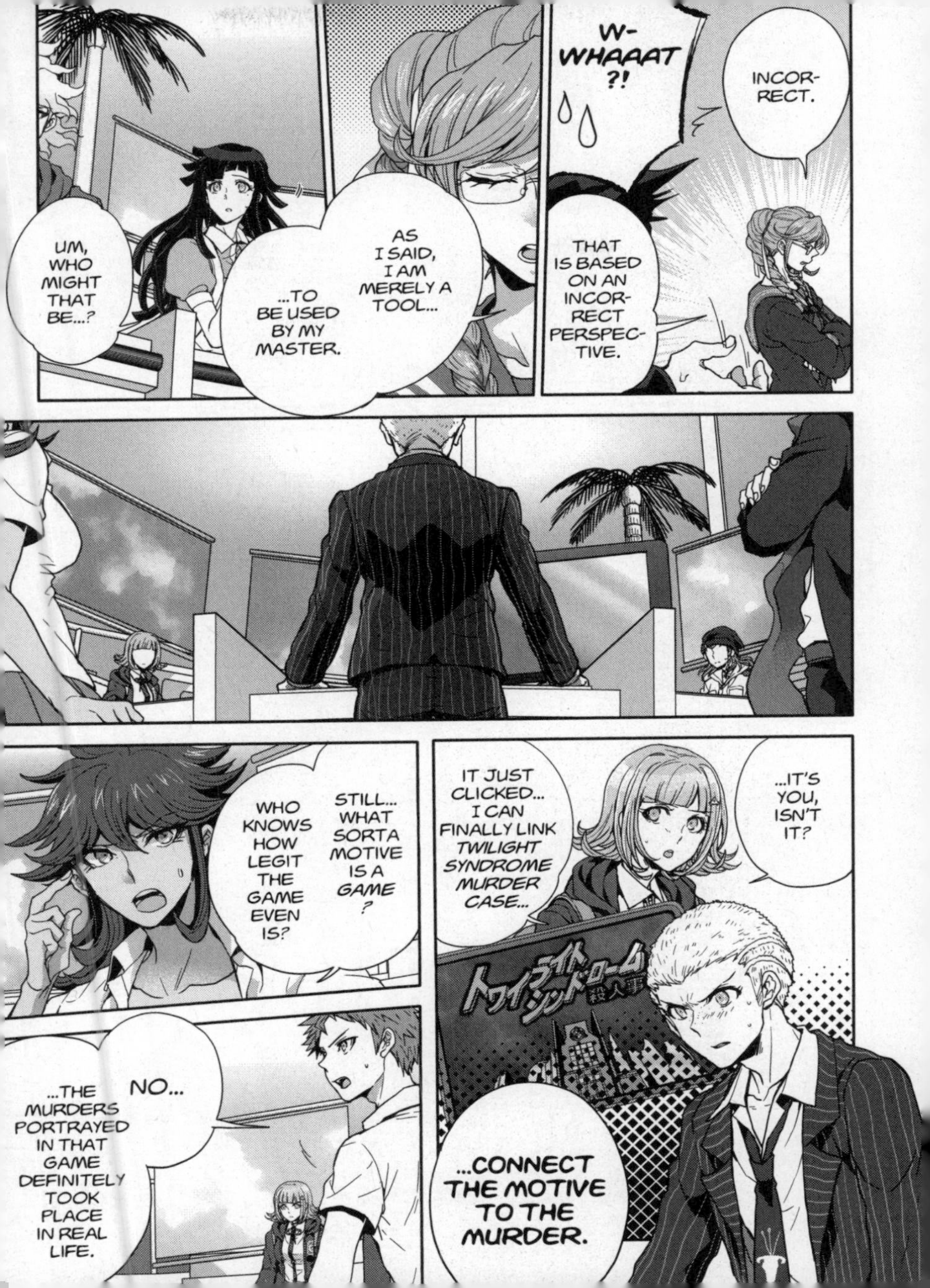
INCORRECT.
W-WHAAAT?!
THAT IS BASED ON AN INCORRECT PERSPECTIVE.
AS I SAID, I AM MERELY A TOOL...
...TO BE USED BY MY MASTER.
UM, WHO MIGHT THAT BE...?
...IT'S YOU, ISN'T IT?
IT JUST CLICKED... I CAN FINALLY LINK *TWILIGHT SYNDROME MURDER CASE*...
トワイライトシンドローム
殺人事
...CONNECT THE MOTIVE TO THE MURDER.
STILL... WHAT SORTA MOTIVE IS A *GAME*?
WHO KNOWS HOW LEGIT THE GAME EVEN IS?
NO...
...THE MURDERS PORTRAYED IN THAT GAME DEFINITELY TOOK PLACE IN REAL LIFE.

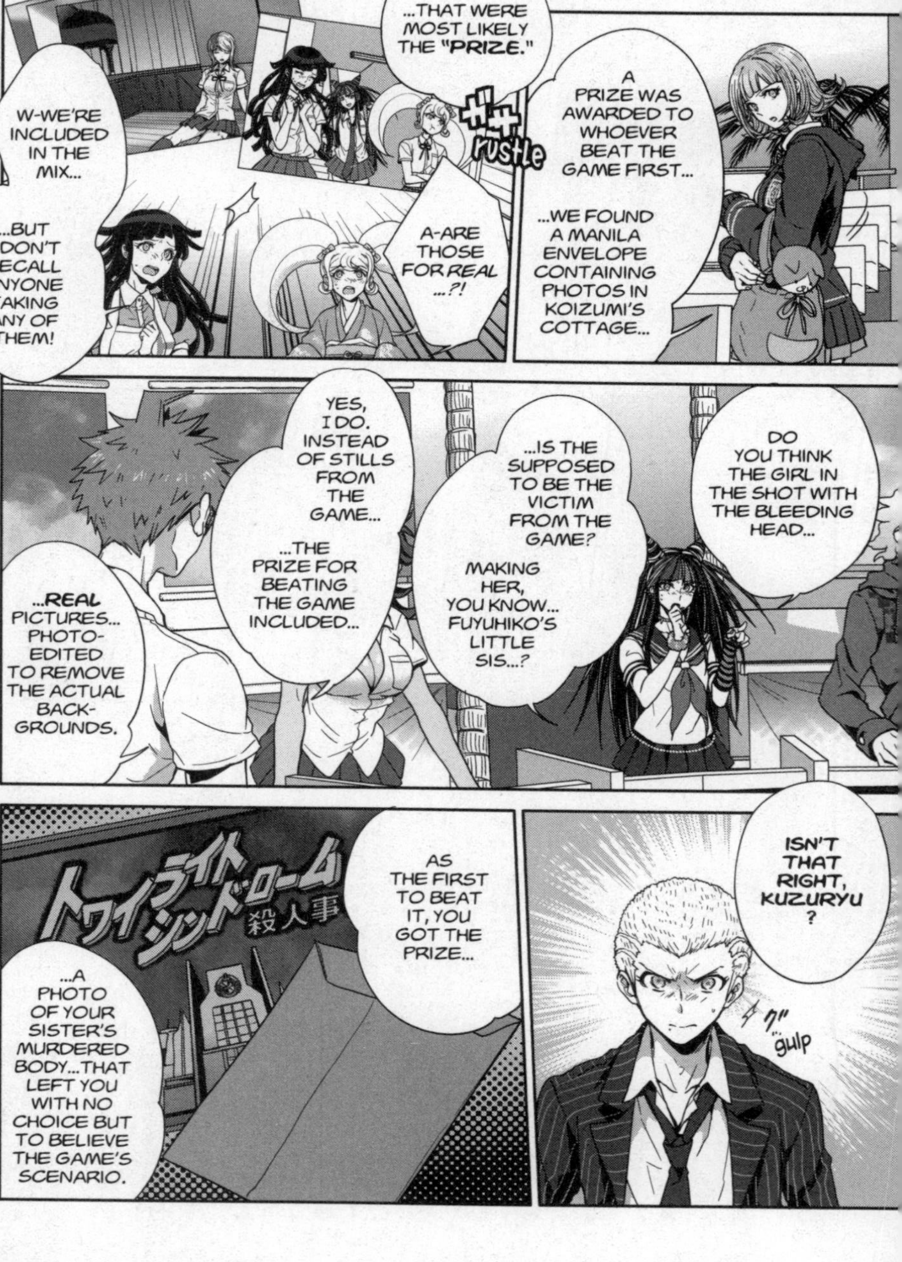
A PRIZE WAS AWARDED TO WHOEVER BEAT THE GAME FIRST...
...WE FOUND A MANILA ENVELOPE CONTAINING PHOTOS IN KOIZUMI'S COTTAGE...
...THAT WERE MOST LIKELY THE "PRIZE."
rustle
A-ARE THOSE FOR *REAL*...?!
W-WE'RE INCLUDED IN THE MIX...
...BUT I DON'T RECALL ANYONE TAKING ANY OF THEM!
DO YOU THINK THE GIRL IN THE SHOT WITH THE BLEEDING HEAD...
...IS THE SUPPOSED TO BE THE VICTIM FROM THE GAME?
MAKING HER, YOU KNOW... FUYUHIKO'S LITTLE SIS...?
YES, I DO. INSTEAD OF STILLS FROM THE GAME...
...THE PRIZE FOR BEATING THE GAME INCLUDED...
...**REAL** PICTURES... PHOTO-EDITED TO REMOVE THE ACTUAL BACK-GROUNDS.
ISN'T THAT RIGHT, KUZURYU?
gulp
トワイライトシンドローム
殺人事
AS THE FIRST TO BEAT IT, YOU GOT THE PRIZE...
...A PHOTO OF YOUR SISTER'S MURDERED BODY...THAT LEFT YOU WITH NO CHOICE BUT TO BELIEVE THE GAME'S SCENARIO.

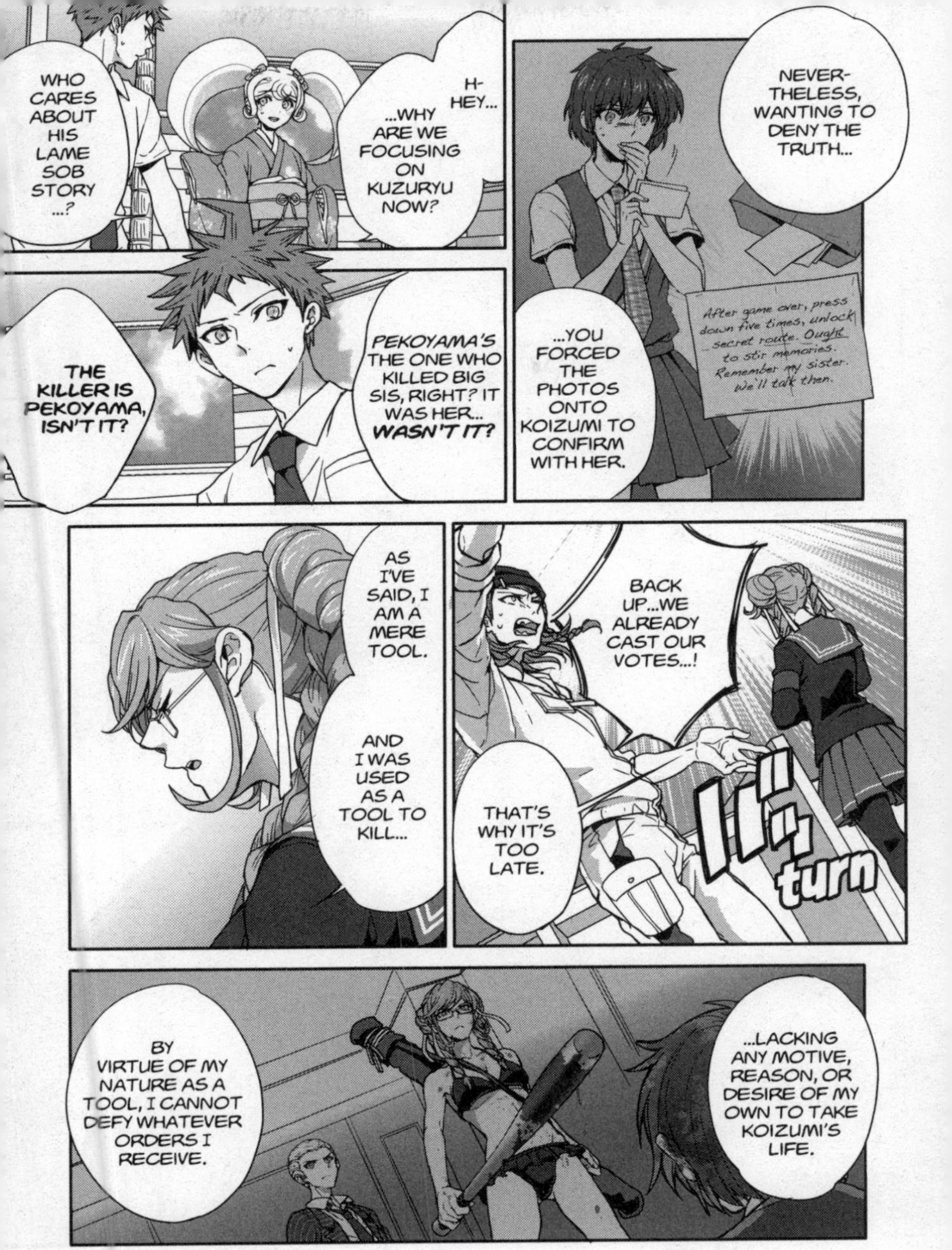
NEVER-THELESS, WANTING TO DENY THE TRUTH...
After game over, press down five times, unlock secret route. Ought to stir memories. Remember my sister. We'll talk then.
...YOU FORCED THE PHOTOS ONTO KOIZUMI TO CONFIRM WITH HER.
H-HEY... ...WHY ARE WE FOCUSING ON KUZURYU NOW?
WHO CARES ABOUT HIS LAME SOB STORY ...?
PEKOYAMA'S THE ONE WHO KILLED BIG SIS, RIGHT? IT WAS HER... WASN'T IT?
THE KILLER IS PEKOYAMA, ISN'T IT?
BACK UP...WE ALREADY CAST OUR VOTES...!
THAT'S WHY IT'S TOO LATE.
turn
AS I'VE SAID, I AM A MERE TOOL.
AND I WAS USED AS A TOOL TO KILL...
...LACKING ANY MOTIVE, REASON, OR DESIRE OF MY OWN TO TAKE KOIZUMI'S LIFE.
BY VIRTUE OF MY NATURE AS A TOOL, I CANNOT DEFY WHATEVER ORDERS I RECEIVE.

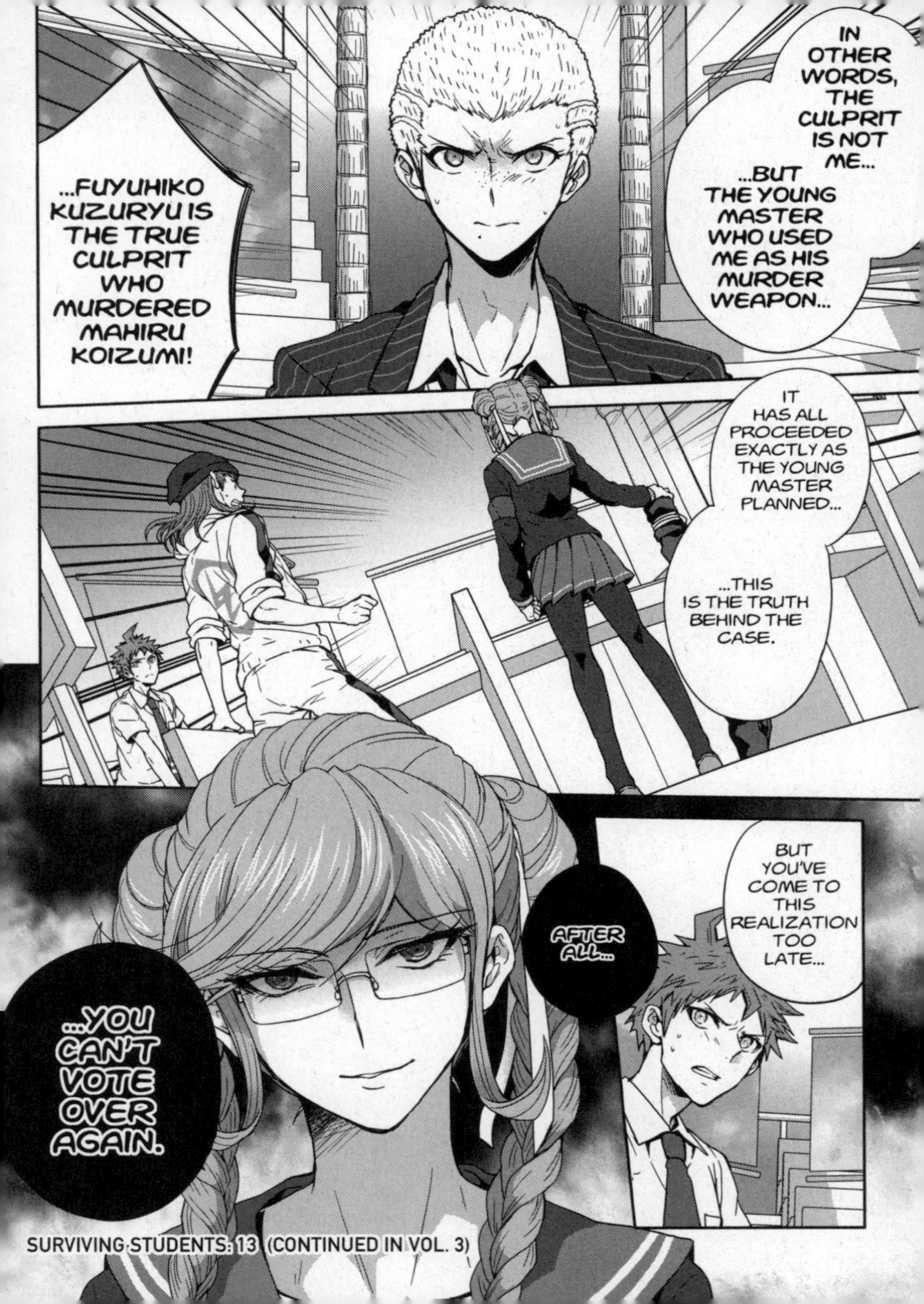
IN OTHER WORDS, THE CULPRIT IS NOT ME...
...BUT THE YOUNG MASTER WHO USED ME AS HIS MURDER WEAPON...
...FUYUHIKO KUZURYU IS THE TRUE CULPRIT WHO MURDERED MAHIRU KOIZUMI!
IT HAS ALL PROCEEDED EXACTLY AS THE YOUNG MASTER PLANNED...
...THIS IS THE TRUTH BEHIND THE CASE.
BUT YOU'VE COME TO THIS REALIZATION TOO LATE...
AFTER ALL...
...YOU CAN'T VOTE OVER AGAIN.
SURVIVING STUDENTS: 13 (CONTINUED IN VOL. 3)

Hello, Kuroki here. It's been quite a while since the last volume. I finally managed to bring the story clear up to the end of Chapter 2 in the game! The tricks only get more and more complex in the world of **Danganronpa 2**... For those of you who have played the game, you can have fun comparing my adaptation with how you remember it, or load up that save file and compare them back-to-back! If this is your first go-round, I hope you try to solve the case with the characters.

It was while I was working on this volume in 2014-15 that the **Danganronpa Another Episode: Ultra Despair Girls** game came out! As much as I wanted to play it, I still didn't have a PlayStation Vita yet... Komaru is so stinking cute!

On another note, I actually got to go see **Danganronpa: The Stage.** Was everyone else able to go? It was a blast to seeing the wonderful world of **Danganronpa** squished into a few short hours. I found it a fun and exciting learning experience to watch how the play gave a fresh interpretation and told the story in a way only possible on stage. Not to mention Sayaka Kanda stole the show! It felt like all of the characters were real. I was blown away by the incredible production quality. I hope we get to see anime and stage adaptions of **Danganronpa 2** sometime! I'd like to look forward to seeing that hope become reality!

Well, until we meet again in the next volume! Thank you for reading all the way to the end!

Kuroki Q

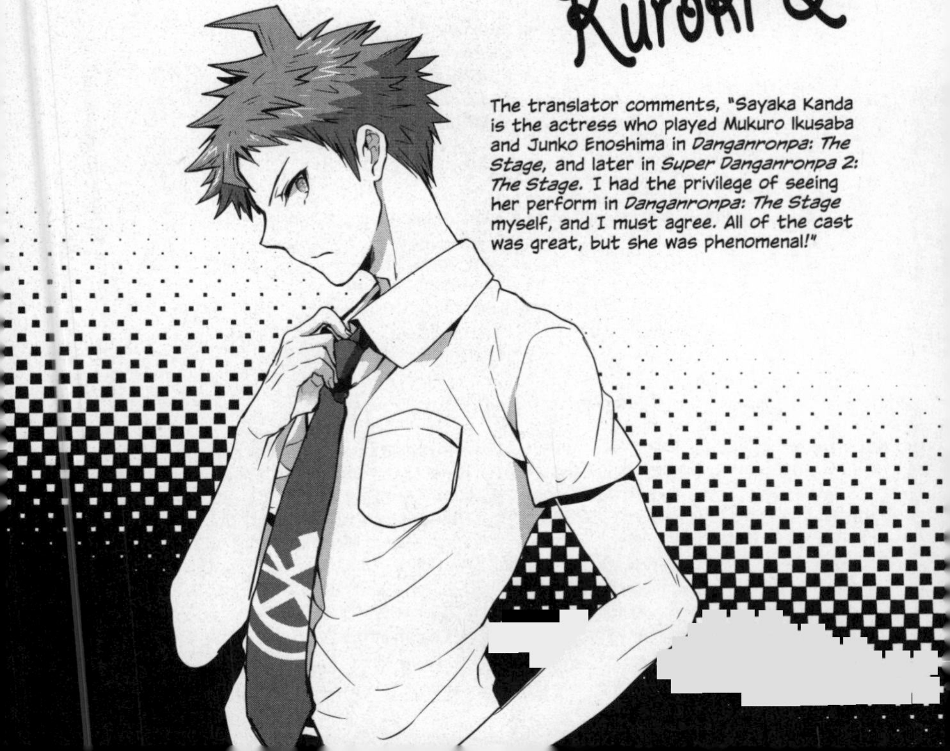

The translator comments, "Sayaka Kanda is the actress who played Mukuro Ikusaba and Junko Enoshima in *Danganronpa: The Stage*, and later in *Super Danganronpa 2: The Stage*. I had the privilege of seeing her perform in *Danganronpa: The Stage* myself, and I must agree. All of the cast was great, but she was phenomenal!"

President and Publisher // **Mike Richardson**

Designer // **Skyler Weissenfluh**

Ultimate Digital Art Technician // **Samantha Hummer**

English-language version produced by Dark Horse Comics

DANGANRONPA 2: GOODBYE DESPAIR VOLUME 2

Published by
Dark Horse Manga
A division of Dark Horse Comics LLC
10956 SE Main Street
Milwaukie, OR 97222

DarkHorse.com

To find a comics shop in your area, visit comicshoplocator.com

First edition: August 2020
Ebook ISBN 978-1-50671-501-8
ISBN 978-1-50671-360-1

3 5 7 9 10 8 6 4

Printed in the United States of America

DESPAIR MAIL

c/o Dark Horse Comics | 10956 SE Main St. | Milwaukie, OR 97222 | danganronpa@darkhorse.com

Don't despair! Even if that's the name of this column. Perhaps in the spirit of certain socially distancing global circumstances you may have heard about lately, it's been requested by our Japanese liaison that we move Despair Mail out of the Danganronpa books and put it online instead, where the whole world can see it, and we can all enjoy our island life together.

Because people have been previously sending in contributions with the expectation of appearing in the books, I will be getting in contact with contributors first and asking them if they're okay with their fan art, cosplay, etc. going up on Dark Horse's social media instead, and hopefully by the time you read this, it will have already happened.

And either way, thank you all so much once again for the support you have given the Danganronpa manga thus far! Things have been a little delayed by events, but don't worry—we plan to keep publishing both Goodbye Despair and Ultra Despair Girls…and maybe other Danganronpa titles as well in the future…

—CGH

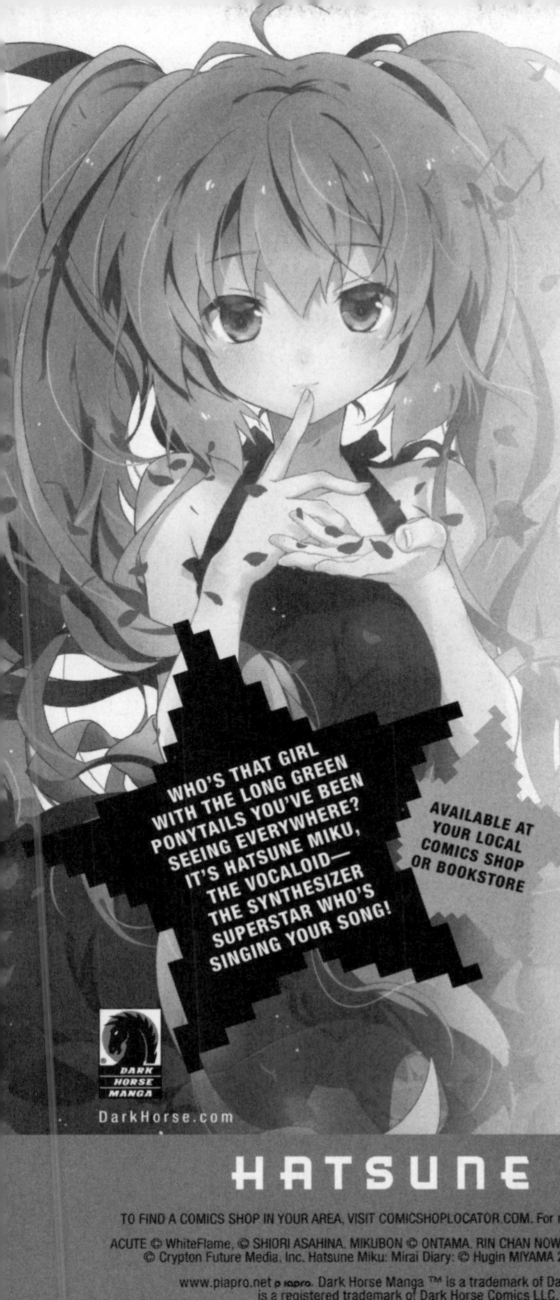
WHO'S THAT GIRL WITH THE LONG GREEN PONYTAILS YOU'VE BEEN SEEING EVERYWHERE? IT'S HATSUNE MIKU, THE VOCALOID— THE SYNTHESIZER SUPERSTAR WHO'S SINGING YOUR SONG!
AVAILABLE AT YOUR LOCAL COMICS SHOP OR BOOKSTORE
DARK HORSE MANGA
DarkHorse.com

HATSUNE MIKU: ACUTE
Art and story by Shiori Asahina
Miku, Kaito, and Luka! Once they were all friends making songs—but while Kaito might make a duet with Miku or a duet with Luka, a love song all three of them sing together can only end in sorrow!

ISBN 978-1-50670-341-1 | $10.99

HATSUNE MIKU: RIN-CHAN NOW!
Story by Sezu, Art by Hiro Tamura
Miku's sassy blond friend takes center stage in this series that took inspiration from the music video "Rin-chan Now!" The video is now a manga of the same name—written, drawn, and edited by the video creators!

VOLUME 1
978-1-50670-313-8 | $10.99

VOLUME 2
978-1-50670-314-5 | $10.99

VOLUME 3
978-1-50670-315-2 | $10.99

VOLUME 4
978-1-50670-316-9 | $10.99

HATSUNE MIKU: MIKUBON
Art and story by Ontama
Hatsune Miku and her friends Rin, Len, and Luka enroll at the St. Diva Academy for Vocaloids! At St. Diva, a wonderland of friendship, determination, and even love unfolds! But can they stay out of trouble, especially when the mad professor of the Hachune Miku Research Lab is nearby . . . ?

ISBN 978-1-50670-231-5 | $10.99

UNOFFICIAL HATSUNE MIX
Art and story by KEI
Miku's original illustrator, KEI, produced a best-selling omnibus manga of the musical adventures (and misadventures!) of Miku and her fellow Vocaloids Rin, Len, Luka, and more—in both beautiful black-and-white and charming color!

ISBN 978-1-61655-412-5 | $19.99

HATSUNE MIKU: FUTURE DELIVERY
Story by Satoshi Oshio, Art by Hugin Miyama
In the distant future, Asumi—a girl who has no clue to her memories but a drawing of a green-haired, ponytailed person—finds her only friend in Asimov, a battered old delivery robot. The strange companions travel the stars together in search of the mysterious "Miku," only to learn the legendary idol has taken different forms on many different worlds!

VOLUME 1
ISBN 978-1-50670-361-9 | $10.99

VOLUME 2
ISBN 978-1-50670-362-6 | $10.99

HATSUNE MIKU

TO FIND A COMICS SHOP IN YOUR AREA, VISIT COMICSHOPLOCATOR.COM. For more information or to order direct, visit DarkHorse.com

REPENT, SINNERS! THEY'RE BACK!

Miss the anime?
Try the *Panty & Stocking with Garterbelt* manga! Nine ALL-NEW
stories of your favorite filthy fallen angels, written and drawn by TAGRO,
with a special afterword by *Kill La Kill* director Hiroyuki Imaishi!
978-1-61655-735-5 | $9.99

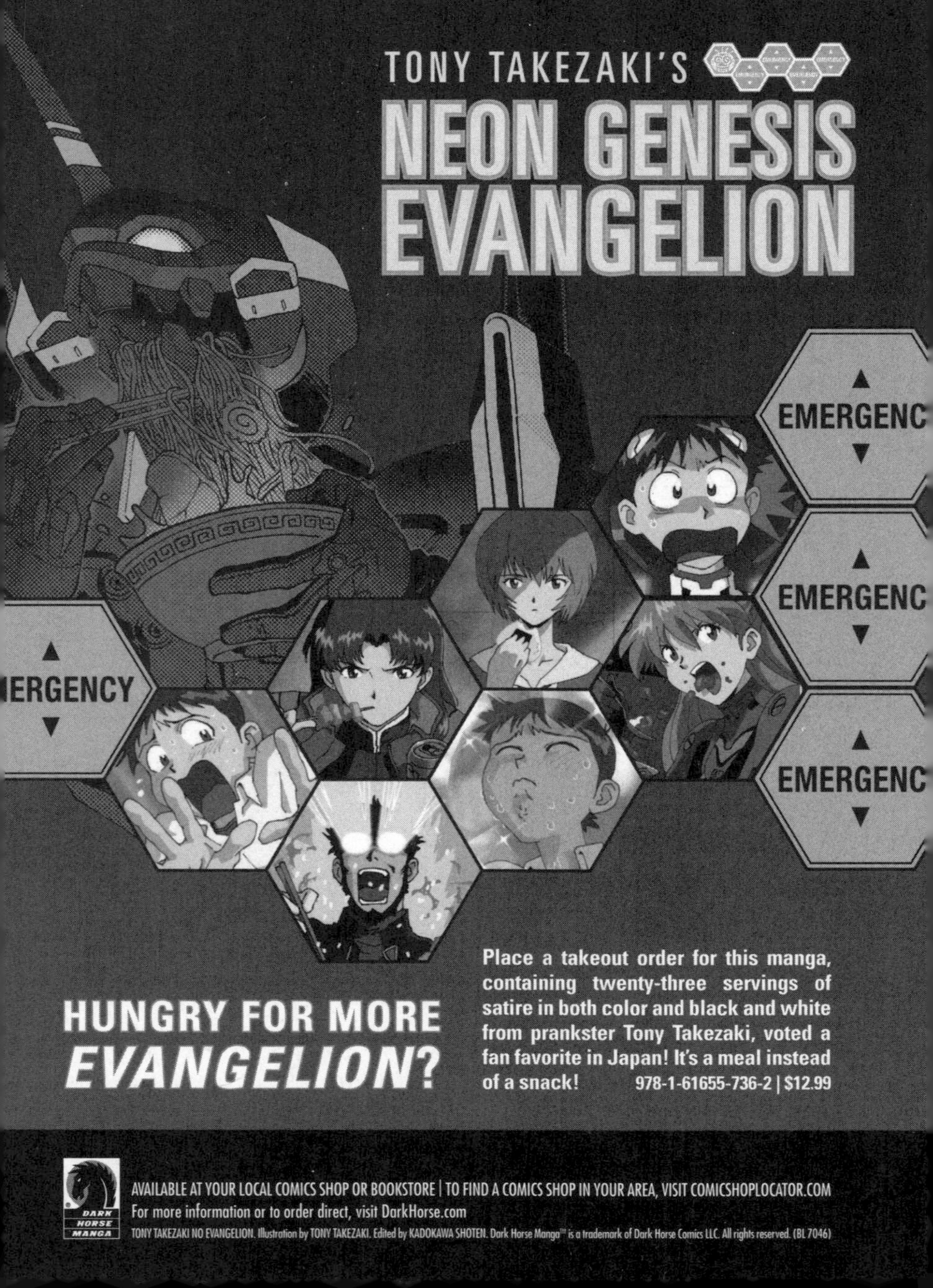
TONY TAKEZAKI'S
NEON GENESIS EVANGELION
EMERGENC
EMERGENC
EMERGENC
ERGENCY

the KUROSAGI corpse delivery service

黒鷺死体宅配便

OMNIBUS EDITIONS

Five young students at a Buddhist university find there's little call for their job skills in today's Tokyo. . . among the living, that is! But their studies give them a direct line to the dead—the dead who are still trapped in their corpses, and can't move on to the next incarnation! Whether death resulted from suicide, murder, sickness, or madness, the Kurosagi Corpse Delivery Service will carry the body anywhere it needs to go to free its soul!

"Nobody does horror-comedy comics better than Otsuka and Yamazaki"
—Booklist

Each 600+ page omnibus book collects three complete volumes of the series!

Vol. 1:
Contains vols. 1–3, originally published separately.
ISBN 978-1-61655-754-6 $19.99

Vol. 2:
Contains vols. 4–6, originally published separately.
ISBN 978-1-61655-783-6 $19.99

Vol. 3:
Contains vols. 7–9, originally published separately.
ISBN 978-1-61655-887-1 $19.99

Vol. 4:
Contains vols. 10–12, originally published separately.
ISBN 978-1-50670-055-7 $19.99

MAY I HAVE YOUR, ATTENTION, PLEA

Your powers of observation will be vital if you want to survive the co
drama (or never mind courtroom—the just plain drama) of *Danganro*
remember that this book reads right-to-left, because that's just the
detail that might REFUTE! someone's trial testimony. Also, remem
this book reads right-to-left, because if you read it left-to-right, the
victims will seem to rise up off the floor and come back to life, wh
be a little disconcerting.

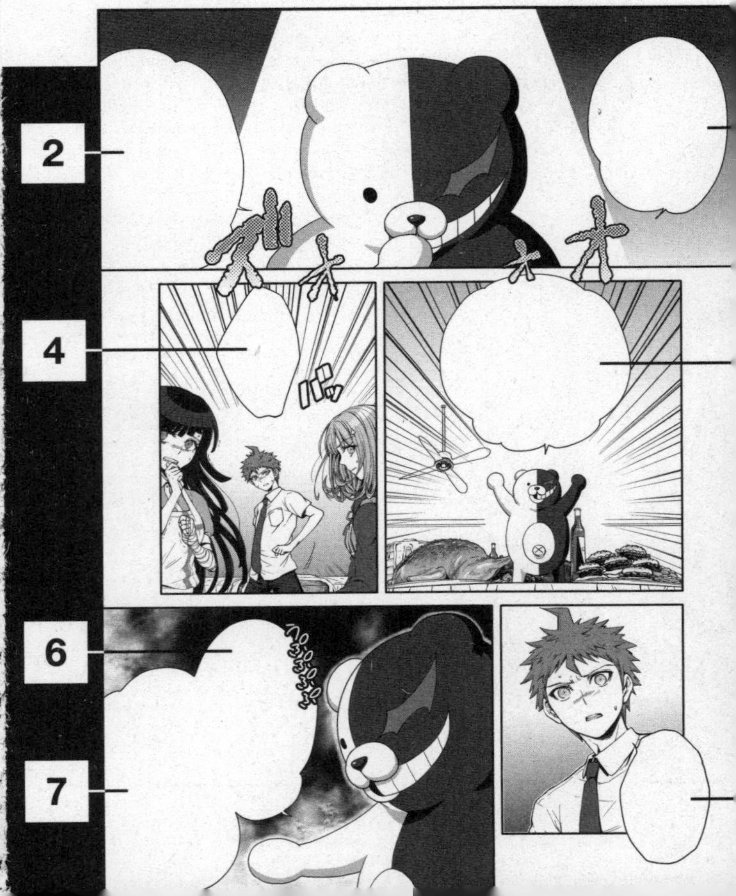
2
4
6
7

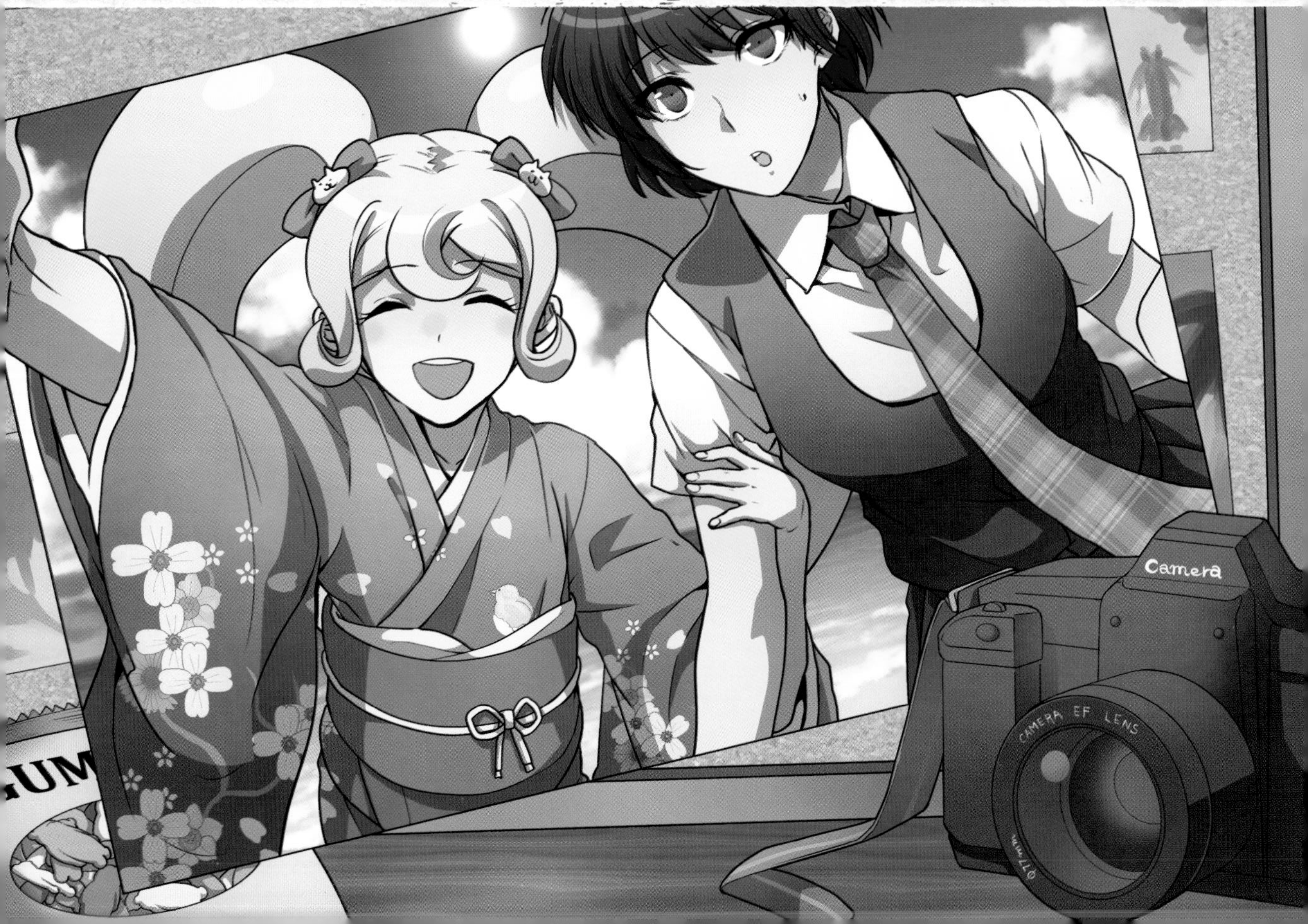
Camera
CAMERA EF LENS
Φ77mm

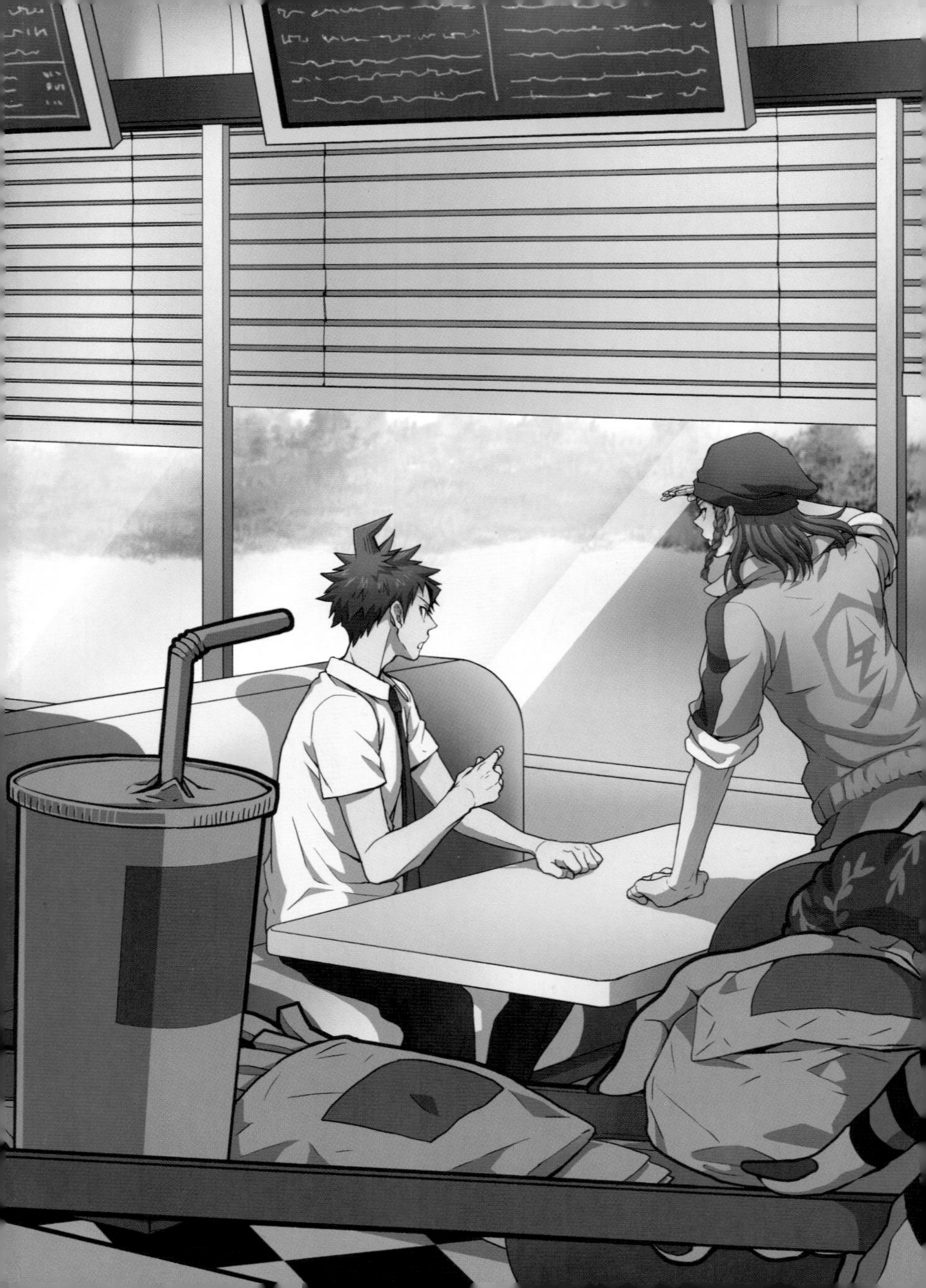